M000280946

Investment Banking

The Art and Science of High-Stakes Dealmaking

Investment Banking

The Art and Science of High-Stakes Dealmaking

Robert Lawrence Kuhn

1817

Harper & Row, Publishers, New York

BALLINGER DIVISION

Grand Rapids, Philadelphia, St. Louis, San Francisco
London, Singapore, Sydney, Tokyo, Toronto

Copyright © 1990 by Ballinger Publishing Company. All rights reserved. No part of this publication may be reproduced, stored in a retrieval system, or transmitted in any form or by any means, electronic, mechanical, photocopy, recording, or otherwise, without the prior written consent of the publisher.

International Standard Book Number: 0-88730-397-8

Library of Congress Catalog Card Number: 89-45768

Printed in the United States of America

Library of Congress Cataloging-in-Publication Data

Kuhn,Robert Lawerence
   Investment banking : the art and science of high stakes dealmaking
/ Robert Lawrence Kuhn.
     p. cm.
   Includes bibliographical references.
   ISBN 0-88730-397-8
   1. Investment banking. I. Title.
HG4534.K78   1989   89-45768
332.66–dc20   CIP

89 90 91 92 HC 9 8 7 6 5 4 3 2 1

Contents

List of Figures and Tables

Preface

My purpose for writing this book is to describe how investment banking really works and how investment bankers really think. I am an investment banker. I arrange mergers and acquisitions, finance companies, and restructure organizations. My doctorate is in brain science. I hold academic positions in corporate strategy and creative management. This background, I believe, helps me make the real world of investment banking accessible to a great many people. Marketplace deals are what I do. Explaining investment banking is what I like.

This book covers all facets of "high finance" from mergers and acquisitions and leveraged buyouts to public offerings and private placements; from international, public, and corporate finance to risk arbitrage, risk management, and deal making. We get into the nit and grit as well, laying out fees and spreads and advising companies "how to build shareholder wealth" and "how to use investment bankers."

We also take a broader view, presenting issues of ethics and proposing a "philosophy of investment banking." Investment banking involves the massive movements of money, flows of capital seeking maximum returns with minimum risks. Here is the energizer of market-driven capitalism, the catalyst of national and international economic development. We show how complex financial instruments actually work and how diverse financings actually happen. This is the essence of investment banking in all its dynamism, complexity, innovation, and excitement.

Chapters are basic yet complete. They began with first principles, easily appreciated by nonexperts. Readers learn the fundamentals of the field, sensing the insight as well as seeing the analysis. The motivations—the "why's" of high finance—are discussed along with the methods—the "how's" of investment banking. Chapters continue with simplifying frameworks to aid understanding and operational techniques enriched by current examples.

The Way of Thinking

We seek *the way of thinking* in investment banking. How can we grasp the bewildering variety of new corporate securities and novel financial instruments? How do investment bankers envision financial scope, create financial strategies, craft financial structures, and make financial deals? It is important to appreciate how professional financiers think, not only to understand what they do. We present the scope, strategies, structures, and deals of investment banking. Our clear emphasis is on practice—what really happens in the real world.

Helpful thought, not latest fads, is what we offer. Method, not fact, is what we stress. Investment banking is an organic process—ever changing, developing, evolving. New techniques arise frequently; new instruments appear regularly. There is no way that any book, with its long production process, can keep accurate in all details. (Changes in tax considerations alone would threaten to invalidate entire categories.)

Have no illusions: We cannot claim up-to-the-minute accuracy, and we do not promise state-of-the-art applications. Investment bankers keep current with *The Wall Street Journal*, various monthly publications, internal memoranda and product descriptions, and, best of all, word of mouth. For immediacy one must contact experts in each area. But our goal goes deeper.

We dig down to bedrock. We want to understand the fundamental reasons why financial products are developed, how they are designed, what purposes they serve, why they change, and how they evolve. This is the guts of high finance, *the way of thinking* in investment banking. Reasons, not guesses; motivations, not mysteries.

We go inside and underneath. By establishing the solid underpinnings of a variety of financing situations and instruments, we enable the reader to appreciate how investment bankers plan and figure, induce and deduce, contemplate and create. Consequently, we describe numerous financial circumstances and products, many in detail, seeking for each underlying mechanism and unifying drive. Discerning development cycles of financial concepts and products is vital; the better one appreciates the past, the better one can anticipate the future. The result, we trust, is a deepening awareness of what investment banking is all about.

Audience

Investment Banking: The Art and Science of High-Stakes Dealmaking should appeal to the following reader groups:

1. Members of the growing financial services community in the United States and worldwide (i.e., investment banks, brokerage houses, commercial banks, savings and loan associations, insurance companies, finance companies, financial service firms, and the like). Whether for initial training or professional review, if your job is in finance, this material is vital.

2. Business and financial executives of corporations and institutions of all sizes. These executives need to understand modern finance techniques and investment banking services. This is what they should know, but often do not.

3. Business people, business students, media people, and general readers who are interested in appreciating the intricacies of investment banking. High finance is no longer an arcane subject. It is always in the news, and nonprofessionals need to make sense of this stuff.

Further Reading and Acknowledgements

No book is complete. For those interested in going further—much further—I recommend the Dow Jones-Irwin's *The Library of Investment Banking*, a seven-volume, 215-chapter professional guide.[1] The *Library* is written by investment bankers for investment bankers. Contributors are those who get things done—leading investment bankers and firing-line financiers.

It is a pleasure to acknowledge the contribution of others to the following chapters: George T. Geis of the University of California at Los Angeles (Chapter 3), Charles Hurwitz of Maxxam Inc. (Chapter 4), G. Clyde Buck of Rauscher Pierce Rafsnes (Chapter 8), Robert Boydon Lamb of New York University (Chapter 10), G. Chris Andersen, Jr. of Drexel Burnham Lambert (Chapter 13), Bruce Foerster of PaineWebber (Chapter 14), J. Morton Davis and Evelyn Geller of D. H. Blair & Co. (Chapter 14), Dorothy Dotson of Prudential-Bache (Chapter 15), Manny Friedman of New York University (Chapter 17), Oliver Abel IV of Kidder, Peabody (Chapter 18), Joanne Hill of PaineWebber and Thomas

---

[1] Having written Chapter 10 on ethics, and having recommended the Dow Jones-Irwin *Library of Investment Banking*, I am constrained to make *full disclosure*. I am the editor-in-chief of the *Library*, and preparing these volumes has consumed a healthy part of my last two years. (I still think it is a good investment.)

Schneeweis of the University of Massachusetts (Chapter 18), Frank X. Stankard of Chase Manhattan Bank (Chapter 19), Keith Maillard of Kidder, Peabody (Chapter 20), Stephen Rappaport of Prudential-Bache (Chapter 21), Gunter Dufey and Taeyoung Chung of the University of Michigan (Chapter 22), and Hung Q. Tran, Larry Anderson, Ernst-Ludwig Drayss of Deustche Bank (Chapter 22). The material has been derived from their respective chapters in Dow Jones-Irwin's *The Library of Investment Banking*, Volumes I–VI.

Fancy theory is not our claim. We present a large number of ideas, concepts, principles, attitudes, approaches, tricks, traps, processes, products, instruments, mechanisms, techniques, regulations, requirements, forecasts, predictions, and opinions. This marvelous, monstrous mass is the real world of investment banking. Allow it to wash over you. Read and learn, but also imbibe and experience. Build inner understanding while argumenting outer knowledge. The outcome is really knowing investment banking.

Robert Lawrence Kuhn

New York
August 1989

PART I

PRINCIPLES AND TECHNIQUES OF INVESTMENT BANKING

PART I

PRINCIPLES AND
TECHNIQUES OF
INVESTMENT BANKING

CHAPTER 1

What Is Investment Banking?*

Investment bankers facilitate the flow of money. They are financial intermediaries, the critical link between users and providers of capital. They bring together those who *need* funds (e.g., corporations that build factories and buy equipment) with those who *have* funds (e.g., institutions that manage money for pension plans), and they make the markets that allocate capital and regulate price in these financial exchanges (i.e., they determine who gets how much money, with what terms, and at what cost). For an exploration of the "essence" of investment banking, see the Appendix: A Philosophy of Investment Banking.

Those who desire to raise capital are called *issuers,* since they issue ownership in their enterprises (i.e., equity) or obligations from their enterprises (i.e., promises to pay debt interest and repay debt principal) in exchange for cash or cash equivalents; those who provide capital are called *investors*, since they invest cash or cash equivalents in exchange for those rights of ownership or obligation (see Figure 1-1). Investment bankers enable issuers to raise capital (i.e., corporations or companies

---

* This chapter has been derived from "The Scope of Investment Banking" by Robert Lawrence Kuhn, Volume II (Capital Raising and Financial Structure), Dow Jones-Irwin's *The Library of Investment Banking* (1990), Robert Lawrence Kuhn, editor in chief.

Figure 1–1. Investment Banks as Financial Intermediaries.

Issuers of Equity or Debt

Investors of Capital

Cash or Cash Equivalents

Ownership or Obligation

Cash or Cash Equivalents

Ownership or Obligation

Investment Banks

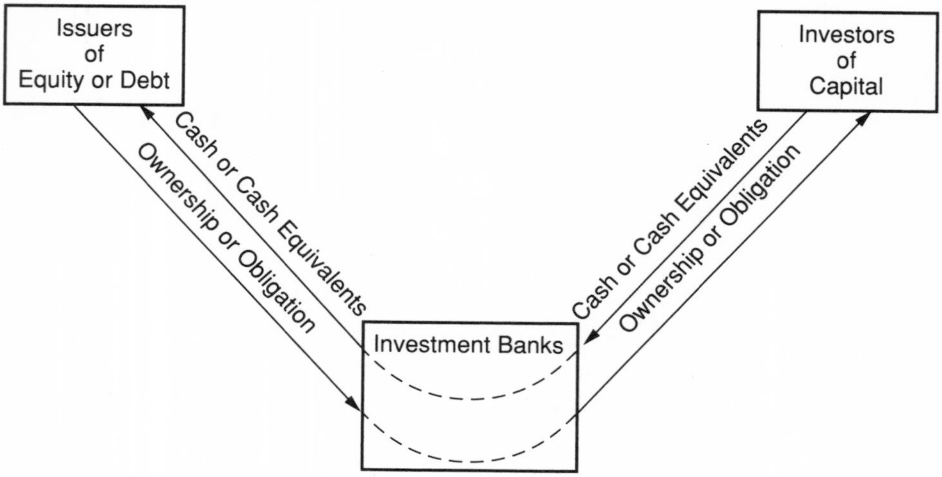

that sell or *issue* securities for cash) and investors to place capital (i.e., individuals or institutions that buy or invest in those securities) in the most efficient manner for both.

Investment banking is a dynamic industry characterized by flux and transformation. Financial instruments have grown more complex as financial intermediaries have become more competitive. Blizzards of innovative instruments are sweeping financial markets. Boundaries among diverse financial institutions are blurring. Barriers between international financial markets are eroding. And—further amplifying the complexity and the competition—financial markets, firms, products, and techniques are merging and melding.

It is in this volatile environment that investment banks of all sizes and strategies struggle with change: They generate change and they are changed by change. Investment banking, long simply synonymous with the domestic underwriting and market making of corporate equity and debt securities, has expanded dramatically. The industry has been transformed—new functions (e.g., the prominence of mergers and acquisitions), new products (e.g., risk management mechanisms such as interest-rate and currency swaps), new techniques (e.g., securitization, or *rolling up* of illiquid receivables), new markets (e.g., Tokyo and London), and new muscle (e.g., merchant banking, where investment banks buy companies for themselves). The result is high drama: a new world of investment banking in turmoil and transition.[1]

This chapter answers the question, "What is investment banking?" by describing investment banking in two sections:

- *Definitions of investment banking,* presenting the range of meanings that the term "investment banking" can imply.
- *Scope of investment banking,* describing the specific areas of investment banking activity.

Definitions of Investment Banking

The scope of the field is determined by definition of the term. We describe four such definitions of investment banking. They range from broadly inclusive of wide-ranging financial services to narrowly restrictive to traditional underwriting. The diversity helps give the industry its dynamism.

1. The broadest definition includes virtually all activities of major Wall Street firms, from international corporate underwriting to retail branch marketing to a host of other financial services (e.g., real estate and insurance).

2. The next broadest definition envisions investment banking as covering all capital market activities, from underwriting and corporate finance to mergers and acquisitions (M&A) and fairness opinions to fund management and venture capital. Excluded, for example, are the selling of securities to retail customers, consumer real estate brokerage, mortgage banking, insurance products, and the like. Included is merchant banking, when investment bankers work and invest for their own account. Also included is the nonretail trading of large blocks of securities for financial institutions.

---

1. Clear evidence for the increasing prominence of mergers and acquisitions and merchant banking, and the decreasing emphasis on underwriting, comes from the new "boutique" investment banks that have been founded in recent years by prominent investment bankers leaving the largest and most prestigious firms. These *new* investment banks do not do any underwriting whatsoever. They specialize in mergers and acquisitions and have raised large pools of capital for investing in their own transactions.

3. Here investment banking is defined to include only *some* capital market activities, stressing underwriting and mergers and acquisitions. Excluded, for example, are fund management, venture capital, commodities, aspects of risk management, and the like. Depending on firm orientation, research may also be excluded if it is used primarily to support retail sales. (Note that the changing profile of investment banking would now include merchant banking in this definition.)

4. The narrowest definition takes investment banking back to its historical foundations, limiting the field strctly to underwriting and the raising of capital in the primary markets, and the trading of securities (broker/dealer functions) in the secondary markets. (It is hard to conceive of a contemporary definition of investment banking that would exclude M&A, so this one is for historians and purists.)

I lean toward the second definition; the connotation of investment banking in this book includes all capital market activities but excludes all retail-oriented selling. We focus on principles and techniques of financing and capital raising, and we discuss securities trading only where it affects these capital market activities. As such, we differentiate investment banking from the securities industry.[2]

Scope of Investment Banking

It would be easy to compile a long list of the dozens of activities that contemporary investment bankers do. Enumerating a short list is a harder trick.[3] Following are 12 categories of investment banking activities.

---

2. Fidelity to this definition of investment banking will not be perfect: I am known to wander in either direction. Sometimes I restrict the definition and make it narrower: Playing the purist I limit investment banking to only *some* capital market activities, eliminating such interlopers as fund management and the trading of risk management instruments. (Never would I exclude merchant banking, leveraged buyouts, or the *creation* of risk management instruments.) At other times I expand the definition and make it broader: Playing the transformer, I encompass all activities of major Wall Street firms. Though some may not classify consumer markets (especially sales and marketing, branch management, etc.) as an investment banking function, I must occasionally do so in order to include what have clearly become investment banking functions (e.g., developing new financial products for individual investors).

3. *Splitting*, seeing the world in ever smaller and more disconnected pieces, is always easier than *grouping*, visualizing ever broader and more organizing principles.

Public Offerings of Debt and Equity Securities

The public offering of debt and equity securities is the foundation of investment banking. Although the term *underwriting* seems to imply an absolute guarantee that the managing investment bank and its syndicate members[4] (i.e., the underwriters) will be legally bound to purchase the securities from the issuing company, the real world is more complicated. Regarding an initial public offering, there are actually only two approaches that an investment bank can take: firm commitment or best efforts.

Firm Commitment or Best Efforts.   When an investment bank "promises" to raise money for a company, how confident can that company be that a specific amount of money will be in their bank account? The degree of confidence depends on numerous factors, primary among them an understanding of the two types of promises.

- *Firm Commitment.* A firm commitment means that the managing investment bank and its syndicate will agree to buy the entire issue at a negotiated price. The underwriter will then resell these shares to its clients, making as its profits the previously negotiated *spread*, which is the difference between the *gross proceeds* paid by the public and the *net proceeds* given to the issuer. This means that the underwriters bear the entire risk of per-share pricing and the amount of total proceeds to be raised. (It should be stressed that a *firm commitment* is often not as "firm" as it appears.[5])

---

4. Chapter 14 and the Appendix ("A Philosophy of Investment Banking") describe the syndication process and its rationale.

5. A firm committment becomes absolutely firm only on the offering day itself (or the night before), when the underwriting agreement is signed by the company and the managing underwriter and its syndicate members. This signing occurs just before the issue "goes effective," which is the moment when the SEC gives its final approval. Until then the firm commitment is not firm, no matter who promises what to whom. (*Even then* the underwriting agreement is not perfectly firm; it has various "outs," for market disturbances, acts of God, and the like.) Furthermore, note the timing of the signing. All the marketing of the issue has already been done; the road shows have been conducted and the underwriting syndicate members know which of their clients are committed to buy how many shares. They know if the issue is oversold or undersold and can make final adjustments to price accordingly. The bottom line is that when the firm commitments of investment banks become *really* firm, it is normally at the very last moment and there is little uncertainty. (However, investment banks *can* lose money on underwritings; for example, this can occur when markets shift after a firm commitment on price has been made and future reputation demands adherence.)

- *Best Efforts.* A best efforts relationship is where the investment bank uses its expertise as structurer in designing the issue
  and as marketer in selling the issue. This means that the underwriters bear no risk in the deal, leaving to the issuing company
  all the uncertainty of per-share pricing and the amount of total
  proceeds to be raised.

Types of Public Offerings.   There are four general types of public offerings that investment banks conduct:

1. Initial public offerings (IPOs) of securities issued by companies that have never before issued any public securities (normally common stock is the first security to be issued in an
   IPO).
2. Initial public offerings of new securities that companies that
   are already public have not previously issued (e.g., a new
   class of convertible debt security issued by a public company).
3. Further public offerings by issuing companies of securities that
   are already publicly traded (e.g., the issuance of additional
   common stock when its price is sufficiently high so that the
   cost of capital is sufficiently low).
4. Public offerings by company shareholders of securities that are
   already publicly traded (e.g., when an original large shareholder, say a venture capital fund, wants to cash out its position).

Types of Securities.   In the past we could differentiate cleanly between
debt and equity securities, putting them each into neatly separate
categories. Today the old distinctions are gone: Debt and equity are no
longer discretely independent entities. They are more points on a continuum than boxes on a chart (see Chapters 12 and 13). For example, a
junior subordinated zero-coupon convertible debenture is actually more
equity than debt, and dutch-auction preferred stock is actually more debt
than equity.

Markets.   Telecommunications have altered forever financial markets.
One result is that some companies prefer the computerbased transactions
of NASDAQ to the specialist-brokered trading floors of the New York
or American Stock Exchanges (which are supposedly more prestigious).

Geography, as well, is no longer a constraint: Companies can reach anywhere in the world to lower their cost of capital, as investors can do to optimize their risk/return trade-off. (See Chapter 22).

The Underwriting Process.   Underwriting is a formal process involving many simultaneous functions, procedures, requirements, and activities. (See Chapter 14 for a complete discussion.) Following are some of the critical steps.

- Company expression of interest and underwriter selection.
- Preliminary analysis of issue structure and securities pricing.
- Due diligence reviews by underwriters and their counsels.
- Legal and accounting analysis and document preparation.
- Preliminary compilation of the registration statement.
- Submission of registration statement to the Securities and Exchange Commission (SEC).
- Circulation of preliminary prospectus to prospective investors.
- Information meetings ("road shows" or "dog-and-pony shows") in major cities for describing the company and its securities.
- Reception and response to SEC comments.
- Final pricing negotiations and signing of the underwriting agreement.
- Final registration statement filed with the SEC.
- SEC approval declaring the issue effective.
- Press releases and tombstone advertisement.
- Closing and settlement.

Public Trading of Debt and Equity Securities

Most large investment banks maintain strong trading capabilities, especially the bluge-bracket firms (the most prestigious investment banks—see Chapter 2). Trading is a significant though volatile profit center—profits are made both from commissions generated by trading for clients and from capital appreciation generated by trading for the firm's own account. Of equal importance is the fact that a firm's trading capability supports a firm's investment banking activities in underwriting debt and equity securities: The stronger a firm's independent power to place its newly issued securities among the general public (both large institutions and individual investors), the stronger its relative competitive position in winning underwriting opportunities and completing these deals success-fully.

Investment banks perform various levels of trading functions. They act as brokers, dealers, and/or market makers (which can differ for different securities).

Brokers.   Brokers are commissioned agents who represent either buyers or sellers and work much the same as real estate agents. Brokers com-municate among each other through actual or electronic stock exchanges and arrange transactions for their clients (i.e., the buyers or sellers of the securities) at prices set by those clients. Stock brokers carry no securities in inventory and therefore assume no risk in price variation or interest charge.

Dealers.   Dealers set bid-and-ask prices for each security they offer for trade. When a bid offered by a dealer is accepted (hit) by a seller (whether broker or institution), the dealer buys the security and takes it into inventory. (By maintaining an inventory of securities, dealers assume a price risk since the market may go up or down during the time they hold the securities. They must also bear the cost of interest carried. Dealers can "lay off" or limit their risk by taking counteracting hedging positions in derivative markets such as financial futures and options. Risk can be reduced, but at a cost.) Over-the-counter markets operate through the dealer system.

Market Makers.   Market makers establish (and support) the entire mar-ket for a security on either buy or sell side of a transaction. Such market making is normally important following its initial public offering before the market becomes sufficiently broad, and it involves the entire system of stock specialists, floor traders, and the like.

Risk Arbitrage.   Risk arbitrage is an important profit center for the trading divisions of many investment banks, although after the insider trading scandals the firms have been keeping a decidedly low profile on this activity. Risk arbitrage is the process of buying the securities of firms that have announced mergers or acquisitions. Since the pre-closing market price will almost always reflect a lower price than that of the deal[6] (embedding a healthy discount for the ever-present risk of

---

6. Exceptions are when the market expects a higher bid to be made; if an auction is anticipated the stock price can run significantly higher than the initial bid.

not closing the transaction as well as for the time value of money), savvy investors can generate a high rate of annulized return—but they must beware the unexpected (see Chapter 17).

Logistics and Support.   All trading functions are backed up by substantial logistical support from a back office operation. Trading requires complex paper processing and record keeping, which are needed for the proper settlement of transactions, the recording and releasing of price and volume data of traded securities, and the reconciliation of cash flows and stock certificate exchanges.[7]

Trading Focus.   The trading focus may differ from firm to firm depending on the specific strategic niche. For example, the large Wall Street securities firms maintain full-line services for retail customers; all bulge-bracket investment banks perform block trading for institutional investors; and those (smaller) investment banks that underwrite initial public offerings of high-risk companies (public venture capital) need to maintain an internal sales staff to distribute and support the stock.

Many Wall Street investment banks began life as securities firms, and the internecine competition and contention between traders and bankers has been the subject of legend and myth at many firms. The current organizational structure of many investment banks is the product or by-product of (i.e., the planned result of, or the fallout from) the historical (and often hysterical) power struggle between securities traders and investment bankers. (Lehman Brothers, it is said, was sold to Shearson as a direct result of severe dissension between traders and bankers).

Private Placements of Debt and Equity Securities

Private placement is the selling of corporate securities to investors without the regulatory requirements of public offerings. The regulations defining private placements are complex, and the securities and investment vehicles offered are numerous. Corporations seeking to place their securities in the private markets engage investment banks to act as their agents on a best efforts basis. Privately placed securities carry a higher rate of return than similarly structured securities that can trade in the public markets. The loss of liquidity (i.e., the capacity to rapidly convert

---

7. Brokers and dealers are regulated by the various exchanges of which they are members and the National Association of Securities Dealers (NASD), which is the professional self-regulating organization to which they all belong.

an investment into cash) enhances risk and therefore requires a proportionally higher return (see Chapter 15).

The universe of investors who consider private placements is decidedly smaller than the universe of investors who consider public offerings. Nonetheless, there has been an explosion in the size of the private markets in recent years. This is due to two factors.

1. *New Capital.* The accumulation of huge new pools of liquid wealth (primarily institutional) has become a great source and supply of capital that must seek profitable investments. The massive growth in pension and insurance funds, coupled with changing tax laws, presents an issuing company with a bewildering number of options for special financing in the private markets.

2. *New Vehicles.* There has been a proliferation of new investment vehicles to meet specific risk/reward/tax profiles. Limited partnerships, master limited partnerships, R&D partnerships, complex real estate deals, sale/leasebacks, joint ventures, and project financing transactions are but a few of the new opportunities that have mushroomed in recent years.

Mergers and Acquisitions (M&A)

This is the high profile area of investment banking—the takeover battles, the hostile attacks, and fierce defenses—generating front-page news and massive fees. But M&A is not all war. The vast majority of mergers and acquisitions are friendly and mutually desirable. M&A has become a major part, in fact a central part, of contemporary investment banking.

Investment bankers seek to get the best price, even when the best price is not the highest for client sellers (e.g., all cash or confidence in closing may be more important) or not the lowest price for client buyers (e.g., certainty of closing the deal may be more vital). Investment banks find, facilitate, price, and finance mergers and acquisitions (Chapters 6 and 7).

We also include in M&A several of the modern incarnations: the tremendous surge of leveraged buyouts (LBOs, Chapter 16), the restructuring and recapitalization of companies (often as a defensive measure against takeovers), and the reorganization of bankrupt and troubled companies.

Merchant Banking

This is where investment banks commit and risk the firm's own capital and seek very high returns. They become equity players and owners of operating companies, and their risks and rewards skyrocket.

Merchant banking is a hot new area of investment banking, energized by the excessive returns (35–50%) that have been attained year after year. It is also a cause of controversy. Committing an investment bank's own capital increases both ends of the risk/reward trade-off. Though merchant banking was eschewed by blue-chip, bulge-bracket firms in the early days, few investment banks today can forgo the opportunity to earn the high returns—for themselves as well as their clients. (Indeed, many of an investment bank's leading clients—the blue-chip institutional investors—are demanding the high-return investment opportunities of LBOs and bridge financing for their funds.)

Such commitment of capital is made for two general purposes: (1) to facilitate a client transaction (i.e., a bridge loan until permanent financing is obtained); or (2) to purchase an operating company for the firm's own account (i.e., equity ownership of the target company— whether 100% ownership by the investment bank, in partnership with a client, or as the manager of a dedicated LBO fund). It should be noted that bridge loans are highly profitable, combining commitment fees, placement fees, high interest rates, and equity incentives ("kickers").

Financial Consulting and Fairness Opinions

Financial consulting per se is not a high-leverage investment banking activity. (Investment bankers do not get paid an hourly fee.) Rather, such corporate finance consulting opens the door for marketing major investment banking services such as M&A and underwriting. (Fees are charged on a fixed scale or with a block retainer and hardly ever on an hourly or per diem schedule.)

Fairness opinions are an important service that have become a significant business, growing in proportion to the increase in mergers and acquisitions, leveraged buyouts, and restructurings. Getting an independent, defensible, expert statement on values and the fairness of those values is an essential part of any M&A transaction involving a public company. In fact, it is inconceivable for the board of directors of a public company to approve a major transaction without an independent fairness opinion.

Investment banks command what may seem to be exorbitantly high fees for giving fairness opinions, especially in relationship to the number of hours allocated (and the amount of paper produced). The reason is the essential nature of the opinion for the public corporations involved on either or both sides of the transaction and the potential liability to the investment bank itself. Such liability can be manifested both in the courts and to the bank's industry reputation. Investment banks assume significant risk in the rendering of fairness opinions. They are often called to testify in legal proceedings, a common occurrence in many public mergers and acquisitions. Furthermore, though indemnified, they may be open to shareholder suits.

Asset Monetarization and Securitization

Securitization is the process by which formerly illiquid assets, mostly small consumer receivables of all kinds, can be liquefied into large, publicly tradable securities. Here is real value added, a clear demonstration of innovative investment banking contribution to the financial markets. Nonexistent a decade ago, the *rolling up* of small, consumer loans that could not be traded in any way into large, institutional instruments that could be traded in public markets has transformed many financial institutions (e.g., savings and loans, automotive finance companies).

The conversion of illiquid liabilities into liquid securities improves the risk/return profile for issuers and investors. Securitized obligations in residential real estate, commercial real estate, and receivables-backed securities (such as automobile and credit card loans) have exploded into a market worth hundreds of billions of dollars (see Chapter 20).

Securitized obligations are highly sophisticated in design and often require statistical analysis and sensitivity testing of key criteria (e.g., default rates, prepayment profiles, interest rate sensitivity). For example, a change from forecasted rates of prepayment (e.g., due to interest rate declines and the resulting refinancing of older, higher-rate mortgages) can result in shocking differences in returns from initial expectations. (Principal itself can suffer significantly.) The features of these securities, from payment schedules of interest and principal to tax considerations of strategy and structure, are continuously being refined to meet more accurately the mutual demands of issuers and investors.

Risk Management

Although we are not focusing on the role of investment banks in securities trading, it has become impossible to divorce one from the other.

New methods of hedging positions in interest rates, foreign currency exchanges, and commodity positions through swaps, options, and futures have permanently changed the financial markets. (See Chapter 18.) Sophisticated, computerized, quantitative methods are essential, and mathematical "rocket scientists" have now become Wall Street partners. Portfolio theory has moved from the ivory towers of academia down to the littered floors of the exchanges.

Swaps have emerged as a radical new mechanism for crafting optimum financial structure positions with respect to interest and currency exchange rates and to the temporal matching of assets and liabilities. Swapping instruments are the mechanisms by which two or more parties exchange their debt obligations in order to control more precisely each party's desired risk/return profile. Swaps work because different corporations have different comparative advantages when pricing different categories of debt in different financial markets. Parties of dissimilar credit ratings or financing needs can exchange their obligations (e.g., from shorter term to longer term and vice versa) in order to optimize their financial strategy and structure (see Chapter 19).

Investment Research and Security Analysis

For many years, the research capabilities of an investment bank's security analysts were often the firm's most prestigious and most visible strength. (In more recent years, M&A, LBOs, and merchant banking have usurped the limelight.) Indeed, many investment banks began life as research boutiques, using the reputation derived from their investment analysis expertise to develop underwriting and money management businesses.

Research is still a foundational pillar of the industry, supporting both the securities trading and investment banking operations. Leading analysts command very high remuneration, and members of *Institutional Investors's* All American Team attain star status. (Investment banks pay heavily to entice stars to change firms. When these financial celebrities make the jump, it's big news in the industry—much like when a big-time free agent switches teams in professional sports.)

It is important for large investment banks to field a top team of investment analyst stars. It symbolizes the investment bank's relative importance and competitive strengths. Such star analysts are not just for image; they are used to attract corporate clients and institutional investors. It is not uncommon for a large investment bank to pass up a major financing or underwriting opportunity because it does not have within the firm first-rate research strength in the potential client's industry area.

International Investment Banking

The opportunities for investment, underwriting, and M&A are extensive in foreign markets (see Chapter 22). All the large investment banks have sought expansion into international finance, with significant representation in foreign markets. Several major American firms have made enormous capital allocations and ongoing investments to establish major offices in London and Tokyo.

Globalization is the new byword of investment banking. Financing has become a multimarket search for the lowest cost of capital for issuers, and a 24-hour-a-day quest for the highest return for investors.

Enhanced Financing Efficiency.   Both issuers and investors seek the optimum level of risk for a given level of return. Such optimizations cover the uncertainties and volatilities of interest rates, currency exchange rates, credit availability (for users of capital), credit instability (for providers of capital), and equity investments. Optimum risk for a given return, or conversely optimum return for a given level of risk, is achieved by using techniques of finance theory such as hedging and diversification. The international expansion of one's investment horizons allows more efficient optimization procedures for both issuers and investors—that is, investment portfolios can be diversified more widely, thereby expanding their risk/return frontier and achieving higher efficiency.

Debt-Equity Swaps.   A new area of international investment banking involves the debt obligations of the Third World and how such complex and emotional issues can be resolved. Debt restructuring plans are one method (they are not unlike corporate restructuring programs for troubled companies). A more innovative approach is debt-equity swaps, in which local, foreign country debt is exchanged for ownership positions in local operating companies. Such swaps are complex and must articulate the diverse interests of multiple parties.

Money Mangement

With the enormous growth in pools of capital (e.g., pension and insurance funds), money management has become a major industry. Several investment banks have set up departments to handle the management of these funds. Although they draw on their inherent strengths in understanding the capital markets for purposes of money management, firms must also be exquisitiely sensitive to any real or apparent conflicts of interest (see Chapter 10).

Venture Capital

Venture capital is the high risk-high return business of investing in young, fast-growing companies. It is a volatile industry with sky-high crests and precipitous crashes. The industry turns in cycles, empowered by recent stories of spectacular success, hot emerging technologies, the opening and closing of windows in the public markets, changing strategies (e.g., financings in later stages rather than in earlier stages), and tax considerations (e.g., existence, rates, and structure of capital gains taxes).

Investment banks are involved at all levels of venture capital investments, from assembling the capital for the funds to taking the portfolio companies public. Regarding management of the funds, there are two approaches: First, an investment bank may simply raise monies for external venture capital funds. Here the investment bank gets a commission for monies raised and may have no further involvement. Alternatively, the investment bank can manage the venture fund itself, setting up a separate subsidiary and management organization.

Investment banks like to involve themselves in the venture capital business since the very nature of venture investments generates a continuing series of financing requirements and investment opportunities in the private and public markets. The various stages, or *rounds*, of financing can involve a bank's financial skills and fund-raising expertise. And certainly the cashing out process—the *exit* or *back end* — is an investment banking activity. Whether through an initial public offering, a secondary stock offering, or by merger or acquisition, an investment bank provides the venture capitalists with the critical cashing out method for liquefying their original investments. (An investment bank can take many bites of the same venture capital apple.)

CHAPTER 2

Structures and Strategies of Investment Banks*

In this chapter, we discuss the importance of structure and strategy for the entire investment banking industry viewed collectively, for specific investment banks considered individually, and for the client companies that investment banks serve.

In the first section, we describe the industry structure of investment banking as a whole; we compare key characterisitics of the leading firms and assess market positioning and relationships.

In the second section, we portray the internal organizational structure of individual investment banks; we take each of the various functions presented in Chapter 1 and determine where it fits into the reporting system or hierarchy of various investment banks.

In the third section, we present the nature of strategy and strategic management in order to make the subsequent applications to investment banking.

In the fourth section, we apply the principles of strategic management to assess proper strategies for client companies. What are the optimal strategies that investment banks should seek to formulate and implement to benefit those enterprises that they advise?

---

* This chapter has been derived from "The Strategies of Investment Banking" by Robert Lawrence Kuhn, Volume IV (Mergers, Acquisitions, and Leveraged Buyouts), Dow Jones–Irwin's *The Library of Investment Banking* (1990), Robert Lawrence Kuhn, editor in chief.

In the fifth section, we apply these same principles of strategic management to the investment banks themselves. What are the optimal strategies that investment banks should seek to formulate and implement to benefit their own organizations?

Industry Structure of Investment Banking

What are the critical structural characteristics of the investment banking industry in the United States? Which are the largest firms? What are the categories that best describe relative size, position, and power? How do the competitors compare?

Categories of Investment Banking Firms

There are two general ways to categorize investment banking firms: (1) relative status, as differentiated by size, expertise, and reputation, and (2) functions offered or emphasized.

Investment banking is a status-conscious industry, with a prestige-based caste system all its own. Who you are is often determined by where you are. (Although caste systems love to protect the status quo, the investment banking variety has been shaken by the changes on Wall Street—such as the rise in recent years of Shearson Lehman Hutton and Drexel Burnham Lambert.) The status of investment banking firms can be classified as follows:

- *Bulge-bracket firms*, the blue-chip houses that are set apart from all others by reputation, size, market power, and client list (i.e., the firms that "bulge" on tombstones).[1]

- *Major bracket firms*, the large national full-line firms that do not have the same investment banking status as the bulge-bracket firms.

- *Submajor bracket firms*, the solid, partnership-owned, often New York–based firms that create a niche by serving special investor groups and smaller issuing companies.

- *Regional firms*, the securities firms that are important in geographic areas outside of New York. The investment banking

---

1. First Boston, Goldman Sachs, Merrill Lynch, Morgan Stanley, and Salomon Brothers are in everyone's bulge bracket. Shearson Lehman Hutton is a more recent entry. Drexel Burnham Lambert was reaching for the bulge before its legal difficulties.

departments of regional firms are usually weaker than their trading departments, which cater to local investors. (It is easier for companies to access the New York firms than it is for private investors.)

- *Specialized firms*, the boutique firms that are strong in only a few focused areas, such as specialists in banking securities or technology offerings.

- *Research firms*, the boutique firms that make their reputation by the quality of securities analysis (their investment banking function is an extension of their research capabilities).

- *Merchant banks*, the boutique firms that specialize in mergers and acquisitions and leveraged buyouts. Many of these highly visible firms have been founded by highly visible bankers who left the bulge-bracket firms; these boutiques do not perform underwritings but have raised large pools of capital for merchant banking and LBOs. (Note that many of these boutiques do not want to grow large; their partners want to be deal makers, not administrators.)[2]

Capital of Investment Banking Firms

Capital is perhaps the most vital of an investment bank's vital statistics. It is a primary competitive weapon in the fight for new business and the search for market opportunity.[3] Investment banks use capital for four primary functions:

- *Underwriting*. In order to make a firm commitment (which is usually required to win an underwriting), an investment bank needs to have the resources to buy an entire issue (together with its assembled syndicate). To have the credibility to become

---

2. Several of these merchant banking boutiques have formed alliances with the giant Japanese securities houses (e.g., Wasserstein Parella with Nomura Securities and Blackstone with Nikko Securities).

3. It is possible for investment banks to have *too much capital*, although investment bankers would not have thought so several years ago, in the last days of the great bull market. With too much capital, and too little investment opportunity, too much money chases too few deals — and the natural result of this mismatch is that risks go up and returns go down. As a consequence of the great influx of capital garnered by many investment banks in the middle 1980s (e.g., from going public, foreign investors), declining returns have become a real issue for the industry.

dealer/manager of a public offering, an investment bank must have the financial capability to purchase the largest part of the issue (and to make up for any shortfall in its syndication process).

• *Securities trading.* Many of the opportunities for securities trading today require the capacity to act as a dealer and take a large block of securities into inventory. This means purchasing the entire block, carrying it in inventory, and then waiting an indeterminate amount of time before reselling the securities to clients. Speed is essential in a global marketplace; there is no time to line up external financing. Capital is essential to take the risks and enjoy the rewards of contemporary securities trading.

• *Merchant banking.* By definition, merchant banking requires the investment of the firm's own capital to facilitate client transactions (i.e., bridge loans) and to purchase operating companies for the firm's own account. Such buyouts will eventually be sold off to third parties or taken public, but the time period may extend several years before the opportune moment arrives. (Bridge loans will generally be financed out in several months—although the risk of being stuck in the loan is always present.) Capital is essential to survive the waiting period.

• *New financial techniques.* Many of the new financial techniques require the investment bank to put its credit at risk in the transaction (e.g., swaps). Even though the guarantees may be contingent and off-balance-sheet, there is increasing call for regulations that would require such risks to be backed by sufficient capital.

Comparisons of Investment Banks

The tables in Tables 2-1 through 2-9, developed by *IDD Information Services, Inc.* and *Institutional Investor* magazine, rank the leading firms in the investment banking industry according to the following criteria:

• Amount of capital (Table 2-1)
• Number of offices (Table 2-2)
• Total securities underwriting (Table 2-3)
• Initial public offerings (Table 2-4)

Table 2–1. Amount of Capital (as of December 31, 1988).

Rank	Name of Firm	Total Consolidated Capital ($ millions)	Equity Capital ($ millions)	Long Term Debt ($ millions)	"Excess" Net Capital ($ millions)
1	Merrill Lynch & Co.	$9,767.5	$3,484.2	$6,283.3	$ 754.7
2	Shearson Lehman Hutton	8,157.0	1,746.0	6,411.0	819.0
3	Salomon Brothers Holding Co.	4,440.0	3,137.2	1,302.8	510.8
4	Goldman, Sachs & Co.	2,771.0[1]	1,876.0	895.0	1,033.0
5	Morgan Stanley & Co.	2,413.9	1,599.4	814.5	429.7
6	Drexel Burnham Lambert	2,143.0[2]	1,292.0	851.0	1,004.0
7	First Boston Corp.	1,864.0	1,130.0	734.0	458.0
8	Prudential-Bache Securities	1,497.8	1,103.7	394.1	292.7
9	PaineWebber Group	1,464.0	1,051.0	413.0	486.0
10	Integrated Resources	1,435.5[3]	530.9	904.6	11.1
11	Bear, Stearns & Co.	1,418.4	1,033.0	385.4	214.6
12	Dean Witter Reynolds	1,343.0[4]	821.0	522.0	475.0
13	Smith Barney, Harris Upham & Co.	978.0	713.0	260.0	253.0
14	Donaldson, Lufkin & Jenrette	950.0	257.0	693.0	186.0
15	Kidder, Peabody & Co.	800.0[5]	463.0	337.0	272.0
16	Allen & Co.	405.7	405.7	—	144.5
17	J.P. Morgan Securities	404.0	404.0	—	130.0
18	Shelby Cullom Davis & Co.	394.0	394.0	—	274.8

[1] As of 11/25/88.　　[3] As of 9/30/88.　　[5] As of 12/26/88.
[2] As of 12/30/88.　　[4] Represents U.S. broker-dealer only.

Table 2–1. (continued)

Rank	Name of Firm	Total Consolidated Capital ($ millions)	Equity Capital ($ millions)	Long Term Debt ($ millions)	"Excess" Net Capital ($ millions)
19	Charles Schwab & Co.	360.0	291.0	69.0	69.0
20	Nomura Securities International	322.0	222.0	100.0	166.0
21	Thomson McKinnon Securities	279.0	204.0	75.0	47.0
22	A.G. Edwards & Sons	259.0	259.0	–	98.0
23	Deustche Bank Capital Corp.	256.0	110.0	146.0	67.0
24	Spear, Leeds & Kellogg	253.0	222.0	31.0	98.0
25	Aubrey G. Lanston & Co.	243.8	243.8	–	86.9
26	Oppenheimer & Co.	238.4	173.5	64.9	86.5
27	Van Kampen Merritt	236.0	236.0	–	75.0
28	Nikko Securities Co. International	227.0	127.0	100.0	166.1
29	UBS Securities	219.0	44.0	175.0	139.0
30	Dillon, Read & Co.	215.0	183.0	32.0	58.0
31	John Nuveen & Co.	213.6	213.6	–	149.7
32	Daiwa Securities America	212.0	112.0	100.0	121.0
33	Alex. Brown & Sons	203.0	170.0	33.0	69.0
34	Yamaichi International (America)	191.0	141.0	50.0	117.0
35	Gruntal & Co.	169.4	122.2	47.2	35.1
36	L.F. Rothschild & Co.	155.0	109.9	45.1	30.1

Table 2–1. (continued)

Rank	Name of Firm	Total Consolidated Capital ($ millions)	Equity Capital ($ millions)	Long Term Debt ($ millions)	"Excess" Net Capital ($ millions)
37	Wertheim Schroder & Co.	150.2	121.6	28.6	54.0
38	Allen & Co. Inc.	143.5	140.0	3.5	35.6
39	Greenwich Capital Markets	138.0	58.0	80.0	66.4
40	Gruss Partners	126.0	126.0	—	105.0
41	Jefferies & Co.	125.0	85.0	40.0	84.7
42	Edward D. Jones & Co.	124.9	69.7	55.2	67.7
43	Neuberger & Berman	124.4	124.4	—	87.0
44	Prescott, Ball & Turben	113.0[6]	103.0	10.0	3.0
45	Stephens	109.4	109.4	—	50.7
46	Brown Brothers Harriman & Co.	102.9	102.9	—	—
47	Lazard Frères & Co.	100.0	100.0	—	55.0
48	M.A. Schapiro & Co.	99.7	99.7	—	72.3
49	SBCI Swiss Bank Corp. Investment Banking	99.4	59.4	40.0	80.5
50	Fidelity Brokerage Services	98.6	98.6	—	26.8

Source: *Institutional Investor*, April 1989.
[6] Unaudited figures

Table 2–2. Number of Offices (as of December 31, 1988).

Rank	Name of Firm	Number of Offices
1	Integrated Resources	1,750
2	Edward D. Jones & Co.	1,395
3	Thomson McKinnon Securities	800
4	Dean Witter Reynolds	691
5	Shearson Lehman Hutton	645
6	Merrill Lynch & Co.	550
7	A.G. Edwards & Sons	368
8	Raymond, James Financial	365
9	Prudential-Bache Securities	330
10	Paine Webber Group	296
11	Charles Schwab & Co.	109
12	Smith Barney, Harris Upham & Co.	94
13	Advest	74
14	Legg Mason Wood Walker	72
15	Blunt Ellis & Loewi	70
	Kidder, Peabody & Co.	70
17	Drexel Burnham Lambert	69
18	Piper, Jaffray & Hopwood	64
19	Quick & Reilly Group	59
20	Wheat, First Securities	55
21	J.C. Bradford & Co.	53
22	Fidelity Brokerage Services	52
23	Dain Bosworth	51
	Interstate/Johnson Lane Corp.	51
25	Ohio Co.	50

Source: Institutional Investor, April 1989

Table 2–3. Total Securities Underwriting.

Full Credit to Lead Manager

1987	1988	Manager	$Volume (millions)	No. of Issues
3	1	Merrill Lynch	$39,649.0	414
4	2	Goldman Sachs	37,106.5	393
1	3	Salomon Brothers	33,929.4	310
2	4	First Boston	29,938.2	311
6	5	Shearson Lehman Hutton	25,737.2	299
5	6	Morgan Stanley	23,048.2	239
7	7	Drexel Burnham Lambert	20,923.4	243
10	8	Prudential-Bache	11,033.7	186
9	9	Bear Stearns	9,149.2	122
8	10	Kidder Peabody	7,110.2	128
14	11	PaineWebber	6,279.0	78
11	12	Smith Barney	4,742.2	65
17	13	Citicorp	3,451.3	71
19	14	Donaldson, Lufkin & Jenrette	2,531.5	60
16	15	Wheat, First Securities	2,425.5	15
—	16	Chemical Bank	2,132.2	11
—	17	BT Securities	1,775.9	4
15	18	Dean Witter	1,723.5	34
12	19	Dillon Read	1,458.9	11
13	20	Alex. Brown & Sons	1,432.6	38
25	21	UBS Securities	887.1	35
22	22	Thomson McKinnon Securities	702.9	25
—	23	Allen & Co.	641.3	4
18	24	L.F. Rothschild	631.5	40
24	25	Edward D. Jones	618.1	65

Full Credit to Each Manager

1987	1988	Manager	$Volume (millions)	No. of Issues
2	1	Merrill Lynch	$67,270.1	595
1	2	Salomon Brothers	61,295.3	469
4	3	Goldman Sachs	58,002.4	530
3	4	First Boston	56,678.9	459
6	5	Shearson Lehman Hutton	44,040.3	428
5	6	Morgan Stanley	36,446.1	327
7	7	Drexel Burnham Lambert	33,984.2	312
8	8	Kidder Peabody	20,244.1	197
9	9	Bear Stearns	17,980.6	165
11	10	Smith Barney	16,379.6	122
10	11	Prudential-Bache	14,177.2	223
19	12	Citicorp	11,662.7	110
12	13	PaineWebber	11,579.8	113
—	14	BT Securities	6,776.2	16
16	15	Donaldson, Lufkin & Jenrette	6,607.5	86
14	16	Dean Witter	6,335.1	61
20	17	Wheat, First Securities	5,702.1	39
—	18	Chase Manhattan Bank	5,213.1	20
—	19	Manufacturers Hanover	4,804.0	10
13	20	Dillon Read	4,779.7	32
24	21	Thomson McKinnon Securities	3,673.7	47
—	22	Blunt Ellis & Loewi	3,406.6	48
17	23	Lazard Freres	3,074.0	16
—	24	Dain Bosworth	2,885.9	25
—	25	Nomura Securities	2,884.0	37

Source: *Institutional Investor*, February 1989.

Table 2–4. Initial Public Offerings.

Full Credit to Lead Manager

1987	1988		$Volume (millions)	No. of Issues
1	1	Merrill Lynch	$4,348.2	28
5	2	Shearson Lehman Hutton	4,043.5	16
8	3	Prudential-Bache	3,193.8	12
11	4	PaineWebber	2,789.1	16
2	5	Wheat, First Securities	2,150.0	2
3	6	Goldman Sachs	1,725.5	15
4	7	Alex. Brown & Sons	1,061.7	15
7	8	Drexel Burnham Lambert	668.1	11
10	9	First Boston	584.8	9
6	10	Salomon Brothers	517.3	7
—	11	Smith Barney	513.2	3
9	12	Dean Witter	500.0	4
—	13	Piper, Jaffray & Hopwood	345.1	4
—	14	Donaldson, Lufkin & Jenrette	215.8	4
12	15	Kidder Peabody	126.2	5

Full Credit to Each Manager

1987	1988		$Volume (millions)	No. of Issues
2	1	Merrill Lynch	$5,642.3	38
1	2	Shearson Lehman Hutton	4,968.9	24
8	3	Wheat, First Securities	4,927.8	9
—	4	Kidder Peabody	4,467.7	12
—	5	Smith Barney	4,033.0	13
—	6	PaineWebber	3,935.2	25
15	7	Prudential-Bache	3,316.4	14
10	8	Drexel Burnham Lambert	2,889.8	19
—	9	Thomson McKinnon Securities	2,836.8	17
—	10	Blunt Ellis & Loewi	2,754.4	18
—	11	Dain Bosworth	2,634.5	11
—	12	Bateman Eichler, Hill Richards	2,573.1	12
—	13	Legg Mason Wood Walker	2,427.8	11
—	14	Butcher & Singer	2,381.1	10
3	15	Goldman Sachs	2,087.8	19

Source: *Institutional Investor*, February 1989.

Table 2-5. High-Yield Debt Offerings.

Full Credit to Lead Manager

1987	1988		$Volume (millions)	No. of Issues
1	1	Drexel Burnham Lambert	$11,906.7	76
3	2	First Boston	3,908.1	16
2	3	Morgan Stanley	3,132.7	11
4	4	Merrill Lynch	2,097.5	11
6	5	Salomon Brothers	1,751.0	9
15	6	Prudential-Bache	1,181.7	7
5	7	Goldman Sachs	805.2	6
8	8	Donaldson, Lufkin & Jenrette	776.3	5
11	9	Smith Barney	696.1	5
7	10	Kidder Peabody	551.0	5
13	11	PaineWebber	359.7	3
9	12	Shearson Lehman Hutton	350.0	2
12	13	Bear Stearns	280.6	2
—	14	R.G. Dickinson	16.0	1

Full Credit to Each Manager

1987	1988		$Volume (millions)	No. of Issues
1	1	Drexel Burnham Lambert	$12,906.8	81
4	2	First Boston	5,485.1	21
3	3	Morgan Stanley	3,132.7	11
2	4	Merrill Lynch	3,000.0	17
6	5	Salomon Brothers	2,198.1	11
5	6	Goldman Sachs	1,805.3	9
13	7	PaineWebber	1,562.2	10
9	8	Donaldson, Lufkin & Jenrette	1,251.3	8
10	9	Bear Stearns	1,205.6	6
14	10	Prudential-Bache	1,181.7	7
8	11	Shearson Lehman Hutton	916.5	5
—	12	Dillon Read	750.0	2
11	13	Smith Barney	696.1	5
7	14	Kidder Peabody	551.0	5
—	15	L.F. Rothschild	274.7	3

Source: *Institutional Investor*, February 1989.

Table 2–6. Mortgage-Backed Securities.

Full Credit to Lead Manager

1987	1988		$Volume (millions)	No. of Issues
4	1	Goldman Sachs	$17,166.7	253
1	2	Salomon Brothers	12,964.6	181
3	3	Merrill Lynch	9,444.2	195
2	4	First Boston	9,435.0	177
5	5	Shearson Lehman Hutton	8,404.8	202
6	6	Morgan Stanley	7,699.0	137
9	7	Bear Stearns	7,569.0	105
10	8	Prudential-Bache	6,206.1	156
8	9	Drexel Burnham Lambert	4,486.3	113
7	10	Kidder Peabody	2,943.4	82
12	11	PaineWebber	2,605.7	47
11	12	Citicorp	1,550.2	54
—	13	Donaldson, Lufkin & Jenrette	1,241.4	45
—	14	Smith Barney	858.4	26
—	15	UBS Securities	738.2	34

Full Credit to Each Manager

1987	1988		$Volume (millions)	No. of Issues
4	1	Goldman Sachs	$18,269.0	268
1	2	Salomon Brothers	15,212.8	212
2	3	First Boston	11,589.9	207
3	4	Merrill Lynch	11,198.9	222
5	5	Shearson Lehman Hutton	9,752.3	221
7	6	Bear Stearns	8,167.2	111
6	7	Morgan Stanley	7,981.2	140
9	8	Drexel Burnham Lambert	6,746.8	130
10	9	Prudential-Bache	6,586.2	162
8	10	Kidder Peabody	3,311.9	89
13	11	PaineWebber	2,735.5	48
11	12	Citicorp	1,898.7	56
—	13	Donaldson, Lufkin & Jenrette	1,511.0	51
—	14	Smith Barney	858.4	26
—	15	Chemical Bank	763.3	14

Source: *Institutional Investor*, February 1989.

Table 2–7. International Bond Underwriting.

Full Credit to Lead Manager

1987	1988		$Volume (millions)	No. of Issues
1	1	Nomura Securities	$18,698.5	144
2	2	Credit Suisse First Boston	14,361.5	84
5	3	Deutsche Bank	12,314.2	86
3	4	Daiwa Securities	10,305.0	83
7	5	Union Bank of Switzerland	8,536.5	75
6	6	Yamaichi Securities	8,396.6	66
4	7	Nikko Securities	7,951.9	64
10	8	Swiss Bank Corp.	6,687.1	55
12	9	Banque Paribas	6,485.4	52
22	10	Merrill Lynch	6,209.5	35
8	11	J.P. Morgan Securities	6,027.1	39
14	12	IBJ Int'l	5,669.0	49

Full Credit to Each Manager

1987	1988		$Volume (millions)	No. of Issues
5	1	Credit Suisse First Boston	$99,530.7	678
2	2	Swiss Bank Corp.	98,184.7	717
1	3	Nomura Securities	95,630.0	672
6	4	Union Bank of Switzerland	94,242.7	660
9	5	Banque Bruxelles Lambert	93,182.0	791
15	6	Merrill Lynch	89,910.3	623
8	7	Deutsche Bank	88,620.0	641
4	8	Daiwa Securities	85,024.9	602
7	9	Banque Paribas	84,682.5	621
3	10	Morgan Stanley	83,853.5	566
18	11	Dresdner Bank	76,152.5	590
12	12	J.P. Morgan Securities	74,026.1	494

Source: *Institutional Investor*, February 1989.

Table 2–7. (continued)

Full Credit to Lead Manager				
1987	1988		$Volume (millions)	No. of Issues
26	13	Bankers Trust	5,307.2	48
11	14	S.G. Warburg	5,276.8	44
13	15	Salomon Brothers	5,106.0	32
18	16	Goldman Sachs	4,057.1	28
16	17	Credit Suisse	3,971.1	37
9	18	Morgan Stanley	3,752.4	31
17	19	Dresdner Bank	3,723.1	24
15	20	Commerzbank	3,456.5	30
25	21	Hambros Bank	2,708.5	46
20	22	LTCB Int'l	2,445.9	26
19	23	Baring Brothers	2,285.6	18
31	24	Kleinwort Benson	2,113.2	15
29	25	Westdeutsche Landesbank	2,022.9	27
		Total Market Volume	$199,493.3	968

Full Credit to Each Manager				
1987	1988		$Volume (millions)	No. of Issues
16	13	Banque Nationale de Paris	72,515.9	519
10	14	S.G. Warburg	72,018.2	458
17	15	IBJ Int'l	66,097.7	446
14	16	Salomon Brothers	65,615.1	399
11	17	Nikko Securities	63,954.6	472
13	18	Yamaichi Securities	62,709.4	438
19	19	Goldman Sachs	62,061.3	396
25	20	Commerzbank	61,348.7	481
28	21	Credit Lyonnais	54,420.1	425
21	22	Westdeutsche Landesbank	54,402.8	459
23	23	Bankers Trust	53,464.5	397
29	24	Shearson Lehman Hutton	51,656.7	308
22	25	Algemene Bank Nederland	51,189.7	424

Source: *Institutional Investor*, February 1989.

Table 2–8. Public Finance: Tax-Exempt New Issues.

Full Credit to Lead Manager

1987	1988		$Volume (millions)	No. of Issues
1	1	Merrill Lynch	$12,532.0	221
3	2	Goldman Sachs	12,468.0	161
6	3	Shearson Lehman Hutton	9,153.2	248
5	4	First Boston	7,490.6	116
4	5	Smith Barney	6,634.1	165
7	6	PaineWebber	4,225.1	72
8	7	Prudential-Bache	3,672.6	161
12	8	Morgan Stanley	3,420.2	37
11	9	Bear Stearns	2,800.5	56
10	10	Drexel Burnham Lambert	2,800.4	84
22	11	Rauscher Pierce Refsnes	1,918.7	43
9	12	Donaldson, Lufkin & Jenrette	1,591.7	35
15	13	Lazard Freres	1,515.0	17
16	14	Chase Manhattan	1,492.7	23
13	15	Citicorp	1,305.5	19
14	16	Kidder Peabody	1,254.1	26
24	17	John Nuveen	1,136.8	64
20	18	Dillon Read	1,105.0	27
29	19	First Chicago	1,083.7	19
25	20	Dean Witter Reynolds	1,051.2	57
17	21	J.P. Morgan Securities	961.0	31
–	22	Manufacturers Hanover	853.6	14
35	23	Bank of America	845.2	15
28	24	Stone & Youngberg	774.0	36
21	25	BT Securities	746.9	22

Full Credit to Each Manager

$Volume (millions)	No. of Issues		1988	1987
$34,259.3	562	Shearson Lehman Hutton	1	1
34,250.2	536	Merrill Lynch	2	2
28,882.9	314	Goldman Sachs	3	4
26,658.8	495	Smith Barney	4	3
21,868.8	252	Bear Stearns	5	8
21,370.5	304	PaineWebber	6	5
20,383.0	235	First Boston	7	6
17,811.4	302	Drexel Burnham Lambert	8	11
17,723.0	399	Prudential-Bache	9	9
16,026.3	307	Dean Witter Reynolds	10	19
15,144.2	134	Morgan Stanley	11	10
11,715.0	184	Donaldson, Lufkin & Jenrette	12	15
11,209.6	212	Kidder Peabody	13	12
9,995.5	100	Citicorp	14	14
9,766.5	79	Dillon Read	15	13
8,468.0	61	Pryor, Govan, Counts	16	18
8,232.1	81	J.P. Morgan Securities	17	20
7,215.5	105	Chase Manhattan	18	16
7,177.5	54	WR Lazard	19	41
7,008.4	93	Ehrlich Bober	20	28
6,986.4	70	Lazard Freres	21	22
6,255.0	76	Grigsby Brandford	22	33
6,137.0	86	First Chicago	23	21
5,858.6	116	Chemical Securities	24	23
5,200.7	66	Manufacturers Hanover	25	35

Source: *Institutional Investor*, February 1989.

Table 2–8. (continued).

Full Credit to Lead Manager

1987	1988		$Volume (millions)	No. of Issues
46	26	Chemical Securities	684.3	28
26	27	Miller & Schroeder Financial	672.0	38
23	28	Cranston/Prescott	666.3	22
19	29	Alex. Brown & Sons	627.5	26
—	30	Stifel Nicolaus	519.1	14
31	31	Northern Trust	464.5	34
—	32	Marine Midland Capital Mkts	445.1	21
27	33	Boettcher	433.7	23
36	34	Dain Bosworth	385.5	24
—	35	First Interstate Bank, CA	371.8	17
39	36	Ehrlich Bober	358.1	34
—	37	William R. Hough	350.7	23
44	38	Clayton Brown	342.4	32
47	39	Underwood Neuhaus	330.3	24
32	40	First Fidelity Bank NJ	315.8	24
50	41	Dougherty, Dawkins, Strand & Yost	304.2	15
40	42	Piper, Jaffray & Hopwood	301.1	13
—	43	Wachovia Bank & Trust	299.9	15
41	44	A.G. Edwards & Sons	288.6	26
38	45	Ziegler Securities	283.3	18
—	46	George K. Baum	239.1	9
45	47	Seattle-Northwest Securities	237.3	24
43	48	Butcher & Singer	234.9	19
48	49	Harris Trust & Savings Bank	218.4	25
—	50	Wheat, First Securities	208.4	7

Full Credit to Each Manager

1988	1987		$Volume (millions)	No. of Issues
26	27	Alex. Brown & Sons	4,652.0	141
27	25	Rauscher Pierce Refsnes	4,201.0	95
28	26	Daniels & Bell	3,904.5	43
29	24	Northern Trust	3,725.0	106
30	31	Cranston/Prescott	3,637.7	74
31	45	Blunt Ellis & Loewi	3,566.1	102
32	37	BT Securities	3,465.9	66
33	34	Thomson McKinnon Securities	3,409.0	74
34	36	Harris Trust & Savings Bank	3,267.8	83
35	30	John Nuveen	3,241.7	120
36	43	Clayton Brown	3,133.8	105
37	—	A.G. Edwards & Sons	3,051.1	132
38	46	Marine Midland Capital Mkts	2,828.4	64
39	38	Interstate/Johnson Lane	2,807.2	55
40	—	Security Pacific	2,571.2	46
41	47	Wheat, First Securities	2,217.0	29
42	29	Howard Weil	2,188.0	37
43	—	Underwood Neuhaus	2,089.4	86
44	—	First Nat'l Bank of Boston	2,084.3	38
45	—	William R. Hough	1,978.2	56
46	—	First Albany	1,941.4	53
47	—	Bank of America	1,811.2	20
48	—	Legg Mason Wood Walker	1,791.6	42
49	49	First Interstate Bank, CA	1,697.3	38
50	—	Russell, Rea & Zappala	1,592.4	27

Source: *Institutional Investor*, February 1989.

Table 2–9. U.S. Mergers and Acquisitions.

1987	1988		$Volume (millions)	No. of Deals
1	1	Goldman Sachs	$81,572.2	129
2	2	First Boston	70,391.3	143
3	3	Morgan Stanley	69,297.4	108
5	4	Shearson Lehman Hutton	66,943.7	184
7	5	Drexel Burnham Lambert	37,838.8	153
—	6	Wasserstein Perella	34,336.5	16
6	7	Lazard Frères	33,136.3	51
8	8	Salomon Brothers	27,486.0	107
4	9	Merrill Lynch	23,518.1	91
9	10	Kidder Peabody	17,001.7	66
—	11	Blackstone Group	9,103.1	7
18	12	Bear Stearns	8,772.6	47
78	13	Hellman & Friedman	7,420.0	1
20	14	Bankers Trust	5,760.0	29
11	15	Donaldson, Lufkin & Jenrette	5,650.1	46
10	16	Dillon Read	5,476.5	31
—	17	Conning	5,308.5	1
24	18	Rothschild	4,738.7	8
16	19	Paine Webber	4,540.5	50
23	20	Prudential-Bache	4,326.3	38
14	21	Smith Barney	3,826.5	39
77	22	Veronis Suhler	3,758.3	7
12	23	Allen & Co.	3,658.0	7
25	24	Alex. Brown & Sons	2,984.3	32
13	25	Wertheim Schroder	2,914.2	20

Source: Institutional Investor, February 1989.
Ranking The M&A Advisers:
The rankings shown here include all deals involving a U.S.–based target company that were completed between January 1 and December 31, 1988. Volume totals include only deals for which the amount was disclosed; deal totals also include transactions for which the amount was not disclosed. These figures do not include recapitalizations, self-tenders, stakes, or restructurings.
Data and rankings supplied by IDD Information Services, New York.

Table 2–10. The Largest M&A Deals of 1988.

Target (Advisers)	Acquirer (Advisers)	Price ($ millions)	Date
1. Kraft (Goldman Sachs, Lazard Frères)	Philip Morris Cos. (Wasserstein Perella)	$13,444.0	12/8/88
2. Federated Dept. Stores (Shearson, Goldman Sachs, Hellman & Friedman)	Campeau Corp. (First Boston, Wasserstein Perella)	7,420.0	6/28/88
3. Farmers Group (First Boston, Morgan Stanley)	Batus (Shearson, Goldman Sachs, Conning)	5,308.5	12/16/88
4. Sterling Drug (Morgan Stanley)	Eastman Kodak Co. (Shearson)	5,100.0	2/29/88
5. Montgomery Ward (Kidder Peabody, Salomon Brothers)	management	3,800.0	6/23/88
6. First Howard Paper (First Boston)	acquisition group (Morgan Stanley)	3,578.7	10/24/88
7. Triangle Publications (Veronis Suhler)	News Corp. (Allen & Co.)	3,000.0	11/1/88
8. Centel Corp. (Morgan Stanley)	investors	2,800.0	9/30/88
9. Wickes Cos. (Bear Stearns)	acquisition group (BlackStone, Wasserstein Perella, First Boston)	2,776.7	12/30/88

Institutional Investor, February 1989.

Table 2–10. (continued).

Target (*Advisers*)	Acquirer (*Advisers*)	Price ($ millions)	Date
10. Sun Exploration & Production (*First Boston, Shearson*)	shareholders	2,767.9	11/1/88
11. Firestone Tire & Rubber Co. (*Goldman Sachs, Blackstone*)	Bridgestone Corp. (*Lazard Freres*)	2,651.9	5/5/88
12. E-II Holdings (*Shearson, Merrill Lynch, Drexel*)	American Brands (*Morgan Stanley*)	2,645.0	3/1/88
13. Macmillan (*Wasserstein Perella, First Boston, Lazard Frères*)	Maxwell Communications (*N.M. Rothschild, Samuel Montagu*)	2,639.1	11/16/88
14. Tenneco—Gulf of Mexico oil res. (*Morgan Stanley, First Boston*)	Chevron Corp.	2,600.0	11/18/88
15. Lucky Stores (*Goldman Sachs, Salomon Brothers*)	American Stores (*Shearson, Drexel*)	2,595.0	6/9/88
16. American Standard (*Goldman Sachs*)	Kelso & Co. (*Kelso, First Boston*)	2,512.2	6/29/88
17. Jim Walter Corp. (*Shearson*)	acquisition group (*First Boston, Drexel*)	2,440.0	1/5/88
18. Borg-Warner Chemicals (*Merrill Lynch*)	General Electric Co. (*Kidder Peabody*)	2,310.0	9/20/88
19. Cain Chemical (*Lazard Freres*)	Occidental Petroleum (*Drexel*)	2,080.0	5/3/88
20. E-II Holdings (American Brands) (*Morgan Stanley*)	Riklis Family Corp.	2,055.0	7/5/88

Institutional Investor, February 1989.

- High-yield debt offerings (Table 2-5)
- Mortgage-backed securities (Table 2-6)
- International bond underwriting (Table 2-7)
- Public finance: tax-exempt new issues (Table 2-8)
- Mergers and acquisitions (Table 2-9)
- The largest M&A deals of 1988 (Table 2-10)

Organizational Structure of Investment Banks

The internal organizational structure of investment banks does not resemble the clean lines of typical large corporations. The hierarchical structure as drawn on classic organizational charts does not work well with entrepreneurial investment bankers. Loose hubs and spokes, rather than rigid military commands, make the best metaphor. The following section takes the *functions* of investment banks (explained above) and describes where each fits in the *structure* of investment banks. Note that structure differs, sometimes dramatically, from one bank to another.

Furthermore, never underestimate the power of politics. Its presence determines the size and structure of empires, forms the shape and territory of divisions, and draws the lines and limits of authority. Who reports to whom is often a question of bargain, jockey, and personal gamesmanship. Corporate politics readily contradicts logic and outmaneuvers common sense.

General Organization

In general, there are two primary divisions in investment banking: capital markets and consumer markets. Sometimes there is a third, research. In addition, there are miscellaneous functions outside the mainstream. [4]

Capital Markets.   Capital markets include all the traditonal investment banking and corporate finance departments (discussed below).

Consumer Markets.   Consumer markets include the distribution and sales of securities, involving everything from the creation of new finan-

---

4. For the purposes of this discussion we exclude all the internal administrative aspects of running an investment bank (back office, data processing, finance, personnel, etc.).

cial products to the management of the branch system. Included here, among other areas, are: products and funds established for retail consumers, products and funds established for institutions,[5] limited partnerships of various kinds (e.g., real estate, research and development, master limited partnerships), and new product and fund development.

Consumer markets are related to mainstream investment banking in that they provide a vehicle for distributing securities. This capability is important for increasing confidence in underwriting, especially for those securities where institutional support would be minimal (e.g., high-risk initial public offerings—public venture capital).

Research. Investment research can be structured in three possible ways: independent of both capital and consumer markets, while serving the needs of both; within consumer markets; and/or within capital markets. Some firms believe that the structural autonomy of research helps ensure its unbiased output. Some firms position research in either consumer or capital markets (often the former). Other firms maintain a separate research capability in both capital and consumer markets, believing that direct responsibility is the most efficient control mechanism for achieving dedicated, focused, and responsive service. Typical subdivisions are global equities and fixed-income.

Miscellaneous. There are often other areas of an investment bank that do not fall within the normal categories. These are ancillary businesses and services from the perspective of investment banking, and we do not deal with them further. Some examples are commodity trading (e.g., gold, silver, coffee, crude oil, various metals, various foods), insurance, mortgage banking, leasing, commercial loan placing, correspondent services (back-office operations such as trading, executing, clearing, and processing securities for smaller firms), and information management products.

Capital Markets

Each of the following functional areas is an independent department under capital markets in at least one major investment bank.[6] Functions

---

5. Financial products and funds established for institutions can be structured either under consumer markets or under capital markets.

6. The capital markets classification is sometimes called *investment banking*, using the second definition.

listed under multiple headings reflect their different reporting structures in different investment banks. (Most of the following areas are described in more detail in subsequent chapters.)

Corporate Finance. Corporate finance is normally the largest subdivision of capital markets and includes securities underwriting, mergers and acquisitions, merchant banking, money markets, perhaps venture capital, and sometimes securities research.[7] Subgroups within corporate finance specialize in specific industries.

Securities Underwriting. Securities underwriting is the process of floating securities of all kinds in the primary public markets.[8] Formal groupings under securities underwriting include departments for the following categories of securities: investment-grade corporate bonds, high-yield bonds, convertible debentures, international bonds, preferred stock, and common stock (listed securities and over-the-counter securities). Some aspects of money markets can be included here, such as commercial paper and medium-term notes. Subgroups within securities underwriting specialize in specific industries.

Mergers and Acquisitions (M&A). All the formal and frenetic activities of mergers and acquisitions are included here: finding, facilitating, valuing, pricing, financing, takeover, defense, leveraged buyouts, restructuring and recapitalization. M&A is often the most visible and dynamic department at investment banks. In fact, M&A has taken on such significance, providing a healthy percentage of corporate profits, that the department is growing toward independence from corporate finance at some investment banks. Subgroups within M&A specialize in specific industries.

Merchant Banking. Merchant banking is the commitment of the firm's capital to equity-level investments and participations. Categories include: bridge loans, (bridging the financing between acquisition and permanent

---

7. Corporate finance is sometimes called *investment banking*, using the third definition.

8. Securities underwriting is sometimes called *investment banking*, applying the fourth and most restrictive definition.

financing), financing guarantees, divestiture guarantees (assuring a minimum sale price), leveraged buyouts (LBOs), and restructurings and recapitalizations.

Leveraged Buyouts (LBOs). Investment banks take four approaches to LBOs:

1. Raising financing for client-led LBOs of specific operating companies
2. Raising financing for third-party general LBO funds
3. Structuring and managing the investment bank's own LBO of a specific operating company
4. Establishing and managing the investment bank's own general LBO fund

Private Placements. Private placement is the process of raising funds from private investors by issuing nonpublic securities. Limited partnerships, master limited partnerships, project financings, and product financings are examples. "Direct investments" is another name for private placements.

Money Market Instruments. This subdivision of capital markets involves the process of raising and trading money market instruments and includes: treasury bills and notes, certificates of deposit, commercial paper, medium-term notes, and synthetic securities (e.g., striped treasuries and interest-only and principal-only instruments).

Preferred Stock. Preferred stock has become a specialized area, with high volume being generated in the so-called money market preferreds (i.e., auction-rate and remarketed versions) where dividend rates change regularly (e.g., every 49 days).

High Yield. Pioneered by Drexel Burnham Lambert, high yield has grown into a large and important component of contemporary corporate finance. Several of the large investment banks have now established high yield departments. The high yield category, labeled "junk bonds" by the popular press, includes a great and increasing variety of financial instruments that fill the everbroadening spectrum between traditional debt and traditional equity (Chapters 12 and 13).

Risk Management. Risk management groups combine expertise in diverse hedging instruments (e.g., futures, options, and swaps) to develop a complete hedging strategy for the financial management of enterprises. (Hedging is the technique of mitigating the exposure to volatility in interest rates, currency exchange rates, or stock prices by purchasing instruments that move in opposite directions to the primary security under different market conditions.) Risk management groups can also be called Financial Strategies Groups. Included in this area can be currency and commodity strategies groups and asset-liability matching groups. Often risk management is handled by departments that are called by the names of their products (futures and hedging; financial futures; options, indexes, and hedging; etc.).

Swaps. Arranging and structuring swaps is a specialized function with its own area, or desk. Primary categories are interest rates and currency exchange rates. The purpose of swaps is hedging exposures, matching assets and liabilities, and improving relative cost efficiencies among different enterprises.

Trading and Arbitrage. Trading and arbitrage is a major division (and an important profit center) of most investment banks. Primary functions include block trading of securities for institutional clients and for the firm's own account.

Asset Management for Institutions. Money management for institutional investors is a growing area.

Innovative Securities. Many investment banks have established a "new product group" dedicated specifically to the development of new financial products (e.g., synthetic securities and instruments).

Asset-Based Finance. Financing secured by corporate assets has broadened into a major activity, catalyzed primarily by the need for asset-based financing to structure leveraged buyouts. (Asset-based finance is usually tied to a specific formula—setting borrowing limits such as 80 percent of receivables, 50 percent of inventories, and 25 percent of plant and equipment.)

Real Estate Finance. Many investment banks have established real estate finance groups to handle the proliferation of large, complex transactions.

Such deal structures often involve multiple properties and the design of specific financial instruments (e.g., strip financings, where various layers of financial instruments offer different maturities, priorities, and interest rates).

Securitization. This division is responsible for the rolling up of small consumer debts into large public securities. Categories include residential real estate securities, commercial real estate securities, and non-mortgage securitization (receivables securitization). Structures include mortgage-backed securities and collaterlized mortgage obligations in multiple variations.

Project Finance. Project finance groups arrange financings for enterprises such as energy plants and natural resources, in which the relatively sure cash flows of those operations are used to service and repay the debts.

Product Financing. This new investment banking area provides off-balance-sheet financing for companies (often high-technology firms) to develop new products and commercialize new technologies.

Sale/Leasebacks. Sale/leasebacks provide alternative financing structures for various corporate purposes (e.g., financial statement restructure, leveraged buyouts).

Venture Capital. The raising and management of venture capital for third-party funds or for the investment bank's own fund is a relatively new area.

Public/Municipal Finance. All the various functions of corporate finance are mirrored by public finance: underwriting (primary markets), trading (secondary markets), and research (see Chapter 21).

Industry Groups. Some capital market divisions establish specific groups concentrating on industries and areas in which the investment bank is strong or wants to become strong. Specialized groups that are established within the capital markets division (or corporate finance) usually serve industries that have particular requirements (e.g., a financial institutions group, a media group, an energy group).

Privatization. A few international investment banks have established expertise in advising sovereign governments on the privatization of government-owned companies (e.g., in the United Kingdom, France, Israel). They can also arrange an underwriting of the securities of these government-owned companies.

Corporate Restructurings. The financial restructuring of troubled or bankrupt companies has been a growth area for investment banking, especially during turbulent economic conditions. Under certain circumstances, swapping newly issued equity for defaulted debt can circumvent bankruptcy and restore a company to fiscal health.

Third-World Debt-Equity Swaps. The enormous debt of Third-World nations, and their inability to meet these obligations, has generated a new opportunity for investment bankers to arrange swaps of equity for debt. Considering the problematic nature of the countries involved, these transactions are often multi-faceted and involve more than two parties.

Strategy and Strategic Management

We have seen that investment banks are financial intermediaries that match economic entities that need capital with those that have capital. The traditional view is that investment banks enable both issuers and investors to raise or invest capital with optimal costs/benefits.

For decades, such activities involved "gentlemen relationships" between captains of industry and their Wall Street bankers. The markets were stable, the instruments were stable, the financings were stable, the spreads and fees were stable, the relationships were stable—all was well with the world.

The traditional investment bank structure worked just fine in the context of such stability. The form and size of the established investment banking partnerships were quite satisfactory. Strategic planning was something that manufacturing companies had to do, not investment banks.

But the world began to change. Markets, instruments, financings, spreads and fees, and relationships have all been transformed and have become exceedingly complex. The economic environment has shifted dramatically, and in order to prosper, or even survive, the strategies of investment banking must also change. It is no longer possible to take a simple, idealistic view of what investment banks should do and how they should do it.

Hence, our emphasis on strategy. We now apply the principles of strategic management to investment banks. We discuss the subject in three parts. We begin with a brief description of strategy and strategic management—what it is and how it works. Next, we present several strategies that investment banks should use for serving the complex needs of their client companies. We conclude by presenting several strategies that investment banks should use for serving their own complex needs.

Strategy is More Thinking Than Doing

Strategy is an ancient term derived from warfare. It connotes the fighting plans of battlefield commanders. One can envision generals hunched over detailed relief maps, moving armies as if they were pawns. One can visualize wars being won and lost by subtle shifts of thrust, parry, and feint. The analogy to investment banking, where every deal must run the gauntlet of tough negotiations, seems apt. (See Chapter 9).

Strategy defines the relationship between an organization and its environment and between the firm and its competitors. It is the critical link between missions and goals above and operations and functions below. It is the method for arraying alternative choices and for driving the resource allocation process.

The Process of Strategy

Strategy is the process by which company longer-term missions and goals are translated into shorter-term objectives and projects. Finding effective strategies is the search for *competitive advantage*, for positions of relative strength from which one can coax, coddle, or coerce favorable outcomes. Competitive advantage seeks to capitalize on your *distinctive competencies*, those aspects of the business situation where your firm excels or can excel relative to other firms.

How is corporate strategy formulated? (See Figure 2-1, which models the following description.) The classic process calls for mapping a firm's comparative strengths and weaknesses onto market opportunities and threats in order to accomplish long-term goals and short-term objectives.

The primary output of this strategy formulation process is the generation of a list of alternative policies, different possibilities of company

Figure 2–1. The Strategic Management Framework.

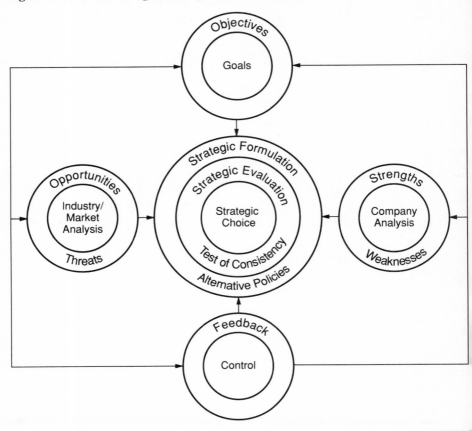

direction for executive consideration. These competing policies are then subjected to rigorous strategy evaluation, using a test of consistency to help make the strategic choice.

Assessing relative strengths and weaknesses of your organization is the key to devising the best strategy. Compare your strengths and weaknesses to those of your competitors in the context of the current industry opportunities and threats. The result of this assessment is the list— desirably a long one—of possible strategies. The various options for strategic direction are then evaluated for probable outcomes, and the best are chosen to be put into action. Internal consistency, especially with respect to company missions and goals on the one hand and resources and capabilities on the other, is a prime test in the evaluation of each alternative strategy.

Three keys to the process follow:

- *Creativity* promotes strategy formulation.
- *Consistency* directs strategy evaluation.
- *Structure* controls strategy implementation.

There is, however, a dark side to strategy. Its presence can fool executives into thinking that they have a good grasp of a situation when they do not have much of a handle on anything. The more the strategic sophistication, at times, the stronger the strategic illusion. The mirage of perfection is the problem of strategy.

It has been said that corporate strategy is like a ritual rain dance. It has no effect on the weather that follows, of course, but it makes those who do it feel they are in full control. Often when companies use strategic planning, they are laboring to improve the dancing, not the weather.

Strategy and Structure

The relationship between corporate strategy and organizational structure is one of the principal advances in business understanding of the past decades. Certain kinds of corporate strategies demand certain kinds of organizational structures; conversely, if these organizational structures are in place, they will exert pressure to induce their complementary strategies. (The classic example is the tight relationship between a multiproduct or multinational strategy with a division structure. In a divisional structure, each division is an independent entity, responsible for a distinct product line or geographic area and maintaining internally its own functional departments—marketing, finance, etc.)

A Way of Thinking: Incremental Versus Strategic[9]

Strategic planning is no panacea, and it does not work under all circumstances. It is simply a way of thinking about orienting an

---

9. Strategic thinking and strategic management are really the application of the scientific method to the world of commerce and organizations. The scientific method involves data collection and analysis, alternative hypothesis formulation, alternative hypothesis testing and eliminations, hypothesis selection, and hypothesis confirmation with further data collection and analysis. Note that in science you "prove" a hypothesis to be correct by the process of elimination; you cannot prove that hypothesis "right"—you must, rather, prove all alternative hypotheses "wrong." (This process is called *falsification* by Karl Popper, a philosopher of science.)

organization. Strategic planning can be best understood in contrast to its opposite, incremental planning. The best executives function well in both modes. While the strategic process leads to original thinking in devising alternative options, the incremental mode can be fertile soil for the spontaneous sprouting of sudden ("Aha") insights.

Incremental Thinking. Operating in the incremental mode, senior executives begin *reactively* by recognizing an immediate problem or some unexpected shock, whether an opportunity or a threat. The person (or team) then searches selectively through a restricted variety of potential solutions, making marginal movements from the status quo, evaluating each tiny step in order. Deviations from current policy are considered sequentially and widened progressively until the first satisfactory solution is found. An agreeable answer is accepted immediately and all other alternatives, even if potentially better, are ignored.

Herbert Simon's idea of bounded rationality applies here.[10] Managers cannot ever know *every*thing; if they want to do *any*thing, they must replace "optimizing," finding the best answer, with "satisficing," finding an acceptable answer. According to bounded rationality, problems in the real world need only be solved satisfactorily, not perfectly.

Strategic Thinking. Operating in the strategic mode, senior executives begin *pro*actively by defining general goals and setting specific objectives. They scan the industry environment, seeking opportunities and threats, and analyze their own firm for relative strengths and weaknesses. The key here is to assess the specific strengths and weaknesses of their particular investment bank in the light of the opportunities and threats in the general industry. The objective is a search for competitive advantages.

What emerges from this dynamic, creative process is a set of alternatives. Each is evaluated for probable consequences. Strategic choice is made with the guideline of internal consistency: Which set of strategies best matches goals and strengths? Implementation (including step and time sequencing), feedback, and review complete the process.

It is a commom misconception to judge incremental decision making as "bad" and strategic decision making as "good." Each is good, but in its own arena. One would not resolve a sudden liquidity problem in the

---

10. Herbert Simon, *Administrative Behavior* (New York: The Free Press), 1976.

strategic mode, just as one would not formulate a comprehensive five-year plan in the incremental mode. Learn when to stay incremental and when to jump strategic.

Strategy and Surprise

Strategic thinking, to be truly strategic, must deal with surprise. The unanticipated must be anticipated, the unforeseen foreseen. If everything is assumed to be known, if your organization's future is expected to emulate your organization's past, then the process is simple extension (trending), and strategy is playing no part.

Strategic management must be concerned with radical change — discontinuity, sharp breaks with the past, and violent twists from current paths. Thoughtful leaders of investment banks must plan for the unplanned.

Strategies for Investment Banking Clients

Following are some strategies that investment bankers consider when contemplating how best to help clients. These are a few of the fundamentals. (See Chapter 3, "Wealth Building and Risk/Return," and Chapter 4, "How to Build Shareholder Wealth.")

Financial Optimization

Achieving the lowest overall cost of capital for issuers and the highest ratio of return to risk for investors is the historical objective of investment bankers. Designing and underwriting financial instruments that optimize the opposing interests of issuers and investors has been the hallmark of the industry.

The goal of investment banking clients is often simple: Issuers seek to raise capital at the lowest possible overall (all-in) cost,[11] and investors

---

11. Whether debt or equity, all capital has a cost. The cost of debt is its interest rate, repayment schedule, covenants, and the like. The cost of equity is the dilution of current stockholders relative to the money raised. The cost of capital is directly related to the overall value of the firm as determined by the market capitalization and to the apparent risk of the firm from both a competitive business (product-market) and financial structure (leverage, debt/equity) point of view. (See Chapter 3 for the mathematical expression of the weighted average cost of capital.)

want to achieve the highest overall return commensurate with a given level of risk. By arranging monetary transactions, exchanges, and relationships among economic entities, investment bankers make the capital markets more efficient. Matching the highly specific profiles of myriad issuers and investors with highly specific financial instruments is the special capability that investment bankers offer.

Financial optimization for business corporations has many specific expressions. Following are just five brief examples from finance theory.

Cost of Capital. Lowering the overall cost of capital is the classic place to start (see Chapter 3). The process of determining the lowest cost of capital (normalized for a given level of assumed risk) involves selecting, monitoring, and modifying the appropriate financial securities and instruments—the right combination of debt and equity and the specific features of each component. The tightly focused, individually unique requirements of issuers and investors—combined with the creative brilliance of investment bankers—have spawned growing multitudes of alternative financial vehicles. (Many financial instruments and products are designed to save companies less than 100 basis points; even though that's less than one percentage point in interest, since the principal is often hundreds of millions of dollars, the incremental profits can be millions of dollars every year.)

Leverage. Leverage is the amount of debt compared to the amount of equity; the higher the relative proportion of debt, the higher the leverage. And the higher a company's leverage, the better its return on equity—so long as it remains profitable (and in business). The proper debt/equity ratio on the balance sheet trades off the return-on-equity benefits of high debt (high leverage) with the lower risk profile of high equity (low leverage). Although the market-approved optimum leverage ratio behaves like a roller coaster, cascading through cycles of high and low visions of what seems best, cautious investment bankers must make a long-term cost-benefit analysis for their clients—an analysis that must be tailored to each company. In fact, a financial marketplace where the boundaries between debt and equity blur, the debt/equity ratio no longer dominates thinking. Ideal ratios have lost their sting and their power. Structures for specific situations are what counts. Investment bankers must therefore craft a specifically sculpted capital structure for each individual company's situation.

Dividend Payouts. Studies differ on the effectiveness of dividend payouts versus retaining the earnings. Theoretically, if the company can grow the money internally at a higher rate that the investors can externally (i.e., the investors' reinvestment rate), then the company should not pay out dividends. (This is especially true considering the double taxation on dividends.)

Pricing Considerations. The lowest cost of capital is not always the best price for issuers, nor is the highest return always the best price for investors. Risk is involved for both issuers and investors. Time is also a factor. The short-term solution may not hold for the long term. The lowest cost of capital for issuers may give investors a bad experience with the company, increasing the cost of capital in the future. Similarly, the highest price for investors may involve hidden risks (e.g., management frustration) that could jeopardize the principal itself. The market is certainly complex, with uncertain and often indeterminable degrees of efficiencies and inefficiencies mingled together. In such an intricate environment, optimization is not necessarily either maximization of return or minimization of cost. It may be, but this is not required.

Offering Strategies. How much stock should be sold in an offering? Clearly, the financial strategy of structuring a public offering is a function of the number of shares and the price per share in relationship to the expected valuation of the entire company. There is always conflict here between the interests of the issuers and investors, though investment bankers can show both groups the benefits of logical analysis. It is often smart for an issuing company seeking a lower cost of capital to hold back the size of its offering, thus keeping demand greater than supply. This reduction in shares to be sold also decreases the dilution of current shareholders. The plan would be for the company to use the capital currently being raised to improve its earnings and public profile so that a subsequent offering can be made to take advantage of the expected higher market capitalizations in the future. (There is a fine line between optimizing cost of capital and being sure that the company raises sufficient capital for its current needs.[12])

Optimization by its very essence demands the input of qualitative insight to modulate quantitative analysis. Investment bankers must

---

12. One must also consider the expenses of the offering, some of which are relatively constant irrespective of issue size (e.g., professional fees and printing costs).

consider myriad issues regarding the financing situation and all proposed financing transactions. Computers could never become investment bankers.

Value Building

The ultimate goal of economic entities is to produce wealth. Investment bankers must be sure that their clients never lose sight of this fact. It is all too easy to get caught up in the glitter and excitement of aggressive acquisitions, new businesses, refurbished offices, media coverage, and all the rest of the executive high life. But corporations are enterprises whose primary task (some would argue sole task) is to build value for their shareholders. Consequently, every decision that is made by corporations should be governed by "value building" criteria. If acquisitions are considered, they must be considered in terms of how they will impact the value of shareholder stock. This valuation is inordinately complex and fraught with uncertainty. Nonetheless, the touchstone of value must always be applied. (Probabilities can be assessed, sensitivities can be tested, etc.)

Value *creation*, a subset of value building, should always be at the forefront of a proper investment banking assessment of client companies. Value creation suggests those kinds of activities that would (or could) add incremental wealth to shareholders beyond that expected from normal operations. The obvious example is mergers and acquisitions, where the additional value generated should well exceed the costs and risks involved (see Chapter 6).

Growth and Development

Valuation in the market is based largely on the growth rate of earnings or cash flow (or, more accurately, the *perceived* growth rate at any given time).[13] Corporate executives are almost always striving to increase the size of their activities and operations. Investment bankers are allies in the process, supplying the necessary capital for such expansion. Cost of capital is optimized when specific liabilities with specific terms (e.g., payback periods) are carefully chosen to finance specific assets with specific uses. Matching the right kind of capital available in the

---

13. This anticipated growth rate is reflected in the capitalization ratios that are applied to earnings (i.e., the price earnings ratios and dividend growth models).

market (e.g., type of equity, timing of debt) with the projected growth and development needs of the company is the special sphere where investment bankers perform their magic.

Robustness and Resiliency

Financing is most efficient for both issuers and investors when there is high confidence in a stable future. More than anything else, the market abhors uncertainty. The capacity of the company to survive economic turbulence is perhaps the prime factor in lowering the cost of its capital. Company financing costs increase as a *multiple* of any increase in uncertainty (i.e., every one-unit increase in volatility triggers *more* than a one-unit increase in cost). Key corporate strengths are robustness, the full-bodied strength of the firm, and resiliency, the ability to spring back after any shocks. Investment bankers must be sure that all financing structures enhance robustness and resiliency.

Growth alone can be dangerous, and rapid growth without proper external positioning and appropriate internal controls is a recipe for certain disaster. The external key is competitive strength, the self-determined capacity to secure a firm's market share and margins. The internal key is administrative information and regulation, the confidence of constant awareness and rapid reaction. Companies that grow quickly are most vulnerable to environmental shocks, and investment bankers must protect their client companies from exposing themselves to such heightened risks.

Robustness and resiliency are equally important in the structuring of financial instruments, especially those that are highly dependent on external factors. For example, securitized instruments (e.g., rolled-up home real estate mortgages) can be surprisingly susceptible to interest rate shifts (which change default and refinancing rates). The same is true for synthetic securities such as principal-only or interest-only instruments. In these cases, sensitivity testing is vital. (See Chapter 20.)

Strategies for Investment Banks

Volatility is the prime characteristic of the investment banking industry, and investment bankers must never forget this ever-present uncertainty. Stock market fads and fluctuations combine with personnel emotion and mobility to generate an erratic and unpredictable environment. Such unpredictable dynamism makes life uncomfortable for investment banking executives but is fertile soil in which true strategic thinking and planning can flourish.

We encourage readers to use the principles of strategic management outlined earlier to develop alternative strategies for their firms, whether investment banks or operating companies. The idea—in one sentence— is to map an investment banking firm's strengths and weaknesses onto its market opportunities and threats in order to formulate, evaluate, and implement the best of numerous alternative strategies so that long-term goals and short-term objectives can be realized.

Following are some specific areas for strategic consideration that investment bankers should consider when contemplating how best to plan their own futures. These are a few of the fundamentals.

Strategic Constraints

There are four primary strategic constraints for investment banks:
1. Capital (e.g., amount, allocation, relationship to strategy, growth).
2. Clients (e.g., sector, size, industry).
3. Services (e.g., underwriting, IPO, M&A, LBO, rate risk management, back-office operations).
4. Personnel (e.g., traders, bankers, rainmakers, innovators).

A firm must start its strategic planning process by assessing itself with respect to all four constraints, and then it must postulate where it wants to be positioned at some future date. Such an assessment must not be done in a vacuum. Investment banking is a highly competitive industry, in addition to being exceptionally volatile. Comparative and competitive analysis is essential at every stage of the process. Remember, distinctive competencies and competitive advantage—together with internal consistency[14]—are the critical criteria for evaluating all strategic alternatives.

Firm/Market Positioning

There are several ways to play the investment banking game. The key is to match the right structure with the right strategy. Several years

---

14. Each part of the strategy must mesh with every other part. It is remarkable how often first-rate organizations devise strategies that contain incompatible elements.

ago the rage was to become a "full financial services" company, with many firms offering every conceivable function from retail brokerage, to real estate services, to insurance sales, to big-money international investment banking. Of those that tried, few made it. (It is certainly possible to be a bulge-bracketed firm servicing large corporate issuers and institutional investors without having a retail distribution capability; note Salomon Brothers and Goldman Sachs. Yet even Salomon could not do everything; its withdrawal from municipal finance was dramatic proof of an investment bank's limitations.)

Firms must position themselves according to their assessment of the economic environment and the coming competitive pressures. Medium-sized firms, for example, seem to be particularly vulnerable to the dual crush of capital requirements and the back-office costs of doing major-league business. On the other hand, smaller firms that stake out strong positions in circumscribed regions can do remarkably well by specializing in smaller local corporations and regional individual investors. Intelligence and service are the keys to success for regional investment banks.

As discussed earlier, one recent development is the formation of boutique investment banking firms. Formed around one or two name personalities (usually leaving a bulge-bracketed firm), these new investment banks desire to remain small so that the full energies of their partners can be devoted to the deal making they love, not to the administration they hate. How can these boutiques compete in this capital-intensive industry? They focus on their expertise—M&A and merchant banking— and by their reputations they raise large pools of capital from financial institutions; as a result they become real players in the great game. They focus their capital on what they do best, and they do not make markets nor inventory securities.[15]

Agent or Principal

Some investment banks are having difficulty deciding who they are— agents or principals. The problem arises as a result of the enormous

---

15. An example of the importance of market positioning and capital focus occurred when Wasserstein, Parella & Company, the M&A/merchant banking boutique formed by the First Boston expatriates, leased some of the magnificent office space vacated after the forced sale of E.F. Hutton to Shearson Lehman.

profits made through the ownership of companies, primarily through leveraged buyouts (see Chapter 16). It's enough to turn any head.

Merchant banking is the new buzzword on Wall Street. As we have noted, this involves risking the firm's capital to make bridge loans for closing acquisitions quickly (many acquisitions requiring bridge loans are made under competitive pressures, and some are hostile). The bridge loan remains outstanding until the permanent financing can be put into place. Merchant banking may also involve taking equity positions in companies (often in partnership with clients).

Merchant banking can clearly generate extraordinary returns, especially compared with the anemic returns on traditional underwriting. Yet there are major problems that arise; the most critical is a blurring of the purely professional relationship that has long characterized the industry. Merchant banking is giving investment banking an identity crisis.

Optimal Size

In some investment banks, the number of employees grew larger than the firm's current market position could support. The outcome, in some cases, was a ballooning organization and a bloated structure that eroded distinctive competencies and lost competitive advantage, resulting in a fast fall into oblivion.

As stated above, the most important factor in implementing a corporate strategy is designing the proper organizational structure to support it. Size is perhaps the most critical criterion here: too small, and you cannot provide the services that clients demand; too large, and you suffocate the firm with excessive costs and frustrate personnel with limited opportunity.

Capital efficiency is an important part of the optimal size analysis. Too much capital is always better than too little, but just the right amount is better than both. Investment banks should be properly capitalized for accomplishing their specific business strategies and financial goals.

Competitive Advantage

Competitive advantage is the key reason any organization survives and prospers. There must be some reason why your firm exists, why employees should work there, why clients should come there. What do you have that your competitors do not?

Perhaps the best definition equates strategy with rent. Rent is payment for a unique piece of real estate; there is no other plot of land, no other space exactly like it. You get paid because you have someplace quite special, a place that no one else has. Likewise for strategy: you are being paid for occupying a unique spot in the company/market spectrum, something that no other firm has. Whether by products or personnel, there are reasons why you get every piece of business. A thoughtful executive understands these reasons. When planning the future, you should examine the present.

The most important thing to remember about competitive advantage is that it must constantly be sought, because without advantage there is no business.

Pricing Fees and Spreads

The pricing of fees and spreads is a critical strategic decision for investment banks. Should a firm buy into a business by underpricing competitors, as the Japanese investment banks did in the Euromarkets? Should a firm back out of an industry because spreads have been squeezed, as Salomon did in municipal underwriting?

How an investment bank prices its services goes a long way toward telling its story and establishing its position. It can be tempting to cut prices in order to win business—after all, bankers must be able to show their stuff. On the other hand, the battlefield must be picked carefully. Shaving prices in the wrong underwriting can generate unacceptably large losses and produce a poor industry image. Furthermore, by offering services for lower-than-normal industry fees, a fee-cutting investment bank might inadvertently signal that its quality is lower than that of its peers—which would be death in the M&A business, for example. (Better, frankly, is to charge a *higher* M&A fee for exceptional performance above an agreed level; such a request will evince strong confidence and can convince the potential corporate client that you can really deliver maximum results.)

Personnel

The importance of personnel in investment banking is so great that it demands a separate category and constant consideration. It is a truism that a firm's primary assets ride down the elevator every evening. Top personnel must be kept content or a bank cannot prosper. Granted, there are always new waves of eager, ambitious young people thrilled to get a shot at the golden ring, but an organization that experiences significant turnover is a company operating suboptimally.

Compensation is part of the story, but only part. Since this is the money game, a person's self-assessed worth is often colored largely in green. How to allocate bonuses is always a knotty problem. One key is to appreciate that opportunity and advancement are also important for investment bankers. The chance to make a personal impact is vital, and the firm should appreciate the importance of such recognition. Giving up-and-coming investment bankers greater responsibility, particularly the opportunity to run their own deals, is an important sign of support.

Internationalization

In the tightly wired world of international finance, the opportunities are great, but the risks may be greater. It is frightfully complex to deal in foreign capital markets, not to mention enormously expensive. A modern investment bank must determine its logical position in the international firmament. Many investment banks expanded dramatically into London and Tokyo, seeing the allure of Big Bang[16] and the rising yen. Tens if not hundreds of millions of dollars in capital commitment were allocated to such expansions. Results have been spotty, and many major banks have subsequently had to curtail these overly ambitious operations. Investment houses considering international expansion should pick their niches and focus their activities.

Strategic Alliances

One approach to several of the strategic issues discussed here is for an investment bank to form a strategic alliance with another, complementary firm. Such an alliance may take several forms. Often, for a U.S. firm, the alliance will be an investment by a foreign financial institution (e.g., Goldman Sachs and Sumitomo Bank, PaineWebber and Yasuda Mutual Life Insurance Company). The financial investment augments the domestic firm's capital base while the strategic alliance provides

---

16. "Big Bang" is the media term for the sudden deregulation of the London financial and securities firms several years ago, allowing increased competition and encouraging the entry of many foreign investment banks.

international presence, visibility, and expertise with a much lower risk profile and cost exposure. Other types of strategic alliances can be considered. When a smaller investment bank manages merchant banking money for a large financial institution, this too can be a strategic alliance. The desire of the institutional investor is to be able to get an early, privileged look at an anticipated series of future transactions in which they may like to participate—in addition to earning the expected equity-level returns. The desire of the small investment bank is to have a ready source of additional financings for forthcoming deals—in addition to the profit-making opportunity of managing the intitial investment.

CHAPTER 3

Wealth-Building and Risk/Return*

Wealth-building is the essence of investment banking. More precisely, it is building the wealth of shareholders within the context of an acceptable risk/return structure that is the central objective of corporate finance. Thus, we focus on *wealth-building* and *risk/return* for issuers and investors as the two primary pillars that form the finance framework of investment banking. Together they organize many of the ideas presented in this book.

This chapter is structured in three sections and an appendix:

1. *Wealth-building*: The essence and nature of corporate wealth, what it means, and how it is measured.

2. *Risk/return*: The essence and elements of risk and return, each from the parallel but opposite viewpoints of issuers and investors.

3. *Tricks and traps in financial analysis*: Some common pitfalls when evaluating the earnings, assets, liabilities, and equities of companies, and the use and misuse of trends and graphs.

4. *Appendix: the nature and measurement of cash flow*. The critical importance of cash flow in determining the wealth and changing value of a corporation.

---

* This chapter has been derived from "A Finance Framework for Investment Banking" by Robert Lawrence Kuhn and George T. Geis, Volume I (Investing and Risk Management), Dow Jones-Irwin's *The Library of Investment Banking* (1990), Robert Lawrence Kuhn, editor-in-chief.

Wealth-Building

Our first task is to understand what builds wealth in for-profit organizations. *We define shareholder wealth as the discounted value of after-tax cash flows distributed by a firm.*[1] This procedure takes the cash flows from future years and divides (reduces) the value of each one by a compounded discount rate in order to generate a present value for each of those cash flows. We then add these present values together to find the company's *wealth*. This procedure can be expressed as follows:

$$\text{Wealth} = \sum_{1}^{Y} \frac{\text{Cash Flow in Year } Y}{(1 + \text{Discount Rate})^Y}$$

$$= \frac{\text{Cash Flow in Year 1}}{(1 + \text{Discount Rate})^1} + \frac{\text{Cash Flow in Year 2}}{(1 + \text{Discount Rate})^2}$$

$$+ \frac{\text{Cash Flow in Year 3}}{(1 + \text{Discount Rate})^3} + \cdots + \frac{\text{Cash Flow in Year } Y}{(1 + \text{Discount Rate})^Y}$$

where

$$\text{Cash Flow} = \text{after-tax cash flow distributed by the firm}$$

$$\sum = \text{sum}$$

We take a productive view of wealth-building, looking at the long term and with a macroeconomic perspective. Such a vision is vital to our framework. It highlights the construction of real, tangible, incremental value in economic enterprises—that is, corporate entities producing additional goods and services. (We ignore completely the myriad ways of making money that investment bankers, market makers, securities traders, money managers, and ordinary investors have discovered in the *simple* movement of paper. In this framework we do not consider the building of wealth through the exchanging of securities and assets and the transferring of such ownership positions.[2])

The concept of corporate wealth-building is important for investment bankers in that it is the primary touchstone for assessing all the financial

---

1. *Distribution* of after-tax cash flows is used in the broad sense of the term and could include any kind of payment such as liquidating dividends.

2. No value judgment is made or implied here. Our definition of wealth in terms of real tangible, producing value is more solid theoretically and much easier to describe.

options and financing alternatives available to corporations. How can we assess and compare the bewildering diversity of financial structures, instruments, and products that are being offered by corporate finance departments? There must be a standard to make such comparisons, and we believe that the wealth formula is a strong candidate.

Consequently, given that our wealth formula is defined as "the discounted value of after-tax cash flows distributed by a firm," it is essential to understand:

1. The *numerator*—what is meant by cash flows and why are they so important?

2. The *denominator*—what discount rate should be applied to future cash flows in order to give them a present value equivalent?

The Numerator—The Cash Flow

Cash flow is finally getting the importance it deserves (and, ages ago, once had).[3] It is cash flow—not earnings per share (EPS)—that sophisticated investors examine in valuing a company.[4] It is cash flow that the Financial Accounting Standards Board (FASB) requires companies to report in the Statement of Cash Flow (for financial statements issued after July 31, 1988).

Why is cash so important? We highlight four reasons.

1. It is cash flow—not earnings—that services debt, pays salaries, purchases inventory, and the like.

2. Accrual accounting (matching revenues and expenses to present and future time periods) may have become too far removed from the underlying cash flows of a firm. Many feel that accountants use too many arbitrary allocation schemes, such as for deferring taxes, depreciating plant and equipment,

---

3. Perhaps it was the power of accrual accounting, with its more accurate description of the revenue and expense-matching and asset/liability condition of the company, which took over from cash accounting and mitigated the importance of cash. Yet many companies have floundered and failed with all financial indicators seemingly in good shape except cash flow. This has been especially true during times of great economic volatility.

4. For example, when Saul Steinberg paid $60/share for Disney, its EPS seemed a dismal $1 (and its P/E was therefore a seemingly outrageous 60), yet its cash flow per share was a very healthy $10.

or amortizing intangible assets. These income-critiquing analysts contend that the resultant earnings figures are not a useful indicator of the operating power or momentum of the firm.

3. Working capital, commonly used in the old Statement of Changes in Financial Position, can mask meaningful liquidity information. A classic case for using cash flow (and not working capital) can be made from analyzing the prebankruptcy years of W. T. Grant, which had reasonale amounts of working capital from operations but poor cash flow. (A great deal of working capital was tied up in receivables and inventory.)

4. The high debt levels of many contemporary firms (e.g., resulting from the many leveraged buyouts) demand more detailed information about the capability of servicing future interest requirements and making scheduled principal repayments.

The Statement of Cash Flow provides useful information for generating a meaningful numerator in the wealth formula. In obtaining a meaningful measure for cash, it is important to classify historical cash flows as recurring or nonrecurring in order to model future cash flows. As described in the appendix to this chapter, adjustments may need to be made to accommodate special situations applicable to a particular company or situation. Some analyses will need more information than is required by generally accepted accounting principles (GAAP) (e.g., those who consider *maintenance* capital expenditures an important distinction from current capital expenditures—see Chapter 3 appendix.)

The Denominator—The Discount Rate

The discount rate is the denominator of the wealth formula, and its power is substantial—a small change in the percentage yields a large change in the outcome. Of course, we know that as the discount rate increases, the present value of the stream of expected cash flows decreases (i.e., the cash generated in the future is worth less as cash equivalents, or wealth, today). Conversely, as the discount rate decreases, the present value of the cash flows increases. In general, the discount rate reflects current expectations of future volatility, uncertainty, and risk in both general macroeconomic conditions of society and the specific microeconomic state of the firm. The higher the expected volatility, uncertainty, and riskiness, the higher the discount rate.

Unfortunately, there is no absolute rule for determining the discount rate. An intuitive sense of the business is as important as a rigorous analysis of the finances. Context is the first criterion. For what purpose is the discount rate being used? For example, to assess the present value of a long-term zero coupon bond, the discount rate is highly dependent on the current expectancies for long-term interest rates. To evaluate a corporate acquisition, the acquiring company might use its own historic return on assets boosted by a risk premium for new projects. (See Chapter 6.)

What is the appropriate discount rate to use for calculating the wealth formula, and for discounting the streams of future cash flows? Recall the objective: the wealth formula will become the standard of comparison with which we can assess and compare all financial structures and financing strategies. Thus, the simplest solution seems to utilize the *firm-specific cost of capital* appropriately weighted by the current capital structure. The following formula computes this weighted average cost of capital[5]:

$$\text{WACC} = K_{STD}(1-t_c)\frac{STD}{TL+E} + K_{LTD}(1-t_c)\frac{LTD}{TL+E} + K_{PS}\frac{PS}{TL+E}$$

$$+ K_{CONV}\frac{CONV}{TL+E} + K_{CS}\frac{CS}{TL+E}$$

where

WACC	=	weighted average cost of capital
K_{STD}	=	cost of short-term debt
STD	=	market value of short-term debt
TL+E	=	market value of total liabilities plus equities
t_C	=	marginal corporate tax rate
K_{LTD}	=	cost of long-term debt
LTD	=	market value of long-term debt
K_{PS}	=	cost of preferred stock

---

5. Copeland, T.E., and Weston, J. Fred, *Financial Theory and Corporate Policy*, 2nd edition, Addison-Wesley, Reading, MA, 1983.

PS	=	market value of preferred stock
K_{CONV}	=	cost of convertible debt or preferred stock
CONV	=	market value of convertible debt or preferred stock
K_{CS}	=	cost of common stock equity
CS	=	market value of common stock equity

This equation is neither resolute nor rigid. It will not yield an absolute, unconditional, unchallengeable number—it is just a starting place. The process is as much art as science. Many issues need to be factored in and considered. Expectations are important. What does the company *expect* will happen to each term of the equation? This assessment is as much educated insight as calculated fact, as much induced as deduced. Perceptive expectancies play a vital part in selecting a truly useful discount rate for the wealth formula.

A logical approach is to select a *target* capital structure—an ideal, reasonably attainable mix of debt and equity financing instruments which gives optimum return on shareholder net worth while incurring an appropriate level of risk. This ideal capital structure can then be used to derive the weighted average cost of capital in the preceding equation.

Such a capital structure will be specifically tailored to meet the special requirements of individual industries and companies. Elements involved include the required levels and mix of working capital, amount and nature of fixed assets, anticipated growth rate, tax structure, sources and uses of cash over time, and the like. Defense contractors, financial institutions, electrical utilities, advertising agencies, and biotechnology startups will all have different target capital structures.

Wealth-Building Conclusions

The wealth-building formula is the central standard of comparison for investment bankers to use in evaluating financing and structural options for corporations. This formula is dependent on the following critical elements:

- A meaningful definition of cash flow—the numerator.
- Estimation of *future* cash flows—which depends on recurring flows from continuing operations as well as from new businesses, operations and investments.
- A firm-specific discount rate—the denominator.

- A target capital structure—needed to best estimate the weighted average cost of capital to be used as the firm-specific discount rate.

Precise calculation of the numerator and denominator is not possible. What is most important is a clear understanding of what generates firm wealth—that is, the sum of future cash flows (numerators), each discounted by the weighted average cost of capital (denominators). Therefore, to appreciate what undergirds wealth optimization one should be comfortable with cash flow definition, able to estimate meaningful future cash flows, and sensitive to the issues involved in formulating the weighted average cost of capital. (Considering the importance of cash flow in the wealth formula, the appendix to this chapter describes further its measurement and analysis.)

Risk/Return Relationships

The wealth-building formula is actually one particular expression of the most fundamental principle in finance—the relationship between risk and return. In the formula, the discount rate (the denominator) and cash flow (the numerator) correspond directly to risk and return. Risk determines the appropriate discount rate (by means of the weighted average cost of capital, which is established by the capital structure), and return determines the required cash flows (which are the future stream of after-tax cash payments distributed by the firm).

The relationship between risk and reward is the central driving force of corporate finance, and investment bankers need to understand its essence and implications. Risk and return are parallel concepts; they are tied tightly together and move proportionately and synchronously with each other (although not always linearly and not always logically). This section will explore various facets of risk and return for issuers and investors. The principles are basic but the implications are profound.

To a first approximation, the relationship between risk and return is a positively sloped straight line (Figure 3-1). This means that as risk goes up, so must return. The actual slope of the line will vary, depending on the specific circumstances of the issuer and the impact of the macroeconomic environment on potential investors.[6]

---

6. For example, return may increase one or two units for every one unit increase in risk or vice versa (Figure 3-1). (Units of risk can be considered arbitrary indicators of increasing riskiness and units of return are traditional percentage points of annual payback, usually in cash or cash equivalents.)

Figure 3–1. Risk/Return Relationships.

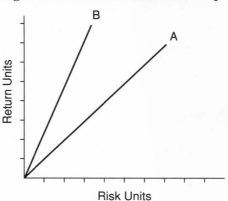

A = One unit of return for each unit of risk.
B = Two units of return for each unit of risk.

Debt and Equity in Terms of the Wealth Formula

From an issuer's perspective, debt is cheap but risky corporate capital, while equity is more expensive (i.e., because it dilutes current shareholders) and less risky (i.e., because there are no interest payments).

Debt. Debt requires debt service (interest) as well as principal repayment—hence the higher risk. But debt does not dilute shareholder ownership, and the interest paid is deductible (i.e., a tax shield)—hence the higher return.

Equity. Equity has no mandatory servicing requirements—hence the lower risk. But equity reduces the percentage of current shareholder ownership—hence the lower return.

Wealth Formula. Both debt and equity can be viewed in terms of the wealth formula. The effects are complex. Consider the following.

Debt decreases the cost of capital (since there is less dilution of equity or ownership) and hence decreases the discount rate (the denominator)—thus increasing the wealth. But too much debt will cause the risk of default to soar, which will demand a very high discount rate to reflect the very high risk—thus decreasing the wealth. (Hence the need for an *optimum* capital structure; i.e., the most appropriate mix of debt and equity given the operating and financial characteristics of the business.) Furthermore, adding to the complexity, debt also reduces the cash flow (the numerator) due to interest payments.

Equity can be also considered in terms of the wealth formula. Equity increases the cost of capital (since ownership is diluted) and hence increases the discount rate (the denominator)—thus decreasing the wealth. But equity makes the company less likely to default, which argues for a lower discount rate—thus increasing the wealth. (Again the need for an *optimum* capital structure.) Finally, equity increases the cash flow (the numerator) since no debt service is required.

We now describe risk and return from the dual and opposing perspectives of investors and issuers.

Risk/Return for Investors

The risk/return profile for investors involves the following tradeoffs (Figure 3-2).

Risk. Risk for investors is the likelihood (or perception) of financial default on the specific securities, the increasing volatility of the securities, the decreasing liquidity (or increasing illiquidity) of the securities, the resultant declining value of the securities, and/or the general financial insolvency of the issuer. This risk is inversely related to the seniority of the corporate security or financial instrument within the financial structure—i.e., the more senior the security or instrument, the less risk it has. (*Volatility* is an especially interesting determinant of investor risk; it has significant influence in defining the risk/return profile. Investors will give up substantial return in order to increase confidence in the stability of their investments. Conversely, few characteristics will scare investors more than increasing uncertainty.)

Return. Return for investors is the expected yield on the corporate security or financial instrument. It is normally expressed as an annual percentage payment in cash or cash equivalents. Over a period of time, return is expressed as a *compound* annual rate (percentage) of return, which assumes the reinvestment of each year's return at the same overall rate.

Figure 3–2. Risk/Return: Investor Profile.

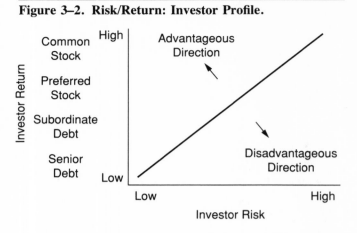

Investor Risk: Default, Volatility, Illiquidity

Graphics. Figure 3-2 portrays the risk/return profile for investors: Low return is associated with low risk and high return with high risk. The corporate securities reflecting this relationship are represented by a simplified security spectrum (i.e., from investor low risk/low return to high risk/high return: senior debt, subordinated debt, preferred stock, common stock).

Risk/Return for Issuers

The risk/return profile for issuers involves the following tradeoffs (Figure 3-3).

Risk. Risk for issuers is the likelihood (or perception) of corporate failure or bankruptcy. This risk is directly related to the general characteristics of the industry and the specific conditions of the firm, primarily its financial leverage.

Return. Return for issuers is the lowest attainable cost of capital, commensurate with an acceptable level of risk. The lowest cost of capital—senior debt at the top of the capital structure—is always the most risky. Conversely, the highest cost of capital to issuers—common equity at the base of the capital structure—is always the least risky (i.e., there is no

Figure 3–3. Risk/Return: Issuer Profile.

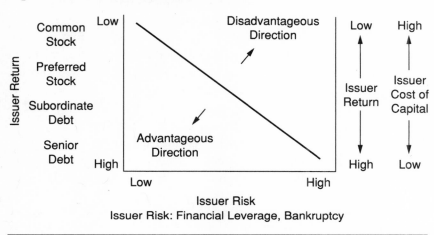

Issuer Risk: Financial Leverage, Bankruptcy

possible default risk since there are no required payments and dividends are optional). Note that equity has the highest cost of capital for two reasons: (1) dividends are not deductible for tax purposes whereas interest payments are deductible; and (2) issuing new equity dilutes current shareholders, thereby reducing substantially their expected rate of return on their stock, which will be considerably higher than the rate that debt holders expect on their interest-bearing obligations.

Graphics. Figure 3-3 portrays the risk/return profile for issuers: Low issuer return is associated with low issuer risk (e.g., common stock) and high return with high risk (e.g., senior debt). Note that low return to the issuer represents a high cost of capital (i.e., equity) and a high return to the issuer represents a low cost of capital (i.e., debt). Note also that high issuer risk is associated with low investor return (i.e., debt) and low issuer risk is associated with high investor return (i.e., equity).

Parallelism Between Risk and Return for Issuers and Investors

There is an inverse parallelism between risk and return for issuers and investors. As risk and return go up for issuers they go down for investors (i.e., more senior instruments in the capital structure). And as risk and return go down for issuers they go up for investors (i.e., more junior instruments in the capital structure). (Compare Figures 3-2 and 3-3.)

For example, secured senior debt may be the least expensive financing available for issuers (lowest interest rates and no equity dilution), but its covenants and constraints will probably be the most restrictive. From the investor's vantage point, this means that secured senior debt has the lowest chance of default (least risk) but also has the lowest interest rate (least return). Conversely, from the issuer's vantage point, this means that secured senior debt has the lowest cost of capital (highest return) but also has the tightest default provisions and protections (highest risk).

In contemporary corporate finance, especially in the structuring of complex acquisitions, there are often numerous levels or layers of financial instruments comprising the firm's capital structure. Yet even within similar instrument classes, the same principle of proportionality between risk and return is maintained: the more senior the instrument or security in the capital structure, the lower the assumed risk and the lower the required return.

For example, senior subordinate debt might yield 12.5 percent while junior subordinate debt from the same issuer might yield 14 percent. Similarly, subordinated debt maturing in one principle repayment (bullet) in nine years would be priced to yield slightly more than the exact same instrument maturing in eight years—the later maturity being more risky. (The inclusion or exclusion of sinking funds, positive and negative covenants, and the like all affect the risk/return profile and therefore affect the expected yield.)

Intersecting Risk/Return for Issuers and Investors

Like supply and demand graphs in economics, the intersection of the risk/return relationships for issuers and investors can help explain pricing and structure of corporate securities (Figure 3-4).[7] Following the economic analogy, the intersection point (where the risk/return profiles of issuers and investors cross) should define a risk/return point of market

7. As in economics, the following graphic representations are highly schematic and are not intended to represent the real world. Relationships portrayed as singular, linear, and smooth are in fact multiple, nonlinear, and jagged. The purpose of these diagrams is to illustrate some basic principles of how risk and return function for issuers and investors under various conditions.

Figure 3–4. Risk/Return: Issuer-Investor Intersection.

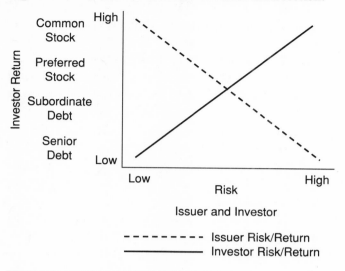

clearance at a specific moment of time. This means that at this specific level of risk and return all the corporate securities are sold.[8]

To be of practical use, we should construct risk/reward graphs and define intersection points for each specific security of each specific firm.[9] The risk axis would now represent the *individual* and perhaps *unique* risk levels implicitly embedded within each security or financing instrument.

Investors and issuers each seek to make their risk/return profiles more beneficial (i.e., more return for less risk); this movement is expressed graphically by shifting the risk/return curves toward the more advantageous direction (Figures 3-2 and 3-3). Different instruments have different risk/return profiles at any given time, and the logic of their compar-

---

8. Note that the issuer/investor intersection point in Figure 3-4 could define the *weighted average* risk/return point of *all* securities in the capital structure taken collectively. As such, this graphic relationship would describe the composite structure of the firm but may not define the risk/return point of any of the firm's actual outstanding securities.

9. We could consider that at each point on the issuer's risk/return line there exists a supply or bucket of securities, where the relative numbers or density at each point of the line represents the firm's target cost of capital. Such a relationship could be illustrated on a three-dimensional graph.

isons—that is, why one is more advantageously positioned than another—is often obscure.

Issuers and investors are constantly searching for the optimum instruments that are on the most favorable edge of the risk/return frontier. For example, from an issuer's perspective a medium-term note of three years might have a lower yield than similar notes for two and four years (i.e., investor demand is highest at the two year tranche at that given instant.)

Tricks and Traps in Financial Analysis

An analysis of risk and return is based in large part on perceptions of the financial status of the firm, both its financial condition at the moment (balance sheet) and its earning power and cash-generating power in the future (income statement and statement of cash flows). From this data, trends are identified and assessments are made.

Yet financial statements have a notoriously poor correspondence to the actual financial status of companies, and using trends to analyze them sometimes compounds the confusion. The numerical nature of financial analysis can beguile the uninitiated. The apparent precision and presentation of accounting and financial information leads to easy misinterpretation.[10]

There are many common pitfalls when evaluating the earnings, assets, liabilities, and equities of companies, and the misuse of trends and graphs is both widespread and contagious. This section points out a few of the pitfalls and highlights some of the misuses.

Tricks and Traps in Accounting

The following topics are just a few of the many areas in financial and accounting analysis that can deceive the naive or fool the cursory.

Earnings Evaluations

The following are example topics that should be monitored closely when evaluating earnings:

- Capitalized costs that should have been expensed and vice-versa (e.g., when already outdated software development costs

---

10. This is especially true with respect to reported earnings—which is one of the reasons why we use cash flows in the wealth formula.

are capitalized it may falsely inflate earnings, when new-product-generating R&D costs are expensed it may falsely deflate earnings);

- income booked from doubtful receivables (e.g., the company that sold time-sharing condominiums booked all its income as 100 percent financed consumer debt—but what happened when those consumers didn't pay?);
- Last-in-first-out/first-in-first-out (LIFO/FIFO) cost of goods sold issues (the valuation of inventories by the last-in-first-out or first-in-first-out methods can disturb margin analysis, especially in a time of inflation);
- timing differences (e.g., delayed and quickened shipments);
- tax deferrals (their cause and resolution);
- net operating losses and tax credits;
- non-recurring profits and losses (e.g., asset sales);
- changing accounting methods and reporting periods.

Asset Evaluations

The following are example topics that should be monitored closely when evaluating assets:

- receivable quality and likelihood of collection;
- inventory quality and aging;
- LIFO/FIFO issues (current value of inventory);
- market value versus historical costs of fixed assets;
- depreciation, amortization, and allocation systems;
- investments in illiquid corporate securities;
- lease values;
- natural resource asset values;
- related-party loans;
- patents, trademarks, and the like;
- goodwill (is it really "good?").

Liabilities Evaluations

The following are example topics that should be monitored closely when evaluating liabilities:

- debt structure and principal repayment schedules;
- loan covenant restrictions and possible penalties;
- off-balance-sheet and contingent liabilities;
- guarantees of third-party debt;
- related-party debt (i.e. debts of executives and owners);
- long-term leases and supply contracts (at above or below market cost);
- underfunded or overfunded pension plans;
- medical retiree obligations.

Equity Evaluations

The following are example topics that should be monitored closely when evaluating equities:

- dividends and covenants on preferred stock;
- dilutions through convertible debt, preferred stock, and warrants (possibly enormous in smaller companies);
- contingent dilutions (such as stock used for acquisitions and dependent on future market price and/or operational performance).

Tricks and Traps in Trends and Graphs

Here we discuss the presentation of data in the context of assessing risk and return for corporate acquisitions.[11]

M&A investment bankers are masters of presentation. Using the same financial records, a company can be made to look either exceptionally desirable (if the banker/broker is representing the seller) or pitifully undesirable (if the banker/broker is representing the buyer). Four principles come into play here: internal comparisons, external comparisons, choice of data, and choice of graphs. Buyers and sellers will view each differently.

Internal Comparisons: Watch Your Base

Assume that Figure 3-5 charts a client company's profit history. A seller will want to make the company look as good as possible by showing high

---

11. A similar risk/return analysis, as described for issuers and investors, can be applied to merger and acquisition evaluations.

Figure 3–5. How Data Selection Changes Perceptions.

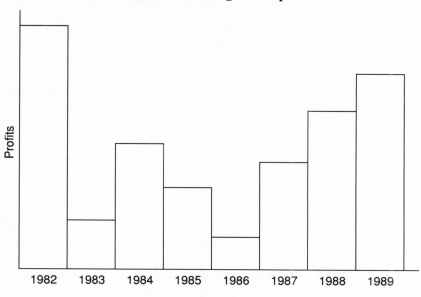

growth. A high rate of growth will justify a high multiple of earnings. A seller might choose to present the four years of consecutive growth from 1986 through 1989. Four years seems fair—but does it present an accurate picture of the company? No matter, go get a premium price for this blazing star.

A buyer will want to make the company look as poor as possible. Showing low growth, or better yet, high volatility, will justify a low multiple of earnings. (Remember, nothing frightens investors more than volatility.) So a buyer is likely to choose to evaluate the eight years from 1982 through 1989. Since the client company's performance varies greatly, the risk must be reflected in a lower price. Go get a deep discount for this panting dog.

The general rule: The seller puts its best foot forward by choosing the base years carefully. The buyer must be sure to look at all relevant years.

External Comparisons: Watch Your Competition

When investment bankers represent a buyer, they like to compare the target company to better-performing competitors. If they represent a seller, they enjoy finding poorer performers. If it is not obvious which companies are indeed competitors, the process gets tricky.[12]

A presentation put together for the Pacific Lumber Company in marketing its long-term debt focused on increasing market control. It was demonstrated that although its 1985 market share of upper-grade, old-growth redwood lumber was a respectable 30 percent, the share would rise to a dominant 65+ percent by 1995. This was not wishful thinking: Competitors were running out of this unique resource and Pacific Lumber's holdings were the world's preeminent supply.

Choice of Data: Watch Your Numbers

Deciding which numbers to highlight and which to hide is also part of the show. Assume a public company is growing by making acquisitions and paying for them with its own common stock. The absolute quantity of sales and profits might evince impressive growth, but if high prices (expressed in large numbers of shares) were paid for the acquisitions (multiples of earnings for the acquired companies greater than that of the acquiring company), then the earnings per share of the acquiring company would be declining (due to dilution) and so might the stock price. Shareholders seeing that the absolute amount of corporate profit was increasing might be perplexed that the market value of their shares was decreasing.

Choice of Graphs: Watch Your Scales

This one can be seen in the newspapers every day. Whether it's the trade imbalance or the national debt, how the scales are drawn affects how the changes appear.

Take a company whose sales were $100 million in 1987, $110 million in 1988, and $120 million in 1989 (Figure 3-6). On a complete graph, the $20 million increase would appear as a 20 percent increase over the three years. If, however, the scale was drawn so that $90 million was the bottom and $120 million the top, the increase would appear to be 200 percent (the $20 million increase from 1987 to 1989 divided by the apparent "$10 million" size in 1987). When graphs are drawn with incomplete scales, all changes are exaggerated.

---

12. You can bet the seller will claim that the companies chosen by the buyer are somehow "in a different market," even though they do sell the same product in the same way. (Maybe they market in Maine but not in Massachusetts.)

**Figure 3–6. How Scale Selection
Changes Perceptions.**

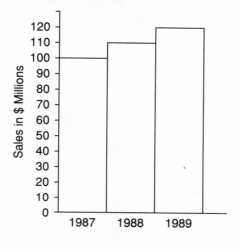

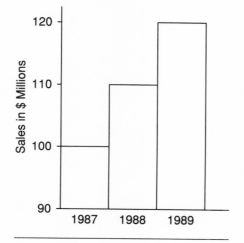

Appendix: The Nature and Measurement of Cash Flow

Although cash has become king and its public reporting has been standardized by the FASB, there still exist some confusion and disagreement about how it should be meaningfully measured.

Cash Flow Definitions

Following are several commonly used definitions of cash flow.

1. *The Classic Definition*: Cash Flow = net income + non-cash charges—mainly depreciation, amortization & deferred taxes.[13]

2. *The Investment Definition*: Cash flow = net income + non-cash charges − capital expenditures. The investment definition reduces the classic cash flow by the totality of capital spending. (Note: In using this definition, some academics add back in the after-tax benefits of the interest deduction, in order to achieve a *pure* cash flow from operations.)

3. *The Maintenance Capital Definition*: Cash flow = pretax income + non-cash charges − maintenance capital expenditures. Maintenance capital expenditures constitute that part of capital spending needed to keep operations at existing levels. This definition is commonly used in corporate takeovers and leveraged buyouts, as some feel it gives the clearest picture of the cash-generating potential of the firm and how much debt the company can support.

4. *The Modified FASB Definition*: Cash flow = net income + non-cash charges + changes in working capital components − capital expenditures. This definition recognizes that increases in current assets such as accounts receivable or inventory drain cash flow, while increases in current liabilities such as accounts payable supplement cash flow.

5. *Other Definitions*: Other definitions of cash flow could be set forth. The key is to determine the specific purpose for analyzing cash flows and to use a definition congruent with that purpose.

Cash Flow Statements

Under GAAP (generally accepted accounting principles), companies must report cash flow classifed according to *operating, investing*, and *financing* activities.

---

13. Deferred taxes are the interperiod timing differences resulting from variances in the way accounting pretax income and taxable income are calculated.

Operating Activities. Operating activities include net income adjusted by certain items not affecting cash (such as depreciation or changes in receivables).

Investing Activities. Investing activities include:

1. cash inflows from the sale of property, plant, and equipment, from the sale of debt or equity, or from the collection of principle on loans from other entities;
2. cash outflows to purchase property, plant, and equipment, to purchase debt or equity of other entities, or to make loans to other entities.

Financing Activities. Financing activities include:

1. inflows from the sale of equity or debt;
2. outflows to shareholders in the form of dividends or the redemption of debt or capital stock.

CHAPTER 4

How to Build Shareholder Wealth*

Financial strategies for corporations are designed by company executives and their investment bankers for the purpose of enhancing shareholder wealth. Such strategies cut a broader path than commonly understood, extending well beyond technical formulations such as optimum debt/equity ratios and dividend payout percentages. The financial strategies we present reach into the heart of corporate strategies, directing managerial attention and suggesting company direction. The impact of these strategies on corporate wealth is high.

In this chapter we present fifteen company-directing, wealth-building, financial strategies for corporations. The sole criterion for inclusion is real-world relevance. Success for companies is what counts: practical business experience—not theoretical academic elegance—is our touchstone. These strategies are building blocks for increasing corporate value. Investment bankers should keep them in mind when representing corporate clients and look constantly for options and opportunities to implement them.

---

* This chapter has been derived from "Financial Strategies I: Techniques for Enhancing Corporate Wealth" by Charles E. Hurwitz and Robert Lawrence Kuhn, Volume II (Capital Raising and Financial Structure), Dow Jones-Irwin's *The Library of Investment Banking* (1990), Robert Lawrence Kuhn, editor-in-chief.

Risk/Reward Ratios are Made to be Skewed

The relationship between risk and return is a fundamental determinant of financial investing. (See Chapter 3.) All things being equal, a given level of risk is expected to be compensated by a given level of reward. But things are never so perfectly equal, and the real world apportions out differing amounts of reward for similar amounts of risk (or differing amounts of risk for similar amounts of reward).

The key is to think *skew*. A skew is a tilt or a tip in your direction. To skew means to shift the risk/reward ratio in your favor. A level playing field is not what you want. One should never approach business without some competitive advantage. A favored position of the risk/return ratio is essential.

All corporate opportunities cannot have the same risk profile, and many good businesses may have higher risks than appropriate for the circumstances. Accepting higher risks is not a mistake per se; the critical question focuses on the potential reward associated with it. When accepting higher risk, it is vital that the expected return be shifted *much* higher. A disproportionate increase in reward relative to risk is essential.

Assessing the risk/reward ratio often depends on one's portfolio of investments. The decision to make one's only business a high-risk-high-reward venture is considerably more serious than when such speculative activities make up only a small part of a large portfolio (e.g., divisions of a diversified corporation).[1]

Play the Percentages

Business, by definition, is a gamble. Free market capitalism requires the chance for all to fail. Risk exists, and nothing can change this fact. But gambling in business is not like gambling in a casino, where the fixed probabilities of payoff in slot machines is established by the house and assures statistical loss for all players taken as a whole group. Business is an active, engaging process, where success and failure rates are influenced directly and dramatically by managers and executives.

---

1. Does requiring a heavily skewed risk/reward ratio preclude taking large risks? Consider those fabled risk-takers who create huge fortunes out of seemingly absurd ideas. (e.g., Federal Express, Apple computers, high-yield bonds, Cabbage-Patch dolls.) Taking risks is fine—just so long as the potential rewards are *disproportionately* greater.

Bet with the odds, not against them. Such skewed betting need not imply chicanery or deceit. Since business is competition, one should not be in business without competitive advantage—some activity that your company can do better than other companies. For example, it is naive (if not futile) to buy a business without knowing how you will make more out of it than others could. There are innumerable ways in which managers build companies. Know as many as possible, and be sure some apply.

Try to Get Lucky

When given a choice between intelligence and luck, intelligent business people choose luck every time. Giving yourself a chance to get lucky is an interesting financial strategy—and it is less capricious than the term *luck* may suggest. It begins by defining a financial floor and assuring that, no matter what happens, you can live with the worst case. You assure your minimum requirements, and then—and only then— you can take some chances.

No-risk gambles are gambles of the best kind. For example, when selling a business, consider getting equity kickers in the acquiring company in order to boost the potential purchase price above an already satisfactory guaranteed price. (Trying to get lucky is like the old chess adage: "Always check you opponent, it might be mate"—i.e., it can't hurt, you have nothing to lose, and, who knows, it might work out better than you think.)

Be Opportunistic

Opportunism in current parlance is an uncomfortable and even slightly ugly word. It has acquired such a negative connotation that few would desire its appellation. To be labelled opportunistic today suggests that one is underhanded or tricky, operating on the fringes.

We buck the connotation and return to the denotation. We use the term opportunism in the sense of simply seeking opportunity. Opportunity is all around if one has the patience to wait and the perception to see. Strange circumstances abound in business. For example, owners may have a multitude of reasons for wanting (or needing) to sell their businesses, and fast-moving buyers can find real bargains.

Seek Strategic Premiums

Sellers should position their properties to maximize any potential premiums. There are usually one or more buyers who may pay considerably higher than what appears to be the expected market value. (This is true whether one is selling an independent company or hard assets.)

Why will a precious few pay a hefty premium? There are various reasons—not necessarily the "greater fool" theory—although the bandwagon effect sometimes plays a part. Often there are strategic premiums involved, such as perceived synergies with other businesses they themselves own (e.g., generating incremental profits due to overhead-sharing) or possible concern for their market position should competitors purchase the business (whether such positive or negative synergies are real or perceived).

At times, special conditions may prevail, such as when a buyer is hungry to invest. For example, in the sale of a solid industrial leader in a relatively stagnant industry, there were a dozen bids grouped within 15 percent of one another, and two outliers some 30 percent higher—one from a competitive industrial company, the other from a leveraged buyout fund. Each outlier had its own reason for making a high bid: the industrial company desired the well-established distribution network to peddle its own languishing products; the fund was willing to accept lower rates of return because it wanted to justify raising more money and needed to have its dollars invested in deals and out of Treasury bills. Searching for strategic premium players is hard work, but almost always worthwhile. When selling assets, look for that strategic player.

Scrutinize Old-time Assets

Assets long ignored may be assets with hidden value. And the longer such assets have been written off the balance sheet, the more valuable they may be. This phenomenon occurs most often in large, diversified companies where isolated real estate holdings and smaller, underperforming divisions may continue to escape top management's attention. (The enhanced value of long-ignored assets has given many corporate takeovers an extra kick—and has shocked the previous senior executives.)

It is remarkable how often value has been discovered in apparently dormant or peripheral corporate assets. Even ancient contracts can have worth. When senior executives do not pay attention to assets they languish. These hidden assets can be revitalized by personal focus, by new management, by merger, or by divestiture. It is important to do something to recapture value.

Entrenched management is often at fault for ignoring assets, although most executives tend to tire over time when plowing the same field. When MCO Holdings was taken over by Charles Hurwitz, he discovered large residual benefits in a coal contract that had been thought worthless. In other companies, the presence of an established sales network, often able to handle other products, can add incremental worth.

Make Money by Not Losing It

It is far better to pass ten good deals than to buy one bad one. Never look back at the big fish that got away. Deals abound; you can see more in a week than you can make in a lifetime. But being burdened by a corporate millstone has buried not a few foolhardy investors. It is better to hit lots of singles and doubles than to risk striking out swinging for the grand slam.

It is usually impossible to assure the success of a speculative venture. An informed judgment before closing can differ dramatically from the company/market reality after closing. When investors do not let a few good deals get away, their hurdle rate is too low or their risk profile is too high.

Many successful investors like to get back their capital rapidly, even sacrificing some longer-term benefits—a low rate of return is unpleasant, a loss of principal is disastrous. In corporate positioning, where long term usually outweights short term, the opposite is normally true: capital investment is often a necessity for protecting market share and future competitiveness.

Assess Relative Valuation

Businesses should only be owned by those to whom they are most valuable (defining *valuable* rather broadly). Falling in love with an investment can be dangerous to financial health. Never forget the primary purpose of for-profit enterprises—to generate maximum financial returns with minimum financial risks. If a division is losing money or market, is out-of-step with current strategy or structure, is draining scarce corporate resources, or is consuming excessive managerial energy, perhaps it should be divested. Divestiture is not failure. It may be the most positive, most aggressive move you can make.

Businesses should only be held when they are worth more to you than they are to *anyone* else—not someone else. That may sound obvious, but the implications are profound. Use any valuation system you like (see Chapter 6), but come up with some dollar valuation for each of your corporate assets. Will another party pay more than this amount to buy this asset? If so, it makes no sense to keep it. The key is to compare value to you versus value to everyone else.

Monitor Swings in Industry and Asset Values

The economy is not entirely rational and markets are not always efficient. Good financial strategy takes advantage of this obvious, imperfect state of the real world. The cyclical nature of business affects the relative worth of different assets at different times. There is constant flux. Whether hard assets (e.g., oil and gas, coal, lumber, and real estate), business assets (e.g., industrial plant and equipment), or intangibles (e.g., customer lists, brand names, media franchises, and patents and technologies)—all values are changing continuously.

A financial strategy suggesting that one should sell conforming assets (at tops of cycles) and buy contrarian assets (at bottoms of cycles) sounds simple and obvious, but it is surprisingly difficult to implement. With the comfort of hindsight, bucking conventional wisdom appears visionary and heroic. But in real time, it is just hard to do. If you follow the crowd and make a mistake, so what? If you fight the crowd and make a mistake, you look like a fool. Financial types fear looking foolish, and thus the crowd psychology gathers its force. Successful financial strategy requires strength of conviction—and nonstop monitoring of relative value.

Optimize Leverage

Leverage is never neutral. Even the term is highly charged. Some praise it; some curse it. The fact is that leverage, properly used, makes sense; it enables a company to shift risk/reward ratios and skew the odds. Not *beat* the odds, mind you, just move them a little in your favor. You can't expect anything more, and over the long run, that's all it takes.

Financial leverage makes all corporate structures riskier, of course, but the key must be the dramatically higher increased rates of return on net investment.

Optimizing leverage means choosing the *right* amount of leverage for each particular situation. It is a mistake to "bet the farm" on every deal — you never know when the roulette wheel will hit zero or double zero.

Protect People Assets

Get, keep, and reward your best employees. Having highly competent personnel is always important; it is especially so for formulating and implementing financial strategy. The leverage here is enormous: The ratio of incremental compensation costs for top people can be a minuscule fraction of the incremental financial returns for the company.

How does one keep the best people? Motivating them is a complex process. Performance is key. It certainly begins (but does not end) with competitive compensation; some say that companies should pay their top producers *more* over the long run than they could earn elsewhere — the most effective control mechanism for retaining superior people are those famous "golden handcuffs." Strive for innovative compensation packages. But compensation, although necessary, is not sufficient; lasting motivation almost always requires more. The best people like doing their jobs; they are committed to personal productivity and company success. The greatest benefit is working with people you like on jobs you enjoy.

Stress Strengths but Eliminate Weaknesses

Do not allow apparent familiarity with this common prescription to undermine its message. The usefulness of the maxim is especially vital when planning financial strategy. Note that we use the verb *eliminate* to describe what action to take regarding corporate weaknesses — we did not say *improve*. Eliminating weaknesses means ridding the organization of the entire area, if possible — not just trying to make it better. *Making better* is bad business — time consuming at best, catastrophic at worst. Business is not a game for the mediocre; it is far better to be great at some things and lousy at others than to be middling at everything. But you must *do* the great stuff and *kill* the lousy stuff.

Test Ideas With Diverse Counsel

Decision makers are lonely people; on their desks the buck stops short. Requesting advice from others is not a sign of frailty and indecision, but one of power and conviction. Executives should refine new financial ideas in the cauldron of critical counsel. Smart, tough associates should offer frank, forceful opinions. Contradicting views and contrary arguments are the only antidote to the ossifying poison of "group think." (Encourage those whose advice is eventually not heeded.) "In the multitude of counselors," say the Proverbs, "there is safety."

Commitment and Persistence

Formulating financial strategy is often easy; implementing it is always hard. Commitment can be defined as the link between personal meaning and company mission—and it is essential for putting strategy into action. It is impossible to succeed in building financial value without dedication, persistence, drive, and determination. The best financial strategists are single-minded in pursuit of their goals; they are focused and intense, and they allow little to impede their progress.

Maintain High Integrity and Reputation

Good financial strategy has long legs. To work today it must work tomorrow. It is never embarrassing—no matter how public the revelation. Only a short-term player would sacrifice integrity and reputation to get an illegal or immoral edge. (*All* ill-gotten edges are short-term, rapidly depleting assets). Remember, a good name brings better business.

CHAPTER 5

How to Use Investment Bankers*

What do corporate issuers and institutional investors think about their investment bankers? How do they choose a firm and how do they obtain maximum benefit with appropriate cost? We explore how experienced executives from issuing and investing organizations optimize their relationships with Wall Street.

Investment bankers have been flying in flack of late. A rather hard time they have been having, what with insider trading scandals, market meltdowns, junk bond castigations, and congressional outcries over bustup mergers and acquisitions. Then there is all that commotion over fees. Investment bankers have been known to pull down well over $10,000 per hour![1] The claim is that such compensation is so immense, so gargantuan, that no honest human labor could possibly be worth so much money.[2]

---

* This chapter has been derived from "How to Use Investment Bankers" by Robert Lawrence Kuhn, Volume V (Mortgage and Asset Securitization), Dow Jones-Irwin's *The Library of Investment Banking* (1990), Robert Lawrence Kuhn, editor in chief.

1. No investment banker ever actually charges $10,000 per hour. The calculation is made by taking fees earned on a particular deal (e.g., for a large merger or acquisition) and divide by the total number of hours worked. A $10 million fee divided by 1000 working hours equals $10,000 per hour. Simple arithmetic. (And $10,000, when you actually play with the real numbers, may be on the lower end of the spectrum.)

2. Ignoring, of course, comparisons to motion picture idols, rock stars, and professional athletes. (How much does Michael Jackson or Michael Tyson earn per minute?)

Investment bankers evince no chagrin. They retort that they are paid only a small fraction of the value they add to a transaction. It is this "value added," they assert, that justifies their hefty emoluments. When they are able to get a few dollars more per share in a corporate merger through their skill and expertise, shareholders can get hundreds of millions of extra dollars. Investment bankers state that their fees are only a small fraction of this incremental benefit.[3]

Does the economy need investment bankers? Do companies need them? Are financial intermediaries promoting their own profession over professional service? What service can they provide, and how can senior executives use investment bankers to their firm's advantage? Although public policy debate will continue, the trick for companies is to learn if, when, and how to use their investment bankers. Investment bankers perform a real service for companies, but knowing how to use these services will make the process more efficient in cost and more effective in results.

Following are tips for tangling with investment bankers—some ideas about how corporate issuers and institutional investors can make maximum use of their investment bankers.

1. Specify Your Goals

Knowing in advance precisely what your company wants to achieve in the financing or transaction is vital. Generalized goals make weak foundations. Proper financial goals should be:

- clear, not vague (everyone should understand them);
- specific, not general (precise and accurate in numerical terms);
- focused, not diffuse (wish lists are fine, but just remember what you really need);
- contained, not boundless (don't reach for maximization before ensuring your minimum goals);

---

3. It's like the joke about the little, old diamond cutter who is asked to cut an extraordinarily valuable stone. After doing a superb job, he sends a bill for $50,000. Exasperated, the owner exclaims, "That's outrageous! It only took you a few minutes!" The little, old diamond cutter apologizes, "I'm sorry, I should have itemized the bill: For cutting the diamond, $10; for knowing where to cut, $49,990."

- difficult, not easy (if you don't stretch, you'll never get the best results);
- consistent, not inconsistent (financial goals must mesh with all other goals);
- measurable, not immeasurable (you must know when it works);
- achievable, not unachievable (living in blue-sky dreamworlds frustrate closure).

You can certainly work with your investment bankers to help clarify your financing goals, but always remember that your goals must be *your* goals.

2. Become Familiar With Comparable Transactions

Know what other companies have done in similar circumstances (the more similar, and the more recent, the better). Learn what happened in the past—but never be satisfied with history. Keep current: the market changes constantly, new deals are going effective daily, and you need to be aware of what's happening.

Ask questions, suggest alternatives, and understand why certain transactions will not work—you must interact with your bankers. Above all, do not be intimidated. The best antidote for the poison of embarrassment is knowledge and aggressiveness.

3. Interview Several Firms

The courting process is important. This is your time to expand horizons. You will never be treated as well as when you have not made your choice. Your prospective bankers will never be more solicitous or more patient. (And if they are not solicitous and patient now, when they want your business, how much worse will they be when they already have it?)

The selection process exposes you to diverse groups and distinct ways of thinking. Different investment banks have different approaches. Although these variances may seem subtle, they are often meaningful and a potential issuer or investor should appreciate them. (A common mistake is to judge all differences in terms of price.) The more you learn, the more you expand your base of knowledge, and this will make it easier to appreciate the variances and assess how each might affect your situation.

4. Select the Firm That Meets Your Needs

Name and reputation are important, but not all-important. How valuable you are as a client to a given firm should sometimes be the most vital factor in the selection decision. (Generally, you want a senior banker at the firm to be intimately involved with your transaction, not just to win the business and then to hand off to subordinates.)

You want a banking house to be well-experienced in the specific kind of transaction you seek. (You do not want them to learn how to shave on your face, no matter how prestigious the firm.) A top-bracketed firm with little commitment to your specific needs may be the worst of all—the illusion of expertise mixed with the frustration of neglect.

5. Maintain Relationships with More Than One Firm

No matter how well you are working with one investment bank, always keep one or two others in your back pocket. Stay in touch with the competition. Don't feel guilty about it. Don't even hide it! Companies maintain relationships with more than one commercial bank; the same principle should be applied to investment banks.

You never know when your investment bank will undergo a radical change—corporate restructure (eliminating your personal bankers), corporate reallocation of resources (going out of your business as Salomon Brothers did in municipal finance), or plainly disappearing altogether (as did several firms following October 19, 1987). Furthermore, by talking to your banker's competitors, you can keep an eye on the pricing markets and prevent your banker from taking you for granted.

6. Minimize Downside Risk; Then Try to Get Lucky

Be sure that you get what you really need. Ensure the bare minimum; secure that bottom line—this takes all danger out of the situation. Then, and only then, go for it.

7. Work Closely With Your Investment Bankers

It is a mistake to assume that your bankers are always working for you, that they are living and breathing your deal. Many investment bankers are working with many clients on many deals (often worrying more about getting the next client than satisfying the current one). Your deal is the most important to you, but it may not be to them. Keep on their tails. Ask questions, check schedules, confirm meetings.

A good approach is to speak regularly to *many* bankers working on your deal, not just to the senior person or even to some of the associates. (You can often learn the most by conversing with those who are running the spreadsheets. Although junior, they are closest to the numbers and may well have the earliest sense of direction and outcome. Try calling them at the office after normal hours or on a weekend.)

8. Maintain Control of the Process

Senior management must participate actively with their investment bankers. Never allow the apparent complexity of the financial structure to pressure you into abdication, or to disenfranchise you from able involvement. This is your company. You know it better than anyone else. Although you may not be a finance expert, you are probably better able to integrate the financial structure with the business structure than any of the hotshot bankers. Only you can sense when a particular transaction, seemingly ideal from a financial perspective, may trigger unpleasant side effects in other areas. The subtleties of the business are often harder to appreciate than the complexities of the finance.

CHAPTER 6

How to Value and Price Mergers and Acquisitions*

The valuing and pricing of business entities in merger and acquisition (M&A) transactions is both art and science. The science is founded on finance theory and models, the art on personal insight and experience. Yet there is a subtle problem emerging today. Our spectacular capacity to process data and analyze numbers on personal computer spreadsheets is undermining the art while facilitating the science. The subliminal message emanating from the thousands of calculations involved in M&A analyses is that precision is possible, that accurate valuation and price-setting is attainable. Such unwarranted confidence is always naive and usually a mistake, even a serious one. Investment bankers specializing in M&A must retain their artistic perception as well as improve their scientific technology.

The purpose of this chapter is to survey the numerous methods of M&A valuing and pricing involved in both quantitative and qualitative analysis. We present these two kinds of approaches to ascertaining M&A prices:

1. Specific models, or numerical valuation techniques that establish price; these are *quantitative models that determine price.*

2. General modifiers or non-numerical elements that affect price; these are *qualitative factors that modify price.*

---

* This chapter has been derived from "Valuing and Pricing Mergers and Acquisitions I: Practices and Techniques" by Robert Lawrence Kuhn, Volume IV (Mergers, Acquisitions, and Leveraged Buyouts), Dow Jones-Irwin's *The Library of Investment Banking* (1990), Robert Lawrence Kuhn, editor in chief.

A primary point is the considerable variety and diversity in practice and technique. No one system or method is inherently more appropriate or more valid under all conditions. Each method and model has its own special slant on M&A transactions, and as such each has its own special application in specific circumstances. Never assume that numbers are inviolate; they may be precise without being accurate. Everything in business is contingent.

The Need for Multiple Mechanisms

The academic literature on valuing companies for acquisition largely stresses *discounted cash flow* (DCF) analysis as the methodologically *correct* route to the *right* answer. DCF calculates the net present value or internal rate of return using the stream of expected cash flow outputs from the business over time, as compared to the initial cash investments into the business (i.e., acquisition payment). It is a highly quantitative, apparently rigorous methodology, and is thus proffered as inherently valid as an economic model of the firm.

But the problem is that companies as complex organizations operating in an even more complex environment are not given to such simplistic portrayal. (Indeed, the apparent sophistication of DCF is in itself deceiving.) Experience proves that no single method of valuing acquisition targets is always proper or truly comprehensive. The M&A process occurs in the real world where multiple forces interact on so many levels as to almost defy analysis; M&A is not sheltered by the highly stylized, well-controlled, idealized models of academics and computer programmers.

We will see how the *softer* less numerical methods can work better than the *harder* more numerical methods. While academic business scholars must prefer methods which are grounded in finance theory (i.e., discounted cash flow analysis), pragmatic investment bankers know from experience that the assumptions necessary to perform such rigorous procedures can generate an impractically broad band of possible outcomes. In such situations—which are not uncommon—the results of the more quantitative techniques become virtually useless and one must utilize other techniques to value and price the deal.

Irrespective of DCF's pure economic soundness, the real world uses additional practices and models for evaluating investments. And when such practices and models produce results that differ from those produced by DCF, they must not be ignored. To deny the existence of other models, techniques, or avenues of analysis is to repudiate potential sources of value or ignore potential areas of risk that must be included in a thorough M&A pricing analysis. It is a fundamental error not to employ multiple methods to assess valuation and price.

Importance of Price

How often have we heard someone say that everything has been worked out in a deal *except the price?* That's like saying that you like everything about the philosophy of Buddhism except the teachings of Buddha.

Price is the quintessential part of M&A transactions. The key to every merger, acquisition, and divestiture is the amount and nature of consideration changing hands. (See Appendix II, at the end of the chapter, for a discussion of how investment bankers evaluate and compare diverse kinds of consideration in M&A offers.)

To make good deals, you have to *find* the right price, that exquisitely fine line between the maximum the buyer can pay and the minimum the seller can accept. Finding that interface, either from buying or selling side, is a creative, exhaustive process.

Creativity is enhanced when options are multiplied, when choices are expanded, and when issues are addressed from diverse viewpoints. Thus, we provide numerous ways, numerical and judgmental, for valuing a business. Each offers its own angles, its own cut of the problem. Choosing the right models, and deciding which modifiers apply and how, is part of the requisite insight.

Seeing a problem from multiple perspectives is the essence of creativity in business. All relevant models and factors should be considered as components of a broadly comprehensive analysis that blends all forces determining price. Used effectively, the combination of these quantitative models and qualitative factors can go far in pricing mergers and acquisitions. Such blending portrays the investment banker's art.

Quantitative Models That Determine Price

Quantitative models focus on generating a hard numerical output to specify price; they determine what businesses are worth and how to value companies. What methods are used, when are they used, how are they used, how do they work, where do they work, and where do they fail? (We do not focus on terms and conditions. The type, timing, features, and constraints of consideration used—such as cash, notes of all kinds, stock of all kinds, earn-outs, participations, personal contracts, etc.— are beyond the scope of this chapter.)

The following models for assessing business value are listed in approximate order of usage or importance. The large number of models and methods is designed to stimulate the art of M&A thinking. Though some are similar, consider the nuances that differentiate among them and under what circumstances might such differences prove helpful.

Discounted Cash Flow

As stated above, DCF is generally considered the most theoretically valid model for valuing and pricing enterprises whose economic life is a description of streams of cash flows going in and coming out. Its application in M&A is derived from its original use in evaluating capital budgeting proposals (e.g. whether to purchase a large industrial tool or construct a new manufacturing plant). DCF is discussed much in the M&A world, although as most investment bankers would admit, it is used less.

The internal mechanism of DCF is simple. It works, as we've stated, by weighing the amount of cash invested for the acquisition against the amounts and timing of all future net free cash generated over the life of the investment (net of depreciation, capital expenditures, working capital needs, etc.). This calculation yields an *internal rate of return* (IRR) (which is actually the implied discount rate when the present value of the cash flows going in are set equal to the present value of the cash flows going out).

Alternatively, the future cash flows can be discounted to present value (using an appropriately selected, though rather arbitrary, discount rate) and compared to the initial investment. This calculation yields a *net present value* (NPV), the difference between what you paid and what you expect to make (in present value terms).

Note that the key difference between the IRR and the NPV is that the IRR calculates the implied discount rate by setting the present value of the in-going (negative) and out-coming (positive) cash flows equal to each other, while the NPV uses independently chosen discount rates in order to compare the net present values of these same cash flows.

Using either internal rate of return or net present value, DCFs require that a terminal value be estimated (using various growth models—see Appendix I), normally about seven to ten years out, which is then discounted back to the present. This logic is similar to the salvage value of a capital asset (e.g., piece of equipment).

DCF analysis is highly dependent on the choice of the discount rate.[1] A difference in one percentage point can be critical. There are four normal approaches for determining the appropriate discount rate:

1. Select the acquiring company's current weighted cost of capital (debt and equity) as the base discount rate (see Chapter 3), and then factor it up by several percentage points (since new projects should require a higher hurdle rate than current operations).

2. Select the acquiring company's historic return on assets as the base discount rate, and then factor it up by several percentage points as above.

3. Utilize current estimates of future interest rate expectations as the base discount rate, which is then increased by a risk factor related to the industry, company, financial structure, and the like.

4. Utilize current estimates of similar companies' weighted cost of capital (from public data) as the base discount rate, which is then increased by a risk factor as above.

The major problem with the DCF, of course, is the inherent uncertainty in estimates and projections. The future is still the future, and forecasts are still forecasts. So many assumptions must be made regarding markets, products, pricing, competition, management, the economy, interest rates, and the like that confidence becomes severely eroded. In this web of multiplied uncertainty, the numerical elegance of the method can be its greatest danger—that is, the gloss of sophistication and the illusion of control can be both deceptive and intoxicating. DCF can be precise (i.e., replicable) without being accurate (i.e., not conforming to reality). It is vital to appreciate this distinction between precision and accuracy.

Nonetheless, one should use DCF in every M&A situation. The process itself is important since it focuses attention on the critical assumptions and uncertainties. Results are important as well, especially when defining the maximum pricing for buyers. For example, if a potential

---

1. See Chapter 6 Appendix I: Merger and Acquisition Formulas for additional discussion of this issue.

buyer's analysis would show that rates of return are still only modest even if actual results would track estimated projections (which they never do), the price is surely too high.

Sensitivity analysis is a necessary exercise in all analytical evaluations. Here, various scenarios are explored by assessing how sensitive your valuation model is to various changes in input. As stated above, the choice of discount rate makes enormous impact on the outcome of the analysis. In fact, one often finds that the largest variations in the sensitivity analysis are produced by testing alternative discount rates.

In addition, since DCF is fundamentally based on the time value of money, it is exceedingly dependent on the timing of cash inflows and outflows. Due to the compounding effect, no mathematical symmetry will be obvious: A simple decrease of 15 percent in margins will not, you can be sure, cause a simple 15 percent decrease in value.

One must be aware of the strange peculiarities of time in determining rates of return; the compounding curve accelerates benefits and costs. In almost every M&A analysis, anticipated rates of return decline drastically after the first few years irrespective of business operations—this is more a conceptual shortcoming of the method than an actual loss of value. It is virtually impossible to maintain excessively high rates of return over extended periods of time since the corporate equity base (i.e., the denominator in the equation—largely retained earnings) swells large as is customary with most projections. Professional corporate financiers would much rather attain a 25 percent compounded annual rate of return for ten years than a 40 percent return for three years.

Price/Earnings (P/E) Ratio

The price/earnings ratio reflects the earning power of the company capitalized by an appropriate discount rate. The formulation is expressed as the P/E *multiple* which is the inverse of the discount rate. An industry-appropriate income statement number—such as earnings before interest and taxes (EBIT) or net profits after tax (NPAT)—is multiplied by an appropriate P/E factor to calculate price. (EBIT is a reflection of the *operational* earning power of the company irrespective of financing and financial structure, while NPAT embeds all current factors including financing and financial structure.)

The P/E multiple is determined by both industry and company characteristics, with anticipated growth rate being the key variable. Indeed, the P/E ratio is virtually a surrogate for anticipated growth rate modulated by an assumed risk factor. P/E ratios for acquisition purchases are usually applied to average earnings over a period of time, about three to five years. This will not work, of course, for young companies. Here, the P/E may be applied to current or even projected earnings. Higher P/Es (or lower discount rates) can be justified (using strict financial criteria) only by higher anticipated growth in earnings. P/Es work best when assessing steady-state companies in industries with similar public firms (so than an average P/E ratio can be determined).

We note that the use of P/E multiples to evaluate and compare company valuations is what has engendered Wall Street's obsession with earnings per share (EPS), since EPS times P/E multiple equals selling share price.

Market Value

For public companies, the stock market gives a daily assessment of value. The current market capitalization of publicly traded companies is central to M&A pricing—share price, multiplied by the number of shares outstanding and factored by an appropriate premium (generally ranging from 20 to 100 percent or more), is generally necessary to acquire a public company with a relatively liquid float. (Thinly-traded companies generate price distortions.)

Premiums are paid by investors to acquire control positions; such stock dominance (not necessarily more than 50 percent) overcomes foot-dragging by incumbent owners or managers and thwarts potential rivals from raising competing offers. Market price is obviously necessary to price a public company since it is almost impossible to buy a company below its market price given the need for independent *fairness opinions* by investment bankers. But market price alone is usually not sufficient. The share-pricing method is grounded on the efficient market theory: that the market is continuously evaluating all information about each company and expressing its current conclusions in up-to-the-minute cash bids and offers for the company's shares.

Yet for acquisition analysis, there is a fatal flaw here. Stock market investors and M&A activists are not conceptually grounded on the same financial foundation and as such should require different analyses. Stock market investors are not buying whole companies; they are purchasing small, highly liquid, minority interests. The investor hopes to gain from market forces, not personal managerial influence, and can close out the position at any time. On the other hand, M&A activists who do buy whole companies cannot enjoy such liquidity and flexibility but can, conversely, dictate future operations through managerial control. These are different concepts requiring different models.

The fruits of control usually command a hefty premium, but that premium may be more or less than the *real* value of the company. Hence the need for other techniques to be used in parallel and conjunction with the market value method. Market value obviously applies to public companies, but can be used to assess nonpublic companies by comparison (see Merger Market Value).

Merger Market Value

In merger market valuation models we compare prices among similar companies, much like comparison shopping for a consumer item among similar retail stores. In the merger market value method, reasonably similar transactions (i.e., similar industry, company size, financial structure, time frame, etc.) are assembled, and these prices are used to judge the relative worth of the target company. Investment bankers favor this technique, generating long lists of comparable transactions to advise clients on both buying and selling sides.

In theory, the M&A market is the true reflection of current interaction between willing sellers and willing buyers. In the real world, however, this is rarely the case. Corporations are not yellow pencils, quickly stacked and easily matched; it is difficult to make true comparisons of complex situations—in one way or another virtually every M&A sale can be considered special or extraordinary. Furthermore, the M&A market often evinces aberrations—companies selling too low when suffering distressed conditions, and companies selling too high when faddish or foolish buyers are over-eager to acquire. The feeding frenzy of M&A in recent years—the search for synergy and the hostile takeover battles—have bid many M&A prices up to unrealistic levels.

Book Value

Book value is the classic accounting determination of net worth. It is a definitive, time-locked, *snapshot* number reflecting a firm's accounting value at a particular time. Book value is important because it is produced by standardized generally accepted accounting principles (GAAP) and prepared by independent, third parties. Yet it is just this apparent precision that makes book value so deceptive and therefore so dangerous.

Book value often means nothing; worse, it can be terribly deceptive. When Maxxam Group bought the Pacific Lumber Company, the value of the latter's world-dominant position in old growth redwood trees was carried on its books for less than 5 percent of real worth. (Historical cost at decades-ago prices—the GAAP principle—was far less than current market value.) On the other hand, many companies maintain ancient plants and worthless inventories, fearing the consequences of large writedowns. In this case, book value would be highly inflated over real value.

Book value may occasionally be used to add tax benefits to a transaction; for example, if the purchase price can be structured below book, additional cash may be generated through tax loss carrybacks or carryforwards—the economic value of the transaction to the seller may then be sweetened in other ways (such as consulting contracts).

Breakup Value

A breakup valuation model assesses the cumulative net worth resulting from selling off all divisions and hard assets of a company (generally in multiple transactions), and netting the proceeds against all remaining liabilities. A breakup valuation is used in two general ways. First, it is considered as downside protection in case the anticipated strategy does not work out. Second, it can be the specific, preplanned strategy of the acquirer (usually in hostile takeovers).

Some companies are indeed worth more dead than alive. The value of the individual parts is higher than the combined sum. This often occurs when companies have little or no business synergies among divisions and mediocre track records for generating healthy returns. Many conglomerates fall into this category.

Breakup value models estimate prices one could get if the various divisions or assets were sold independently as viable businesses. Often these businesses are highly desirable to potential acquirers who would pay a substantial premium for them (but would not be interested in buying the entire company). The ideal goal of some acquirers is to recover most or all of the full purchase price by selling off parts of the target company, and thereby wind up keeping some desirable parts for a nominal investment.

Real Asset Value

Real asset value determines the market value of all *hard assets* of the company—what you could get for the plant, property and equipment, any natural resources or reserves, and the like. This does not include the *business premiums* for earning power or divisions. Real asset value defines a baseline, a floor, on which the liquidation value model can be estimated.

Liquidation Value

A liquidation valuation model can be used as a pricing benchmark, or the lowest realistic value for any target company. The key factor here is the company's realizable net asset value judged according to the following procedure: All assets are sold individually to generate the best obtainable prices and all liabilities are paid off as they are due—with both sale of assets and payment of liabilities assumed to be conducted in an orderly, businesslike fashion. (Note that the difference between *orderly sales* and *firesales* can be shocking.) What remains, theoretically, should approximate book value—but variance is wide and one should not be surprised if there is great disparity.

Often the analysis does not assume maintenance of any division or subsidiary as a going concern. The company is simply liquidated for its raw assets: receivables are collected, inventories are sold off, and fixed assets (including advantageous leases) are given to brokers for sale or auction—all assets are converted to cash. (Don't forget intangibles such as patents, trademarks, etc.)

Debts are then netted against the likely gross cash generated to determine a floor for the purchase price. Don't forget hidden liabilities such as underfunded pension plans, retiree medical benefits, and other contingencies. Never underestimate the costs and problems of liquidation—running the company as it is being closed down—from poor collections of receivables (people just won't pay) to managing unmotivated personnel. (Watch the vultures circle.) Remember: Debts are sure; assets are not.

The liquidation model should be used when estimating the lowest value for a company (the "downside")—especially when acquiring troubled companies. Getting some sense for the ultimate floor is a worthwhile exercise when evaluating all companies. DCF and other going-concern techniques do not contemplate sale of assets and therefore provide no sense whatsoever of liquidation value. Liquidation analysis often requires the assistance of appraisers, brokers and actuaries.

Perceived Growth

Perceived growth differs from actual growth. In this model, forecasts and projections are crucial—and here's where anxious acquirers can really fool themselves. In these situations, the acquirer must pay a price higher than historic or current earnings can support. What is the worth; what is the justification; and what price can be offered? Assumptions are key; numbers on computer screens mean nothing of themselves. Numerous possibilities must be considered: market growth, competitive position, potential substitutes, and changing technology to name just a few.

Synergy Value

Buying a company for its potential synergy value is dangerous. Many a stratospheric price has been lavished on a pipedream. The assessment process evaluates the operational impact of the proposed acquisition on the acquiring company's current business.

Ask if the combination can yield benefits to either acquirer or target or both. Can the target's sales force sell the acquirer's products? Can the customers of one buy the products of the other? Can the acquirer's plants produce the target's products? Can our overhead support their needs? Can our management help them, their management help us? Will two plus two equal five—or three, as often happens?

Such *anti*synergy is the autoimmune disease of the M&A body. All too frequently, especially when one acquirer completes many deals, the headstrong attempt to achieve an unrealistic or impossible level of synergy can destroy the original health of both companies.

Investment Value

An investment value model takes a more passive look at the acquisition, and evaluates the target company as if it were merely a small stock purchase to be put into a large investment portfolio. Although the analysis will use many of these same techniques described above, the *attitude* and *approach* will be different. Passion will be less, as will assumptions of managerial magic. Here the acquirer forgets about synergy value on the one hand and breakup value on the other.

Going Concern Value

A going concern valuation model is a hybrid. First it takes net asset expectations (whether break-up or liquidation value) and then adds any excess rates of return anticipated for operating the business. This technique hedges assets and earnings.

Competitive Value

The competitive valuation model is used to assess how much the target company might be worth to competitors. What would be the amount that a company would be willing to pay in order to lessen competition, to gain share, to shore up prices—to thwart you? For example, magazines are occasionally bought by competitors and closed immediately—the point being to incorporate acquired subscription lists into the acquirer's existing ones in order to enhance the acquirer's existing properties. Competitive valuation is generally applied to industrial, not financial players (though financial players can use the competitive model to assess potential resale values, especially given some operational and market share improvement).

Replacement Value

The replacement value model estimates the cost of replacing the target company with *all new* plant, equipment, materials, and the like—which is obviously more expensive than the following two similar valuation models. Replacement valuation only applies to industrial companies requiring the target's facilities and/or are contemplating entrance into the target company's business.

There are two kinds of replacement value analyses: (1) only assets (fixed and current) are considered; and (2) the entire conduct of the current business is assessed, including hiring and training personnel, designing and producing products, establishing markets, building customer lists and service operations, installing control systems, and the like. This analysis is similar to the make-or-buy decisions of industrial manufacturers.

Reproduction Value

Reproduction valuation is an estimate of the cost of totally replicating the target company in exactly its present form. A similar plant and equipment are assumed to be bought in their current condition, personnel must be hired and trained, new product names must be established, and the like. This technique, as with the previous and following ones, is used primarily by industrial buyers who are considering entering the target's industry.

Build-or-buy analyses should accompany all corporate acquisition programs, and one should determine the relative advantages of buying ongoing companies or starting similar businesses from the ground up. Time delays, asset availability, personnel training, and market recognition are critical factors in the cost comparisons.

Substitution Value

The substitution value model is an estimate of the cost of buying the same *output* as the target company currently produces without having to purchase any of its specific elements. Ends and not means are judged— a decidedly less expensive proposition.

Rules of Thumb for Multiple Values

Each of the above quantitative models that determine price are used in conjunction with prevailing rules of thumb to convert numerical output into actual pricing values. These rules, by definition, are creatures of the market to be discerned by common knowledge and constant monitoring.

Rules of thumb are generally expressed in multiples—industry-specific integer multipliers of operational data such as net profits after-tax (NPAT), earnings before interest and taxes (EBIT), and net free cash flow. They are also expressed as industry-specific integer multipliers of unit values such as price per barrel of oil reserves for an energy corporation, price per bed for a health care company, or price per subscriber for a cable television concern.

Rules of thumb are tricky, and perhaps unreliable. Procedures and fingers change, as do multiples, and one must keep attuned to the latest notions. Even more importantly, not all companies in a given industry are equal. Differences in market share, brand name, reputation, management, cost structure, and myriad other elements are critical. The same multiple paid willingly for an industry leader would yield an absurdly excessive price for a follower. The bottom line is that numerical techniques are necessary to get some sense of the situation, but they are inadequate to fix a final price. For that, we must look beyond numbers.

Estimating Earnings Projections

Estimates of future earnings are vital in M&A valuation and pricing. After all, multiples in the above quantitative models must multiply *something*. One should work with five-year financial data, normalized to adjust for changes in accounting principles, mergers and acquisitions, non-recurring events, and the like. Percentages should be calculated so that trends become easier to spot.

Critical trends and deviations from those trends should be noted over the five years in general and the most recent two years in particular. Special attention should be paid to sales growth (by product line), gross margins, general and administrative costs, and all the traditional ratios of liquidity, leverage, activity, and profitability.[2]

By incorporating the previous five years into the trend analysis, one can make a first estimate on what the next five years might be like. The fundamental assumption, of course, is that the future will emulate the past—a dangerous decision under the best of circumstances.[3] With earnings estimates made, growth rates and discount rates can be calculated (see Appendices to this chapter). These are then transformed into the proper multiples to use in the quantitative models (e.g., for P/E ratio models, the growth rate surrogate is applied to the net income; for DCF models, the discount rate is applied to the yearly cash flows).

Qualitative Factors That Modify Price

Valuing and pricing M&A transactions cannot be done independently of the context in which the deal is being done. Knowing why a certain deal is desired facilitates knowing which quantitative models and qualitative factors to consider. For example, industrial and financial buyers would have different motivations to pursue the same deal, would make differ-

---

2. Example ratios for trending and deviation analysis—*Liquidity:* current ratio and quick ratio; *leverage:* debt-to-total assets, debt/equity, times interest earned, and fixed charge coverage; *activity:* inventory turnover (cost of goods sold to average inventory), average collection period, sales to fixed assets turnover, and sales to total assets turnover; *profitability:* gross margin on sales, net margin before interest and taxes on sales, net margin after interest and taxes on sales, return on total assets, and return on net worth.

3. For mature companies in mature industries, this assumption is less speculative than for early-stage ventures in young industries. One's confidence in making five-year projections for, say, a large furniture or pipe manufacturer would be considerably higher than for a start-up firm in superconductivity or expert systems.

ent assessments, and would be willing to pay different prices. Client motivations, therefore, are important for investment bankers to assess.

Client motivations for pursuing M&A are many:

1. *Financial M&A*—for example, stock enhancement, balance sheet/earnings improvement, leveraged buyout, management buyout, and going private.

2. *Strategic M&A*—for example, horizontal integration, vertical integration, market share growth, product/market protection, plant utilization, overhead amortization, technology leaps, and diversification.

3. *Managerial M&A*—for example, company restructure, desired growth, chief/senior executive interest, and personal ambition.

Price is the universal currency of the international M&A economy. A price that is too high or too low, even though calculated by microprocessor and printed by laser, does not generate exceptional value for M&A activists—either buyer or seller.

In general, there are two categories of qualitative factors which affect value—operational factors and transactional/financial factors. The two are interrelated, and in most transactions acquirers look for both sets of benefits. Operational factors—such as market position and presumed synergy—tend to relate to specific companies at specific times and are less susceptible to general rules. Consequently we focus on transactional/financial factors.

Following are transactional/financial factors that impact M&A valuation and pricing. Each must be evaluated in the specific context of acquirer and target.

Do-Ability

This is my first choice—the top of the list. Can the deal get done? No matter how attractive a situation, no matter how right the price, the deal has to be feasible. There are virtually an infinite number of reasons that make a deal *in*feasible—even after terms and conditions are generally agreed.

How can a deal come unhinged? Anything can slam the door—from bad chemistry and personal piques to over-eager lawyers and potential lawsuits to changing business conditions and interest rates. Deals disintegrate, even at the last moment. It is much easier to uncover a dozen attractive situations than to consummate one of them.

How can one assess do-ability? There is no cookbook list of secret recipes and special ingredients. The best advice is to optimize benefits for both sides, strive for simplicity, and assess major sticking points (deal breakers)—and use your nose (does the deal *smell* right?).

Financibility

The ability to finance an acquisition is usually dependent on two factors: the general creditworthiness of the acquiring company and its credibility with lenders and/or security holders; and the specific confidence of financial institutions that the proposed deal is a good one. (If equity interests in the acquirer and/or seller paper are the consideration being used, this problem becomes less important and perhaps moot.)

The initial financial strength of both acquirer and target are critical. Factors to consider include history of earnings, quality of assets, and absence of encumbrances. Projected streams of income, from which cash coverage of interest and amortization of principal will be derived, must be scrutinized. (Always remember that debts are paid with cash and not earnings, so cash flow is always more important than accounting income.) *Haircuts* will be performed on company projections (reductions in estimates) so that lenders can be confident that their loans are safe even under almost-worst-case conditions.

Financial Structure

Acquisition price, if independent of financial structure, can be misleading. How deals are financed can greatly affect appropriateness of price. For example, an all-cash payment financed entirely with three-year senior debt would merit a very low price from the perspective of the buyer, whereas the use of owner-carried notes, zero coupon bonds, and preferred stock would support a much higher price for the same transaction.

Sometimes a deal is actually worth more than the acquiring company can afford to pay. In a well-known billion-dollar acquisition of a natural resource company, interest charges in the highly leveraged structure amounted to twice the preacquisition cash flow. The deal could not have been completed without the substantial use of zero coupon notes which would mature as the target's assets could be converted to cash over a 15-year period.

Many of the advances in modern M&A have involved the creative development of novel financial instruments that match company cash flow with debt requirements and balance risk and return for various levels of lenders and investors. The three traditional levels—senior debt, mezzanine, and equity—are often segmented into a dozen or more *strips* in larger and more complex transactions (see Chapters 12 and 13).

Tax Considerations

Taxes are a great concern in all M&A transactions and are fraught with opportunity and threat—and they incur high professional costs.

Tax issues for the buyer include: how do anticipated taxes affect the net free cash available for operating the company and amortizing debt? What will the new tax basis of the acquired assets be, and how will they be allocated? Are there any special tax considerations in the industry or company? any hidden tax liabilities? any recapture? any net operating loss carryforwards?

Tax issues for the seller include: What is the after-tax, realizable, net free cash generated? What is the most efficient structure to minimize tax liability? What about tax-free exchanges, taxable transactions that generate losses, installment structures, capital gains treatment, contingent payouts, consulting arrangements, liquidations, spin-offs, and blanket tax exemptions? It is usually important to control timing such as when taxes would become payable on the exercise of options or on constructive receipts of dividends; the worst case is the mismatch of the receipt of cash and income so that a tax liability is incurred without generating money to pay it.

The key to many deals is to find the win-win structure that minimizes the collective tax liabilities for both the acquiring company and the selling shareholders. In this manner, more value will be available to distribute between the parties.

Cost of Capital

A company's cost of capital is one of its key characteristics, in which the weighted cost of debt and equity are embedded. Required rates of return must be evaluated in light of the acquirer's cost of capital, and additional returns above the cost of capital such as a new, more risky project would command must be factored in.

Hurdle rates, the estimated rate of return over which the company must jump, differ. A company selling for a high P/E in the market can afford to pay a higher price (in cash as well as stock) than a comparable company selling at a low P/E. The higher P/E company has, by definition, a lower cost of capital. (The implicit assumption, although not completely valid, is that the pooled future earnings will be capitalized by the public markets with the same high multiples.) Conversely, if corporate or investment fund money is languishing in low-return, short-term instruments, hurdle rates for a potential acquisition might be lower.

Liquidity

Liquidity factors for the buyer include two types—operational and transactional. Operational liquidity issues include: What are the immediate cash requirements for operating the business, including working capital (seasonality) and capital expenditures? Many new owners have found themselves desperately short of operating cash the day after closing, having calculated only the direct acquisition costs. Transactional liquidity issues include: What are prospects for turning the business into cash? Can it be sold easily? taken public? or refinanced? (Liquidity issues for the seller are only meaningful if they were not paid fully on closing.)

Competitive Bidding

Competitive bidding factors for the buyer include: How strong are competitive bidders? How serious are they? What are their primary motivations? If the M&A interests of a competitor's company are complementary with those of your own company's, might there be some cooperative effort such as agreeing to break up the target so that each partner would obtain a desired division while keeping the overall price within reason? If competitors' interests are not complementary, how likely are they to remain interested (and hence be available to buy the business should the acquirer change its mind or seek a quick profit)? What about risks of getting outbid after incurring high costs, primarily in a contested public area? Can you get a *lockup* on some stock or key asset of the target?

Competitive factors for the seller include: Can the price be raised by competitive bidding? Is a formal auction appropriate? How can all bidders be encouraged to participate in the process?

Defense

Defensive factors for the buyer include: Would purchasing the target make the acquiring company *less* risky, perhaps by becoming countercyclical, by protecting key markets and customers, or by securing sources of supply? Or would the acquisition create a *more* risky company with higher operational costs and exposure to a given market (in addition to the greater financial strain)? Would the target be dangerous if acquired by a competitor?

Control

Control factors for the buyer include: Are there any special positions that require controls—such as stock of other companies, market share, key customer relationships, long-term supply contracts, or key real estate? Is there any value in buying a control position in the target company, but not buying the entire company? (For example, preserving a net operating loss carryforward [NOL]—which becomes severely attenuated with more than a 50 percent change of ownership.[4]) If only a control position is sought—not the entire company—a different analysis is required. Control of any kind is valued highly, and control premiums are common.

Understandability

It is shocking how often acquirers do not understand the business they have just bought. Hundreds if not thousands of hours of time will have been lavished on completing the deal while only a small fraction of that time has been spent on appreciating the business or its strategies. Understandability factors for the buyer include: How well do you know the industry, from the nature of the business to the key people in it? Could your management take over the target if their current management resigned? The history of M&A is littered with good deals gone bad

---

4. There are many technical aspects to the determination of NOL utilization and its limitations. It is a minefield requiring expert assistance.

because the acquirer was just not aware of the critical issues in an unfamiliar industry or organization.

Desirability

We delude ourselves if we think that personal desire does not wield substantial influence on M&A decisions. Owning a new company is one of the great ego boosts in modern society, not only for the chief executive but for the entire management team. Never underestimate the importance of enhanced power and prestige.

Desirability factors for the buyer include: How strongly is the target wanted or needed? How far will your company reach to get it? How important is it for business position? How is it important for CEO/executive interests?

Synergy

Synergy factors for the buyer include: What are benefits to the current company if combined with the intended target? What are the procedures, timeframes, roadblocks, and dangers of generating the planned-for synergies between acquirer and target? What could happen to destroy such hoped-for incremental benefits? Should the deal be pursued even if the expected synergies do not materialize? (This is especially critical if synergistic increases in revenues or decreases in costs are part of the projections that support the purchase price and its financing.)

Business Timing

Business timing factors for the buyer include: Is this the right part of the cycle to acquire this company? If at the top of the cycle, are you paying top dollar? If at the bottom of the cycle, what are the target firm's immediate business prospects? What are the trends? What is likely to happen to target's relative cost of doing business over time? For example, will labor become progressively more expensive relative to foreign competition?

Payment Timing

Payment timing factors for the seller include: How important is cash up front? Are you willing to take back notes? Even when equating price with market rate interest, a seller who waits for full payment can demand a higher (present value) price due to the assumption of inherent risks.

Acquisition Timing

Acquisition timing factors for the buyer include: How fast *must* you move? How fast *can* you move? Must money be raised from new third parties, or is it currently available with established credit facilities?

Acquisition timing factors for the seller include: How quickly should the transaction be completed? Who is under more time pressures — buyer or seller?

General Risk

General risk factors for the buyer include: What is the likelihood that business and financial expectations may not be met? How volatile are the industry and the company? What are the environmental and competitive threats? How important is management? what is their attitude? and what happens if they resign?

General risk factors for the seller include: What is the likelihood of receiving a better offer? Conversely, what is the likelihood of the current best offer vanishing? If the transaction is not all cash, what is the probability of not receiving full payment? In any case, what is the likelihood of closing?

Integration of Valuation and Pricing Practices

There is no simple formula for valuing and pricing M&A. In determining the *best price* for a business from either buyer's or seller's side, a wide-ranging, creative analysis is prescribed. Such an analysis must reflect responses to a wide variety of stimuli; only a cyclical, looping, systems-oriented, organic approach can protect against simplistic or deceptive conclusions.

For example, an acquiring company could do a discounted cash flow analysis based on best-guess forecasts for the target. But should an astute buyer be tied to the price that emerges from the computer model? Not necessarily. The DCF value may be twice the stock market value — so why offer double up front? On the other hand, the DCF may be far less than the breakup value — other companies may put strategic premiums on various divisions — so why lose the deal?

Alternative valuation approaches can be correlated with one another to assess acquisition pricing strategies and concomitant risks. An *if/then* analysis seeks an array of recommended actions based on generally known conditions. Consider the following logic: If comparable M&A market prices are below liquidation value, acquisition risks are minimal; but if market prices are above DCF and break-up values, acquisition risks are substantial. *If/then*s are not new and not magic. Rather they reflect the complex processes that occur among acquirers examining a potential transaction. Serious buyers will always use sophisticated quantitative techniques, but the canny ones will not be bound by them. They will always plug a range of intuitive, qualitative factors into the valuation process.

It is good practice for both buyer and seller to assess the other side's position with a series of scenario-planning exercises— absolute worst case, probable minimal requirements, desired deal level, and realistic best case. Other companies should be included in the analysis. The buyer can evaluate what competitors might pay for the target (and why), as well as which other companies might make a better alternative candidate for acquisition. The seller should do likewise, exploring all possible suitors. Even if they are questionable, alternative possibilities for M&A transactions make both buyers and sellers better negotiators—see Chapter 9.)

A thorough and effective valuation and pricing analysis would include using many of the *quantitative models that determine price* and *qualitative factors that modify price* in various combinations. Matrices can be generated by matching one against the other, the models against the factors, so that each point of intersection has the potential for generating new thinking. Then multidimensional matrices can be designed so that cells include several models and factors working together (or fighting against one another).

Sensitivity analysis should be conducted utilizing many models and factors, testing what happens under various scenarios (e.g., sales down 20 percent, margins eroded by 15 percent, interest rates jump up to 17 percent). Such computer-based analysis should analyze the cross-impact of various factors working together (or fighting against one another). In this manner, a fuller appreciation for price can be realized. Additional insights into the business will also be gained.

In summary, valuing and pricing M&A demands multiple levels of attitude and approach. It is a mistake to allow one method to dominate thinking. Conversely, it is impractical to calculate every quantitative model and weigh every qualitative factor in every transaction. Pick only those models and factors most appropriate and explore them in depth. Good judgment, honed by experience, will enable investment bankers to assess which models and factors to use and how to use them. Yet it is always advisable to test a few of the more obscure models and factors in order to expand horizons. You never know what you might find.[5]

Appendix I: Merger and Acquisition Formulas

Earnings Growth Formula

The formula for determining the earnings growth rate is:

$$(1 + g)^t = \frac{e_t}{e_i}$$

where:

g represents the growth rate through the forecast

period t (say five years)

e_t represents the after-tax net income in the

tth period (say in the fifth year)

e_i represents the after-tax net income in the

ith time period (the first year)

Solving for g we find that, if trended earnings are doubled over the five years, this is the equivalent of a compounded annual rate of earnings growth of about 15 percent; if earnings are tripled, about 25 percent; if increased four-fold, about 32 percent; if five-fold, about 38 percent; if six-fold, about 43 percent; if seven-fold, about 48 percent.

Discount Rate Formula

The appropriate discount rate for calculating DCF reflects the risk profile of the acquisition. The general formula is:

$$d = r_f + r_p$$

---

5. A list of the largest corporate mergers and acquisitions in recent history, as of mid-1989, is presented in Table 6-1.

Table 6–1. The Largest Corporate Mergers and Acquisitions (as of July 1989).

Target Company	Acquiring Company	Merger and Acquisition Value (in billions)	Year Completed
RJR Nabisco	Kohlberg, Kravis, Roberts[1]	$24.5 billion	1989
B.A.T. Industries	Hoylake Investments[2]	$21.0	Pending[3]
Warner Communications[4]	Time, Inc.	$14.0	Pending[3]
Gulf Oil	Standard Oil	$13.4	1984
Kraft Foods	Phillip Morris	$13.4	1988
Time, Inc.[4]	Paramount[5]	$12.2	Pending[3]
Getty Oil[6]	Texaco Oil	$10.1	1984
Dome Petroleum	Amoco Canada	$9.0	1988
SmithKline Beckman	Beecham Group	$7.8	Pending[3]
Conoco Oil	DuPont	$7.4	1981
Federated Department Stores	Campeau	$7.4	1988
Marathon Oil	USX[7]	$6.5	1982

[1] Kohlberg, Kravis, Roberts (KKR) is the most famous leveraged buyout (LBO) firm. They have completed many successful LBOs, from Houdaille Industries (the first major LBO in 1979) to Beatrice Foods, making enormous profits (and spectacular returns on equity investments) for themselves and their partners.

[2] Hoylake Investments is a partnership lead by Sir James Goldsmith, Jacob Rothschild, and Kerry Packer. Although the outcome is far from clear as we go to press, the situation exemplifies the contemporary M&A game for large investment partnerships led by entrepreneurial financiers (or, depending on one's view, corporate raiders).

[3] Pending transactions are subject to change.

[4] In this well known corporate battle, Time and Warner originally announced a merger. Paramount then made an unsolicited acquisition offer for Time, following which Time made a friendly acquisition offer for Warner. Although Time appears to have won the battle as we go to press, the transaction has not yet closed and the situation exemplifies the contemporary M&A game for large corporations.

[5] Paramount is the former Gulf + Western Corporation.

[6] This is the famous (or infamous) case whether Pennzoil sued Texaco for disrupting Pennzoil's own acquisition of Getty. Pennzoil was awarded $10 billion, Texaco filed Chapter 11 bankruptcy, and a settlement was eventually reached at $3 billion.

[7] USX is the former United States Steel Corporation.

where:

d is the appropriate discount rate

r_f is the *risk-free* rate of return (normally indexed by the highest return on currently available Treasury bills)

r_p is the *risk premium,* the incremental rate of return (above the risk-free rate) that the acquiring company must earn in order to accept the risk inherently involved in making the acquisition

The critical issue is to determine r_p, the risk premium or the required incremental rate of return. Various theory-founded methods can be employed; these usually relate to the capital asset pricing model and/or the stock market beta:

1. The capital asset pricing model relates the risk premium to the expected value of return and to standard deviations of return for the current portfolio of corporate assets.

2. A beta-weighted adjustment relates the risk premium to the stock market beta, which defines the relationship between the excess returns on the common stock of the target company and the excess returns of a market portfolio. (*Excess returns* are simply the difference between the expected return and the risk-free rate.) Beta is simply a representation of the systematic risk of the target company—the risk that is intrinsically related to the company itself and cannot be diversified away.

As discussed, most companies in the real world do not employ these theoretically more rigorous but less practical methods. Rather, they set an artificial hurdle rate related to their current cost of capital or historic return on assets, and adjust both upward for the inherently higher risk of new projects.

Acquisition Valuation Formula

There are numerous formulas for valuing a business. Most are based on discounting and/or capitalization rates of streams of cash flow and/or income. (Variations relate to the specific variables chosen, and how they interrelate.) Following is the model I prefer (at least currently).

The acquisition value of a company (present value), AV_{pv}, equals the present value of its stream of net free cash flow, CF_{pv}, plus the present value of its terminal value, TV_{pv}, at the end of the cash flow period.

$$AV_{pv} = CF_{pv} + TV_{pv}$$

The acquisition formula values the target company strictly from the perspective of the acquirer. Thus, the first term (CF_{pv}) uses the net free cash flow generated, representing the actual cash that would be available for the acquirer to take out of the acquired company and dividend to shareholders during the term of ownership, discounted to present value by an appropriate discount factor.

The second term (TV_{pv}) represents a terminal valuation at the end of the period of cash flows (usually when the company is sold or assumed sold), and then this terminal value is discounted back to present value. The terminal value is often based on the earnings (not cash flows), since the multiples-of-income method is used to evaluate companies in the public markets and in third-party sales[6].

Appendix II: Evaluating Merger and Acquisition Offers

Since many transactions involve considerations other than total cash at closing, investment bankers for the target company are required to evaluate the absolute and comparative values of the consideration (especially in a competitive situation where alternative offers usually have different characteristics). The basic technique is to equate all considerations to *present value cash equivalents*.

Evaluating cash is easy—cash is cash, and so all payment of cash are valued at 100% (unless there are any contingencies). Notes and other interest-bearing instruments must be evaluated as to their term, stated coupon, payment schedules (interest and principal), covenants, seniority, security, default likelihood, insolvency likelihood, remedies, and ratings (if applicable). This analysis yields an independently evaluated market rate for the note. If this market rate is below the stated coupon on the

---

6. For M&A evaluations, I prefer to use earnings *before* interest and taxes (EBIT), rather than earnings after interest and taxes, since EBIT factors out the financial structure of the company and focuses on the business operations. Since we assess terminal value using EBIT, we must subtract out the balance sheet debt (compensating for interest) and/or choose a higher discount rate (compensating for interest and taxes). Alternatively, we could arrive at the same valuation by factoring out the taxes and using the normal discount rate. We would do this by multiplying the pre-interest-pre-tax cash flow by a term that subtracts out the effective taxes—one minus the effective tax rate $(1 - t)$—and not forgetting the tax-shielding effect of the interest.

note, then the note must be discounted by the difference and is thus valued below par.

Common stock is evaluated according to similar principles. If the stock is of a large public company and is not restricted, it will be assessed close to market value but a bit below it. (Even the most blue-chip stock cannot be valued exactly at market value, since the market can change at any moment; and even though the share price may just as easily go up as down, it is this volatility itself that demands a discount.) If the stock taken as consideration in an M&A transaction is not publicly traded, or is thinly traded, or if there are restrictions of any kind, then appropriately larger discounts are made.

Contingent payments (which are often used as consideration elements when private companies are acquired) are the most complicated to assess since they are based on future events and are uncertain by definition. Investment bankers make reasonable assumptions regarding the key industry, business, and operating criteria and then discount the resulting numbers rather heavily to compensate for the substantial uncertainty and risk.

CHAPTER 7

How to Buy or Sell a Private Company*

The merger or sale of a private company differs in style and substance from the merger or sale of a public company. Such a transaction is usually a unique event in the life of the owners of that private company who are often the entrepreneurial founders or their families. Most likely, the entrepreneur will never have sold his or her business before and the prospects are both bitter and sweet. On the one hand, it is time to enjoy the financial rewards after years of hard work. On the other hand, selling your company feels like selling your baby.

In most respects, private company M&A is not much different from traditional M&A. Virtually all of the issues involved in finding, facilitating, valuing, pricing, strategizing, and structuring M&A deals apply equally well to private companies as to public companies. But there are differences: personal motivations for selling, personal motivations when selling, business analysis, financial analysis, and structuring the

---

* This chapter has been derived from "Mergers and Acquisitions for Private Companies" by Robert Lawrence Kuhn, Volume IV (Mergers, Acquisitions, and Leveraged Buyouts), Dow Jones-Irwin's *The Library of Investment Banking* (1990), Robert Lawrence Kuhn, editor in chief.

deal. These differences may seem subtle, but whether or not the deal is completed often depends on whether or not such subtleties are sensed.

Personal Motivations for Selling

From the viewpoint of a private business owner, there are four primary driving motivations for merging or selling his or her business: personal liquidity, expansion capital, personal liability, and generation transition.

Personal Liquidity

Foremost is the desire to liquify one's personal holdings. In many cases, the seller is the founder of the company and his or her personal wealth is almost entirely tied up in the business. Here is the first opportunity to reap the financial fruit of one's labor, to diversify one's portfolio ("take some chips off the table"), and to enjoy the material benefits of building a successful business.

In many cases, achieving security and confidence rather than making maximum monies is most important. Many entrepreneurs have been living on the edge for years—their risk/reward profile has shifted far toward the high-risk upper end—and they look forward to reducing the incessant pressure.

Expansion Capital

The second reason for sale is the recurring need for expansion capital. The only thing more financially taxing than a stagnant business is a growing business. Growth demands capital—for research and development, plant and equipment, inventory and receivables, distribution and service, and a host of administrative necessities.

Oftentimes, good growth companies outrun their internal financial capabilities (even when supported by commercial banks), and the public markets are either not available or not desirable. Suddenly, these small and medium-sized companies find themselves competing against larger players in larger markets. Success has catapulted them into a different league, and competing in the new league requires new strengths. Many companies have discovered, to their chagrin, that success at one size does not guarantee success at another size.[1]

---

1. See *Creativity and Strategy in Mid-Sized Firms*, Robert Lawrence Kuhn, Englewood Cliffs, NJ, Prentice-Hall, 1989.

Personal Liability

The desire for financial reward and the need for expansion capital are not the only motivations for private company merger or sale. The elimination of personal liabilities can be a powerful stimulant. The most common kind of personal liabilities are personal guarantees of company debt.[2] Many owners of private businesses are required to support their company's credit with commercial banks by giving their own commitments; this pledge means that they are legally obligated to use their own private assets to pay back any bank debt that the company is unable to pay for any reason whatsoever. (The owners' signatures may even be required for real estate mortgages.) In many cases, such personal guarantees originated years before, in the early, risky days of the business and were just never removed. (There are few things harder to do in business than taking security away from a bank once they have it.)

Successful entrepreneurs are self-confident to a fault and may not give those guarantees a thought or a worry. That is a serious mistake: Such guarantees may put at risk a family's entire net worth. In business, there is no certainty. You never can control the future. Eliminating personal guarantees and liabilities is an entirely appropriate motive for selling a business.

Generational Transition

Generational transition is another reason why owners of privately-held companies seek to sell. Private businesses are often sold as part of the estate-planning or settlement process. They are also sold to resolve family disputes, generally occurring when the founders' progeny encounter fundamental disagreements (both personal and professional).

Motivations of Acquirers

From the viewpoint of potential acquirers of privately-held companies, motivations are more traditional. Good private companies may have proprietary products or technology. They may have a solid position in a small market niche and enjoy strong customer loyalty. Often such companies have product lines that can be expanded dramatically when supported by adequate resources—both organizational and financial. There can be high market leverage in privately held companies.

---

2. Other forms of personal liability include tax obligations (e.g., employee withholding taxes), product liability (on occasion), and personal damages.

Personal Motivations When Selling

In most cases involving the sale of private companies, emotions run high. When it comes to their businesses, owners of closely-held businesses usually think beyond dollar signs. Their motivations encompass more than the simple maximization of purchase price.

Broad Concerns

Consideration to founder/owners takes on broader meaning, expressing itself in nonfinancial terms as well as financial numbers. For example, a continuing involvement in the business is desired by many selling entrepreneurs. In these situations remuneration may play a more minor part. Participating in the business and assuring its continuing success is what counts.

The nonfinancial concerns of selling shareholder/managers frequently reach beyond themselves and involve their employees and even their customers and vendors. The company founder feels a sense of family for those with whom he or she has long worked. Loyalty is a typical trait that entrepreneurs value in employees and associates, and at the time of the sale many come to realize that loyalty should be a two way street.

Comfort with New Owners

It is important for founder/owners to feel comfortable with the new management and owners. Will they do right by the company and its people? Will they preserve what the founder built? Private company transactions often fall apart when the founders or their families just didn't *feel* right about the prospective buyers. (For example, this hesitation might develop if part of the new owners' plans would involve plant relocations and employee layoffs or a cheapening of the quality image of the company's products.) Conversely, more than a few private company transactions were made in which the new buyers were not the highest bidder but were the *best* people.

Business Analysis

Due diligence analysis is critical to all mergers and acquisitions, and there are standard systems of business reviews that are an essential part of the process.[3] We assume that such a detailed analysis has been

---

3. All major accounting firms publish comprehensive due diligence checklists.

done successfully. The key criterion to assess when doing due diligence analyses of privately held companies is the personal importance of the owner or owners (i.e., the selling shareholders).

How important are the current owners to the continuing operations of the business? Are they involved actively in management, and if so, in which aspects? (Sales is generally the most sensitive area.) There are some serious traps here. Assume that the previous management/owner is critical for business success, at least for the short term. A long-term consulting contract with the former owner is no guarantee of his or her continued participation. Nor is a contingent payout based on performance for part of the purchase price. (To that former owner, the difference between no million dollars and one million dollars in purchase price is far greater than between one million and ten million.) There are psychological factors at work here, some outside of the owner's control, intent, or even awareness.

When Owner/Managers Are No Longer Owners

What happens when the entrepreneur puts real money into his or her pocket for the first time? The fact is that no one can predict what happens. Work habits may not change one iota, or on the other hand a penchant for exotic travel and strange companions may suddenly emerge.

Another factor is the diminished sense of personal ownership. The realization of loss has a slow but insidious impact on the performance of many former owners. Identity is blurred and estrangement breeds, and productivity becomes severely depressed. Said one entrepreneur so afflicted, "What seemed to be my normal job on the outside was bothering me terribly on the inside. It was something like being asked to continue living with my wife after she had just married another man."

Entrepreneurial founders of companies are a feisty lot, not being accustomed to working for anyone. Organizational structure and bureaucratic procedures are not things with which they identify. Following directions is not something they do well. There are too many things to rub them the wrong way. It is a simple historical fact that most arrangements for entrepreneurial founders to work with their companies after its sale will terminate, for one reason or another, short of the original contract date.

Business Importance of Owner/Managers

Consequently, it is vital for investment bankers representing buyers or sellers of privately held companies to appreciate the business importance of the selling shareholders. The more important they are for the continuing prosperity of the company, the less that company should be worth. This means that the business significance of the owner/managers is a vital modulating force on the normal quantitative techniques and qualitative factors in valuing and pricing mergers and acquisitions (Chapter 6).

When considering the importance of the selling shareholders on the business, the following areas of potential concern should be considered: relationship with customers, relationship with suppliers, technology and product development, management and labor relations. For example, how much of the company's revenues does the shareholder/managers generate or influence strongly? Are there particular customers with whom they have a special relationship? Are they the vital force behind new product development? Might there be labor problems without their paternal or maternal guidance?

On the other hand, some companies may be more valuable *without* the former owners involved. (Witness the stock jump of some public corporations when the founder/chief executive retires or dies.) Sometimes founders cannot see beyond their own prejudices and once-wonderful ways of thinking. For example, when the old guard is no longer holding the reigns, younger executives may be inspired to do better work ("to bring the company into the modern world," as one liberated manager put it); freedom from the shackles of fear can stimulate creative and innovative thinking. For another example, unprofitable lines of business may be closed since new owners will have no emotional attachment to them.

Noncompete Clauses

Noncompete clauses are an essential part of virtually all purchases of privately held companies. It would be the height of folly to buy a company only to have its key people go out and start a competitive company. Noncompete clauses normally run from three to seven years and are usually related to a contemporaneous consulting contract.[4]

---

4. One problem with noncompete clauses is that they are difficult to enforce. Courts are reluctant to deprive an individual of his or her only means for making a living. So although noncompete clauses are critical and essential, be aware that they may be unenforceable.

Financial Analysis

There are three general ways in which the particular financial analysis of privately-held companies may differ from the general financial analysis of all M&A companies: (1) differences in financial reporting motivations (e.g., tax minimization procedures); (2) personal compensation and benefits for the owners and their families; and (3) business changes that should or might be made. Investment bankers must be attuned to these issues and, whether representing buyers or sellers, use them to best service their clients in the requisite financial analysis.

Reconstructed Income Statements

The normal procedure for conducting a financial analysis of privately-held companies is to prepare a *reconstructed* income statement, giving effect to all changes that would be immediately instituted (or could be easily implemented) once new buyers take over.

It is commonly acknowledged that privately held companies have different financial reporting objectives than public companies. Nonpublic firms have no incentive to maximize reported earnings—there are no stock prices to worry about and no financial analysts with which to bother.[5] In fact, there is a major *disincentive* for showing high earnings— taxes. The higher the earnings a company shows, the higher the taxes a company pays. The more money that appears as income, the more money that is paid out to the government—with the paradoxical result that the more a company shows in earnings the less it is actually worth!

Consequently, private companies do everything legally appropriate to diminish profits for tax purposes (and sometimes that fuzzy line between legal and illegal is shaved rather closely). There are two primary methods that private companies use to reduce earnings; compensation to owners and their families, and evaluations of inventories.

Compensation to Owner/Managers

High compensation of manager/owners is virtually universal in all profitable private companies. For owners to draw low salaries and take out their profits as dividends, they must pay a double taxation—first at the

---

5. Of course, financial institutions and creditors are concerned with the financial status of the company—but they are used to dealing with private companies.

corporate level and second at the personal level. That hardly makes sense, especially to aggressive entrepreneurs.

What is there to do? Owners of mature profitable businesses seek to take money out of the businesses in tax deductible form—salary and expenses. Salaries are often higher than those found in comparable public companies. (Note: The Internal Revenue Service [IRS] will challenge *excess* compensation). There may be numerous ways in which general expenses are charged to the business (e.g., travel and entertainment, automobiles, and the like) with questionable benefits for operating the business. (The IRS has become much more strict in disallowing personal expenses as business deductions).

Nepotism

Nepotism, the employment of family members, is a common custom in private companies. And although the word connotes an activity somewhat shady, there is nothing intrinsically wrong with families working together to build a business and make it prosper. We do not suggest that nepotism is merely a circuitous route for reducing taxes. Family members are often exceptionally hard workers, feeling a great sense of commitment to the business. Indeed, the business becomes in many cases an extended family, with the positive results beneficial for all.[6] Nonetheless, a new owner may not feel the need to employ so many members of the family, and perhaps those jobs could be replaced at lower pay scales.

Pitfalls of Income Reconstruction

In reconstructing an income statement for a privately held company, be aware of the problems. It is clear that the salaries of owners and their families can often be added back to income. What is easily forgotten is that most of those jobs must be done by *someone*. Other people—new people—must be hired to do those jobs. The reconstruction needs to make provisions for the new compensation packages required for the replacements.

---

6. Studies suggest that there may be some special benefits of family-run companies. There seems to be more commitment to the company, more pride in its success. For example, employees seem to prefer the working environment.

Inventory Evaluations

Regarding the evaluation of inventories, private companies can be tempted to understate their values—for example, taking aggressive write-offs to reduce profits and hence taxes. (Such write-offs might be praised in a public company as conservative management.) Although inventory should be judged at market value, this value is often difficult to estimate and value judgments are almost always required.

There is an interesting trap in inventory evaluations for unwary buyers. Private companies may choose to let out the built-up cushion in their inventories in preparation for a merger or sale (or for going public). In these cases, profits in the last year or so might appear *greater* than they would normally be.

How should one assess the numbers and get at the truth? The key is to compare the gross margin percentages. If this margin has jumped up in the last year, though there may be other explanations, suspicion should be aroused. (Making comparisons with industry averages is one method of corroboration.)

New Operating Strategies

Potential buyers should evaluate M&A candidates in the light of how new owners might run the business. This analysis takes on added weight when appraising private companies since there are often rather obvious business decisions that the original owners were just unprepared to make. (Often the old owners tell the new owners exactly what they should do.) These decisions are usually unpleasant ones disappointing employees, customers, and/or vendors—dropping unprofitable product lines long associated with the company, closing inefficient plants, getting competitive bids for supplies, transferring lackluster executives, firing unproductive staff, and the like.

There is also the stagnancy factor. Many founders like to keep doing business the way they have always been doing business. The power structure considers change uncomfortable, if not downright dangerous. It is hard to be creative and innovative in such an environment. Founders of companies can exhibit high inertia to fresh ideas. The challenge of the new appears to be an attack on the old—and the old is what made the business successful in the first place. Some founder/managers act as if all new ideas are a personal affront.

In such stifling situations, new owners can come in, do what has to be done, and improve the business substantially. Yet it is difficult to project up front, before the deal is made, the impact of such benefits. Consequently, buyers should not count on making significant improvements in the company—but should rather consider the potential opportunities as incremental profits.

Structuring the Deal

Making deals with private companies is often more complex than making similar deals with public companies. The number of elements and options for consideration, financial and nonfinancial, can be greater with private company acquisitions. When acquiring public companies, cash must be, by far, the primary consideration. It is possible to use stock in mergers with large companies, and sometimes debentures can play a part, but cash is almost surely king.

When acquiring private companies, investment bankers on both buying and selling sides have more with which to work. Cash, of course, is still king. Indeed, many entrepreneurs will have an inherent distrust of anything else than hard dollars. Nonetheless, there is more flexibility here. In fact, there has to be room for structural elasticity since it is often difficult to harmonize price.

To find any overlap between the lowest price the founder is willing to accept and the highest price the buyer is willing to pay is a formidable task. After all, the founder is giving up his or her life's work and the buyer is incurring severe risk when purchasing a relatively unknown business. Often, there is no chance whatsoever of overlap if the purchase price must be paid all in cash.

How can the gap between sellers and buyers be bridged? Frequently it is the noncash portions of the consideration that work the harmonizing magic. In a typical case, perhaps 50–75 percent of the purchase price may be paid in cash or highly liquid securities (see below). The remainder may be composed of the following elements.

Seller Paper

Seller paper is where the former owner takes back debt as part of the purchase price (much as in real estate transactions). This debt can be structured with great variety and creativity. It usually pays a market rate of interest (or slightly less) and has an acceptable amortization schedule of perhaps five to seven years.

Seller debt is often subordinate to any senior financing that is part of the buyout. Though owners and their bankers may squawk, subordination is usually the rule in leveraged buyouts (but not in sales to corporate acquirers). Occasionally, there may be a grace period in which the amortization of the seller's principal is postponed for several years and/or the seller's interest is accrued but not paid, thus giving the new owners some cash flow breathing room.

If the sellers agree to take back paper in order to assist the buyers in financing the transaction, the sellers always seek to maximize the likelihood of getting their money. Sellers desire guarantees for their debt. Ideal are third-party guarantees, such as irrevocable bank letters of credit or insurance company guarantees—but such security is rarely achieved. More customary is that the sellers take a second position on the assets and stock of the company behind the senior debt. This would mean that, in the worst case, the sellers would have a chance of getting their company back if the buyers would default on the debt.

Earnout-Contingent Compensation

Earnout-contingent compensation is the trick that gets impossible deals completed; it is the vehicle that spans the unbridgeable gaps in private company transactions. In earnouts, the additional compensation is related directly to some future performance or event, thereby harmonizing the disparate interests of sellers and buyers. The contingent formula for the additional purchase price is often based on financial performance, which is preset by formula and payout schedule.[7] Earnouts can take many forms, though it is most often figured as a percentage of earnings.[8]

---

7. Earnouts could also be based on nonfinancial criteria, such as the commercialization of a technology (e.g., triggered by federal approval to bring a new drug to market) or the number of subscribers to a magazine or cable television system.

8. Experienced M&A specialists representing a private company seller are usually uncomfortable with profit-based contingency formulas since the new owners have full control of the company (and the books) and can alter the profit picture significantly. Even if a major accounting firm is doing the audit, there are too many ways in which profits in any given year can be severely depressed—such as increasing managerial bonuses, R&D, advertising, and capital expenditures and consequent depreciation. To make matters more complicated, many of these decisions may be in the best long-term interests of the firm. Furthermore, sellers do not want to be forced to delve into the books of the buyer. Better for many sellers is to devise a formula based on operational information, such as gross revenues or numbers of items sold.

Stock of the Acquiring Company

There are two general conditions where shareholders of private companies will take the stock (preferred or common) in the acquiring company as consideration in the transaction. First, stock can be used as additional compensation—as a mechanism of reaching a mutually acceptable price. (Stock is often used as the medium for paying the earnout contingency compensation.) Second, there are occasionally tax considerations that make it desirable for founder/owners to take all stock (less likely when there is no distinction between capital gains and ordinary income). But whenever a seller agrees to take all the consideration in stock, it is essential that the stock must be in a well-capitalized public company whose shares are highly liquid and traded daily on a major exchange. (In all cases, the float should be large relative to the seller's total position.)

Note that when some companies give their stock as consideration in the acquisitions of other companies, they may require certain restrictions to be placed on that stock. Such restrictions would decrease its value, perhaps substantially. Private companies are ill-advised to take restricted stock as a major part of their consideration when selling. If the transaction is a merger in which they have or share control, the story may be different.

Assumption of Liabilities

When a buyer accepts a selling company's liabilities, this kind of consideration can be just as important as if that buyer were paying cash for assets (all the more so if some of those debts are personally guaranteed by the owners). Although it is often hard for founder/owners to accept, the fact is that sometimes the assumption of liabilities is even more important than being paid cash (e.g., when all seller responsibilities for ongoing law suits are eliminated). A private company's bankers will strive to eliminate all possible legal and financial responsibilities of the previous owners in any M&A transaction.

Related-Party Transactions

Owners of private companies often have various relationships with their business. For example, they or their family members may own the land on which the factories are built or the buildings in which the retail stores are leased. These relationships give opportunity for more creative structuring which takes advantage of win-win tradeoffs such as tax benefits. The entrepreneur can continue to own these properties, and long-term contracts can assure the former owner and family of long-term income (and relieve the new owner of having to finance a larger purchase price).[9]

Employment Agreements

Employment agreements are common when founder/owners sell their businesses. After all, the buyer wants to assure continuity and the seller is looking for additional consideration (and probably meaningful work). Depending on the actual situation, it may be mutually beneficial to put more dollars into the employment agreement and less into the purchase price. The terms of employment contracts are often tied to the payment of final obligations; for example, the contract can be structured to last until the *later* of either five years or the final payout of the seller's debt.

Consulting Contracts

Multiyear consulting contracts are common in the sale of private companies. Such contracts normally last as long as the necessary non-compete clauses and may involve other members of the family as well as the founder/owners themselves. The amount of actual work done under these consulting contracts is usually minimal.

Fringe Benefits

Offering fringe benefits, though minimal compared to other elements in the merger consideration, can be an important psychological assist in making a deal with a founder/owner. Continuing to maintain an office or provide health insurance can be a powerful incentive to someone who has never had another corporate home other than this company.

Employee Benefits

Finally, founder/owners will likely bring their employees into the deal. They might have given some stock to personnel at very low values. They might require pledges of employment. They might insist on contracts for key people. They might even opt to go for an Employee Stock Ownership

---

9. Such an arrangement is like an automatic, pre-existing sale/leaseback.

Plan (ESOP) when selling their businesses, even if it doesn't generate the most money with the best security.

Role of Investment Bankers

Most entrepreneur/founders of small and medium-sized companies have never worked with an investment banker in their lives and the prospect probably does not thrill them. All they know about Wall Street they have learned from the mass media.

What benefits can investment bankers bring to private companies seeking merger or sale and how can these be communicated? First of all, the very inexperience of entrepreneurs should be stressed—especially in relation to potential acquirers who are almost always highly experienced in negotiating acquisitions (whether large industrial corporations or financial investment groups). Entrepreneurs understand expertise: They are experts in their business and should appreciate that investment bankers are experts in mergers and acquisitions.

Next is the matter of secrecy and discretion. It is vital to respect the confidence of clients. This is a central ethic of investment banking (see Chapter 10), but it takes on special significance in private company M&A. There is often some reticence if not ambivalence on the part of the seller. Any premature disclosures may disrupt the entire process. Unauthorized exposure may cause personal and professional embarrassment and could damage the client company's business relationships with customers and vendors. Frankly, investment bankers provide a buffer between the company's manager/owners and the public. If there is an accidental leak (often from the manager/owners themselves), the blame can be placed on the firm's overly aggressive investment bankers. (It is easy to blame investment bankers for their overanxious rapacity; everyone will believe the excuse and belt the scapegoat.)

Selling a business is a sophisticated process, demanding the highest professional standards. Investment bankers should be able to fulfill the following services for private companies.

Understand the Business

The investment bankers should really get to know the company—its products and people and the reasons that make it all work. They should examine all facets of the business—market, products, product development, manufacturing, distribution, service, reputation with customers, image, advertising, management, organization, finances, and the like. Go for the jugular issues, the critical success strategies—what makes this company special? what are its distinctive competencies? what are its comparative advantages and competitive strengths?

Since the company is private, getting inside (figuratively speaking) will be more difficult than with public companies. Manager/owners will be reluctant to talk openly—even though they have invited the investment bankers to come in. After all, a private company is not used to confiding in outsiders (a public company, remember, deals continuously with the insistent and incessant questions of shareholders and analysts). M&A bankers must be patient, and evince sincere human interest and warm human compassion. Conducting due diligence analysis on a private company is much like running a group therapy session for first-time patients.

But don't become a Milquetoast and forget about the company's weaknesses—the product/market soft spots, company defects, and organizational problems. You do not want to appear negative (or a boor), but finding the truth is your responsibility. Explain that, as their representative, you are professionally bound both to maintain secrecy and to present them in the best possible manner. In the M&A process, it is best to assume that investment bankers who represent potential buyers will uncover all skeletons, so investment bankers who represent sellers must be ready with all answers and explanations.

Understand Owner Priorities

As M&A representatives, the investment bankers must know what their client owners want to achieve. Not everyone's objective is similar. In fact, not everyone's objective is logical.[10]

Some owners want to get their money and get out totally. Others desperately want to stay in the company and remain a part of their life's work. Still others want to enable their family members to continue in the business in some way. It is even possible to develop a transaction

---

10. I once knew an owner who was not happy unless he was personally guaranteeing the company's indebtedness. Such risk gave him the feeling of total commitment—which was what he required to remain highly motivated and energized. Talk about a risk-seeking personality—this was the pinnacle! (The end of the story was not a happy one—and emphasizes the importance of *eliminating* personal guarantees for owners of privately held companies.)

in which owners can cash out most of their value from their company and still maintain control (whether themselves or through their families). Deals can be structured to accomplish virtually all interests.

Business Presentation

Investment bankers are known for the professionalism of their presentations. They generally prepare a book portraying the company in the best possible light, which would include a description of the business and industry, products and markets, competitive positioning and market share, management and organization, operating history, financial history and current condition, future opportunities, and the like. (The book is presented quite elegantly, with thick dividers, embossed lettering, and perhaps a hard cover.)[11]

Special attention should be focused on recasting the financial statements so they reflect properly how a traditional business would appear without the special owner benefits. Such a recasting should not include the hypothetical results of assumed business decisions—such as curtailing unprofitable product lines or closing inefficient plants—no matter how obvious or easy. The effect of implementing such cost efficiencies as well as developing growth opportunities should be described in a different section and can include appropriate financial estimates of what the company would look like if the stated changes would be made.

Buyer List Development

First-rate investment bankers can interact with a large universe of potential buyers, calling on the experience of its internal team and the information of its external network. In addition, investment banks have access to sophisticated public and private databases with enormous amounts of data on industries and companies. From these vast resources, investment bankers should be able to bring dozens of potential candidates to the table, international as well as domestic. In addition, they should be able to develop lists of comparative transactions that give ballpark estimates of values and general categories of structures. Such unbiased data helps bring both buyers and sellers closer to the real world.

---

11. Not infrequently the covers and dividers are much thicker than the papers and documents, giving rise to some unpleasant remarks about form and substance.

There are various factors to consider in evaluating a long list of potential buyers. Degree of interest in the client's business is obviously first, and the financial capacity to complete the deal is a close second. But other factors should also be involved. For example, suppose that the founder/owner insists on retaining a minority share (say 20 percent) of the company for his son; such a demand would eliminate many potential buyers, but not all. The corporate culture of potential purchases could be another important factor in that most owners want their employees to be happy in their future home.

Buyer Contact and Evaluation

Minimum interference with business operations is vital in the early stages of all M&A situations, and this is especially true for smaller private companies. It is highly disruptive to have waves of potential buyers stomping through the offices and arousing uncertainty and worry. (After many years of working for the founder or his family, most employees would needlessly fear for their jobs.) Why allow the merely curious to agitate your people? Investment bankers have a responsibility to minimize such disruptions.

Negotiating the Deal

How a deal is negotiated depends on company conditions. Sometimes it is best to evaluate buyer interest and then work with the two or three most serious candidates. At other times, a controlled auction makes the most sense. This is where potential buyers submit one round of bids based only on the book prepared by the investment bankers—and then only the few leading bidders are invited to participate in the next round, which involves on-site analysis and interviews. (See Chapter 9.)

The negotiating stage is where many founder/owners begin to get nervous. They imagine they are losing control of their businesses (and their lives). They seem surrounded by swirling, simultaneous meetings of multiple buyers on a feeding frenzy. It may appear that all decision making has passed to these fasttalking, fancy-dressed, hot-shot investment bankers whom they barely know.

Investment bankers working with private companies must be sensitive to the special concerns of manager/owners. Care must be taken never to slight their clients, no matter how irrelevant their questions or how pressing the situation. Investment bankers must always be cognizant of the fact that they are agents and not principals. Owners should never lose control of the process and it is the responsibility of their bankers to give such assurances.

Legality, Accounting and Tax

Here is where the professionalism of investment bankers should shine. The places for possible pitfalls in structuring a deal are innumerable. For example, the simple decision whether to sell stock or assets is fraught with complex ramifications involving tax, continuing liabilities, and future plans of both buyers and sellers. Since this sale is probably the most important transaction that the owner will ever make, and since most of his or her net worth is probably tied up here, nothing less than the best professional advice must be used.[12]

Investment Banking Fees

You get what you pay for. Investment banking fees are calculated as a percentage of the transaction size. They are normally set as a sliding scale downwards as the transaction increases in size (see Chapter 8).[13]

Since investment banking fees are a percentage of the entire deal, they can become quite large. Such numbers can only be justified if they are a very small percentage of the incremental value that the investment bankers add in a transaction. (Value added is most often reflected in a higher purchase price—derived through attracting better buyers and negotiating better deals. It is also reflected by a smarter structure for both sides, a greater likelihood of closing a transaction, and a lesser likelihood of legal and tax foulups.)

---

12. This is another example where investment bankers are far better equipped to handle mergers and acquisitions than business brokers, who are often just glorified matchmakers. Investment bankers bring an integrated, professional approach to the most important decision of a company's life.

13. The traditional "Lehman Formula" is the standard on which most fees are based: five percent on the first million, four percent on the second million, three percent on the third million, two percent on the fourth million, and one percent on the fifth million and thereafter. However, as with everything else in M&A, many modifications are made. In small, difficult deals, the five percent may extend for several millions or for the entire deal; alternatively, the fee may start as high as ten percent and scale downward from there. In very large deals, the total fee will amount to less than one percent. Innovative, incentive-based fee structures may offer investment bankers a lower amount, say one percent, below a certain trigger and a higher amount, say two percent, above that trigger. Such an incentive fee structure really encourages the bankers to *top out* the price.

Many investment bankers currently seek an up-front retainer before they begin M&A work with a company, especially a private company where owners have been known to change their minds halfway through the process (or just before the end). Should such retainers be charged, or should the only fees be contingent on the successful conclusion of a transaction? (Out-of-pocket expenses, from travel to computer time, are always billed to the client company, irrespective of transaction outcome.)

There are two sides to the issue: On the one hand, a retainer seems coercive and nonreflective of industry tradition where only success is rewarded and failure means failure for the banker as well as the client. On the other hand, a retainer separates the serious from the curious. An enormous amount of work is involved and opportunity costs are high; consequently, an investment bank must be assured that should a reasonable deal materialize its client is committed to close the transaction (or must pay for the priviledge of backing out).

Investment Banking Attitudes

It is important that investment bankers treat their private company clients properly. The fact that the deal may be small should not affect the handling of the deal at all. Even the appearance of a condescending or patronizing attitude must be avoided. Granted, the entrepreneur/founder is not financially sophisticated. But, he or she is a significant success (and is probably worth *more* than the banker!). Unless investment bankers are going to do their best possible job, they should not take the assignment.

Each transaction should be given the attention of a senior investment banker, one with significant experience handling either private companies or firms in the specific industry (or both). Although the proverbial young MBAs will be doing much of the work, they must be guided continuously by an experienced dealmaker.

Indeed, the fundamental difference between investment bankers and business brokers is that the bankers must be able to provide significantly more services and expertise. Private company M&A is generally not the grist for page one news or even the inside pages of *The Wall Street Journal*. Some investment bankers, accustomed to the megamerger spotlight, cannot get themselves up for smaller deals. However, these are the exceptions.

To true investment bankers the deal itself is the thing, its size being of little matter. Most M&A specialists just love doing deals and doing them well. Indeed, some bankers enjoy negotiating smaller, private company deals more than larger, public company ones. It is in the private company deals where investment bankers can take more personal responsibility and thus gain greater satisfaction from a job well done.

CHAPTER 8

Commissions, Fees and Spreads*

Investment banking compensation—commissions, fees and spreads—is one of the juicier topics in the industry. Nothing satisfied the media more than reporting megabuck payments for what seems to be preciously little real work. There is much misunderstanding here, along with some to-be-expected abuses by the industry. In general, however, capitalism's market mechanisms establish value-related prices for all goods and services. Let's see how it works in investment banking.

Pure investment banking (defined as excluding securities brokerage, trading, and research) involves a wide range of revenues and fees, all of which relate to a specific transaction or project being handled by a firm. The terms of such fees are usually set forth in a formal underwriting agreement, engagement letter, or letter of intent which may also describe indemnification, expense reimbursement, and certain timing aspects of the project. These agreements are usually drafted by the investment banker and then reviewed and accepted (after possible modifications) by the client.

---

*This chapter has been derived from "Spreads and Fees in Investment Banking" by G. Clyde Buck, Volume I (Investing and Risk Management), and "Pricing Public Offerings" by G. Clyde Buck, Volume II (Capital Raising and Financial Structure), Down Jones-Irwin's *The Library of Investment Banking* (1990), Robert Lawrence Kuhn, editor in chief.

Initial Public Offerings

The most significant normal source of investment banking revenue is from arranging public offerings. A typical gross spread or underwriting commission on an initial public offering of $15 million of common stock, for example, might be 8 percent or about $1.35 million. (This percentage decreases with increasing offering size, so that for a $50,000,000 common stock offering, the gross spread would be five–seven percent) This amount may seem large to first-time corporate clients who may not realize that many weeks and hundreds of people are involved in making the offering successful—not to mention the significant risks of disruption or failure. All gross spreads are negotiated by representatives of the issuer and the managing investment banking firm, with final negotiations taking place immediately prior to the actual offering date. Several investment banking firms are usually involved in the distribution of any public offering, and each of these firms must pay a significant portion of its share of the underwriting commission to the salesmen participating in the offering.

Some of the questions considered in negotiating compensation for arranging a public offering (which usually is finalized immediately prior to the official offering date) are as follows:

1. How large is the public offering? (A normal size for regional and national underwriters might be $5–35 million.)

2. How difficult has it been (or will it be) to distribute the securities? (Sometimes the company is well-known and much of the offering can readily be sold to institutions.)

3. What have recent gross spreads been on comparable public offerings? (Usually 20–30 offerings are considered.)

4. How important is the gross spread (in comparison to the offering price of the securities) to the client company? (Usually it is not nearly as important as the offering price.)

5. What prior discussions have taken place with the client regarding the underwriting discount? (Often this topic arises in early conversations about normal offering procedures.)

6. Have other investment banking firms given the client company any opinions or estimates of appropriate underwriting discounts? (Sometimes such estimates are part of initial proposals by prospective lead underwriters.)

7. Are co-managers involved in this offering? If so, what percent of the management fee portion of the underwriting discount will be paid to such co-managers? (A normal management fee is 20 percent of the total underwriting discount.)

8. What expenses are expected to be incurred by the underwriting group (such as legal fees, travel, advertising, and aftermarket stabilization expenses)? (These vary widely.)

9. What gross selling concession is expected by the individual brokers who participated in selling the offering? (This is normally 50–60% of the total underwriting discount.)

10. What risk is anticipated in making a market for the securities after the offering? (If the issue is difficult to sell and to price, the risk can be very large and the underwriter may ask for a higher gross spread.)

11. How difficult has it been to conduct appropriate due diligence analysis and prepare legal documents involved in the offering? How difficult has it been (or will it be) to sell the offering? Was the offering distributed primarily to retail or institutional customers? What degree of risk is involved in the securities? How uncertain are future quarterly earnings per share? (Again, greater risk or greater difficulty translates into a logical need for a higher gross spread.)

12. What do other firms in the underwriting syndicate think the gross spread should be? Why? (If a member of the proposed syndicate feels strongly that the spread is much too low, that firm might drop out of the syndicate.)

13. What does the client company think the gross spread should be? Why? (Normally the client company has not had much experience with such matters and is not as up-to-date as the lead underwriter.)

14. How aggressive has the client company been in seeking a relatively high offering price? (The more pressure for a high price, the more the underwriters may feel entitled to a higher underwriting commission if added selling difficulty is involved.)

15. What are current market conditions for offerings of similar securities? (Sometimes there are two or three very comparable offerings that occurred recently.)

For small, risky initial public offerings, many lead underwriters ask for added compensation in the form of due diligence fees or expense reimbursement provisions of perhaps $20,000–$50,000. These special fees can be an important supplement to the normal 20 percent management fee portion of the gross spread (i.e., the entire underwriting commission).

Common Stock Offerings

Initial public offerings involve a greater percentage of compensation to investment bankers than routine public offerings of common stock for companies that are already publicly traded in an active market. Comparable gross spreads for typical public offerings of common stock (for public industrial companies not "utilities") might be five to seven and one-half percent for offerings of $15 million and two to five percent for offerings of $50 million.

Fixed-Income Securities

Fees for public offerings of fixed-income securities of public companies vary widely because of the relative risks and complexities involved in each offering. A rough indication of possible gross spreads on corporate debt securities (with a typical offering of "A" rated corporate debt with a maturity of 10 years) would be one and three-tenths percent on $20 million and about seven-tenths percent from $50 million to $200 million.

Since *convertible* debentures are somewhat of a hybrid between a fixed-income security and common stock, typical underwriting commissions for public offerings of convertible debentures would fall between the higher fees for common stock offerings and the lower fees for typical offerings of long-term notes or debentures. The same situation applies to high yield debt, where three to three and one-half percent spreads are typical.

Private Placements

The term *private placement* as used in investment banking generally refers to arranging the private sale of long-term debt securities to substantial financial institutions, such as leading insurance companies who have private placement departments specifically organized to review and purchase such securities (see Chapter 15). Fees to investment bankers for arranging such private placements vary depending upon the size and degree of difficulty of the project, but normal fees for placements of senior debt might be one and one-half to four percent for placements of $5–10 million, one to three percent for placements of $10–25 million, seven-tenths to two percent for placements of $25–50 million, and one-half to one and one-half percent for placements above $50 million. Fees for more risky subordinated debt would be higher, perhaps two to three times the preceding fee schedule.

If a banker were concerned about whether or not the placement could be done at all, he might ask for a larger fee plus an initial non-refundable retainer. In a somewhat similar vein, investment bankers often ask for a *busted deal fee* of perhaps one-third or one-half of the normal fee if the private placement is cancelled by the issuing company due to circumstances beyond the control of the investment banking firm— such as a significant increase in prevailing interest rates or a serious deterioration in the financial condition of the company. It is also normal for investment bankers to be reimbursed for all out-of-pocket expenses and to be indemnified by the company against litigation involving the private placement project.

Venture Capital

A special form of private placement that warrants its own category involves small placements of speculative securities for risky, emerging growth companies. Many investment banking firms consider raising venture capital to be an important service to their corporate clients. Their corporate finance personnel develop personal relationships with certain venture capital firms and assist their clients with the entire process of raising money from such venture capital firms. Usually the preparation of a business plan or placement memorandum is involved in the project and perhaps two or three dozen venture capital firms are contacted before serious due diligence and negotiations are conducted with a small number of venture capital firms, depending upon the amount of the financing. These projects involve a high degree of uncertainty; and, in many cases, no financing takes place due to the inability of the venture capital firms to agree with the issuing company on an appropriate price for the securities (the securities are typically either convertible preferred or straight common stock).

Again, the percentage investment banking fee depends in large measure upon the size and degree of difficulty involved in the project, and could be as high as eight to ten percent on a small transaction. An average fee might be five to six percent, and it would not be unusual for the investment bank to also receive warrants as part of its compensation. Such warrants might be, for example, for the purchase of new securities equal to ten percent of the amount of the securities issued in the venture capital financing at a price of 120 percent of the price being paid by the venture capital investors, with the warrants having a life of five years. It is also not unusual for investment bankers to seek a right of first refusal for arranging subsequent private placements or public offerings as part of their consideration for arranging difficult venture capital financings.

Mergers & Acquisitions

Fees for arranging mergers, acquisitions, and reorganizations also involve a wide range of fees, depending upon the size and degree of difficulty anticipated and the specific role played by the investment banking firm. Over the years, many firms have suggested the *Lehman formula* as a typical fee for selling a company: five percent of the first $1 million, four percent of the second $1 million, three percent of the third $1 million, two percent of the fourth $1 million, and one percent of any amount in excess thereof. Accordingly, this so-called five-four-three-two-one Lehman formula would involve a $150,000 fee for the first $5 million of proceeds to a seller plus one percent of any amount in excess of $5 million. Due to inflation, many investment bankers have adjusted that formula to five percent of the first $2 million, four percent of the next $2 million, and the like. Another formula is five percent of the first $5 million, two and one-half percent of the next $10 million and three-fourths of one percent of any proceeds in excess of $15 million.

Many investment bankers prefer to suggest a flat percentage fee (e.g., 2% or 3%), and many clients prefer to negotiate a flat fee or a fixed dollar amount. Another increasingly used structure would also add to the normal incentive of a larger fee for a larger transaction the further incentive of a *higher percentage* fee if the selling price exceeds a certain amount (such as a normal price for the company being sold). For example, if a seller thought the value of his company was approximately $150 million, the contingent compensation of the investment banker might involve an added one percent of the total amount of the transaction if the price exceeds $160 million and an added two percent of the entire transaction if the price exceeds $170 million. This incentive fee could also be reduced substantially by having the added one percent or two percent only apply to the proceeds in excess of a certain amount. (The latter is employed more frequently.)

Investment bankers can represent either buyers or sellers in merger/acquisition transactions (thus resulting in two fees to two firms), and fees could well be less than one percent of the amount involved on large transactions. Retainers and *busted deal fees* are sometimes involved in merger/acquisition projects, depending upon the philosophy of the investment banker and client company involved in the project. Merger/acquisition fees for large transactions are major pieces of revenue for an investment banking firm, but the degree of difficulty, risk, and responsibility is also quite major on such projects.

An astute investment banker in the middle of heated negotiations between, for example, a buyer who has made a final offer of $200 million and a seller who absolutely must receive $250 million can often help break the deadlock and may affect the outcome by ten million dollars or more by making exceptional structural suggestions or by knowing how to handle difficult personalities. Many people feel that really good merger/acquisition specialists are well worth the high fees they seek. Perhaps that is why their fees have not declined in recent years in spite of greatly increased competition in investment banking and the overall financial services industry.

Leveraged Buyouts, Merchant Banking Deals and Other Special Financings

The range of size, uncertainty, and capital commitments involved in arranging special projects such as leveraged buyouts (LBOs), merchant banking deals, leveraged leases, project finance deals, and the like is so great that no useful schedule of typical fees can be suggested other than by comparison to private placements and venture capital financing. Where substantial investments or risk of the investment banking firm's capital are involved on either a temporary or a long-term basis, the need for compensation is obviously significantly greater and the form of compensation can involve not only fees and percentage commissions but also potential gains on the resale of securities. In analyzing the fairness of such fees, one must consider that relatively few people are properly qualified to initiate, analyze, structure, and arrange a successful LBO for a large company.

LBOs may involve either a single overall fee or several separate investment banking fees such as:

- merger/acquisition, sponsor's or advisory fees (for finding the company being acquired and structuring a proposal, the fee might be one–five percent of the value of the company, and might have a minimum amount, such as $300,000–500,000)

- bank financing placement fee (for arranging senior bank debt, the fee might be one percent of the amount involved or might be included in an advisory fee)

- subordinated debt/mezzanine financing placement fee (for arranging unsecured junior debt, the fee might be three–five percent of the amount involved)

- bridge financing fee (for arranging temporary debt, the fee could vary widely, depending on the uncertainty of expected take-out financing)

- commitment fees (for providing various degrees of confidence or assurance that a proposed LBO financing will be arranged in a reasonable length of time, the fee could vary widely, in line with risk)

- other advisory or fairness opinion fees (especially if a substantial part or all of a public company is being sold)

Financial Advisory Fees

In addition to the aforementioned types of projects, investment bankers may have special advisory or consulting projects where raising capital or selling a company is not involved. Financial advisory projects might include fairness opinions, analyses of alternative financings, expert testimony, and valuations. Usually a flat fee is negotiated for the project, but sometimes it is more appropriate to charge a fixed fee per hour (e.g., $200–350), per person-day (e.g., $1,500–3,000), or per firm-month (e.g., $10,000–30,000). As with all investment banking projects, the exact form and amount of the investment banker's compensation is determined by his negotiations with a client, taking into consideration normal fees charged by other investment bankers for comparable projects.

With respect to fairness opinions, where an investment banker is saying that a certain transaction is fair from a financial point of view to certain shareholders, the fee not only must cover the time spent in analyzing the transaction (and usually several other comparable transactions) but also must compensate for the responsibility being assumed and the risk that someone will file a lawsuit against everyone involved. Fairness opinion fees for transactions involving public companies normally range from a low of perhaps $50,000 (where only a few million dollars are involved) to $1 million or more on larger transactions.

Whereas these sums may seem to be excessive compensation for generating what amounts to a few pieces of paper, there is substantial value being added. The fairness opinion represents the only independent third party involved in the proposed transaction (usually a merger or acquisition), and it is the expertise and reputation of the investment bank which prepares it that protects the interests of all stockholders.

Summary

The bottom line is that investment bankers believe that they are always adding *incremental* value to all transactions in which they participate. Fees at their highest are only a small fraction of the wealth-generating power that shareholders obtain from the capital-raising and financial advisory services of investment bankers. High value demands high compensation. Capitalism would have it no other way.

CHAPTER 9

The Deal-Making Process*

My purpose for writing this chapter on deal making is to express some personal ideas about the most important process of investment banking—where negotiating transactions is an everyday obsession. Deal making is so important to investment banking that it has come to epitomize the field, even to caricature it. The perceived image of the rapacious shark is a distortion of the truth and a disservice to the industry. The best deal makers combine optimal information and analytical skills with artistic intuition and human sensitivity.

To live life is to make deals. Deal making is constantly in session. No organization goes unaffected. No individual is immune. From boardrooms to bedrooms, you can't avoid doing deals. You can either do them poorly or do them well. This chapter is about doing them well in business, professional life, and personal life.

Every aspect of deal making is exhilarating—the thrill of a new deal beginning, the satisfaction of a good deal closing. Making deals intrigues and inspires: the electric sparks of planning, creating, nurturing, and achieving. Nothing is as satisfying as a good deal executed well (well, almost nothing).

It's not all roses and medals. Some transactions are bombs—good deals that were never closed and bad deals that sadly were. Why do good ones fall apart? Why do bad ones come together? One learns from failure as well as success.

---

* Note: This chapter is derived from *Dealmaker: All the Negotiating Skills and Secrets You Need*, Robert Lawrence Kuhn, New York: John Wiley and Sons, 1988.

What the best deal makers do, often by the feel of their gut, can be grasped, absorbed, and applied. To be a great deal maker, you need perspective, insight, and techniques. Intensity and guts must amplify strategy and structure. What's here is what works. What's here is what counts.

Deal Fallacies

Let's start in reverse. What common assumptions about deal making are wrong? What is real deal making *not*?

Not Just Edge-Getting

The popular press harangues us with a getting-the-edge stereotype. Predatory propaganda is the way of our world. If you don't know the craft of negotiation, you're a dolt and a doormat. If you don't conquer through intimidation, you're a pushover and a placemat. If you don't watch out for Number One, you're a flake and a dishrag. No one wants to be a blockhead or a pansy or a nerd with a wet noodle for a backbone, so we are all compelled, actually bullied, to play the one-upmanship game.

But it's all so futile, so short-sighted. Today's quick buck chokes off a thousand tomorrow. Streams of dollars that could flow in the future are never seen. The irony, of course, is that what is not seen is not known; no negative reinforcement ever occurs, and no long-term consequences of short-term actions are ever appreciated. The deal making edge-getter goes blithely on his or her devious way, smug that he or she has mastered the craft of negotiation, conquered through intimidation, and watched out for Number One—whereas, in reality, he or she has flubbed the deal, blown the negotiations, and flattened Number One.

Not Just Negotiations

What constitutes a deal? Clever negotiations, if you believe popular wisdom. This is true—but not truth. Deal making requires greater talent and demands broader technique. Deal making means more than negotiating. Learning how to make deals means more than learning how to negotiate. How to get what you want in trading and haggling is only part of our story.

Deal making describes the whole process whereas negotiation defines specific skills. Deal making involves far more than is usually assumed, and when you commence with the techniques of negotiation, you've already conceded half the battle. Negotiations, if you think about them, start in the middle, taking for granted that a certain deal should or must be made. But *which* deal should or must be made? How do you know? It makes no sense to negotiate in a make-believe world, however nice the imagined fairyland.

It is better to negotiate the right deal badly than the wrong deal well. Think about that.

Not Just Tactics

Deal making is strategy as well as tactics—how to plan ahead as well as how to carry out. It is creative choice as well as shrewd manipulation. Choosing the right deal—knowing in advance which deals are "doable," which deals can be consummated, and which cannot—is more important than negotiating that deal. You need to be much more than a good negotiator to be a good deal maker.

Are you not a clever negotiator? Do not worry. You don't need to be one to be a good deal maker. Are you surprised? Certainly the skills of adroit bargaining are valuable. But one can be a good deal maker *without* being especially wily in negotiations, and a smart negotiator may be winning minor victories on the wrong battlefield.

Defining a Deal

What, actually, *is* a deal? Let's frame some basic definitions. A little precision can't hurt. *A deal is an exchange of value and consideration among two or more parties.*

- *Value* means anything whatsoever that at least one side thinks has some kind of worth.
- *Consideration* means whatever things are used to purchase that value. A tangible or intangible something must change hands.[1]
- *Parties* refers to the participants in the deal.

---

1. Value and consideration can be *tangible* (i.e., items that have physical substance) such as property, plant, equipment, and inventory; and they can be *intangible* (i.e., items that lack physical substance) such as copyrights, brand names, customer lists, and licenses.

The value and consideration of the exchange may include goods, services, assets, liabilities, cash, cash equivalents, promissory notes, stock ownership of all kinds, patents, rights, royalties, or responsibilities and commitments. Each side seeks to achieve specific objectives and may include any combination of tangible and intangible value and consideration in the deal.

In a traditional corporate deal, one party exchanges cash or notes to purchase the stock or assets of a company. In a less traditional corporate deal, a weak business might be exchanged solely for the assumptions of its liabilities.[2]

In a traditional personal deal, an employee gives his or her work time and effort to a company and receives a salary and other benefits in exchange. In a less traditional personal deal, an indicted criminal bargains for a less severe punishment in exchange for admitting guilt and/or cooperating with authorities.

Deal Complexity

Complexity is a killer in deal making. It sucks time and saps strength. Deal makers should fear its ominous advance.

There is an *inverse* relationship between complexity of deals and probability of closure. This means that the more complicated the deal structure the less likely it is to work. The KISS principle—Keep It Simple, Stupid—is as valid with giant corporate transactions as it is with small, personal arrangements. (In fact, small deals are no easier to make than big deals. Sometimes they are even harder since personality and ego can more easily foul up the works and choke off progress.)

Transactions may be disarmingly simple or tortuously complex. A purchasing agent and a vendor can agree on price without need for written confirmation. Some corporate mergers cannot be closed without consuming hundreds of turgid legal documents. But a deal is a deal is a deal, and every point in every transaction must be sifted and selected, dissected and analyzed, considered and decided, no matter how large or small the numbers.

---

2. Assumptions of liabilities to acquire businesses can be worse for the acquirer than paying an equivalent amount of cash since it introduces more uncertainty and risk.

Deal Components

Stripped to basics, all deals are similar. Simple or complex, all deals look the same inside and underneath. Reaching agreement with your kids on their weekly allowances is analogous in structure to hammering out terms of a corporate acquisition, both of which parallel discussing a raise with your boss.

All deals have common components: distinct parties with differing interests, value and consideration to be exchanged, terms and conditions to be discussed, a process of negotiation, a closure or consummation event, and an execution or implementation of the agreed-upon terms and conditions.

Mutual agreement is the key idea. This is easy to say but hard to do. Determining terms and conditions is the crux of most deals. It is the area of greatest conflict, yet it offers the greatest opportunity for dynamic creativity—for bridging unbridgeable gaps and climbing unclimbable cliffs.

A first step in devising good terms and conditions is to understand their compositions. We present the seven components needed to establish deal terms and conditions, followed by two example applications, one corporate and one personal.

The Seven Component Questions

1. *What kind of stuff?* What is the nature and character of the value and consideration being exchanged in the transaction? This means the specific types of goods, services, assets, liabilities, ownerships, intangibles, rights, responsibilities, commitments, and the like.

2. *How much of the stuff?* What are the amounts of the value and consideration being exchanged? This means the precise number of the things, tangible and intangible, changing hands in the transaction.

3. *What's the stuff really worth?* What is the relative benefit of the value and consideration being exchanged? How does each side of the transaction relate to the other?

4. *What's the stuff really like?* What promises and assurances (representations and warranties) are given to the value and

consideration? These are the legal declarations about the state of the value and consideration being exchanged—the mutual promises by the respective parties, their rights to make the transaction, and the like.

5. *What's certain and what's not?* Which terms and conditions cannot change (noncontingent) and which can change (contingent)? Contingent aspects of transactions depend on future events or conditions (such as income in later years in an acquisition). Noncontingent aspects are set forth absolutely and cannot be altered.

6. *How can compliance be assured?* How can it be provided that each side lives up to its side of the bargain? These are the methods for generating confidence in deal completion by fulfilling the terms and conditions through security interests, guarantees, performance requirements, and the like.

7. *What's the timing?* What is the schedule for completing the transaction? This describes the sequence of events for executing and activating each aspect of the terms and conditions, the time frame when exchanges and transfers of value and consideration all happen.

Example of a Corporate Transaction

Assume Company A is buying a small subsidiary of Company B (call it SmallCo). How would each of the components fit and apply? The following is a simplified summary of the terms and conditions organized in answer to the seven questions.

1. *What kind of stuff?* Company A purchases from Company B all the assets and current liabilities of SmallCo for cash, notes, and profit participations; Company B keeps SmallCo's long-term debt and stock.

2. *How much of the stuff?* It costs $12 million to be paid as follows: $2 million in cash at closing, $2 million in Company A stock, $5 million in promissory notes to be paid at a rate of $1 million per year for five consecutive years, and $3 million in Company A stock to be paid as a percentage of future profits of the SmallCo division.

3. *What's the stuff really worth?* The $2 million cash is easy; cash is cash. Company A stock is more difficult— it can be valued at market value if Company A is public, if the stock has a ready market, if there are no restrictions, and if there is reasonable stability in the stock—a lot of *ifs*. The $1 million for five consecutive years must be discounted to present value if no interest is being paid. Thus the $5 million of face value on the promissory notes would be only worth about $3.6 million (using a 12 percent discount factor). The $3 million based on profit participation is worth substantially less than its face value since, in addition to the present value discount, its ultimate valuation is completely dependent on indeterminable elements: SmallCo's future prospects when controlled by other parties, and the double doubt of uncertain profits in the SmallCo division and uncertain valuation of Company B stock.

4. *What's the stuff really like?* Company B asserts that all assets and liabilities being transferred are in good condition. Company A provides an acceptable method for determining the division's future profitability. Each company assures the other of its legal right to complete the transaction.

5. *What's certain and what's not?* All but the profit participation is certain (noncontingent); the profit participation is dependent on uncertain events (and is highly contingent).

6. *How can compliance be assured?* The $1 million per year for five years can carry the corporate guarantee of Company A. It may also be backed up by security interests in the assets being sold or even the independent guarantee of a financial institution (e.g., a letter of credit).

7. *What's the timing?* The schedule for transfer of ownership of Company B value (SmallCo's assets) is stated clearly (usually at closing) as is the schedule for transfer of consideration (the various payments of cash and stock at closing and over time).

Example of a Personal Transaction

These same components exist in every deal, although in smaller, more personal transactions, several are more implicit than explicit. For example, watch the seven components at work in a deal between you and your boss regarding last year's bonus.

1. *What kind of stuff?* You transfer to your employer last year's productivity and the implied promise of next year's productivity in exchange for certain financial consideration.

2. *How much of the stuff?* The length is your implied employment arrangement; perhaps one year. The quantity of each type of financial consideration is specified for your bonus; say, $30,000 in cash and $50,000 worth of stock options.

3. *What's the stuff really worth?* A logical relationship should relate work performance to financial bonus.

4. *What's the stuff really like?* Assertions are more assumed than stated. Each side (you and your boss) agrees to the exchange of bonus for continued work.

5. *What's certain and what's not?* The bonus is generally certain (noncontingent) for the previous year. It is usually uncertain (contingent) for the coming year (i.e., it is based on specific or unspecific factors such as the company's profitability, the relative performance of your division or department, your own personal productivity, and, often, the whim and caprice of your boss).

6. *How can compliance be assured?* Confidence in receiving the bonus is often its verbal promise; confidence in your continued work effort is assumed. (However, it becomes problematic if you deem the bonus to be too low.)

7. *What is the timing?* The schedule for bonus payment is based on corporate tradition (e.g., at the end of the year when performance can be assessed).

What's a Good Deal?

Good deal making is like good love making: When both parties are satisfied, each party enjoys it more—and wants to do it again! Being satisfied, however, does not necessarily mean being satisfied at the same time, to the same degree, or in the same manner—on either side of the analogy. Deal making, again like love making, involves a complex mingling of personality and passion, a mysterious mixture of individuality and desire.

A good deal means different things to different parties: To a company enjoying high growth, a good deal might require a 25% or more annual return on investment. To a company threatened with bankruptcy, a good deal might mean selling off inventory at a loss in order to generate survival cash. To an independent consultant, a good deal might mean selling services at low-ball fees in order to establish a reputation in the market. To a governmental agency, a good deal might mean speeding up spending in order to justify a larger budgetary appropriation.

Larry Hagman and the rest of the *Dallas* cast get paid bundles for each original episode, but share none of the residual income from the hit television series. Lorimar, the producing company, loses big money on each first-run episode but gets fat from successful syndication. It's a good deal for both sides. The actors take no risks and pocket their cash up front; the producers take high risks (since most series are not hits and losses are never recovered) and hope to score big from reruns. That's the nature of deal making: lower risk for lower reward and higher risk for higher reward. (Although in this case, the actor's lower reward is nothing to cry about!)

In the short run, a good deal is whatever makes *you* happy. In the long run, a good deal is whatever makes *everyone* happy. The short run deal boosts ego. The long run deal promotes career. In making deals, one often has to choose between ego and career. It's a tough call: Conceit never likes second place.

When *Bad* Means *Good*

In the language of the street, *bad* means *good*, something tough and strong; and *good* means mediocre, something soft and weak. The same reverse sense often applies in evaluating deal making. A good deal maker is often glamorized as a ruthless manipulator, a cold-blooded predator of the concrete jungle who devours all without mercy.

By some quirk of character, evolutionary or social, we admire the tough guy. Macho is cool. The masculine image is steel and ice, not silk and satin. The feminine image is warm and sensitive, and few deal makers have the ego strength to survive such compliments.

How can accolades and respect in this media-blasted world of saber-toothed virility be won? Pressure and squeeze the other side. Pummel and pulverize them. To trick your opponents and seize more for yourself is the touchstone of success, the proverbial pot of deal-making gold at the end of the wily tactician's rainbow. Building the business takes a back seat when personal ego does the driving.

Too many business people pride themselves on besting their buddies. They must twist an advantage to feel productive; they must feel the turn of the screw to sleep a satisfied sleep. You know the type. A fair price is never fair. Grinding never stops. Agreements are changed constantly. Power plays never end. A fully agreed-on deal is altered on signing. Payment is delayed deliberately. Simple meaning is confounded by calculated obfuscation and legal pyrotechnics. The pounding is relentless.

Some of these characters browbeat and coerce. Others prefer to dupe and deceive—the former like to see you squirm, the latter enjoy the painless slice. Priorities are always inverted, objectives pulled inside out, goals flipped upside down. Getting the edge is the goal and shaving points is the game. Edge-getters are often haughty and swell-headed (legends in their own minds), with more vanity and arrogance than acumen and intelligence. When these types fancy themselves deal makers, they are often more addicted to the clever kill than to the extra meat. What counts is not the spending power of the bigger payoff but the puffing power of the smoother stroke. It's the edge itself that's sought, the intoxicating elixir of Darwinian dominance brewed with sublimated sexuality, and not necessarily the amount.

But the entire deal becomes more tenuous and the likelihood of closure less sure. Commitment is weakened, confidence is shaken, and time is lost. Problems can erupt; days are wasted, deals delayed, relationships ruptured, and reputations ruined—all silly sacrifices on the high altar of ego worship and gamesmanship.

Morality is not the issue here. Straight pragmatics is what we promote. We count numbers and keep score, with no special points given for being fair or nice. Know, however, that the race we run is a marathon—our time frame extends well beyond the close of the current deal—and what will be a good deal tomorrow defines what must be a good deal today.

Describing a Good Deal

A deal is good when it optimizes objectives. This general definition means that solutions must be found for most problems under consideration. But *optimal* is different for each party and for the deal as a whole. From each side's separate viewpoint, a good deal fulfills most of that side's wants and needs—irrespective of the impact on the other side. In other words, as long as your side is content, it matters not a whit how the other side comes out.

The best deal, then, is the maximum you can reasonably expect to get combined with the minimum you can reasonably expect to give. This is what you give in deals:

- The value and consideration, the cash and stuff you paid or received
- The risks assumed, such as the potential default by the other side
- The opportunity costs incurred, such as the lost chances to pursue other deals

When both sides of the deal are assessed at the same time, a deal is good when it optimizes objectives of both parties. A deal is best when it achieves the maximum number of goals for all sides while sustaining minimum risks. Using this collective definition, a good deal is not all that common and a best deal is indeed a rare commodity. Most deals have uneven value to the opposing sides. A best deal for one side is likely to be only a good deal for the other.

Good deal making is a means to an end, not an end in itself. Although it is indeed satisfying to make good deals, the source of that satisfaction should be the higher goals being attained— not a showcase for advancing ego. All parties to a deal should be satisfied on signing, enthusiastic during execution, delighted on completion, and pleased on reflection. Solution sets that achieve nonconflicting objectives are always present in deals and should be sought aggressively.

A deal can be considered good when it fulfills at least the minimum goals of all participants. A good deal is as good ten months after closing as it is after ten minutes. Good deals should stand the test of time and be remembered fondly ten years hence.

Unequal Roles in Good Deals

Don't misunderstand. We build no safety nets under weaker parties. Social support has no place in this definition. Bleeding hearts we bar. The toughness of the marketplace must dominate. Deal makers must consider the other side simply because it makes smart business sense in the long run—not because it is a nice thing to do. This point is vital.

Unequal outcomes result from unequal positions. Each side is seeking good, better, and best for itself in an adversarial and win/lose situation (i.e., if one side has one dollar more the other side has one dollar less). The rules of the game, even when known, are not always fair. You play deal maker, therefore, very much at your own risk. Final decisions are yours alone.

A good deal does not require each party to play an equal role, to achieve a similar degree of success, or even to make money. Natural power is distributed according to preexisting patterns. For example, if a liquidator buys end-of-the-season merchandise below cost the manufacturer seems to lose money. But if the manufacturer's overall costs are covered, the conversion of the unsalable inventory to ready cash produces a profit.

In another example, when a company with a tax-loss carryforward and low profits pays a whopping price to purchase a company with substantial profits, the deal can be good for both sides. The buyer thinks in terms of the acquired company's pre-tax income (which it shelters from tax) and the seller thinks in terms of receiving top dollar.

How about a more extreme example? Assume you are able to purchase a company in serious financial trouble by assuming only part of its outstanding liabilities. The previous owners wind up with residual debt and a negative worth. Is this a good deal by our definition? The answer is yes, if it is the arrangement the sellers can construct under the circumstances. In these dire situations, good deal makers like to find ways to give something positive to those on the other side. Here a multi-year, personal consulting contract is one possibility.

Relativity Makes Deals Good

Variety in deals is endless. No two are exactly alike. Good deals, however, have one facet in common: comparisons are always made and assessements are always relative. Satisfaction is achieved to the extent that each party feels relatively positive about the outcome. The key word is *relatively*. To find out what it means, we explore a peculiar aspect of human nature.

Human beings are creatures of comparison. We react emotionally to recent events, even when it makes no sense to do so. Consider the following situation.

You own 1000 shares of a stock selling for $20 per share. On Monday you are hopeful but neutral. Suddenly, on Tuesday, there is a rumor of an unfriendly takeover and the stock shoots up to $30. You are elated. You are also $10,000 richer, at least on paper. You tell your spouse, kids, relatives, friends— perhaps plan some long-wanted pleasure purchase— you're a hero. Then, on Thursday, the target company sues and the raider backs off. While there may be other suitors, no one surfaces and the stock drops to $24 where it closes on Friday.

You are depressed. *Even though you are $4,000 richer on Friday than you were on Monday*, you feel terrible—after all, you just *lost* $6,000. This emotional relativity is the point. Your mental attitude with the stock at $24 is controlled by your mental attitude when the stock was $30 (however momentary the event) and not when it was languishing at $20.

Now, for the sake of argument, we make the middle of the week disappear. There is no dramatic announcement of an unfriendly raid. Rumors of merger or acquisition build slowly. The company states it would consider negotiating with interested parties. The stock moves smoothly from $20 to $24 over the course of the week. And come Friday, you are feeling fine—after all, you just *made* $4,000.

The same relative emotions dominate in deal making. Absolute assessment of deals carries less weight than logic would suggest. Good is appraised, consciously or unconsciously, in relation to other real or imagined alternatives. The closer you think your deal is to the best deal, the better you feel. The better you feel, the likelier you are to make that deal.

There is another invidious kind of comparison skulking around deal making, a malady to which investment bankers are particularly susceptible. This is the comparison *between* or *among* parties. All too often, one side blows a superb deal simply because it feels that the opposing side is getting a better deal. The truth or falsehood of the attitude is irrelevant. Judging motivations of the other side is impossible. Furthermore, it doesn't matter how successful the other side is if your objectives are achieved. Nixing a deal because of ego imbalance is akin to cutting off your nose to spite your face. Good deal makers evaluate what *they* get, not what others get. They like their noses uncut.

Why Work Good Deals

At first blush, completing deals seems unlikely. How can human nature allow it? Agreement on terms and conditions appears impossible. Yet dozens of healthy-sized deals, hundreds of mid-sized deals, and perhaps thousands of smaller ones are consummated every day. Deals get completed because, ultimately, each side comes to believe that they are getting more than they are giving. Making each side believe they emerge as winners is the critical essence of making good deals.

Good deal making is the way of dynamic action, potent growth, and competitive edge. This is the frontier, the comparative advantage for contemporary business people. Good deal making is intense, gutsy, spirited, and aggressive. Good deal making, in short, propels companies and catapults careers.

Edge-getters, however, often wind up with few deals and fewer friends. They can be found spinning endless hero-stories of long-forgotten transactions. In deal making, if you pardon one more love-making analogy, you can play by yourself but, well, it just isn't as much fun.

Learn the Skills

The five deal making idea-skills discussed here set leading negotiators apart from haggling hacks. These idea-skills should live inside you and form the core of your natural deal making instincts. They should become second nature, loading automatically into your subconscious whenever you commence deal making behavior.

Know the Attitudes and Elements of Deal Making

Knowledge builds confidence and competitive edge. Your capability for using each deal skill and secret effectively will increase as you appreciate the structure and detail of the deal making process. Picture this image: each deal skill and secret is a tree and the deal making process is a forest. Your task is to see how each tree builds and blends with the entire forest and how the forest gives context to the tree.

Seat-of-the-pants deal making is fine for some sharpies, but the rest of us mortals need some assistance—for example, in grasping the subjective aspects of each deal skill and secret.

Know What You Want to Achieve

It's self-defeating to judge by comparison. Jealousy and envy are distractions for deal makers. They erect obstacles for conducting good business.

So, worry about yourself, and let the other side worry about itself. Don't become angry over what your opponents receive and don't be annoyed by their apparent satisfaction. Be pleased with what your side receives and be content with your own satisfaction.

Good deal makers can separate their own needs and wants from those of others. To do so, however, you need proper preparation and self-confidence. For instance, if you sell your business at the price and with the terms you want, you have no gripe when the buyer makes even more money over time.

Discern What the Other Side Wants to Achieve

Project yourself to the other side of the table. Float down into the seats of those with whom you are dickering. What are their real requirements? What's on their "wish list?" What are they looking for in the deal— bottom line—and how important is it? Most critically, what are their priorities?

Often, giving others what they want will *not* take away from what you can get for yourself. But gaining such insight does not come quickly or easily: You must develop sensitivity to people and awareness of situations. Remember mood and feeling, the fuzzies and tinglies. Make no mistake: How your stomach is churning influences how your head is working.

For example, if the owner of a closely-held company wants to sell out in order to retire, there is meaning beyond money. Maximum price can become secondary to special terms and conditions. Such an owner might well sell the business—a beloved baby—to a buyer offering a lower price if the owner believed that these new managers would take better care of the family legacy (including employees, products, customers, community, and reputation) than those offering a higher price. The best deal makers always go for the emotional heart of the other side's interests—especially when it's not price.

Seek Win-Win Solutions

Search for areas where each side can achieve certain of its goals without adversely affecting the other side. In the language of game theory, such sectors are called win-win, since one side is not compelled to lose (i.e., give up something it likes) whenever the other side wins (i.e., gets something it likes).

How to find a win-win solution? Establishing common ground is the key. Examine each aspect, element, and component of the deal. Analyze all the pieces and particulars of the transaction several times—you never know where these optimal regions will turn up. Win-win intersections can be surprisingly broad if one has the foresight to search for them, the insight to develop them, the perception to recognize them, and the resolution to employ them. When one structures deals with innovation and intelligence, win-win solutions emerge constantly.

For example, a company acquiring a family business might replace some of the cash purchase price with its own equity stock. Such a modification may win for the selling parties by giving them a sense of participation and continuance, and win for the buying parties by diminishing the amount of cash they must raise and pay. What happens here can happen often: In a very real sense, the buyer pays less, and the seller receives more.

Think of Alternatives and Solution Sets

The best deal makers multiply their options. They think on several levels at the same time. They are always planning for contingencies. The unexpected they expect; the unimagined they imagine. They are always watching over their shoulder with one eye and over the horizon with the other.

Experienced negotiators keep diverse alternatives always in readiness, like having several relief pitchers constantly warming up in the bullpen. They play *what-if* scenario games, devising creative responses to dummied-up problems. Expecting surprise at all times, professional deal makers are never surprised. They know how to hit curve balls even while waiting for sliders.

A *solution set* suggests a family of related ideas available for bridging gaps and resolving conflicts. No professional ever relies solely on one perfect solution to bargaining disputes. Perfection is impossible in the crazy quilt of human bargaining. Total control can never be exercised in deal making. There are too many issues, too many people, and too many agendas—many of which can be hidden and all of which can be contentious. Deal makers that are trained to think in terms of solution sets are better able to fine-tune the deal structure to optimize the interests of both buyer and seller. That's the meaning of win-win.

Keep the Secrets

What are secrets in deal making and why should you keep them? *Deal Secrets* is my way of directing attention to real deal making in real situations. It stresses knowing and doing, remembering and applying. More particularly, it underscores the *active* accumulation of deal making knowledge, the internal storing of fresh ideas. Practice, not theory, cuts ice.

You must feel it inside. Often there's no time for studied response. If you stop to think, you're stopped forever. If you hesitate, you could be lost. Deal makers must be driven by instinct to react properly under all circumstances. How can you train those instincts? You need proper reflexes. That's the point of secrets. The following seven deal making secrets train your instincts for rapid response.

Be Fair but Be Frank

Some of the toughest business people around are also some of the fairest. Getting the upper hand should be gotten out of your head. But *conceding* the upper hand should be stricken from your mind. Don't seek personal domination. But don't appear frail, fragile, feeble, or flimsy either. Doormats, remember, get stepped on. Placemats, eaten on. Dishrags, wiped with. None of these textile-types make good deals (the soles of shoes, bottoms of plates, and dirt from dinner don't build negotiating strength).

Being fair does not mean being weak. Weakness disrupts deals by tempting the other side to expand expectations and swell demands. Creating false hopes—building appetite without satisfaction—is not conducive to good deal making.

Let the other side realize that you know the nature of their game, the way they change the rules, and what their players have in mind. For example, if you decide to do business with a certain company regardless of price, be sure that they know that you know the score. If that supplier thinks they've pulled a fast one this time, they will try to pull a faster one next time. The price, already high, will go even higher. (As in the jungle, weakness is attacked mercilessly, and the nick will swell to a gouge.)

However, if the supplier realizes that you know what's happening— that you've decided to do business in *spite* of the high price (for whatever reason, say quick delivery), they will respect your strength. You may get a more reasonable price the next time. Remember, respect encourages fairness.

Avoid Hype

Hype helps? Well, that depends. Hype can sometimes sell a first deal, but never a second one. (Fool me once, shame on you; fool me twice, shame on me!)

Exaggeration is a short-term, rapidly-depleting asset—and a long-term, quickly-accruing liability. It's usually either a bad habit or a desperate act. Neither, be advised, is good for deal making. Just try negotiating again with someone you've duped. The French Resistance was no tougher than what you'll face.

If all you have is one deal to make, be my guest, make my day— have at it. Although I admit I've done it myself, I don't recommend hyping; nor have I ever met a person who has only one deal to make.

Be Conservative

Always be moderate in projecting your most likely results. Make reasonable and restrained public pronouncements. Aim forecasts below the center. Strive to exceed a pessimistic projection rather than fall behind an optimistic one.

Develop Alternative Scenarios

Allow the other side choices in assessing your analysis. (This transfers some of the burden.) Give them room— and keep your options open.

What impact would various internal surprises or external shocks have on your company? For example, what might happen to cash flow if sales rose or fell 10 percent? 20 percent? 30 percent? What if competition pressured prices? What if interest rates escalated? What if two surprises or shocks hit simultaneously? Such sensitivity analysis is particularly apt for buyers and sellers of businesses and for lenders and borrowers of debt.

Sensitivity analyis should also be used to examine the position on the other side of the table. Such an appraisal will probably be qualitative in character, providing more insight than fact. What are the best guesses of your opponent's current position and possible options? Are they really at the wall or can they be coaxed just a bit further back?

Admit Uncertainty

Don't be afraid to admit uncertainty about parts of your package. Point out, for example, where some of your numbers or statements may be slightly suspect. Business information cannot be perfect or precise. Honesty enhances credibility, and careful admissions can be most disarming. (Try using such high-powered honesty when battling a cynic; it can melt even the most hard-bitten deal maker.)

In preparing a proposal for bank financing, for example, a company should enumerate all assumptions precisely, pointing out areas of difficulty or ambiguity. Potential problems should be exposed by design, rather than be hidden by default. The honesty shown will be a potent force for augmenting confidence.

I am not advocating, of course, spilling the beans, singing like a canary, hauling skeletons out of the closet, picking through your garbage, or turning over all the rocks (and other such tattle-tale cliches). Taking truth serum is not the idea here. Improving credibility is.

You don't have to tell all the truth, but be sure that whatever you do tell is in fact true. Deal makers are grown-ups. The rules of the game assume each side carries its own weight.

Address Questions Nobody Has Asked

Use this one for surprise, but use it cautiously. Few moves are more impressive than when one side brings up sensitive subjects regarding its own position that the other side has not considered. It enhances credibility enormously—not to mention how the shock value can disorient the other side.

Such frank actions are good counterattacks to credibility problems. Say the company has fallen behind its sales projections, and as a result its bank is beginning to question everything. A daring technique is to show your account officers something *else* they missed about the company, perhaps a collection problem with minor accounts. Such credibility enhancers can become credit enhancers. (This technique, be advised, is a bit of brinkmanship; there is danger that your new admission will pull down an already shaky house.)

One must be careful not to go overboard here. Most people are conditioned to assume that their deal making opponents aren't telling the whole truth anyway. Some deal makers always shave (haircut) projections by 10 to 30 percent. By giving a pessimistic reading as your most

Principles and Techniques of Investment Banking

likely case, you run the risk of having this low-ball projection subjected to the same financial clippers. A double haircut you don't need; baldness in transactions does not mean deal making virility.

Think Image, Not Ego

Act as if your deal opponents have become your new public relations agents. In a way, they will be. No matter how confidential the negotiations and no matter how secret the deal, other people will hear about it. Regardless of how you envision yourself, what circulates about you is how others see you. Your reputation is cast by the look in their eyes when your name is mentioned out of your presence. A deal maker's reputation is his or her most valuable asset. Such an asset is not to be hidden away but made manifest.

It's in poor taste to parade your supposed superiority. Such conceit will return and bite you on the backside. Whatever you dish out, so will you be dished. It all comes down to this: What turns you on—getting the edge and puffng your ego or building the business and promoting your person? You can win the battle of making one deal, and still lose the war of making many. Make your decision: Which do you want, a career or a caper?

Appendix: Deal making in the Bible

The Bible is a rich case book of famous deals:

- God giving Adam and Eve the Garden of Eden paradise with the one condition being not to eat from the forbidden tree
- God's covenant with Abraham to make of him a great nation in exchange for his obedience and, well, a very small piece of very sensitive skin ("You want what. . . ?!" "That's the deal, Abe, it's my best offer")
- Jacob wrestling with God and refusing to let go until receiving a blessing
- God at Mount Sinai offering ancient Israel blessings for obedience and cursings for disobedience
- God granting David a choice of punishment for his sins (he chose to fall into the hands of God and receive a plague rather than fall into the hands of man and flee from enemies)

- God allowing even the most wicked king (Manasseh) to repent and be forgiven

Some deals worked for these biblical deal makers, such as when Jacob bought his brother Esau's birthright for a bowlful of porridge. And some deals did not work, such as when Sarah gave Haggar (her handmaiden) to Abraham (her husband) in hopes of having the promised son through this surrogate mother (a particularly modern issue, only back then the insemination process was natural, not artificial).

CHAPTER 10

Ethics for Investment Bankers*

Ethical problems in investment banking came to center stage in the late 1980s in ways not seen since the Great Crash of 1929 and the imposition of the original securities acts of 1933 and 1934. Media pictures of handcuffed arbitrageurs and indicted investment bankers, being led away by police from trading floors and personal homes, spread fear in the Wall Street community. The specter of law enforcement officers and FBI agents tapping phone lines, interrogating suspects, debriefing informants, and wiring confessed felons became serious matters for not a few companies.

The careers of highly-respected investment bankers evaporated overnight in these ignominious exposures. The reputations of major investment banking firms have been tainted. (It is descriptive of the ethical environment that some of those caught in insider trading or other criminal violations have worn wires to spy on their colleagues—in order to ameliorate their own sentencing.) A significant number of criminal prosecutions, SEC investigations, and U.S. congressional inquiries continue as this book goes to press.

---

* This chapter has been derived from "Ethics for Investment Bankers" by Robert Lawrence Kuhn and Robert Boyden Lamb, Volume I (Investing and Risk Management), Dow Jones-Irwin's *The Library of Investment Banking* (1990), Robert Lawrence Kuhn, editor-in-chief.

The harsh glare of legal and media spotlight has focused on Drexel Burnham Lambert, E.F. Hutton, and individuals at Kidder Peabody, Goldman Sachs, Morgan Guaranty, and other well-known firms. But the fact is that the entire industry is involved. Investment bankers have no monopoly on scandal; money management firms, law firms, accounting firms, and private individuals have all been caught up in the clamor.

Such criminal investigations, indictments, and convictions (not to forget hard time in prison) have changed the way all investment banking firms now conduct their internal affairs. Throughout the organization, policies and procedures have been modified: hiring methods, training programs, information processing, data base monitoring, surveillance, and control functions have all been toughened.

Ethics on Wall Street

Wall Street deserves higher ethical standards. In reality, the scope of such a legal and ethical shift on Wall Street goes far beyond the insider trading scandals. This legal/ethical problem reaches to the very heart of investment banking precisely because it is an industry epitomized by the phrase "your word is your bond." Trillions of dollars change hands each week before any papers or contracts are exchanged. If any substantial portion of these verbal deals, trades, and sales were to be viewed as ethically or legally tainted, such concern would present a serious danger to the markets. Ethics is a central, not peripheral, issue of investment banking.

The time period is important here. These ethical/legal problems were underscored just when the securities industry came under multiple investigations in the wake of the October 1987 stock market crash. The capital markets are being increasingly criticized as virtually a private insiders' casino. There are, it seems, a surfeit of tricks and treats leading to unfair personal gain: market manipulation, program trading, two-tier stock issues, corporate payments of greenmail, poison pills to entrench management, golden parachutes to enrich management, and the like.

The integrity of the capital markets has become suspect. The general public, professional investors, legal authorities, congresspeople, the SEC, and other regulatory bodies sense that the game may be rigged, the playing field not level. Such distrust reduces liquidity, adds volatility, and raises costs to issuers and investors—all to the detriment of our financing system.

What is the solution? Ethics must be a primary concern for investment bankers.

Ethics

Ethics is the study of standards of conduct and moral judgment. No longer the private provence of philosophy and theology, it is a subject of considerable interest throughout the business world.[1] The study of ethics has come out of the closet or down from the ivory tower (take your choice of metaphor).

Our focus is on investment banking, an area where the import of ethics must supercede its recent controversy and intense media attention. No mere fad, ethics forms the foundation on which investment banking is built. Ethical conduct generates confidence, and without the confidence of clients investment banking cannot exist.

Granted, the investment banking community was rocked by the insider trading scandal of 1986 and subsequent indictments. The calamitous events triggered both external critique and internal reflection. While public voices from Washington to Hollywood blasted Wall Street as greedy and unscrupulous, investment bankers themselves wondered quietly about the future of their profession.

Had the power of vast wealth distorted proper values? Had the massive movements of monies corrupted an entire industry? Whatever had happened in the past, the future was what counted: What are appropriate ethical standards in investment banking and how should they be set?

The fact is that ethical issues in investment banking far transcend the garish gloss of insider trading. There are many moral questions and few easy answers.

Objective and Organization

Although ethics for investment bankers have been subjected to both heated polemics and sarcastic humor,[2] there has been little formal

---

1. See *Corporate Ethics: A Prime Business Asset*, published by The Business Roundtable, New York, NY, February 1988. This landmark study gathered information from 100 major corporations and examined the philosophies, policies, and procedures of ten of them in depth (Boeing, Champion International, Chemical Bank, General Mills, GTE, Hewlett- Packard, Johnson & Johnson, McDonnell Douglas, Norton, and Xerox.)

2. Such as, "Famous thin books: *Ethics on Wall Street.*

thought given to the subject. Progress can only be made when areas are organized. Scope and issues can best be made clear in the context of models and frameworks.

The following is our framework for ethics in investment banking. We structure this chapter in three general sections.

First, we describe the *ethical environment* of the investment banking field. These are the critical characteristics that drive the moral issues as they affect the various subdivision such as management, banking, trading, sales, mergers and acquisitions, arbitrage, back-office operations, accounting and financial controls, and the like.

Second, we enumerate some of the prevalent *ethical issues*, problematic areas requiring moral judgment.

Third, we offer some *ethical recommendations*, operational solutions intended more to stimulate thought than to legislate behavior.

Ethical Environment of Investment Banking

Investment banking is an intense, high-powered industry, with enormous stakes and immense wealth amplified by compulsive competition and swollen egos. We suggest that in this emotional pressure-cooker there are six primary factors that influence the ethical environment:

1. *Law and Regulation*: the legal regulations and prevailing securities law enforcement policies

2. *Company Codes and Traditions*: the security firms' own ethical codes, procedures, and traditions

3. *Profit Maximization*: the personal drive for generating the largest income

4. *Inefficiency Exploitation*: the degrees of efficiency in the market and the potential for seeking and taking advantage of inefficiencies

5. *Money, Power, and Career*: the gross amount of money, power, and career advancement that can result from the skirting or outright violation of ethical standards

6. *Current Moral Climate*: the present ethical standards of both the general society and the specific culture in which a person does business

Law and Regulation

Investment banking exists within a changing environmental and industrial structure. Legal regulation and prevailing securities law enforcement policies create the framework within which ethical issues arise. Institutions that comprise the regulatory and enforcement system include the courts (Federal and state), FBI, Congress, SEC, and others— regulatory bodies, agencies, and authorities involved in policy making, investigation, and enforcement both in the United States and abroad. Each of the securities exchanges are major players: New York Stock Exchange, American Stock Exchange, National Association of Securities Dealers (NASD), Chicago Board Options Exchange, Chicago Board of Trade, and the like each imposes its own rules, codes, and procedures.

Company Codes and Traditions

Each investment banking house or securities company also has its own rules, codes, and procedures. But here there is even more influence and impact. First, these rules, codes, and procedures differ from firm to firm. More importantly, there exist within such organizations very particular (even peculiar) ethical norms, traditions, idealized goals and aspirations, stories and myths, and aspiration targets that have been developed over years if not decades. Bureaucratic procedures may conflict with entrepreneurial desires. There may be excessive control through enumerated rules and codes or a more freewheeling style with the absence of such specific standards of conduct. Individual human beings are products of the collective culture. How one behaves is influenced heavily by what the group accepts.

Profit Maximization

No one claims that investment banking has cornered the market on making money. But, to be frank, nowhere else is income generation as singular a source of business raison d'être. In other industries products or services are sold to produce dollars. In investment banking the products and services *are* dollars. An investment bank is a financial factory. Money is on everyone's mind all the time. The numbers are huge, the stakes are immense. It becomes easier for dollars to swamp morals.

Inefficiency Exploitation

Investment bankers seek competitive advantage. Although finance theory talks of *efficient markets* (where all information is known, and everyone has even access to the same opportunities), the goal of all investment bankers is to find *inefficiencies* in the market—cracks in the system, flaws in the gem. Irregularities that can be exploited are the sweet savor of the hunt (e.g., getting a price higher than expected for a divestiture, financing a deal for 50 basis points lower than the competition, creating an innovative hedging instrument, or finding a new technique to attack a corporate target or defend a corporate client). Indeed, finding such inefficiencies is trumpeted as the special sign of the best denizens of Wall Street—those investment bankers, researchers, traders, arbitrageurs, and sales people at the top of their class.

Money, Power, and Career

Money, power, and career are virtual synonyms in the investment banking lexicon. This is neither good nor bad. It cannot be a value judgment, since the game is played with money—that's how the score is kept— with the winner accumulating the most cash and with it the most power. Winning is just the way the system works—it's the great energizer and the highest good—and the fierce competition that is generated can alter behavior and blur standards.

Human beings are creatures of comparison. Context is often more important than content. How we feel inwardly is affected by how we appear outwardly. How we did last year (or week) is judged in comparison with how our friends and peers did in that same time period. And when friends and peers make more money than we do, even huge personal compensation can be depressing when seen through the insidious lens of comparative wealth. More, as they say, is never enough.

Current Moral Climate

Whether we like it or not, not all ethical standards are absolute. Some probably are, but not all. Few would defend the virtues of suitcases of cash being exchanged for insider information on Wall Street side streets. But there are areas of gray—such as the same investment bank representing clients on both sides of a transaction, or investment bankers personally owning and trading the securities that they are underwriting. It is in the gray areas where general perceptions change. What had seemed to be a clever idea yesterday (unorthodox, but neither illegal nor immoral) can suddenly look downright shady today.

Proper human behavior, to some degree, is the product of its times. Slavery and the role of women, for example, are two categories in which the advance of civilization has heightened ethical standards. On a less grand scale, the same phenomenon is occurring in investment banking. Actions applauded in the past as *tough* business would today be condemned as *bad* business. Ethical issues move by quantum jumps. What was recently quasi-justified is now excoriated; what was condoned is now condemned. Exposure to public scrutiny is often the touchstone. There is no better pressure for raising moral standards than the threat of media revelations.

This is not an argument for moral relativism. We do not say that there are no absolute standards in human behavior. But the fact remains that as society grows more complex in general, and as investment banking advances into new areas in particular, novel situations arise. How to deal with these new questions of moral judgment is the essence of ethics.

Ethical Issues in Investment Banking

The following thirty-three categories are ethical issues in investment banking. They are designed to stimulate thought. (Do not expect all questions to be answered, nor all questions to be asked.) This list is representative, not exhaustive; there are more potential issues than these.

Conflict of Interest

This is the largest and most inclusive category. Conflicts arise when a banker might have more than one participation in a particular circumstance. Perhaps he represents clients on opposite sides of a transaction. Perhaps he has personal financial interests that would benefit from a particular outcome. Perhaps a relative or close friend is involved. Perhaps career advancement favors a different result. It is easier to define a nonconflicted situation—where the banker has only one conceivable objective, normally maximizing a single client's interests.

Confidentiality

Confidentiality is a prime characteristic of investment banking. Keeping information private is important in all aspects of business, but it is absolutely essential in the financing and securities processes. Information must be respected as if it were a precious stone. Misplaced statements or misappropriated data can often cause more damage than mistaken facts. Revealing a critical secret (e.g., a forthcoming transaction) can have an enormous adverse impact. But keeping confidences is not a simple task in the complex world of investment banking. Information needs to be shared for deals to be completed. It is not always easy or obvious to know what to tell whom.

Disclosure and Due Diligence

Disclosure is the opposite of confidentiality, yet both accomplish the same goal—maintaining the fairness of the capital markets. It is the responsibility of all issuers of public securities to present information that is both accurate and complete. Material omissions can be as unethical (or unlawful) as erroneous statements. It is the responsibility of investment bankers to make sure that, to the best of their abilities, issuers make proper public disclosures of all relevant and material information of a quantitative and qualitative nature.

Due diligence is the process of discovering all relevant information in order to assure proper disclosure, and investment bankers are required to conduct an appropriately thorough review. Due diligence involves the verification of all company claims and representation, from technical ones (i.e., legal and accounting) to business (e.g., products, markets, distribution, customers, research and development, manufacturing, management, and systems). It is important to note that due diligence is the test for limiting legal liability in addition to maintaining the ethical standards of the profession.

Inside Information

There are actually several different kinds of insider trading. All are immoral as well as illegal, but the differences are meaningful. When large investors run elaborate operations and with malice aforethought solicit inside information, it is worse than when individuals happen to come across the same secrets and cannot resist the temptation to profit from them. But more serious than either offense is when an investment bank engages in illegal practices—such as stock manipulation—as part of the normal conduct of its business. Such unscrupulous actions pollute the entire industry.

Although some might claim that restrictions on insider trading infringe on free markets, overwhelming opinion desires to protect the integrity of markets. Speaking strictly in terms of economic efficiency, any justification of insider trading is spurious. If the level playing fields of capital markets are allowed to tilt to insiders, then many investors will pull their money out of the markets; the result would be decreased liquidity and increased costs of capital.

Gathering Information

How far can bankers go in finding helpful information? Planting listening devices in offices is clearly wrong. Is checking the garbage of law firms? monitoring flight paths of corporate aircraft? using private detectives to expose the personal lives of corporate raiders—are these proper conduct?

Communicating Information

Is it wrong for a banker to leak false information in order to create market inefficiencies and thereby gain a competitive advantage? The individual leaker may gain in the short run, but the system (and even the individual) will lose in the long run. No one trusts a liar. When you tell the truth, you never have to remember what you said.

Client Relationships

How should investment bankers treat their clients? As lambs to be shepherded—or fleeced? If a banker can obtain an overly large spread in a negotiated debt offering, is that the right amount to charge? The client may be desperate and the banker may be their only salvation. Should an investment banker represent more than one company in the same industry? advise a company known to be participating in criminal activities such as fraud? (Not that the investment bankers would be specifically aiding and abetting the fraud, rather that the client company is engaged in illegal activities of some kind while the bankers are working with the firm.) Finally, what about the poaching of talent from clients? or clients making an employment offer to a banker?

Self-Dealing

Self-dealing combines conflict of interest with client relationships. For example, using client trust funds to promote personal interests of any kind is clearly unethical. Yet not a few investment bankers have fallen into the self-dealing trap with rationales such as making a knowledgeable investment or a temporary loan. Self-dealing is an insidious enemy; it is frighteningly easy to justify.

Corporate Opportunity

Investment bankers are constantly conditioned to be opportunistic, to take advantage of situations, and to get the best deal. However, sometimes the line between client and self blurs. If an interesting acquisition opportunity arises, to whom do you show it to first—your client in a related industry or your firm's leverage buyout group? Similarly, with *hot* securities, is it appropriate to hold some back for executives and employees of the investment bank—and then sell them into a demand-driven market?

Competitor Relationships

In a competitive environment, it is expected that each firm will promote itself over its competitors. That's normal. But how far does one go in undermining the opposition? Should one slant the facts of a busted deal? spread gossip about personalities? start rumors of dissension? Should one investment bank sue another for stealing clients? for interfering with business relationships? Should bankers short the stock of competitors' initial public offerings in order to stretch their opponent's capital and impugn their opponent's reputations? How should the practice of investment banking houses raiding and recruiting one another's star bankers be viewed?

Getting New Business

How far should investment banks go in winning new business? In competitive debt offerings, should bankers set prices very low to get competitors' business? (And what should be done about the practice of then going back, after having underbid everyone else and won the business, and re-negotiating the price?) It's easy to promise, but it's harder to deliver. How close should a banker match conviction of promise with certainty of performance?

Winning

What should be the price of victory? To what extent should you go to win a corporate acquisition? In the page-one corporate megadeals, reputations rise or fall. A corporate war is the blood lust of investment banking. Everything is sacrificed for success. But what happens when principles are compromised in the quest for triumph?

Loyalty

Does loyalty have any meaning in investment banking? Should a bank (commercial or investment) ever side with a new client against an old client in a corporate takeover battle? Corporations have become furious at their bankers when such circumstances developed — long-standing relationships were strained or severed. Regarding the bonds between investment bankers and their firms, does the individual have any moral obligation to the firm beyond the current deal and the expected bonus? What happens when bankers switch firms? Should they take their client lists — and their clients — with them? And should competing firms poach personnel to attract new clients?

Fees

When is enough enough? Is there no limit to the size of fees? Should fees have some appropriate cap, or should market supply and demand tell the whole story? Are multimillion-dollar fees for merger and acquisition advice good for the industry? What about when M&A work is not in the best interest of the client? Can an investment banker give advice *not* to make a deal, when such advice flies in the face of enhancing firm reputation and maintaining personal pay?

Merger and Acquisition Churning

The enormity of generated fees cannot help but cast M&A activity in a new light. In recent years M&A has produced an abnormally high percentage of investment banking profits. There is great danger of churning — constantly identifying ("teeing up") companies and initiating procedures for M&A (putting them "in play") in order to collect fees. As conglomerates are built, sold, and dismantled, investment bankers make money at each stage. They take several bites of the same apple.

Trading and Securities Churning

Brokers are paid by commission; the more trades they make, the more money they make. If there are no trades, then there is no money. In a game scored exclusively with money, one can be tempted to make more trades than are necessary for optimum performance. (Indeed, several studies have shown that the cost of securities transactions is an important factor in overall returns, and that turnover minimization produces the best long-term results.) One can even delude oneself into rationalizing that the churning is in the best interests of the client. The churning of accounts is a classic problem. This is why it is better for managers of funds to be paid as a percentage of net profits (which is even better than a percentage of assets under management).

Loss Leaders

Is it appropriate to price an underwriting close to cost (or even below) in order to win the business, planning to make it all back and more as a result of establishing a relationship with a new client company and expecting to profit by securities trading, subsequent financings, M&A relationships, and the like? Japanese security firms have come to dominate the Euromarkets through very aggressive pricing policies that have driven back their competition. Certainly, the cost of capital for issuing firms has come down. But what are the long-term effects of squeezing out competitors? Should running an investment bank be like running a department store? The jury is still out.

Ownership

Should investment banks own operating companies? Investment banks are becoming more entrepreneurial of late. But should they become players, competing against their own clients or acquisitions? What about sharing ownership with client companies? Some investment banks like rolling over part of their fees into equity. (This way they cannot lose.) But when investment banks become partners with clients, what happens to the fiduciary relationship?

Merchant Banking

Merchant banking is extraordinarily profitable. When a firm's capital is on the line, or when it accumulates vast financing fees, does its advice maintain the same level of quality? When an investment bank puts up its own capital, does the character of the relationship change?

Risk/Reward Tradeoffs

Understanding risk/reward tradeoffs is the essence of finance (see Chapter 3). The more successful financial participants and players shift the tradeoff well to the reward side. But is there a limit to the shift? Investment bankers that underwrite very risky companies take very high percentages of the proceeds in fees, expenses, and warrants. Granted, the risks here are very high. The question is who should get the extra rewards to compensate for the extra risks—the investment bankers or the actual, check-writing investors?

Mistakes

Investment bankers, like normal human beings, make mistakes. Should they admit such errors? Should they try to make amends? Sometimes the amounts are enormous and the potential liabilities would be staggering. (In our litigious society it is dangerous to admit error.) What should an investment bank do when it incurs a multimillion-dollar trading loss through incorrect trades? A cover-up may dig the hole deeper.

A different kind of mistake occurs when an investment bank just does not know what it is doing. Misjudging the prepayment rates of certain mortgage-backed instruments or not realizing the volatility of interest-only/principle-only products can result in enormous losses even before one realizes what is happening (see Chapter 20).

Misleading Statistics

Figures lie, they say, and liars figure. Using misleading statistics is a common business practice, but the flagrant abuse of such deceit is an art form on Wall Street. Cherry-picking underwriting cases and M&A stories are commonplace. Similarly, firms may only report the best-performing of their many investment funds. They may choose their time periods with exquisite precision to maximize apparent returns.

Restructuring financial statements of sale and divestiture candidates can yield illogical results based on logical assumptions. This is especially true for private companies (see Chapter 7). It is possible that while each hypothetical restructuring assumption may be reasonable individually, the simultaneous effect of all of them produces artificial profits that may appear plausible but are actually impossible.[3] And what if a prospective buyer believes the pro forma nature of the numbers? Are vigilance

---

3. Restructuring assumptions made when corporate divisions are being divested often subtract out all head office allocations in order to boost the division's operating profit line and induce a higher sale price. Yet there may be vital functions and services included in the eliminated expenses such as insurance, personnel, legal services, and the like.

and intelligence a buyer's only protection, or do the seller's investment bankers have a broader responsibility than just optimizing price for the client?

Personal Compensation

How do investment banks allocate income to personnel? Should senior bankers take the greater majority? What should a banker do when he or she must choose between a deal in which a personal bonus is promised and one where the firm will benefit more? (or one where the client will benefit more?)

Personal Life

Investment bankers work long hours. They will go nonstop to complete a deal, especially when power and prestige are on the line. But when does such sacrifice become unethical in the broader sense of the term? Is it morally right to ignore one's family in quest of investment banking glory?

Cultural Relativism

Should a banker impose personal standards on others? Irrespective of circumstances, are ethics always the same? Many American business people have erred by trying to impose American values on non-American cultures. On the other hand, in many countries it is almost impossible to do business without bribery and kickbacks. However camouflaged or disguised, should one violate one's own ethics (not to mention American law) by engaging in such accepted behavior?

Superiority and Condescension

Contemporary finance is highly complex, and the technical knowledge has become arcane and virtually inaccessible to ordinary corporate people. Although not often intended, it is easy for investment bankers to make their clients feel inferior, treating them as if they were children. It is embarrassingly easy for investment bankers, especially young hotshots, to irritate older, operating executives.

Justifying Position and Fees

The huge fees paid to investment banks and the enormous compensation packages paid to investment bankers create a vicious cycle of unrealistic expectations. The banks and the bankers now must justify these monumental payments. This means that they may feel compelled to make huge returns, which often entails taking huge risks. Some of the largest trading losses have occurred because the traders' giant salaries had to be justified.

Similarly, many investment banks (and bankers) have become hooked on the financing highs of huge M&A fees. No longer an unexpected bonus to the individual bankers, to the M&A department, and to the firm as a whole, these fees are now considered normal income and any decrease in dollars is accompanied by a proportional increase in depression. The natural result of this greatly heightened expectation is substantial pressure for investment bankers to stimulate, instigate, initiate, and inaugurate new M&A deals. Previously assistants and advisors to their corporate clients, M&A bankers have become supervisors and overseers. (The tail-wagging-the-dog cliche does seem to fit.)

Special Consideration

Are there any circumstances where special consideration should be given? For example, should minority-owned companies or personnel be encouraged in affirmative action–type programs? Should investment banks be deterred from participating in hostile takeover situations due to opposition from various special interest groups (e.g., unions and local communities)? Recall the flap when Shearson Lehman Hutton joined with Beazer PLC to go after Koppers Co. Pittsburgh civic leaders and Pennsylvania politicians came after the large investment bank with a vengeance, including national advertisements and the stoppage of financial relationships. Does Wall Street have social responsibilities other than providing capital for commerce?

Political Campaigns

How actively should investment bankers participate in politics? Should bankers be finance chairpersons for political candidates? Should they participate in political action committees (PACs) and lobbying trade associations? Wall Street firms have extensive lobbying operations in Washington. Regulation and tax law have a heavy impact on investment banking.

Boycotts and Social Conscience

Should investment bankers participate in boycotts? For example, should a banker refuse to finance companies doing business in South Africa?

Should they honor the Arab boycott against Israel? Should they deal with tobacco companies?

Whistle Blowing

Should investment bankers report the infractions of peers? subordinates? superiors? friends? If one knows that a colleague is acting irresponsibly or immorally, does he or she have a moral responsibility to intervene? Should the person be approached privately? And if the improper action is not stopped, then should the firm be informed? Should the legal authorities? The issue becomes more difficult when the improper action is more unethical than illegal. For example, when a research analyst questions a security that his or her firm is selling (as happened with the defaulted WPPSS bonds), he or she should not hesitate to publish the report.

Legal Boundaries

How close do you get to the edge? Is *chicken* a game for investment bankers who play with other people's money? For example, is it ethical to test new theories of law in order to gain personal acclaim even though the risk is great for the client?

Firm Status: Who Are We and What Do We Stand For?

Good ethics are predicated on a strong sense of self. One cannot establish standards without knowing one's identity. Several investment banks have maintained a strict proscription against participating in hostile takeovers of any kind. Other banks have joined the fray more recently, only after watching both the generation of enormous fees and the movement of hostile takeovers into the accepted mainstream of business finance. An investment bank that primarily represents clients seeking acquisitions will have a different mentality than a merchant bank that largely manages its own money. It is vital for investment banks to have a clear sense of purpose and niche.

Ethical Recommendations for Investment Bankers

The following 15 categories are ethical recommendations for investment bankers. They are designed to stimulate thought. (Do not expect these recommendations to answer all questions.) This list is representative, not exhaustive. There are more potential solutions than these.

Competence

Competence is not often considered part of ethics. That is a major mistake. One of the most damaging ethical errors characteristic of investment bankers is promising more than they can deliver. Sometimes it's a matter of wanting to win the business. Sometimes it's a matter of over-estimating their abilities. At all times, it's a serious betrayal of client confidence. Ethical investment bankers must always believe that they can deliver exactly what they promise. They cannot always live up to these promises, but they should always believe them when they make them. (Because of the critical nature of investment banking—a company's financial future is at stake—a healthy dose of realism is a desirable personality trait. Investment bankers should think more like physicians than marketeers.)

Optimization

Optimize does not mean *maximize*. The latter means getting the *most*, the former getting the *best*. The best is often not the most, although it can be, of course. The best is always conditional and contingent (i.e., the best under the circumstances, the best given current constraints). Arranging a merger or acquisition may generate the greatest fee for an investment bank but it may not be in the best interest for either buyer or seller.

Similarly, getting the highest price for a client company in an initial public offering (IPO) is clearly the *most* (maximum), but it may not be the *best* (optimal). If the after-market price of the securities falls and the company's market reputation becomes tarnished (i.e., investors grow sour and the future cost of capital rises) then that great price would not be as great. An optimal solution to IPO pricing would be obtaining the highest price that still allows investors to make decent money and feel good about the company; such an outcome would reduce the company's ultimate cost of capital by favorably affecting future financings.

Confidentiality

The simplest rule is never to tell anything about clients that does not need to be told. The less said the better. A client should never have to ask its banker to maintain confidentiality. Such secrecy should always be assumed unless specifically excluded. A need to know is the only reason to ever tell. Even within the investment bank itself, strict confidentiality

194 Principles and Techniques of Investment Banking

must be respected. Most investment banks impose rigid, restricted lists of those particular corporations that they are advising or working with in a confidential manner (such as on M&A deals). This restricted list means that no trader, sales person, M&A associate, or any other employee of the firm may buy or sell securities of those listed corporations either for client accounts or for their own accounts. The investment bank (or bankers) cannot benefit from securities trading as long as that company remains on the restricted list.

Compartmentalization

Confidentiality is facilitated by compartmentalization. This is the famous *Chinese Wall* that divides traders from bankers. When corporate finance people know of an imminent bankruptcy in which their trust department is heavily invested, their obligation of silence is no less than if the upcoming event was a major merger. Illicitly minimizing loss is the same as illicitly maximizing gain.

Respect the Law

To *respect* means more than to obey. Investment bankers, as finance professionals, must take the high road and set the proper example for clients and colleagues. Such an exhortation must be more than a platitude because, in the financing and securities business, the high road is sometimes hard to take. In a business where making more money means everything, illegal acts often seem like clever shortcuts to success. Always remember that investment bankers have no obligation to support a client's illegal or immoral activities. Indeed, helping a client commit criminal or unsavory acts makes a banker and his or her firm accomplices in the crime or corruption, and makes him or her criminally liable and/or morally defiled. Investment bankers have a resolute duty to advise clients on even minor infractions.

Judgment

No plan is perfect; few solutions are without flaw. Investment banking is an art as well as a science; insight is as important as analysis. Investment bankers are paid for their experience and sense and must exercise their best judgment in all situations. Shrinking from giving advice because of fear of failure is almost as unethical as giving advice known to be wrong.

Integrity and Forthrightness

Investment banking is a business based on confidence. Client companies pay enormous fees because of the critical nature—and high financial leverage—of the advice. Investment bankers have an absolute obligation not to abuse that confidence by exaggerating their sense of certainty. When offering advice, they should take pains to articulate their degree of confidence in that advice. If they are unsure, they should say so. If they are guessing, they should admit it. Clients appreciate such honesty; it builds confidence and relationships; it will not destroy them. Be open without being naïve. Be sure that all that you say is true, although you need not say all that is true. The best way not to be caught in lies is not to tell them.

Singlemindedness

Singlemindedness is the only antidote for the pernicious poison of conflict of interest. Objectives should be clear, focused, and resolute. Complex issues should always be evaluated in the context of one client's purposes and welfare. Investment bankers should rarely have to weigh the interests of opposing forces or parties. In virtually every investment banking situation, conflicts should be absent and interests undivided. (Sometimes conflicts cannot be avoided. Here the clear duty is full disclosure.)

Consistency

Consistency is one of the true tests of professionalism. You always do your best, irrespective of client or compensation. Investment bankers may not always give *the* best, but they should always give *their* best. Peak performance should be a regular event. Also, one must bend backwards not to take advantage of client weaknesses or vulnerabilities. (This can be difficult since an investment banker's mind is conditioned to take advantage of such weaknesses or vulnerabilities in competitors.) Similarly, one must avoid the tendency to churn accounts or companies, whether in securities trading or M&A. (Consider the analogy to a surgeon performing unnecessary operations.)

What an investment bank will and will not do should also be consistent (and hopefully founded on good values and sound logic). The original condescending air of moral revulsion voiced by certain investment banks toward large, junk-bond-financed leveraged buyouts was quietly forgotten once the success of such ventures became apparent (not to mention the gargantuan fees.) Such inconsistency taints the entire moral tone of an organization. Morality should be maintained with at least some absolute standards and not as the flamboyant cheerleader for parochial interests.

Respect, Patience, and Sensitivity

Investment bankers should respect their clients; they should treat them with consideration and courtesy. Patience is also important. Investment bankers are much like physicians. They should develop their bedside manners with operational officers of client companies. Investment bankers deal with the life's work of these senior executives, who have every right to understand fully what is happening. Sensitivity to differing cultures (whether corporate or national) is also important. Remember, investment bankers start out with a negative reputation that is part haughtiness and part greed. They must work hard just to get back up to zero.

Investment Bankers are Human Beings

The broad view of ethics encompasses attitudes as well as actions. Investment bankers should be able to vote their consciences like other members of the body politic. If they are opposed to doing business with South Africa, they should not do so. If they object to sexist or racist remarks or prejudices of any kind they should not remain quiet.

Ethics Inside the Firm

Interpersonal relationships within firms are also areas of ethical concern. Indeed, the moral atmosphere of the internal organization will influence greatly how each member of that organization behaves on external assignments. Competition personifies investment banking, both with respect to the firm's position in the industry and the individual's career in the firm. Politics can get rough in investment banks. Political gamesmanship is to be expected in any organization and obsessive concern for one's career is particularly strong when the financial stakes are so high.

It is the responsibility of top management to establish the right corporate environment, the exquisite balance between morality and rivalry. Value ethics; but do not dull the competitive edge.

Personal Characteristics

How does one keep the competitive spirit strong and not give in to the temptations of easy answers and tricky triumphs? Many successful investment bankers take their work but not themselves seriously. They inject humor into their life, often on the self-deprecating side. They radiate a quiet confidence, not needing the artificial boosters of strut and swagger, put-down and put over. Domineering personalities are shooting stars—big flash and fast burnout. Team success is important. Credit and glory should flow in all directions.

Appearance is Reality

Form is substance. There is no way that having the risk arbitrage and the M&A departments report to the same executive can appear proper—since perceived (or real) self-dealing or stock manipulation would become readily apparent. Similarly, when firms allow employees to purchase hot securities for their own accounts, this gives the impression of favoring one's self over one's clients (even of penalizing one's clients). Finally, we would all do well to follow the wisdom of the wise: Assume that everything that you ever do will be reported in full on the first page of the *Wall Street Journal*—then make your ethical decision.

Full Disclosure

Full disclosure is most important. It is the touchstone of ethics for investment bankers. We list it last because we want you to remember it. If there is any one test that could cleanse almost any ethical impurity or that could make moral almost any questionable circumstance, full disclosure is it.

Full disclosure means what it says: Tell everything; let it all hang out. If you have related-party transactions between a public company and its officers, you must reveal them. If your firm puts out a research report on a company but is also marketing (or owning) its securities, you should tell the world. If you recommend an acquisition in which you have a healthy equity position, say so up front. If you are representing all sides in a three-company transaction and if everyone on all three sides knows everything, you are clean. (Not squeaky clean, but clean nonetheless.) Your wisdom may be questioned, but not your honesty.

Responsibility and Action

Ethics in investment banking revolves around corporate culture, rules and regulations, and individual compliance. Investment banking houses can be envisioned as a loose collection of strong-minded entrepreneurs, each of whom is committed to (or obsessed with) task achievement and personal advancement.

In such a complex organizational environment the role of management is especially crucial. Leadership here must be won; it cannot be dictated. Attitudes are established more by example than by command.

What control methods can top management of investment banks use? Codes of conduct should be discussed and debated, not just printed and posted. Specific examples should be thought through; vague generalizations make eyelids grow heavy.

There should be a tough internal system of surveillance and control. Specific systems should be established and special personnel should be assigned to make them work. Practices should be policed, and infractions should be punished. The penalties for transgressions should be known and publicized.

But such enforcement must not be heavy-handed. An investment bank cannot be a totalitarian state. Individual freedom is the life force of creative, dynamic action. Individual freedom must be protected, not truncated. So we stress this point: Administered properly, ethical systems will actually engender more freedom, not less—freedom from fear, freedom from unfair competition, and freedom from uncertainty. Ethics should be viewed as a great liberator in investment banking.

Hiring practices and training programs should make ethics central, not peripheral. Employers must explain explicitly to all recruits from day one of their employment what conduct will be tolerated, what latitude will be permitted, and how severely ethical or legal problems will be viewed.

Stress the positive side: Ethics in investment banking is an asset, not a liability. It is a sure way to enhance company reputation, increase company business, and augment personal value. With ethical issues in business so visible, clients are more sensitive to their investment bankers' standards of conduct—and more appreciative of upright behavior. Increasingly, clients want to be represented by firms that are known for their high principles and impeccable morals. Ethics in investment banking has become a new weapon of competitive power.

CHAPTER 11

Personality of Investment Bankers*

Investment banking is a people business, and good people make it work. But good people are not random events: they should be properly recognized, positioned, encouraged, and appreciated. Investment banking is a service industry and a firm's primary assets walk out the door every evening. The bottom line is that human relationships overwhelm technical knowledge.

In this chapter we consider individual personality in investment banking from three perspectives: (1) the importance of diversity in background and temperament, (2) a description of personality types required in large organizations, and (3) a personality profile of traditional investment bankers.

Strength in Diversity

Despite the common perception of personality stereotypes in investment banking, diversity is more important than conformity to any contempo-

---

*This chapter has been derived from "Individual Personality in Investment Banking" by Robert Lawrence Kuhn, Volume I (Investing and Risk Management), Dow Jones-Irwin's *The Library of Investment Banking* (1990), Robert Lawrence Kuhn, editor in chief.

rary organization. A portfolio theory approach can apply as much to personnel as it does to securities: A certain amount of variety generates more reward for less risk.

Diversity should cover all the facets of personnel characteristics. Broad backgrounds should be represented in investment banking organizations—avoid any exclusivity of gender, race, religion, geography, academic background, work experience, or outside interests. The only characteristics that all investment bankers should share are high competence, high energy, and professional commitment.

Why the need for diversity? While this might make good public policy, the motive in investment banking here is pure profit. Look at the long term: the world is changing.

New Thinking

New thinking is a prime reason for encouraging diversity. People from different backgrounds have different approaches to common problems and fresh views on current issues. In any given situation, music or math majors might not react in the same way as would economics or finance majors. An MA in comparative literature might see angles that an MBA would miss. Diversity is the best antidote to the poison of group think.

New Energy

In an economic environment cauterized by constant and often dramatic change, the status quo can be a deadly enemy of investment banking vitality. Here is where personnel diversity makes a positive contribution. When dissimilar people come together, a certain tension normally develops. This can be beneficial. The status quo is disrupted; everyone is more alert, more expectant, and more ready to make and accept changes.

New Business

New business is another reason for encouraging diversity. The investment banking universe is changing. New clients—from international corporations to domestic municipalities—are being run by more heterogeneous leaders, and investment banks must deal with the new realities. The greater the scope of its bankers, the greater the reach of the bank. One never knows from where new business will come.

Personality Types in Investment Banks

Though the range of human personality is exceptionally broad, we deem four categories especially important to investment banking organizations. While not everyone can be grouped into one of these categories (and some might make multiple categories), most investment bankers fit one of the following descriptions.

Business-builders

These are the rainmakers—the people who develop the client relationships, who maintain the flow of business, and who generate the opportunity to provide service and collect fees. Business-builders have strong, magnetic personalities, but their strengths and lines of force do not always flow in the same direction. Again, this is good. The scientific chief executive of a high technology medical company might like discussing particle physics or neurobiology more than social events or charitable affairs. Business-builders do not have to be good golfers or join exclusive country clubs, yet many are and many do. The one unifying factor among rainmakers is an intense desire to achieve and a real interest in people.

Analysts

These are the eggheads—the people who make the models, calculate the numbers, solve the equations, program the computers, and run the spreadsheets. They generally operate in a supporting role, but can be taken to clients as part of a presenting or implementing team. Do not underestimate analysts: Business-builders make the promises; analysts deliver the goods. Builders procure the first assignment; analysts secure the repeat business. Analysts value substance over form. They desire financial compensation as much as anyone else, but they glow when someone appreciates their technical excellence.

Innovators

These are the creative ones—the people who devise the new client products, the novel financial instruments, and the fresh merger and acquisition ideas. Innovators do not hit many home runs; failures outnumber successes by wide margins—but a good batting average is not what is important here. One good innovation can generate enormous amounts in direct investment banking fees, not to mention the incalculable indirect benefits to image and reputation. Innovators are not easy to employ. They may irritate and aggravate, but they will never sit or stagnate.

Administrators

These are the managers—the people who maintain the organization, who enable each banker to do his or her best job, and who pull the team together. Getting hot-shot investment bankers to work together is no trivial matter. Ego and emotion match deal size and bonuses. Personality conflicts abound. More than one firm has been shaken by uncontrolled traders running wild or back-office snarls grinding down. Good administrators must monitor, regulate, and restrict; they must steer, guide, and control; they are essential in investment banking.

Personality Characteristics of Good Deal Makers

Good investment bankers must make good deals. The reverse is also true: Good deals are made by good investment bankers. What personality traits determine a good deal maker? Demeanor, disposition, and manner are critical success factors. A would-be investment banker deal maker who maintains poor personal character traits starts every inning with two outs, two strikes, and a knuckleball zig-zagging toward his leaden bat. Why start a tough game at such a disadvantage?

The following seven categories of personality characteristics are important for being (or becoming) a good deal maker. They are exemplified in the best investment bankers working today.

Achievement and Accomplishment

Good deal makers are like successful entrepreneurs. They are motivated more by inner glow than outer show. They have a never-ending sense of urgency and are attracted to challenges, not risks. Power is important, but it is the power to make things happen, not the power to boss subordinates. They would rather consummate a deal from their makeshift, garage office than command a huge corporate division from an elegant, executive suite.

Commitment and Dedication

Good deal makers invest themselves in all their deals. Psyche and ego are always on the line. They consider their current deal, whatever the size or substance, to be just about the most important thing in the world, and on it alone does the sun rise and set. The day begins early and ends late. Fervent conversations with other deal participants proceed virtually nonstop. There is tension, insistence, and compulsion. The commitment must be wholehearted and the dedication monastic. These traits will not assure deal success, but omitting them can almost guarantee deal failure.

Focus and Intensity

Good deal makers shoot rifles, not shotguns. They define tight targets and never allow their eyes to waver from the bullseyes. To change the metaphor from shooting to fishing, hook good deal makers on good deals and they will swallow the line and sinker as well as the hook. They may miss other deadlines or appointments, but they blaze a one-track path for completing their deal.

Patience and Perseverance

Good deal makers never give up. Bulldogs all, they do not rest until every avenue and alternative is explored to exhaustion. A lost deal must be lost long before it is lost forever. They know how to wait, but they do not know how to quit. They have an exquisite sense of timing and have learned through experience that acting too quickly is as dangerous as reacting too late. They can read the verbal and nonverbal signs of deal participants on both sides of the table. They can discern the right moment for movement. Professionals know that sometimes no action is the most aggressive and powerful action that can be taken. The hardest thing for novice deal makers to do is nothing.

Sensitivity and Perceptiveness

Good deal makers read people well. They translate emotions and feelings into plans and action. They appreciate the potentially negative impact of seemingly innocent suggestions and off-handed remarks. They rarely have personality clashes and never turn opponents off. They find and push *hot buttons* of allies and adversaries. They genuinely like people and thereby achieve competitive advantage.

Integrity and Consistency

Good deal makers can be trusted. They say what they mean and perform what they promise. They are not volatile or mercurial. They know from experience that truth is easier to remember than fiction, and that a reputation for honesty is the best advertisement for future business.[1]

Creativity and Innovation

Good deal makers try new tacks if old ones stall. They are never at a loss for fresh suggestions to circle obstacles, bridge gaps, and scale walls. They use diverse techniques to devise unexpected responses to troublesome situations. Originality in deal making becomes both a process facilitator and a content contributor, stimulating helpful interaction among people as well as suggesting specific ideas to resolve deal points.[2]

---

1. There is an Armenian proverb that asks whether one can trust going down into a well with the person in question holding the rope. With a good deal maker you can descend deep.

2. But what happens when more investment bankers develop into vibrant new deal makers? Am I concerned that the cluttered marketplace will make my own deal-making life more competitive? No. The more really good deal makers are working, the more really good deals are made. Good deal makers do not require bad deal makers as their natural prey. Rather, good deal makers on both sides of transactions increase the overall quantity and improve the overall quality of deals being made. Good deals enhance the reputation of all deal makers. I look forward to meeting you.

PART II

FINANCING AND CAPITAL-RAISING IN INVESTMENT BANKING

CHAPTER 12

Financial Instruments and Products*

Corporate finance, for all its modern complexity, is built on the twin principles of focus and purpose. The reason why so many financing securities exist is that each fulfills a very specific objective better than does any other security. But just trying to remember all the instruments, vehicles, and products—much less understand how they all work—is a daunting task. This chapter offers several classification systems which may assist both memory and comprehension.

Elements of Corporate Finance

Corporate finance has three essential elements:

1. obtaining the lowest cost of capital (financial strategy),
2. obtaining capital that most properly matches sources to uses (financial structure), and
3. obtaining optimum value for investments (financial return).

The fundamental principle of linking risk with return applies to all three: Seekers and providers of capital each desire to obtain the highest

---

* This chapter has been derived from "Financial Securities and Instruments: Classifications and Characteristics" by Robert Lawrence Kuhn, Volume III (Corporate and Municipal Securities), Dow Jones-Irwin's *The Library of Investment Banking* (1990), Robert Lawrence Kuhn, editor-in-chief.

returns commensurate with acceptable levels of risk (see Chapter 3). Financial strategy, structure, and return all benefit from a deep understanding of the instruments.

Catalysts of Financial Innovation

The last decade has witnessed an explosion of new financial products as investment banks compete for power and prestige. There have been at least five catalysts:

1. the volatility of financial markets, primarily the unprecedented swings in interest and exchange rates,
2. the progressive deregulation of financial markets in the United States, Europe, and Japan,
3. the penchant for higher liquidity on the part of holders of small debts (e.g., mortgages, car loans, etc.),
4. the desire for greater financial flexibility to handle the dynamic structure of contemporary business,
5. the demand for substantial levels of financing to support the aggressive advance of corporate mergers, acquisitions, and ventures.

The process is continuous and recursive. No longer can investment bankers be satisfied with simply locking in long-term rates for their clients at some local low point. Now they must hunt continuously for optimum borrowing conditions and be ready to exchange old instruments for new ones as if trading in used cars for new models.

Classification Systems and Chapter Purpose

The purpose of this chapter is to organize financial instruments into understandable classes with similar characteristics. Organization helps understanding. We intend this framework to offer some perspective on the bewildering assortment of financial securities, instruments, vehicles, and products available currently. Our objective is comprehension, not comprehensiveness (if the former is difficult, the latter is impossible). The more investment bankers appreciate the internal logic underlying and unifying the instruments, the better they can consider and suggest which ones make sense.

There are numerous possible classification systems for financial instruments. None has intrinsic superiority. Since our purpose is to give perspective, we present *several* classification systems. The benefit of these multiple and diverse systems is that each presents a view of the issue from a different outlook, and the multiple images so generated produce a three-dimensional portrait rich with detail. Such a picture enhances understanding.

We present five different classification systems, based on the following critical criteria: security heirarchy, product category, primary characteristics, payment pattern, and term period. (Many of these corporate securities and risk-related instruments are discussed in detail elsewhere in the book.)[1] Each of these classification systems, remember, describes the *same* financial instruments, but does so from different perspectives.

Classification by Security Hierarchy

The traditional categories used to group financial securities are characterized by their vertical position within the corporate hierarchy—a top-to-bottom description of the capital structure (i.e., secured debt, senior debt, high-yield debt, subordinate debt, convertible debt, preferred stock, convertible preferred stock, and common stock.)

Figure 12-1 portrays a hierarchy of corporate securities that forms a spectrum flowing from high risk/high return to low risk/low return (from an investor's perspective—investor risk/return is usually inversely proportional to issuer risk/return [see Chapter 3]).[2] The general categories of equity (common and preferred stock) and debt (high yield and investment grade) are blurred by a larger category of *quasi*-equity that includes virtually all of the preferred stock and high-yield debt. Many of the specific securities/instruments listed in Figure 12-1 are discussed later in this chapter and elsewhere in the book. (Note that secured debt is illustrated separately, since it is not directly related to the time line of the corporate life cycle or current corporate strength.)

---

1. *All* of the corporate securities and financial instruments presented in this chapter are described in depth in the seven-volume Dow Jones-Irwin *The Library of Investment Banking.* Numerous cases and numerical examples are provided to give working knowledge and practical understanding of these financial mechansims.

2. The linearity of the hierarchy is more a teaching tool than an actual fact. There is extensive overlap among these securities and instruments, and it is a mistake to think that instruments which occur later on the corporate time line cannot be used at earlier stages of a company's history.

Figure 12–1. Hierarchy of Corporate Securities.

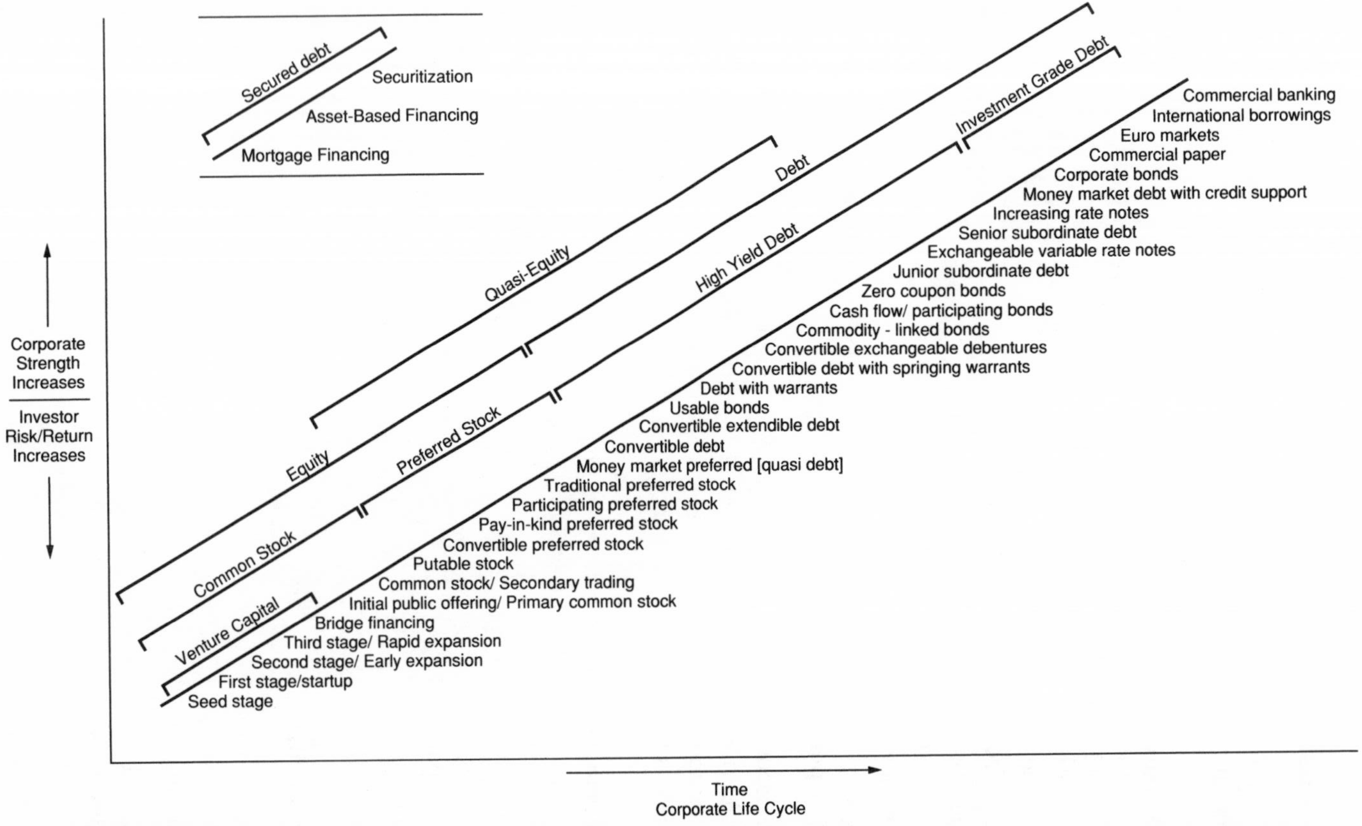

Corporate Strength Increases

Investor Risk/Return Increases

Time
Corporate Life Cycle

Secured debt
Securitization
Asset-Based Financing
Mortgage Financing

Debt
Investment Grade Debt

Commercial banking
International borrowings
Euro markets
Commercial paper
Corporate bonds
Money market debt with credit support
Increasing rate notes
Senior subordinate debt
Exchangeable variable rate notes
Junior subordinate debt
Zero coupon bonds
Cash flow/ participating bonds
Commodity - linked bonds
Convertible exchangeable debentures
Convertible debt with springing warrants
Debt with warrants

High Yield Debt

Quasi-Equity

Usable bonds
Convertible extendible debt
Convertible debt
Money market preferred [quasi debt]
Traditional preferred stock
Participating preferred stock
Pay-in-kind preferred stock

Preferred Stock

Convertible preferred stock
Putable stock
Common stock/ Secondary trading
Initial public offering/ Primary common stock

Equity
Common Stock

Venture Capital

Bridge financing
Third stage/ Rapid expansion
Second stage/ Early expansion
First stage
Seed stage/startup

Classification by Product Category

The following classification of financial instruments is structured by product category.

Money Market Instruments

Money market instruments are what comprise the wholesale market for low-risk, highly liquid, short-term obligations. Represented are the debts of the federal government (Treasury bills, notes, and bonds) including the federal agencies,[3] negotiable bank certificate of deposits, bankers' acceptances, municipal notes, and commercial paper. Eurodollars and *repos* (repurchase agreements or secured loans) are also part of the money market.

Corporate Instruments

Corporate instruments are issued by for-profit entities. The spectrum of securities ranges from the most senior secured debt to the most junior common equity. The variations are myriad, and the distinction between debt and equity has become blurred.

Partnership Instruments

Partnership instruments are direct investments in assets held for income generation, capital appreciation, and/or tax considerations. Limited partnership instruments are usually private placements, while master limited partnerships are publicly traded. Partnership instruments are almost always debt securities with high relative returns and convertibility or participation features.

Securitized Instruments

Securitized instruments are debt securities that are supported by real or hard assets. These collateralized instruments are the product of the pooling (rolling up) of small-denomination obligations and debts into instruments that look like traditional bonds. By repackaging small, illiquid, consumer receivables into large, liquid, publicly-traded securities—

---

3. Such as Government National Mortgage Association (Ginnie Mae) and Federal National Mortgage Association (Fannie Mae).

securitizing them—an issuer can attract a broader investor market and hence achieve a lower interest rate. (The creation of liquidity is the key, which, along with the explicit collateralization, reduces investor risk and hence issuer interest rates.)

These collateralized securities, issued primarily by financial institutions, are backed by pools of assets, the cash flow of which cover the interest and principal payments due on the securities. Investors rely on the collateral and not the issuer's credit, for assurance of debt service and principal repayment. The majority of outstanding collateralized instruments are mortgage-related (i.e., residential and commercial real estate receivables), primarily those guaranteed by the three federally-supported housing agencies. These instruments permit savings-and-loans to sell their mortgages and gain the greatly desired liquidity.

A proliferation of securitized products has used a variety of other assets to back securities: car loans, credit card obligations, insurance premiums—conceivably, receivables of all kinds. In theory, securities can be written on any asset for which the cash flow and risk can be predicted.

Hedging Instruments

Hedging instruments are products that mitigate risk that arises from volatility in interest rates, currency exchange rates, commodity prices, individual stock prices, and stock market movements. By nature, hedging instruments are highly leveraged. The primary products are options, futures, swaps, and indexes. Many of the recent innovations in finance have been in hedging instruments.

International Instruments

International instruments are financial securities floated outside an issuer's own national market. Even companies that do not have foreign operations can now access money overseas. Companies can raise capital and hedge risk wherever optimal irrespective of domicile, geography, or currency.

There is an enormous variety of international financial products arrayed across the debt-to-equity spectrum. (Government debt is the largest source of international financial securities.) Borrowings from commerical paper to long-term debentures can be in Eurodollars, Swiss francs, or Japanese yen almost as easily as U.S. dollars. Bonds may be denominated in one currency (e.g., Swiss francs) and interest paid in another (e.g., U.S. dollars). Foreign-currency-denominated bonds may be sold to investors in that foreign country or in other places (e.g., sterling-denominated bonds issued by foreign companies in the U.K., called bulldogs; yen-denominated bonds issued by foreign companies in Japan, called samurai; non-yen-denominated bonds issued by foreign companies in Japan, called shogun). By taking advantage of fleeting opportunities in foreign financial markets, some companies have been able to borrow at rates lower than even the U.S. Treasury can obtain.

Municipal Instruments

Municipal instruments are issued by national, state, and local governments to fund a variety of general and specific obligations. Such governmental debt comprises a good part of the world financial markets. (There may be tax benefits associated with municipal instruments.)

Classification by Primary Characteristics

The following classification of financial instruments is structured by primary characteristics:

Fixed-Rate Instruments

Fixed-rate instruments are traditional income-generating notes and bonds that are immutable in structure. The terms and conditions do not change following purchase. For example, fixed-rate debt has a given coupon and that coupon remains constant for the life of the instrument.

Flexible-Rate Instruments

Flexible-rate instruments are income-generating notes and bonds that have a coupon that can change. Such a change may relate to a wide variety of independent variables: prevailing interest rates, issuer's performance, commodity prices, stock prices, payment schedules, and the like. Two examples are floating-rate notes with interest-rate caps (upper limits) or collars (upper and lower limits),[4] and continuously offered long-term securities (COLTS) where the interest rate is set daily in accordance with a market rate.

---

4. Investors require some discount for bonds with interest-rate caps, and depending on the specific terms of an interest-rate collar, a discount or a premium may be appropriate.

Exchangeable Instruments

Exchangeable instruments are income-generating debt and equity that, at the election of either issuer or investor, can be changed into another instrument. An example would be a preferred stock that can be exchanged for a subordinated debt (with similar features, interest rate, and convertibility). A company with a tax loss carryforward may be able to offer preferred stock as its instrument of lowest capital cost (considering the tax benefits to some investors)—but may want the right to exchange the preferred stock into subordinated debt (where the interest paid would be deductible). Preferred stock may be better in the short term (when the company is not a taxpayer), while subordinated debt may be better in the long term (when the company becomes a taxpayer).

Participating Instruments

Participating instruments are securities that entitle the bearer to share in the financial output of the issuer. Such participations can relate to revenues, profits, and/or cash flow as established by some preset formula. Two example securities are cash flow bonds and participating preferred stocks. Partnership interests, including master limited partnerships, are generally participating instruments.

Convertible Instruments

Convertible instruments are income-generating debt (usually subordinated) and preferred stock that can be changed into another instrument, normally common stock at a preset price or formula. Issuers reduce interest or dividend rates by offering investors upside participations. The convertibility factor adds value to the original instrument, thereby enabling a lower-than-market interest rate to be realized. (Convertible instruments are, in essence, a fixed-income security combined with a free call option.) Bonds with warrants, either detachable or cemented, are similar to convertible instruments (although detachable warrants are obviously more flexible and therefore more valuable).

Convertible instruments are often used for mezzanine levels of finance (i.e., debt layered in between senior bank lending and equity investments). Such high-risk debt, common to venture capital and leveraged buyouts, usually demands rates of return between 20 and 40 percent. Since few companies can afford to pay such rates of interest, the convertible feature allows some equity-level participation to augment the stated interest rate.

Primary Equity Instruments

Primary equity instruments represent the shareholder ownership of a company. Equity involves the least risk to the issuer (its priority is last in liquidation) and the highest risks and returns to the investor. Holders of common stock may have diverse voting and valuation participations. Supervoting classes of stock (e.g., 100 votes per share) enable control to be ensured while selling equity to raise capital.

Swapping Instruments

Swapping instruments provide a method for exchanging debt obligations between two or more parties in order to reduce the risk and/or increase the return for both parties. Swaps work because different entities have different comparative advantages when pricing various categories of debt. Parties of dissimilar credit ratings or financing needs can exchange their obligations (e.g., from floating-rate into fixed-rate instruments and vice versa) in order to optimize their financial strategy and structure. (See Chapter 19.)

Forward-looking Instruments

Forward-looking instruments place a financial bet on the future price of some interest rate, currency rate, stock price, commodity price, index, and the like. Futures and forward contracts can be categorized within this classification. Such bets can be naked, highly-leveraged gambles (whether informed or intuitive) or carefully structured parts of a complex hedging program to optimize the risk/return tradeoff (i.e., reaching the most efficient sector—the outer limits—of the risk/return frontier).

Derivative Instruments

Derivative instruments are products that are second-order reflections of primary securities. For example, options are second-order reflections of the underlying stock. Derivative instruments are highly leveraged, augmenting risk and return.

Synthetic Instruments

Synthetic instruments are artificial securities constructed by combining or pulling apart real securities. For example, Treasury notes and bonds can be stripped into a series of yearly tranches that meet the highly focused requirements of investors who must match maturities of assets with liabilities.[5] Other examples are the (highly volatile) principal only and interest only instruments that are the disaggregate components of more traditional bonds.

Tax-Advantaged Instruments

Tax-advantaged instruments—debt that offers tax benefits to investors—can produce financial efficiency. The results are simple: lower taxes for investors mean lower rates for issuers. Industrial revenue bonds (IRBs) have long been used to reduce the cost of capital by giving investors tax-free interest and therefore lower coupon rates. Dutch auction preferred stock (DART) enables corporate investors to exclude 70–85 percent of dividends while still receiving close-to-market rates due to the frequent auction process. Multinational companies with profits in numerous countries should consider borrowing in those countries with higher relative tax rates in order to maximize the debt's tax shield (although local tax law may not be that cooperative and repatriation of funds may not be that simple).

Classification by Payment Pattern

The following classification of financial instruments is structured by payment pattern:

Guaranteed Pay Instruments

Guaranteed pay instruments require payment of a specified amount on a specified schedule irrespective of circumstances or conditions. For example, most investment-grade corporate bonds require quarterly interest payments no matter what.

Securitized Pay Instruments

Securitized pay instruments are similar to guaranteed pay instruments in that they require payment of a specified amount on a specified schedule

---

5. To continue the example, a $100 million 10-year Treasury note paying nine percent interest could be stripped into ten synthetic zero-coupon-bond tranches, each paying $9 million in one-shot bullets as they mature in sequential years, and one $100 million synthetic zero-coupon-bond tranche paying the entire $100 million face value at maturity at the end of the tenth year. Investors who purchase such specific instruments have extremely specific financing needs.

irrespective of circumstances or conditions. Securitized instruments differ in that they are collateralized by hard assets (e.g., mortgage-backed bonds). Examples range from traditional asset-based financing to innovative securitization products.

Contingent Pay Instruments

Contingent pay instruments require payment of a specified amount on a specified schedule only if certain conditions are met. For example, a cash flow or participation bond would relate payment to the performance of an enterprise; a formula is set and payment is made. Another example is an earn-out security given as consideration in an acquisition.

Resetting Pay Instruments

Resetting pay instruments are structured so that their coupon rates or yields can change according to a specific formula, time period, or set of events. For example, auction-rate preferred stocks are reset every 49 days; increasing-rate notes are often adjusted upward every quarter,[6] and some convertible bonds have a reset price for conversion into common stock if the stock price drops below a specified amount in a specified time period.

Mismatch pricing is a technique for pricing debt that resets the interest coupon rate at more frequent periods than the rollover period. For example, an instrument with a twelve-month rollover period may be reset monthly. Fixed-rate notes can have rates readjusted at one (or more) specific time or when triggered by specific events. Floating-rate funds are tied to various indexes such as the prime rate, London Inter-bank Offered Rate [LIBOR], and the like. Even long-term bonds can have interest rates set each day. Numerous formulas can be used; typical formulas involve spreads over specified Treasury instruments.

Increasing-rate notes are used frequently as bridge-financing facilities. Refinancing is forced since the increase is punitive, growing at perhaps 50 basis points per quarter (or month) until full repayment. Exchangeable variable rate notes are reset regularly (e.g., quarterly) and can be exchanged at the issuer's option for fixed-rate notes with predetermined characteristics (price relative to Treasury bills, maturity, call price, sink-

---

6. Increasing rate notes are designed to force redemption at an early date. They are often used as divestiture financing in acquisitions where certain assets will be sold.

ing fund, etc.); often after 5 years, the *fix* becomes mandatory. An interesting variant is a note that resets interest rates in the *opposite* direction from the market (i.e., goes up when rates drop and vice versa); such an upside-down reset formula is used to hedge other interest-sensitive instruments.

Optional Pay Instruments

Optional pay instruments do not require payment unless the issuer's authoritative body decides to do so. For example, the payment of dividends on common stock is at the discretion of the board of directors.

No-Pay Instruments

No-pay instruments are financial products, the purpose of which does not involve periodic cash returns. The financial benefit of ownership is usually the appreciation of market value. Most of the hedging vehicles (e.g., options, futures, indexes), fall into this category. Swaps involve the exchange of obligation between two parties and are, in essence, a no-pay arbitrage product.

Classification by Term Period

The following classification of financial instruments is structured by term period of existence.

Fixed-term Instruments

Fixed-term instruments have an established maturity date; they exist for a definite period of time that is preset at the time of issuance. Traditional bonds are fixed-term, with clear, defined amortization schedules of principal repayment.

Variable-term Instruments

Variable-term instruments exist for a flexible period of time. One example is preferred stock, the redemption schedule of which is related to business performance. Another example is a *flipflop* bond which allows an investor to switch back and forth between two types of securities (e.g., flipping from a perpetual, floating-rate note into a six-month note bearing a lower rate of interest and then flopping back to the floating-rate note when the short-term instrument matures).

Permanent-term Instruments

Permanent-term instruments are intended to exist for the entire life of the issuing enterprise. Common stock is the classic example—though even common stock may be bought back into treasury shares, reverse-split, or retired.

Perpetual-term Instruments

Perpetual-term instruments exist for an indeterminate period of time; they do not have a defined redemption schedule. Two examples are remarketed preferred stock and perpetual bonds. (An example of a perpetual bond is an instrument that is denominated in Swiss francs and pays interest in U.S. dollars—every ten years issuers may purchase or call the bond, and investors may sell it back to the issuer.)

Categories of Newer Financial Instruments

There is a large number of innovative securities refining and combining the classifications and characterisitcs presented above. Most of these seemingly countless new instruments involve variations on three primary themes: bonds with options/warrants (e.g., options to convert into equity and warrants to purchase new debt), swaps, and collateralized securities. Our sampling of the newer financial instruments that follows can be classified into three general categories: options/warrants and associated instruments, high-yield instruments, and hedging instruments.

Options/Warrants and Associated Debt Instruments

Options. Options are the right to purchase a security (call) or sell a security (put) for a specified period of time, most often in the public markets. Companies can use options to offer greater flexibility and leverage to investors and thereby attract more investment into their stock—which lowers the firm's cost of capital due to the increased liquidity.

Companies also use options to hedge their own investment positions. Mathematical models (e.g., the Black-Scholes option valuation formula) are used to evaluate the current worth of options. Program trading— using computers to exploit minute differences between stock prices, options, and indexes—can produce guaranteed returns (and cause market perturbations).

Warrants.   Warrants are rights to buy securities at predetermined prices (the strike price) directly from the issuer for a specified period of time. They can be detachable (able to be used or sold independently of the original note) and therefore more valuable to investors. Warrants may give the bearer rights to purchase common stock (at some premium above market value) or additional bonds (with same or different terms).

Debt with Kickers.   Debt with kickers are debt instruments (or preferred stock) with additional benefits (that give the kick—e.g., warrants, royalties, profit participations, premiums, and the like). Issuers reduce the interest rate (and thereby the current risk) by trading off some return. Investors absorb some of the current risk (by accepting a lower-than-market interest rate) in hopes of attaining a higher ultimate return. (Issuers would not mind paying the upside since reaching the triggering variable—the key criterion or indicator to which investors' return is linked—would usually mean that the issuer's business would be prospering.)

Bonds With Warrants.   Traditional bonds with warrants offer equity warrants along with the debt instrument. For example, equity-linked bonds have proven attractive for foreign investors in the Japanese markets, who prefer such an indirect participation in Japanese equities for tax and other reasons.

Many recent innovations in finance involve bonds with debt warrants. Several variations have interesting nicknames: *Bunny bonds* are bonds with attached warrants that enable holders to reinvest the interest into bonds with the same terms and conditions (named *bunny* since the bonds can multiply like rabbits). *Harmless warrants* give holders the right to purchase a similar security with the same maturity as the host bond. *Harmful warrants* give holders the right to purchase additional bonds which may have maturities and principal amounts different from the host bond.

Usable Bonds.   Usable bonds are debt instruments that can be used at face value (par) in lieu of cash to exercise specific warrants. When linked with these underlying warrants, these bond units have been called *synthetic convertibles.* Usability can give bonds added value when investors seek to exercise the warrants. In this case, no price is too high for the usable bond as long as it can be purchased below par (including forfeited accrued interest) since this is the cash exercise price. Companies have used these bonds to convert debt into equity by flushing out warrants; the company simply reduces the warrant exercise price below the underlying stock trading price (throwing the warrant *in the money*).

High-Yield Instruments

High-Yield Debt. High-yield debt—so-called junk bonds[7]—is debt issued with ratings below investment grade and consequently higher coupon rates. Studies conclude that such spread premiums have more than compensated for the heightened risk, giving investors enhanced long-term return. High-yield debt has had a dramatic impact on corporate America. By paying higher coupon rates on notes, companies previously unable to raise capital have raised billions. Pioneered by Drexel Burnham Lambert, high-yield bonds catalyzed the explosive increase in mergers and acquisitions (especially leveraged buyouts).

High-Yield Commercial Paper. High-yield debt's success has invaded the commercial paper market in the form of unrated paper. Such commercial paper provides low-cost, fixed-term sources of cash previously unavailable to unrated companies. Borrowings can be custom-tailored, by maturity, to the firm's precise cash flow needs (literally to the day). The borrower can access the market at its discretion, with almost

---

7. How did junk bonds get their pejorative name? Originally, any debt that was below investment grade in quality (as defined by a bond rating service such as Standard and Poor's [where investment grade is considered as BBB or above]) was the result of a fallen angel, a once large, solid company that had come upon hard times. This debt was indeed junk in that the certainty of payback had declined (the previous investment grade might have been AAA), and this decline was often precipitous. Many of the infamous rust belt companies of the 1970s were unfortunate examples of fallen angels whose debt became junk. (See Chapter 13.)

The junk bond market today is radically different. This vigorous market of almost $200 billion is composed of two kinds of companies: businesses that are growing, not shrinking, but have not yet reached investment grade (e.g., MCI in its early stages), and strong businesses that have been leveraged financially by management buyouts or recapitalizations (e.g., RJR Nabisco and Macy's). The risks are still apparent—the growth companies may never reach investment grade and the highly leveraged companies can suffer rapid deterioration—but the reasons underlying these risks suggest a different characterization. Hence the preferred name *high-yield*, where the added risk is compensated with added return.

no advance notice. All transactions are structured and priced net of transaction fees so comparisons can be made easily. The issuance of commercial paper offers companies continuous exposure to institutional investors in money and capital markets. This visibility can enhance success of future debt or equity offerings. Commercial paper can also provide benefits for future negotiations on bank pricing.

Zero Coupon Bonds. Zero coupon bonds are debt instruments for which the service, repayment, interest, and principal is deferred for a number of years. As accrued interest is compounded, the principal amount increases (accretes). Zero coupon bonds are essentially bonds stripped of their interest coupons and selling at a deep discount to face value (say 73 percent off for a 10–year maturity—an implied interest rate of 14 percent per year); the deep discount reflects the present value of the principal at maturity, discounted by the implied interest rate. From the investor's position, zero coupon bonds provide a guaranteed reinvestment rate which current pay instruments cannot. On the other hand, these bonds involve higher risk since current interest is accrued and not paid.[8] Zero coupon bonds, therefore, command higher interest rates.

Zero coupon bonds match current company financial needs with future payback capacity. Many financings in recent times, particularly leveraged buyouts, could not have been done without zero coupon bonds. A variant allows investors the option of investing interest with the same terms and conditions as originally set or with terms and conditions extant in the future (the bond may have warrants as well). By transferring the reinvesting option to investors, interest is lower than on a normal bond for the same reasons that interest on a regular zero coupon bond (no option) is higher.

Hedging Instruments

Interest-Rate Risk Management. Interest-rate fluctuations on floating notes can be bounded with upper and/or lower limits by setting floors, ceilings (caps), and collars (combined floors and ceilings or minimax). Companies can set absolute limits on interest-rate exposure while getting the benefits of floating rates. Of course, issuing companies pay

---

8. One variation on the zero coupon bond gives investors the option to sell the bond after a fixed amount of time at a specified yield that rises over time.

a premium for caps on floating-rate notes. A variant is a floating-rate bond that converts into a fixed-rate bond when market rates fall below a certain level.

Futures. Futures are the promises to deliver certain items, usually commodities or government securities, at specific times in the future. Companies buy and sell futures to hedge exposure to fluctuations in commodity prices, interest rates, and exchange rates. For example, a company can hedge its long-term bond position by buying Treasury bond futures. Futures can stabilize any company that depends on the price of commodities, whether a seller (e.g., a food producer of wheat or oranges) or a buyer (e.g., a textile firm using cotton or an electronics firm using expensive metals). For multinational companies or importers/-exporters, the commodities that most needs hedging are foreign currency exchange rates.

Swaps. Swaps are the exchange of debt obligations among two or more entities, often through a third party such as a major commercial or investment bank. Swaps lock in interest and exchange rates; they can convert floating to fixed rates and vice versa; and they can alter the maturities of obligations. Swaps exploit the relative borrowing strength of different borrowers and can produce complex variations in defining specific constraints for interest rates. They can be linked, for example, to sinking fund debentures. (Amortizing swaps are like sinking fund debentures in that the interest is used to pay back the principal.)

Indexes. Indexes link financial rates to the price of certain indicators (Treasury bills, the prime rate, LIBOR, currency exchange rates, stock market values, etc.) or commodity prices (gold, silver, etc.). Companies employ indexes to hedge their positions. Issuers can pay lower guaranteed rates since they offer a potential bonus: they will gladly pay higher rates if the chosen indexes rise (which would mean that their products would be generating greater profit). An example is an oil company bond paying a premium at maturity if the price of oil exceeds $25 per barrel for a specific period of time. Another example is the so-called *heaven and hell bond* where the principal amount to be paid at maturity is tied to the performance of a currency or an index; investors may win big (heaven) or lose big (hell)—although generally such risks are hedged.

Example Innovation: Securitized High-yield Instruments

The combination of two important and relatively new financial concepts—high-yield bonds and securitization—can generate an innovative offspring that expands financial flexibility and extends the market. We explore an interesting example: securitized high-yield instruments — highly-rated securities (triple A) backed by pools of junk bonds.

The concept is simple enough. Issuers offer significantly greater value in bonds than the value of the securities they desire to issue. How much overcollateral is required? The rating agencies evaluate the quality of the high-yield bonds backing the new securities, the diversity and maturities of this asset pool, and the frequency at which the pool changes in composition and must be reevaluated to reflect alterations in value or credit. Obviously, the riskier the collateral, the more overcollateralization is required.

Securitization may bring to the high-yield bond market many of the same advantages as it has brought to the mortgage and receivables markets. The huge high-yield market offers an enormous new reservoir of assets with which to construct investment-grade securities. Here investors look to the collateral, not to the issuer's credit, for confidence of debt service and timely repayment.

The concept of repackaging high-yield bonds into investment-grade instruments would increase the total amount of capital available for the high-yield market. This increased size and consequent liquidity would result in a lower cost of capital for issuers and a more efficient investment for investors.

An important development in the securitization of high-yield bonds occurred when Standard and Poor's Corp. decided to rate high-yield backed bonds by looking to the cash flows resulting from the underlying high-yield instruments rather than the market value of those high-yield bonds. Market values can fluctuate wildly, while the cash flows are tied directly to the fundamental capacity of the originally issuing companies to pay interest and repay principal. The new approach is similar to the one used by the rating agencies to evaluate collateral mortgage obligations, although it is more complex due to the fact that high-yield instruments are much less homogenous than home loans.[9]

Since high-yield bonds generate yields from 200 to 500 basis points over triple-A securities, an efficient arbitrage can be established. Thus an issuer could repackage its higher-yielding below-investment-grade bonds into a lower-yielding investment-grade instrument—and make a healthy

---

9. On the other hand, mortgage securities have been significantly more volatile than junk bonds.

return on the differential in interest rates. The amount of interest saved on the yield difference would more than compensate for the required overcollateralization.

For example, assume an issuer with a $200 million high-yield bond portfolio with an average yield of 13.5 percent annually; the issuer might use this portfolio to issue $150 million of single-A rated bonds paying 10.5 percent per year. With no defaults in the portfolio the issuer would earn an interest rate differential of $11.25 million [(200 × 0.135)−(150 × 0.105)] that is saved by issuing the higher-rated, lower-yield bonds; this interest savings of $11.25 million yields an incremental return to the issuer of 22.5 percent on the $50 million [200–150] in additional high-yield bonds used as collateral.

CHAPTER 13

Innovative
Corporate Securities*

The last two decades have witnessed unprecedented volatility and change in financial markets. Wide fluctuations and unexpected shocks in inflation, interest rates, currency exchange rates, and stock market valuations have destabilized traditional corporate finance. In addition, the economic world has become highly competitive, and markets have become global. Geography is becoming transparent as multinational companies operate in dozens of countries and technological breakthroughs shorten product life cycles. The result is that financial planning has become exceedingly more complex for corporations and investors alike.

The central problem of contemporary corporate finance departments—helping client companies cope with the volatility and change—cannot be solved by relying on traditional financial instruments. Complex economic problems demand complex financial solutions. Today, corporate finance requires that issuers and investors alike target their risk and return profiles more clearly, thereby minimizing the cost of capital to companies and enhancing the confidence and participation of investors.

---

*This chapter has been derived from "Developments of Innovative Corporate Securities" by G. Chris Andersen, Volume III (Corporate and Municipal Securities), Dow Jones-Irwin's *The Library of Investment Banking* (1990), Robert Lawrence Kuhn, editor-in-chief.

In this chapter, we review some of the major innovative developments in corporate securities, giving the rationale for their invention. Matching risk and return among issuers and investors with great specificity is the critical concept.

Historical Perspective

Innovation has not always been essential in finance. Indeed, over most of the last 50 years, investment bankers have avoided change. They represented, generally, the bulwark of the status quo. After the 1929 Stock Market Crash, new laws and regulatory bodies served to constrain financial innovation and thereby protect the marketplace. All our traditional financial instruments date from that period. Most importantly, the Glass-Steagall Act of 1933 forced commercial banks to get out of the underwriting business. That gave rise to an oligopolistic investment banking industry, an elite group that dominated wholesale investment banking through the 1960s.

The four decades after the Crash were a time of syndicated transactions built on personal relationships. The oligopolistic wholesale firms had strong ties to the large industrial corporations that issued investment-grade securities; they also exercised almost feudal power over brokerage firms who distributed these securities. Investment-grade securities were then, as now, bought and not sold. Investment bankers created pieces of paper for investment-grade credits, then priced them where the market wanted to buy them—and called this *distribution*. It was that simple. Corporations were stable; financial markets were stable; investors were stable. Hence, investment bankers had little incentive to innovate.

But the financial instruments created in this period all depended on the stability of a single premise—that the U.S. dollar was and would remain a reliable store of value. And that premise had two important corollaries: (1) there would be no serious degree of inflation, and (2) there would be no serious volatility in interests rates.

For many years these assumptions were perfectly valid. The U.S. dollar was strong, inflation was low, and interest rates were stable. During the 1950s, for example, there were long periods (months) when yields on Treasury bonds did not vary more than 10 basis points. An investment banker back then might not have seen as much variation in Treasury yields in his entire career as his counterpart today may witness in a single afternoon. The older generation of investment banker was perfectly content to live in the cocoon that government regulators devised. They happily issued plain vanilla securities for their largely blue-chip clientele.

But Wall Street's era of cozy contentment ended in the 1970s. First, in 1972 the U.S. closed its gold window, ushering in a new era of floating exchange rates. A year later came the Arab oil embargo and a great global surge of unprecedented inflation. Faith in the U.S. dollar began to erode. The deregulation of fixed-rated commissions forced on Wall Street in 1975, combined with the growing power of large institutional investors, led to massive consolidation in the securities industry, wiping out the mid-sized investment banks that previously had catered to the public equity needs of the country's mid-sized corporations.

By the 1980s, worldwide competition had become a pressing reality as European and Asian economies raced ahead. Meanwhile, advances in telecommunications and transportation made the world smaller. Suddenly, U.S. businessmen had to contend with tough new competition all over the world. And Wall Street has experienced a changing of the guard. The older generation that grew up in the era of the efficient oligopoly has stepped down; a new, more competitive generation has taken charge.

We live in a time of dynamic economic flux. Today, no currency is considered a permanent store of value, and with the fall from grace experienced by such giants as Penn Central, U.S. Steel, and Continental Illinois, no corporate security, no matter how prestigious the issuer, can be considered completely safe. Once upon a time, a conservative investor might reasonably buy a AAA-rated bond and put it into a lockbox for thirty years, confident that his investment was bulletproof. Nowadays, such an act would be unthinkable. Never before have investors been so skittish or so short-term oriented—with good reason. The ambient level of risk in our capital markets system has increased dramatically.

Fortunately, our free market system offers us the means to cope with all of this change. Some investors are more amenable to risk than others; and factors that represent risk for one party may not represent similar risk to another party. On an increasingly competitive new Wall Street, investment bankers have begun inventing new mechanisms that allow individuals and institutions to hedge their investment bets and reduce risks through the use of innovative instruments and by investing in diverse marketplaces. Creating new instruments and markets that more closely reflect the risk-return profiles of issuers and investors is the essence of contemporary investment banking.

Investment bankers thus have an expanded role: serving as intermediaries for issuers and investors (public and private) who wish to make increasingly diverse kinds of financial contracts with one another. In effect, Wall Street looks for innovative ways to create specific instruments to serve the needs of those willing to assume a higher degree of risk for a commensurate reward, as well as those willing to pay for higher levels of certainly. These new market methods allow for increasingly refined definitions of risk and reward and correspondingly refined gradations in seniority, security, and pricing. In this manner, investment bankers help investors cope with instability while lowering the cost of capital for issuers.

High-Yield Bonds

Perhaps the epic event of the past ten years in the U.S. capital markets has been the acceptance and expanded use of high-yield bonds, the area in which Drexel Burnham Lambert has been most prominent. Under the old order, only the largest corporations could access the public debt markets because they, and they alone, qualified for investment-grade credit ratings—that is, ratings of BBB− or higher. Those credit ratings are awarded by bond rating agencies that have traditionally put tremendous faith in a company's size and longevity. In a survey in the late 1970s, Drexel Burnham Lambert was unable to find any companies with investment-grade ratings whose shareholder equity was less than $250 million. Indeed, only some 600 U.S. companies have issued securities that now quality as investment-grade, and most of them are financial institutions or low-risk public utilities. The rest, including those smaller and mid-sized companies providing most of the growth in our economy, are rated below BBB− or else have no credit rating at all.

Until 1977 the only below-investment-grade paper consisted of debt issued by large corporations like Ford, Chrysler, and U.S. Steel that, at least temporarily, had gone into serious decline. Hence, the pejorative name *junk bonds*. The debt of smaller companies, with presumably lower credit quality characteristics, was held primarily by institutions in the form of either bank loans or equally illiquid private placements. Drexel's pioneering work made it possible for these issuers to sell debt in the public marketplace. By securitizing bank loans and private placements into liquid high-yield bonds, Drexel gave investors a chance to trade freely in the debt instruments of mid-sized companies, thereby greatly expanding the available pool of capital for issuers and broadening the terms and conditions under which it could be obtained.

Before the development of this new marketplace, the debt securities of troubled companies—*fallen angels* as they are called—traded at a discount from face value (par) but earned superior rates of return for the wealthy, sophisticated individuals and private investment groups who qualified to invest in them. An overwhelming majority of these companies succeeded in meeting their debt obligations, notwithstanding their lowered credit ratings.

One Drexel employee, Michael Milken, took an interest in these downgraded securities while still in business school, and he confirmed earlier studies by the National Bureau of Economic Research demonstrating that the U.S. bond markets were irrationally averse to risk. These studies noted that the yield premium demanded by bond buyers for lower-rated bonds had consistently exceeded the incremental risk, and the conclusion was that a bond buyer would come out ahead by buying lower-rated issues—provided that he kept a diversified portfolio.

What Milken did, in effect, was to point out the discrepancy between the real value of these fallen angels and their perceived value in the market place. Because investment-grade bonds sold at too high a premium, below-investment-grade bonds outperformed them. The perception in the debt markets was one thing: a triple-A bond was the most secure financial instrument available. The reality was quite another: a triple-A bond was the riskiest investment because it probably was overpriced to begin with. With non–investment-grade bonds, an investor could earn a dramatically disproportionate return for the level of risk assumed—especially if the investor used a little judgment.

A few investors were willing to give the theory a try. The time was right, because in the severe inflation of the 1970s, the nominal yields on traditional, investment-grade bonds had, for many years, resulted in negative real returns (i.e., inflation was higher than yields, especially on an after-tax basis). The performance results of the first portfolios composed of these discounted securities confirmed Milken's studies, and demand for higher-yielding, non–investment-grade bonds soon began to outstrip supply. To meet the growing appetite, Drexel began to underwrite new debt issues for smaller, younger corporations with many of the same credit ratios and characteristics as companies that were in decline—except that these issuers were growing rapidly, not deteriorating.

The classic example of this discrepancy between perception and reality was MCI's debt-with-warrants issue which Drexel underwrote in 1983. The issue was the first $1 billion underwriting in the U.S. The company was a single-B credit at the time, but it was investing great amounts of money in new technology that would enable it to become a major competitor in the rapidly-deregulating telecommunications industry. Most other investment bankers thought Drexel was reckless to underwrite such a huge issue for a single-B company. But remember, the conventional wisdom back then also held that Western Union, with its Baa rating, was a wonderful credit. A few years later, MCI was among the small number of investment-grade credits; Western Union, it is sad to say, was handled by Drexel's workout department as a less-than-investment-grade credit. All's well that ends well, however; Western Union subsequently completed a complicated exchange offer reorganization which converted a portion of its once investment-grade debt into equity and dramatically improved its prospects.

Innovative Financial Instruments: Between Debt and Equity

The introduction of underwritten high-yield bond issues marked the beginning of an unprecedented era of innovation on Wall Street. A new breed of investment bankers, many of them recruited from the country's finest business schools, began finding ways to let various parties with divergent interests make many different kinds of contracts with one another. These financial engineers invented new financial structures, dividing, say, single financings into multiple pieces of paper (layers or strips of different seniority, maturity, security, risk, and yield) for sale to different people with different needs. This new generation of investment banker blended traditional securities with options and commodities to devise products such as currency swaps, interest rate swaps, indexed bonds, limitless varieties of convertible bonds and debentures with staggered or fluctuating maturities, and variable, floating, or zero coupons. Yet all of these instruments have two common purposes—helping clients raise capital at minimum cost in a volatile financial world and helping investors carve out strategies appropriate to their tolerance for risk.

The lesson to be learned from the criss-crossing pattern of MCI and Western Union is simple: in today's world, traditional notions of credit are obsolete. One major reason is that the line between dept and equity has blurred. Today, there is a continuum of financial instruments stretching from traditional long-term debt to traditional common equity (see Chapter 12). As you increase the level of risk, these new instruments take on more characteristics of equity; as you increase the level of safety, they take on more characteristics of pure debt—that is, a smaller coupon rate but a lower risk of principal.

Much of the paper labeled below-investment-grade or non–investment-grade should not be evaluated as pure debt. It is actually a cross between debt and equity. The riskier the piece of paper, the more its potential payoff should resemble that of common stock.

There is no sharp dividing line between debt and equity, but rather a *spectrum* of positions stretching from pure, riskless debt on one end (e.g., obligations of the U.S. Government) to pure, high-risk equity on the other (e.g., venture capital). To complicate matters, all issuers' credit is either improving or deteriorating at all times. Therefore the analysis of debt and equity characteristics of outstanding issues constantly changes in response to the increasingly volatile and changing general environment; yes, that does even include riskless government issues of sovereign states. Importantly, in an institutional marketplace with real depth, it is increasingly clear that no one cares whether the instrument is called debt or equity. It is not the name that is important; it is the risk/reward profile.

Credit Analysis: Security Seniority

There must be, however, a line on the corporate balance sheet which divides debt and equity. That line is just below the most junior level of subordinated debt. Should the balance sheet deteriorate to the point of bankruptcy, a court would begin to reorganize the capitalization by moving this line upward and, in effect, converting some portion of the lower-ranking debt into equity. Creditors who held the most senior-ranking debt instruments would be the first to reclaim their principal; those with subordinated debt would be left to take their chances, much like common shareholders, though ahead of shareholders on the line. Thus, along with the evolution of new securities has come a change in the basic practice of credit analysis. Besides determining an overall credit rating for each company, analysts must now attempt to discover where each security issued by that company stands within the spectrum between pure debt and pure equity.

Until recent years, most credit analysis was predicated on the notion that the capital markets were essentially just financing the construction of bricks and mortar—plant and equipment—or some other tangible asset. That was fine in earlier times, when a new steel plant had a useful life of perhaps forty years. But such assumptions are inappropriate in the modern era of hyperintense global competition and collapsing technological time, when the average new product has a useful life of only three or four years.

Perhaps the biggest change in credit analysis has been a de-emphasis on accounting book value. There was an acute realization in the late 1970s and early 1980s that a company's stated earnings are generally less important than its cash flow or its cash *availability*. Cash, after all, can come from many sources other than operations; a company like MCI can, if need be, derive cash from its heavy equity capitalization in the public markets. At the time of MCI's first huge debt issuance, the stock market valued MCI at more than $5 billion, even though the company's book value was less than $1 billion. The difference between MCI's $822 million book value and its $5.3 billion market capitalization represented a source of cash it could readily access that appears nowhere on its balance sheet. However, this financing option has obvious major credit risk implications. In short, the *availability* of that cash source was much more important to any credit analysis of MCI than the accountants' estimate of its book value.

Questions about cash availability and cash flow are also intertwined with questions about corporate management. If an investor is financing only plant and equipment, the quality of management may not matter much; bricks and mortar can always be sold off when they are not being properly utilized. But an investor who finances cash flow rather than tangible assets is making an investment based on the management itself. And in a period of cash stringency, a chief executive officer who personally has a heavy equity stake in the company and who has the proven ability to get the most from his capital is generally a better credit risk than the chief executive officer who owns no stock and whose principal motivation may be to maintain an empire.

Because credit research has become more astute, analysts can now define levels of risk more precisely for non–investment-grade debt. This, in turn, has led to a more liquid market for these instruments. For the first time, investors have the tools to make rational decisions about high-yield bonds and other nontraditional credits. And once armed with those tools, they continually demonstrate willingness to take higher risks for commensurately higher returns but still short of the ultimate risk of common equity. The result is a dramatically expanded capital market as both investors and issuers gain greater confidence and experience.

Because the marketplace now accepts new levels of risk, the possibilities for securities innovation have become almost endless. Investment bankers now design financing instruments to fit a company's precise needs. Our role now is to design the optimal security for each corporation, then fine-tune it to lower the company's cost of capital as much as possible, and, finally, to break it into tightly tailored components that can be sold to investors with varying appetites for risk, maturity, and the like.

Innovative Financial Instruments: Some Examples

Following are a few examples of innovative financial instruments—to give vision to this expanding universe.

Commodity-Linked Bonds

Commodity-linked bonds are a prime example of the process outlined above. Drexel Burnham Lambert designed the first such bond for Sunshine Mining Company in 1980. Borrowing costs were forbidding at the time because of double-digit inflation, but Sunshine happened to produce a metal that is itself believed to be among the best inflation hedges. Drexel lowered Sunshine's coupon rate by giving investors either $1,000 principal at maturity or the price of fifty ounces of silver—whichever was greater. The security allayed investors' inflation fears at minimum cost to the company since a silver mining company already owns the silver it has pledged at maturity. Investors would receive a higher yield if the price of silver exceeded a predefined level ("upside" protection) and therefore accepted a lower guaranteed yield; the coupon was reduced by approximately one-half. If the price of silver had risen substantially, affording the investor an excellent return, then the company, owning ample silver production, would have been more than able to pay. The risk/reward tradeoff was appropriate for both issuer and investor.

The important point is that factors representing market risk for one party may not present significant risk for another. In the Sunshine Mining case, investors were wary of long-term bonds because of the inflation factor. But Sunshine itself had little fear of inflation because of its inflation-beating assets underground. On the contrary, Sunshine's biggest worry was the short-term volatility in its cost of capital. Sunshine therefore traded away to investors some of the long-term, inflation-hedging price protection inherent in its silver in order to get a lower up-front coupon rate and consequently a more stable short-term cost of capital.

Convertible Bonds

Up until the late 1970s, companies that were less than investment-grade credits could not access public straight debt markets, but they could sometimes raise capital by issuing convertible bonds. Historically, if we assume that a corporation's senior debt might be privately placed with institutional investors at a coupon of perhaps 11 percent, its *subordinated* convertible 15-year to 20-year public debt issues might carry a coupon of eight percent, with conversion premiums of 15 to 18 percent; that is, they were convertible into a fixed number of common shares at a price 15 to 18 percent above the then-current market value. Convertible bonds have special investor appeal because they offer potential long-term capital gains if the share price appreciates.

Convertible bonds were an early way of blending debt and equity in a single financial instrument. The trouble was that, periodically, the market would not accept a standard convertible bond from those companies most in need of capital—small and medium-sized growth companies that expected rapid growth in their stock value as well as revenue and profits, if only they could raise capital to fuel expansion.

The first step in helping these companies was a new type of convertible bond—the high-coupon, high-conversion, premium convertible bond. A market for this new instrument emerged in the high-interest-rate environment of the late 1970s. On one hand, companies were reluctant to pay the high cost of long-term, straight bond financing; on the other, they were unwilling to sell equity in a depressed stock market or at levels they thought were undervalued. But by offering coupon rates that were lower than those on straight bonds yet higher than those on traditional convertibles, these issues attracted investors who were eager for a measure of competitive yield. And in return for yields better than those on traditional convertible bonds, investors were willing to accept conversion premiums that were perhaps twice as high. Obviously, the higher the coupon rate an investor receives, the less he relies upon the equity portion of the investment to enhance its overall rate of return. For companies that could enjoy a rapid appreciation of stock value, the instrument was good for the investor as well as the issuer.

Before long, chief financial officers discovered that they could choose their coupon rates by adjusting the conversion premium and vice versa. For example, assume that there were two companies whose shares exhibited similar trading patterns and that each could expect to pay a coupon rate of approximately 13 percent on straight bonds. One of those companies might elect to issue convertible bonds with an 8 percent coupon rate and a conversion premium of 15 percent; the other, perhaps desirous to delay conversion of debt to equity, might offer a coupon rate of 10 percent with a conversion premium of 25 percent.

Such a scenario, by the way, exists in the real world. In 1984, Houston-based Texas Eastern Corporation and New York–based SCM Corporation, two companies of comparable investment quality, each issued convertible subordinated debentures on the same day. SCM's $60 million offering had a 10 percent coupon and a conversion premium of 15.79 percent, while Texas Eastern's $175 million offering had a 12 percent coupon and a conversion premium of 28.29 percent.

Debt with Warrants

The next variation on the convertible theme was debt with warrants. Traditional convertible bonds had been issued for terms of 15 years or longer, but in the late 1970s companies began seeking ways to reduce the cost of intermediate-term financing using equity features. By literally dissecting a convertible bond—that is, by separating the debt component from the equity component—companies could get better value for each piece. Warrants give debtholders the right to purchase underlying stock at a set price for a given period, typically five years. And because they are detachable from the associated debt instrument, the warrants have extra value for investors who want to speculate on the equity of the debt issuer while receiving steady income from the interest payments.

In early 1984, Del E. Webb Corporation of Phoenix needed to raise $25 million for four years to fund several new real estate development projects. At the time similar credit companies were paying about 15 percent on straight debt issues, but Del Webb was confident that its stock, then trading for around $16 a share, would show significant appreciation in the next few years—and the investment community generally agreed. Accordingly, to each $1,000 note the company attached 20 four-year warrants to purchase common stock at a strike price of $26 per share. (The stock subsequently traded above the $26 mark.) Despite the comparatively high conversion premium—$10 on a $16 stock (62.5%)—Del Webb raised the funds it needed with a coupon rate of only 11.5 percent, thus lowering its interest expenses by some 350 basis points (25%) versus a straight debt offering.

Naturally, the lower the exercise or strike price at which investors can exercise their warrants (making the warrants worth more), the lower the coupon rate they will accept (making the debt worth less). The point is that debt with warrants offers companies tremendous flexibility, allowing them to fine-tune a debt/warrant package to almost any desired coupon level by adjusting the warrant premium or maturity and the number of warrants. This fine-tuning process, in essence, moves the instruments back and forth along the debt-equity spectrum in order to locate the optimum risk/reward profile for both issuers and investors.

Additional value was later added to the straight debt portion of the unit by making it usable with the warrant. (This synthetic feature allowed the owner of a warrant to pay the strike price of the warrant in either cash or the equivalent face amount of the debentures). Since most of the units are offered at face (par) value, the stripped-units debenture is, in effect, sold at a discount. This discount effectively lowers the strike price and premium of the warrant. Importantly, however, the usability of the debenture also tends to support the market price of the debentures in a period of rising interest rates. Therefore, the value of the debenture itself is also enhanced. With this feature one completes the cycle from the traditional convertible bond back to the unbundled package of synthetic convertible debt with warrants.

The next logical extension of the synthetic convertible bond would be a deep-discount usable debenture with warrants. This would allow for a very high warrant strike price because of the deep discount on the usable debt. Perhaps the most interesting use of the concept is found in the creation of deep discount debt with springing warrants which can be part of a defense against unsolicited tender offers.

Debt with Springing Warrants

As with most issues of debt with warrants, this debt is usable with the warrants to purchase common stock at a given price over a specified period of time. But the springing warrant feature provides that the deep-discount debt is usable at the accreted value of the debt under normal circumstances but may be used *at par*—a much larger number in the early years—after some specified triggering event such as a hostile tender offer, a major block purchase of stock, or some other event designated by the board of directors.

Thus, if the company is put into play by a bidder, the ability to use deeply discounted debt to exercise the warrants makes conversion attractive and increases the number of common shares outstanding. This dilution of the bidder's position can make the price of acquisition substantially higher. Consequently, debt with springing warrants can be a highly effective weapon against unsolicited tender offers or other hostile acts.

In 1984 Gearhart Industries, Inc. successfully placed an issue of subordinated debentures with springing warrants as part of its defense against an acquisition bid by Smith International. The notes had a face amount of $99 million but were sold for about 68 cents on the dollar. The warrants could be exercised with cash or, under certain circumstances, by utilizing the notes at their face value. The basic idea behind the issue was to drop the warrant strike price if the company faced a hostile offer, thereby increasing the number of shares dramatically and raising the cost of acquisition proportionally. Since the company had the power to designate the triggering event, the issue did not affect the cost of a friendly acquisition. In effect, this was the original "poison pill" tender defense. It succeeded better than the current conventional poison pills because it had at its base a logical, financial reason for its creation.

Exchangeable Debentures

Though the high inflation rates of the 1970s subsided in the 1980s, investors continued seeking new ways to combine debt and equity features in order to maximize the risk/return trade-off in their portfolios and to secure an equity stake in certain companies. One type of instrument that attracted them was the exchangeable debenture, a type of security that can be exchanged or converted—at the issuer's option—for another type of security at some future date. A corporation might even want to issue a convertible bond and have the option of exchanging it for a ten-year note after five years. Conversely, the company might want to issue a five-year note that later will be exchangeable for a convertible bond. The advantage to the company is clear: enormous flexibility in attempting to match future assets and liabilities in light of expected interest rate movements and tax liabilities. And in order to sell an instrument with such flexibility, the issuer must attract the investor with a commensurate return.

A somewhat specialized example of this variation was used for Pantry Pride, Inc. The company emerged from bankruptcy in 1981 with a tax loss carryforward of more than $300 million, enough to last many years. In 1983, the Florida-based supermarket chain needed to raise capital. Convertible preferred stock would have been the natural choice because Pantry Pride had no worries about the negative tax consequences of paying dividends (which are not deductible). The problem: the company was constrained by the terms set forth in its bankruptcy proceedings, which precluded it from paying dividends until 1985.

The solution: the company floated $42.5 million worth of convertible exchangeable debentures with a coupon rate of 8.75 percent. Then, in 1985, it exchanged that debt for convertible preferred stock. The most important aspect of this strategy was that it allowed Pantry Pride to take advantage of the favorable climate for equities that existed in 1983, even though the company could not issue preferred stock at that time. The equity conversion feature of the debentures attracted investors who wanted the potential for capital appreciation. Moreover, Pantry Pride avoided the extra time and expense that a second issuance in 1985 would have entailed.

Putable Stock

All of the new securities discussed above involved taking debt and driving it toward equity. The next major step was to take equity and drive it toward debt. The first important innovation of that type was putable stock, also called *superstock*. It consists of a common share paired with a *put*, or an investor's right to sell the common share back to the issuer for a specified sum.

In November 1984, when there was little market enthusiasm for any new equity offering, Drexel underwrote a unique, $6 million issue of putable stock for Arley Merchandise Corporation of Taunton, Massachusetts (a leading manufacturer of curtains, draperies, and bedcoverings). To allay investor fears about the stock, Arley gave buyers the right to require the company to give them the value of their original purchase price two years after the original issue. This could be done at the company's option in (1) cash, (2) debentures with an equivalent market value, or (3) sufficient additional common shares to bring the aggregate current market value up to the original offering price.

Conceptually, putable stock trades like a common stock if market expectations are positive for the company (upside), but if market expectations are negative for the company (downside), it trades like a piece of paper that just represents a specified sum at a certain future date but yields no income along the way. In other words, the possibility of loss (downside) is the same as that of a zero-coupon bond. That makes it simple to analyze. On the possibility of gain (upside), what matter are the same questions about growth and opportunity that apply to any equity; on the downside, the questions are the same as those that would apply to any deep-discount zero coupon bond of less-than-investment-grade credit. In effect, in this putable stock instrument we have combined the market characteristics of debt and equity but without their normal contractual characteristics (i.e., you have a stock with the downside floor of a debt security).

Recapitalizations, Reorganizations, and Leveraged Buyouts

The potential for innovative securities that blend debt with equity is by no means limited to the half dozen examples described above. Indeed, the possibilities are endless, provided the investor knows where the security stands in the debt/equity continuum and therefore has a sound basis for deciding whether the risk is justified by the potential reward. It was the maturation of the market for purchase of subordinated debt in the 1970s that provided the base in the 1980s for the recapitalization and restructuring movement in corporate America: It was subordinated debt that provided both the framework and the potential capital for leveraged buyouts (LBOs) and recapitalizations (see Chapter 16).

The takeover movement resulted from the disappointing performance of U.S. businesses and hence their equities during the 1970s, which created great disparities between the public market value of many companies and the prices that knowledgeable private investors felt was the intrinsic value of their assets. And these entrepreneurial investors were willing to back their beliefs with capital and pay large premiums over market prices.

How does one finance such huge, highly leveraged acquisitions? Once again, improved credit analysis and more flexible uses of high-yield debt were the keys. Entrepreneurs like T. Boone Pickens, Jr., Carl Icahn, and others understood the defects in more traditional methods of securities research, and by the early 1980s were using high-yield bonds to finance their acquisition bids. Subsequently, savvy senior corporate managers began to emulate these strategies with their own corporate restructurings, recapitalizations, and leveraged buyouts.

Most *shark repellents* devised by lawyers—poison pills, staggered boards of directors, and the like—proved ineffectual against determined takeover artists often using straight cash. The most dependable means of defusing takeover threats usually turned out to be through the voluntary adoption of the raiders' financing techniques before the raiders could impose them. Stockholders benefitted whenever stock value was enhanced.

Among the most effective ways of defusing a takeover threat, for example, is the equity-for-debt swap. By exchanging a chunk of its long-term debt for equity, a company can dilute an unwanted bidder's position in the company while leaving its total capitalization unchanged. The swap lowers the target company's debt-to-capitalization ratio, and since the company's level of debt is reduced, the money formerly paid in interest expense will now contribute to net earnings.

For example, a company with 15 million shares outstanding swaps $37.5 million of debt at $25 per share to add an additional 10 percent to the number of primary shares outstanding. In the event of a proxy battle, the bidder would have to contend with an additional 1.5 million votes. If the bidder attempted to tender an offer at $30 per share, the additional equity would raise the cost of acquisition by $45 million. Furthermore, the company could place those newly issued shares into friendly hands.

Conversely, a debt-for-equity swap makes the company more highly leveraged, making it less attractive for raiders (and potentially a better return for stockholders). Here a company borrows heavily on its assets (much like an LBO) and then uses the cash to buy in stock (reducing the number of shares outstanding). Alternatively, the company can declare a huge special dividend.

Risk Management

By opening a major market for below-investment-grade credits and for instruments that can be analyzed on a fixed-rate basis, Drexel helped develop a continuum in the cost of capital. High-yield bonds in their many combinations and permutations lower the cost of capital for corporations by allowing investors to intelligently take on high levels of risk for potentially greater reward.

Today, abrupt cycles of economic change, growing internationalization of markets for goods and services, and a revolution in communications technology have led to unprecedented volatility in virtually all financial markets and the need for new or better instruments for intelligently managing these risks. Therefore, bankers have been forced to develop new methods that investors and issuers alike may use to control risk and reward more reliably.

Not surprisingly, the growth of markets in financial futures and options has parallelled and enhanced the development of high-yield bonds and other new securities, and vice versa. The growth of market options and futures instruments that permit interest rate and currency risk to be effectively managed has been tantamount to a revolution for corporations and institutional portfolio managers alike. (See Chapter 18.)

The development of interest rate and currency swaps beginning in the early 1980s has as dramatically extended the time horizon in which corporations and investors can effectively target their risk/reward parameters as high-yield bonds extended corporate capital availability. By allowing borrowers and lenders to change the character of assets or liabilities without changing the underlying source or placement of funds, swaps allow industrial companies and financial institutions around the world to escape the boundaries of both national markets and differentiated domestic markets in order to customize both the asset and liability sides of their balance sheets. (See Chapter 19.)

Options and swap markets initially tend to function most efficiently for companies with top credit ratings. Until recently, for instance, the cost of getting a guarantee from a bank or other intermediary tended to be prohibitive for companies with lower credit ratings in the swap market. But with the increasing globalization of world financial markets and the rapid maturation of the currency swap market, we are beginning to see mid-size companies take advantage of sophisticated risk management strategies through investment banks. Meanwhile, advances in hedging technology are promoting experiments in the use of a combination of interest rate and stock index futures contracts to hedge away a significant portion of a high-yield portfolio's price risk, while still capturing a large portion of the high-yield bond credit premium.

Just as financial futures and interest rate swaps have evolved in response to increased market volatility, other markets have responded to the related problem of illiquidity. Just as we saw that high-yield bonds are really just securitized borrowings that are tradeable and liquid, so have a whole host of assets undergone the securitization process because lenders demand more liquidity. Beginning with the securitization of mortgages in the early 1970s, which occurred after the creation of the federal mortgage guarantee corporations led to standardization of mortgage investments, markets have developed for a variety of receivables including automobile loans and credit card debt. (See Chapter 20.)

Asset securitization has vast potential because of the numerous assets that remain illiquid. Even pools of less-than-investment-grade loans are being securitized. The trend towards new solutions to markets change and volatility seems healthy and is continuing. Of particular interest is $650 billion of third-world debt now outstanding. This debt, selling at discounts of 10 to 90 percent from face value, represents obligations of some 130 countries ranging from Afghanistan to Zimbabwe. By restructuring the debt of some credits among less developed countries it may be possible to create outstanding investment values through both direct and pooled participation in the debt and equity instruments of these countries. And in the process, the free market may help to alleviate a problem that has confounded governments and financial institutions around the world.

Summary

Today, investment bankers are continually seeking new ways to help their clients control their capital costs and deal with abrupt cycles of economic change. The innovative instruments developed over the past ten years do not create new risk; they transfer it to investors who are willing to assume a higher degree of risk for a commensurate higher rate of return. This ability to transfer risk, allocate it, and price it accurately is the bedrock of a healthy financial system.

CHAPTER 14

Initial Public Offerings*

An initial public offering (IPO) is the first offering of a corporation's securities, usually common stock, to the general, investing public. It is an important milestone in the lifecycle of a company. While an IPO can theoretically be handled by the issuing company, IPOs today are almost always managed by underwriting professionals—investment bankers—and properly so, since the mishandling of any aspect of an IPO can seriously and permanently damage the financial and competitive standing of the company *going public*.

Why Companies Go Public

Companies are taken public for a variety of purposes. In general, one or more of the following five objectives is usually cited in published reports of new equity offerings: debt refinancing, financing of capital expenditures, financing of corporate growth, use for general corporate purposes, use for miscellaneous other reasons. More specifically, companies go public in order to

- Raise cash with which to finance a merger or an acquisition; add new products or services; increase working capital; expand investment in plant and equipment or research and develop-

* This chapter has been derived from "Initial Public Offerings I: The Underwriting Process" by Bruce Foerster, and "Initial Public Offerings II: Public Venture Capital" by J. Morton Davis and Evelyn Geller, Volume II (Capital Raising and Financial Structure), Dow Jones-Irwin's *The Library of Investment Banking* (1990), Robert Lawrence Kuhn, editor-in-chief.

ment, or repay debt (including debt resulting from a management-led leveraged buyout).

- Provide current owners with greater liquidity and personal wealth by securitizing their stake in the company, establishing a market for their stock, and enabling them to sell some or all of their stock for cash.

- Establish the value of the company for estate and inheritance tax purposes.

- Create a medium of exchange that can be used in place of cash for mergers or acquisitions, for employee benefits such as options and stock appreciation rights that assist in retaining and recruiting key personnel, or for collateral that can be used to obtain personal loans.

- Facilitate future funding—debt or equity—by means of subsequent public offerings.

- Permit borrowing on more favorable terms based on an improved debt-to-equity ratio.

- Permit valuation of the company by the public market, rather than by an outside consultant hired by a handful of private investors.

- Enhance corporate visibility and credibility, in part by making available to current and prospective customers, investors, and others, information about the company through required Securities and Exchange Commission (SEC) filings, an annual report, and periodic public relations releases. (Note: this reason can be a two-edged sword in that what heretofore had been proprietary information may no longer be shielded from competitors.)

- Deepen the commitment of employees by permitting them to hold a stake in the company.

- Facilitate the exit of founding entrepreneurs from the business.

Costs, Risks, and Complications of Going Public

Also associated with going public are certain costs, risks, restrictions, and duties which prospective issuers should review carefully with a responsible investment banking firm before proceeding with an IPO. Matters to consider include:

- Substantial costs in management time—commonly six to nine months of continuing activity by most of the key senior executives (chief executive officer, chief financial officer, treasurer, corporate counsel, and many others).

- Considerable IPO-related fees and expenses. The underwriters' gross spread—the difference between the fixed price the investing public pays for any IPO stock and the net proceeds the issuer receives—averages 7 percent of the gross proceeds of the IPO and can exceed 10 percent for certain very small issues. Attorneys' and accountants' fees can consume several hundred thousand dollars. Issuing companies also incur legal expenses and registration costs associated with SEC, National Association of Securities Dealers, and state Blue Sky regulatory filings. Printing and mailing costs associated with filing the registration statements, distributing preliminary and final prospectuses and underwriting agreements can run from $100,000 to $250,000 (and occasionally, for complex transactions, even higher). An allowance for so-called unaccountable expenses sometimes granted to the lead underwriter in smaller, more speculative, or start-up deals—reimbursable expenses not itemized or otherwise specified in advance—may reduce net proceeds to the issuer by as much as an additional 3 percent.

- Substantial ongoing expenses for required quarterly and annual SEC filings, exchange listings, annual reports, investor relations activities, taxes, key-man life insurance, outside directors fees, directors and officers (D&O) liability insurance, and the like.

- Ongoing investment of management time for investor and public relations activities.

- The need to divulge potentially sensitive information concerning sales, profits, executive salaries and bonuses, competitive strengths, and overall corporate strategy.

- Constraints on management decision-making, since executive actions are subject to review by public shareholders, the board of directors, regulatory bodies, and others.

- Possible damage to a thriving entrepreneurial culture (as a result of tighter legal constraints, public exposure, quarterly reports, etc.).

- Diffusion of corporate ownership that could increase the possibility of a hostile takeover.
- Increased pressure to produce favorable short-term financial results even during business downturns and sometimes even at the expense of long-term growth and development.

Investment bankers may also point out to prospective IPO clients that there are many available financial alternatives to going public. These alternatives include, but are not limited to, borrowing from commercial banks, savings and loans, or other short-term lending institutions; private placements; venture capital opportunities; government grants; research and development partnerships; equipment leasing rather than outright purchase; merger or outright sale of the business. Nonetheless, it is not often that a company that can go public (with a reasonable valuation) chooses not to go public. The financial rewards, corporate and personal, are usually too large to forsake.

Candidates For Going Public

What kinds of companies are well suited for IPO's? In general, investment bankers look for exciting companies in growth industries; companies with a solid record of achievement and profitability; and companies with outstanding potential based on mastery of a complex technology, a unique product or service, or ownership of patents or exclusive licensing agreements. Companies possessing one or more of these characteristics are good candidates for going public.

If interest in a particular industry (e.g., biotechnology) is sufficiently strong, an IPO may be successful even if the company going public is years away from having a salable product or service. Conversely, a general downturn in investor sentiment in a given industry may militate against proceeding with an IPO, even if the company and its plan to go public are otherwise sound in every respect.

The first criterion for going public is high ambition. If an entrepreneur says, "I'm going to make $50,000 the first year, $70,000 the second, and $95,000 the third," investment bankers say, "Wonderful! That is a good *private* business. Keep it and build it and have lots of luck."

But if that entrepreneur seeks to earn $1 million in profits the second year, and $5 million the third year, and $25 million the fifth year, then those bankers take a serious look. Because even if the entrepreneur is not completely accurate, he or she has an exciting vehicle. If the IPO raises $6 million for half the company, setting a $12 million valuation on it, the potential return is highly attractive. If, five years out, the company is earning, say, $10 million in profits, it could be selling at a $200 million valuation in the public market. The $6 million that the public puts up for half the company, then, could be worth $100 million in the marketplace.

The main justification for going public is the company's promise of growth. Some indications of growth potential are a consistent earnings history with impressive profit margins, an increasing backlog, and large contracts that have to be financed.

The prospective IPO may have an entrepreneur at its head who has already taken companies public in the past and wants to repeat his or her earlier successes. A company may have a new product and require more capital to market it. It may have a patent or proprietary position in a promising field. The company need not be in a high-technology field, but it should have the potential for substantial future growth into large and expanding markets—markets with room for intense competition.

Offering Range

Going public is not the route for everyone. However, the size of a company is not the most important indicator of whether and when to go public. The criteria for eligibility are numerous. In the middle 1980s roughly a third of the companies going public generated $10 million or more in revenues, almost 60 percent of companies had less than $2.5 million in revenues, and almost half were startups with at most $400,000 in revenues. The size of the average underwriting was $6.5 million, and the range for the majority between $4 million and $8 million.

Large underwriters are not likely to undertake offerings of less than $20 million. When Apple Computer went public in 1980 after three years of explosive growth, it was generating over $117 million in sales; Morgan Stanley and Hambrecht & Quist, working with a large underwriting syndicate, raised over $101.2 million in the initial public offering. With Home Shopping Network, which had suddenly jumped in size after completing a merger, Merrill-Lynch raised over $36 million in 1986.

At the other end of the spectrum are small underwriters and penny stock houses that will accept offerings of $2 million or less. Small amounts of capital can probably be raised with less red tape and at less expense in a private placement, albeit with the sacrifice of liquidity.

Private and Public Venture Capital

Historically, the sponsorship of fledgling enterprises was the province of venture capitalists like the Whitneys through their investments in new businesses and the Rockefellers through Venrock, their aggressive investment vehicle. Men like Fred Adler and dynamic firms like Kleiner Perkins on the West Coast were leaders in new high-technology enterprises. These risk-takers provided entrepreneurs with capital, set up companies with and for them, and built them up, even if the companies were not initially profitable or were at the very early stages of developing new products. After these firms had become profitable, and often at the peak of their growth, these venture capitalists brought their companies to Wall Street—to the Morgan Stanleys and the L. F. Rothschilds—and raised public capital. Right there, at the first public offering, the venture capitalists would realize a high-multiple return on their investment. For example, Venrock Associates provided venture capital for Apple Computer and Kleiner Perkins for Genentech.

In recent years, a number of private venture capital funds have been launched to tap the lucrative potential of this activity. D. H. Blair, among other small investment banks, has taken that concept one step further. They sponsor the same entrepreneurs, but involve the public at the earlier, high-leverage (high risk–high return) state. And they use the vehicle of initial public offerings rather than private placements to generate these early-stage investments. Thus, with a much smaller outlay, the broader public can participate in the kinds of gains that venture capitalists have enjoyed.

Advantages of Public Venture Capital

Public venture capital has several advantages over private placements. By definition, no public market exists for private investments. Private venture capitalists have their funds locked up until the companies go public. Public venture capital situations, however, enjoy some liquidity. Investors in early-stage companies need no special arrangement to find a buyer to whom they can sell their position in a private transaction. They do not have to wait until their company finally does go public— if indeed it ever does. When they think their stock has reached a good price, they can liquidate their position. Or, on any particular day, if they are not comfortable or psychologically want to be out of the market, or if they simply feel out of sorts with the world or the particular stock, they can sell. The investors may not get a great price, but at least they can protect themselves and realize either a small gain or a tax loss. And if the stock has made a large move, they can take profits that may be unparalleled anywhere.

A great disadvantage to entrepreneurs, venture capital investors, and IPO investors alike is that they may be selling the baby (their stock) before it matures. Some people buy the company stock at $6 and sell it a few days later at $8, pleased with their profit of 33 percent. Or if it goes up only a point, about 17 percent, in a few weeks, they'll say, "That's 1,400 percent annualized. Stratospheric! I'll sell it." Then they may miss the big move. Nova Pharmaceuticals is a case in point. It came out in 1983 at 6\frac{3}{4}$ a unit. In a month or two, it was up to $10. Then it dropped back, and you could have purchased all you wanted at about the offering price and sometimes less. Within three years, it hit a high of $187. It may have been an advantage to enjoy liquidity and a 30 to 35 percent profit in a few months. But those who were patient did far better. They realized the returns that venture capitalists seek.

Very High Risk

At the same time, public venture capital embodies perhaps the highest risk for the investor. Most obviously, these firms may become total failures. They may never develop into full-fledged companies. Some are not even companies in the complete sense of the term, not having sales or earnings. Their industries may never develop. The hazards of any business enterprise are magnified in small or startup companies. Patents are challenged or are violated without the companies having the resources to defend themselves. They may run out of funds before they have completed their products. The timing for their entry may be poor, or the market for their product or for the investment may change.

It would be a mistake, however, to judge the potential of a company from the stock price for the first year or so. Anyone buying emerging companies must recognize the fact that you are buying an infant that must learn first to get up, then to walk and run, and finally, to reach its full height. You want to hold for the time when the company has moved into the dramatic growth pattern that the market extrapolates into the future.

A few years ago, a company (Daxor) that was developing banks of frozen semen went public. After opening at $6, it dropped to 3\frac{1}{2}$. That can occur when a company is just starting out and the market for the stock is thin. Daxor stayed at 3\frac{1}{2}$ or $4 for two years. Then, in the spring of 1987, it suddenly moved up 20 points in two days. Since the stock also had an accompanying warrant, the unit including the shares and warrant moved up 50 points. Something that had cost $6 at the offering and had gone lower multiplied about eight times. Two and a half years after the offering, Daxor was discovered. What happened?

What caused the sudden jump?   Daxor benefited from belated recognition. It stores frozen blood as well as semen, and today, people are so terrified of transfusions because of AIDS that many families are freezing their own blood. They want to be able to draw upon their private blood bank when they need it. Suddenly, because institutions became excited by these prospects, the stock started trading hundreds of thousands of shares per day. The maximum loss for the investor was six points; the gain potential, for the one who did not sell out in disgust, was over ten times the initial investment. That's the risk/reward profile.

The Investment Bankers

The amount of money raised in an underwriting is a balance between what the issuer wants to raise, what the general market will absorb, and what the investor wants to pay. The job of the underwriter, or investment banker, is to bring together the entrepreneur-client, who brings in the growth company, and the investor-client, who puts up the risk capital, and to mediate between them.

Choosing an Investment Bank

It is important to choose an investment bank with a solid track record— a house that does more for its client than file with the SEC, take the company public, and collect a commission. The banking house should care about its reputation and the aftermarket success of the IPO and of the company being underwritten, and it should want to remain involved with the management on a continuing basis. It should also have a real stake in its companies. Underwriters sometimes take equity positions in early-stage companies that they will take public, purchasing these positions at a discount to what the market value will be. Another practice followed by some underwriters, especially in taking early-stage companies public, is to purchase inexpensive underwriters' warrants. These warrants permit the investment bank to buy stock typically at 20 percent *above* the offering price. This practice gives the underwriter a vested interest in the companies' aftermarket performance. If the company does poorly, the warrants are worthless. If it does well, the investment bank makes more by exercising the warrants than they do with the underwriting commissions, and the company collects another round of financing.

Timing

Timing is a key element in the process. An issue must be taken public when the market is good and that type of security is in favor, or no one will buy it. Although growth companies, by definition, can expand independently of the economy and of conditions in the securities markets, a bad market will dampen the issuing of IPOs.

The underwriter must be decisive in order to capitalize on market conditions and to bring an issue out promptly. If the delay is too long, the market may shift and the window of opportunity will close. A bad market does not merely determine if and when a company will be taken public. It may keep the company from raising as much capital as it wants, may reduce valuations, and may generate problems in the aftermarket.

Getting the Highest Valuation: A Common Mistake

It is a mistake to choose an underwriter just to receive the highest valuation possible. Although it is common in underwriting to take the maximum amount of what the market can bear and thereby please the client with a high valuation, nothing could be more detrimental to the public and, ultimately, to the corporate client itself. If a company is overpriced, the founders and venture capitalists may be happy at first, but they will be dismally sorry after the shares have dropped back to their fair value. On the other hand, if the stock is priced fairly and reasonably and it starts to perform and is well received, the insiders will be able to sell their shares at a much higher price. Public attitudes have an important influence here. A declining price will sour the public taste and greatly reduce its appetite for new shares. An increasing price, conversely, can cause a feeding frenzy.

It is crucial for the underwriter to price an issue well for the benefit of the public and not just for the corporate client, because it is the public investors who are putting up the risk capital. They deserve a big reward if the speculative company works. If it does not, they are certainly going to lose a lot of money. This is not a matter of altruism. There is one tenet that is central to this business: *Investment bankers are only as good as the last two or three issues that they have handled.* For that reason, underwriters should price the shares as if they themselves were investors.

The Basic Investment Bank Conflict

There is a basic conflict between the entrepreneur-client and the investor-client in which the underwriter must see himself as arbitrator. The investor in a growth situation wants a premium for his or her risk. He or she wants the opportunity to get in on the ground floor in an exciting growth situation. When the entrepreneur comes in and asks: "How shall I price my company? What is fair, and what do you recommend?" the underwriter must play the role of King Solomon and do what is right for both of them. It requires a tough selling job to get the point across, but when a company is priced well for the public, for the risk investor, and it does well in the aftermarket, everybody wins.

Merrill Lynch's underwriting of Home Shopping Network is a case in point. The stock at the IPO was priced at $18. The issue opened in the aftermarket at $42 and immediately went much higher, eventually reaching $150. Soon after it came out the media started asking: Hadn't Merrill-Lynch underpriced the company? Didn't it render the company a disservice? On the contrary: everybody benefited from this underwriting: Merrill Lynch, because it had a winning stock; the public, because they had bought the company at the IPO price and in the aftermarket and made substantial profit; and the insiders, because they still owned a big portion of the company (about 84%) on which they made enormous profits, and because the public would be eager to subscribe to subsequent offerings.

The entrepreneur must be made to realize that his interests are not in conflict with the risk investor's, because when the stock does well and he realizes a huge profit, he also develops a following. He wants to develop that image. Essentially, what we are pricing in an initial public offering is only the tip of the iceberg, not the iceberg itself. That is the difference between being acquired and going public. When an entrepreneur sells his company outright, he is giving up his rights (completely or largely) to an entire stream of future profits that the company will bring. Even if he remains part of management, he relinquishes much of his financial interests.

But going public is a landmark in a firm's history. The entrepreneur retains and intensifies his efforts to make this company the greatest achievement of his life. What he has heretofore invested is only seed capital. What has been sold to the public is just a fraction of his potential wealth. If the investment banker represents an entrepreneur seeking to sell his entire company (and not just a piece of it) to a major corporation, it makes sense to fight for every last penny. But if the public is being invited to buy part of the company, it must be so exciting that the momentum of pricing it properly and building a following on Wall Street will support the stock.

Consider the Aftermarket: Where the Big Money is Made

What is true for the investor is also true for the entrepreneur. The big money is made in the aftermarket. When Home Shopping Network went from $18 to $150 per share, the initial price that the founders and initial investors gave away as a bargain was only a small fraction of the company. That initial offering was what made the whole company more valuable. And the company was able to make acquisitions with its highly valued stock.

Once stocks become glamorous, they retain a high multiple, even when they do poorly. The semiconductor companies are as cyclical as in any industry. Yet they command high multiples because they are seen as forefront technology firms. Even though they have enormous competition from the Japanese and still more from new entrants like the Koreans and Taiwanese, they still retain their glamour. They are glamorous even though, if you average out their earnings over the years, they hardly ever make money—that is, they make money for two or three years and then lose money for several years. Texas Instruments in 1986 earned less than two dollars a share, yet was being recommended at $100 even before the turnaround.

First impressions are vital. Investors remember the initial activity, whether up or down. The owners should want to start out with a *hot* image, so that the stock will always be viewed as a glamour stock selling at a high multiple. Then no one has to worry about the price. The owners' interests coincide with those of the risk investor because they also want to bring it out at a price so exciting that it will appreciate and gain the company both a reputation for success and the ability to generate big money. Perhaps most importantly, when the firm comes back to the market for more capital, it can do so at a higher price and with a happy following.

On the other hand, if an issue is priced too high, everybody loses. The underwriter renders a disservice to the investor, because it has already fully discounted the IPOs future value. The price is so high that even if the company works, it will only then be worth what the public paid originally. And when enough firms are overpriced, then nobody can make any money. The market dries up. Even the venture capitalists can no longer form companies. They have a hard enough time saving the companies in which they have already invested. After all, they invest with the idea of seeding a company for two or three years and then bringing it public. But if the public market evaporates, investment bankers themselves have killed the goose that lays the golden egg. When the public risk-takers say, "I pass—because I have been hurt on the last three issues," then there is no place for underwriters to go. In fact, with the public market dead because investment bankers have killed it, the venture capitalists must go to their own pocketbooks to provide the new funds these companies need for later-stage financing. It becomes very tough.

Pricing for Performance: Structuring an Issue

The basic questions any entrepreneur must face are what to give up for the resources he needs and in what form to seek funds. The entrepreneur may prefer a debt issue (so he does not give up equity) but finds that interest rates are high or, more likely, that straight loans are impossible. He may then seek a compromise between debt and equity in the form of convertible debentures or preferred stock.

For an initial public offering, straight equity works best. An equity issue does not impose more debt and risk on an already speculative company. It improves the balance sheet considerably. It is cheaper than debt as a way of raising capital. And it increases the company's leverage in obtaining further financing.

If the company has an earnings history, or is close to commercialization, the offering can consist of straight shares of common stock. If the company is a startup company, however, and may wish at some time to raise more funds, a unit structure, offering a package of shares and warrants (options to buy shares), may be especially attractive for both issuer and investor. For early-stage companies, underwriters usually look for a structure in which about half the company will be sold to the public. This is not a challenge to management. Since, in the final analysis, all are investing in the company's management, it is in everyone's interest that the management remain in charge. Control can be ensured in many ways other than by confining the shares to insiders.

The owners are certainly entitled to a premium for their ideas, the capital they have invested so far, and the considerable energy they have put into bringing the company to the point of going public. They receive that premium in the immediate, substantial increase in book value and in the unprecedented opportunity for growth that they will now enjoy. Their company will be able to sell at a substantial multiple of its earnings. Given these benefits, they should allow the outside investors the opportunity to catch up. If the outsiders experience a 50 percent dilution, the equity will have to double for them to break even (assuming minimum pre-offering equity). That is not an unreasonable expectation. But if they have only 10 or 20 percent of a company, the future value has been overly anticipated (discounted) in the shares.

Giving half or more than half of the company to the outsiders is often an inducement to investors because it leaves relatively fewer *insider shares* (shares held by the founders and other owners before the company goes public) outstanding and shows that management has confidence in its own performance.

How can management control be protected? Various strategies exist. Several classes of common stock can be created, some with multiple voting privileges. Stock dividends can be structured for management that are contingent upon stock or earnings performance. Special classes of options or warrants can be made part of the offering. Shares of the company can be held in escrow, to be issued to insiders after the stock's performance or a company's earnings meet predetermined targets.

Company Capitalization

Management Technology, as an example company, shows how an initial pubic offering can transform a company's capitalization, prospects, and future. The firm offers sophisticated software systems to international banks and financial institutions. Before the offering, the company had about $1 million in debt and $1.5 million in stockholders' equity. In 1987 it had several hundred thousand dollars in profits on revenues of about $3 million and was running a small working capital deficit.

When the chairman of the company met with the brokers prior to the IPO, he pointed out that the banks he was soliciting for business would be intrigued by the product and services he offered. Then they would look at the size of his company and its balance sheet and back off!

Before an offering can be sold to the public, the company has to sell itself to the broker community. In this case the chairman accomplished just that. He portrayed the huge market potential for his services and encouraged his investment bank to work out a structure that would win sponsorship in house and on the street. Half the company was sold to the public for $4,347,000 net of underwriting commissions.

The pro forma adjustment showed that after the offering, the company would have paid off part of its debt and would have, in all, $4.7 million in equity, with a much stronger debt/equity ratio. Even more importantly, the balance sheet would establish the firm's credibility with the banks with which it was trying to gain contracts. (See Table 14-1.)

The company has since concluded a number of important agreements around the world, including long-term agreements in Australia and Scandinavia, and with companies like Olivetti and the Bank of Montreal. The underwriting was the impulse that triggered what could be explosive growth. It opened new vistas for a company with grand designs. The units, which opened at $6 in May 1987, traded in January 1988, after a two-for-one split, at $21.50—the equivalent of $43.

Risk Factors

The *risk factors* are written in the registration statement to stress the *negatives* to investors. In the process, they protect the company, the underwriter, and the brokers from liability for false and misleading information. The risk factors may include any negative factor that could inhibit the company's plans—dependence on major clients, working capital deficiencies, lack of an earnings history, or critical dependence on one customer or executive. In fact, some of these risk factors are so standard that they appear in prospectus after prospectus with identical language—a laundry list. Here are some that are most typically found in prospectuses of early-stage companies preparing for an IPO.

Continuing Losses and Capital Deficiency

This condition is not uncommon for a development-stage company that has spent years developing a new product. It alerts the unsophisticated investor to the risks involved; the sophisticated investor will realize that the losses also represent research and development and other expenses whose value cannot appear on a balance sheet.

Table 14–1. Management Technology Capitalization Changes (from the 1987 Prospectus).

CAPITALIZATION

The following table puts forth the capitalization of the Company as of January 31, 1987, and as adjusted to give effect to the issuance and sale of the Units offered hereby and the application of a portion of the proceeds to reduce certain indebtedness.

	January 31, 1987	
	Actual	As Adjusted
Current liabilities	$1,047,607(1)	$ 709,743
Stockholder's equity:		
Preferred Stock. $.01 par value: 1,000 shares authorized and issued	10	10
Convertible Preferred Stock. $.01 par value: 1,000 shares authorized and issued	10	10
Common Stock. $.01 par value: 10,000,000 shares authorized:		
1,401,200 shares issued and outstanding at January 31, 1987	14,012	
2,801,200 shares issued and outstanding as adjusted (2)		28,012
Capital contributed in excess of par	1,707,788	5,018,788
Deficit accumulated	(274,069)	(274,069)
Treasury stock	(1,300)	(1,300)
Total stockholders' equity	$1,446,451	$4,771,451

(1) Includes a revolving line of credit established in August 1986 with ABN-LaSalle in the sum of $250,000, payable on demand at prime plus 1.5% of which $210,864 was outstanding as of January 31, 1987. As of May 11, 1987 the entire credit line had been utilized. In addition, the credit line has been exceeded by approximately $50,000.

(2) Does not give effect to the exercise of the Class A Warrants, Class B Warrants, Over-allotment Option, or Unit Purchase Option, or up to a maximum of 40,000 shares of Common Stock which would be issued to NNS Development Corporation upon such entity's conversion of up to $60,000 of Company indebtedness into shares of Common Stock at a conversion rate of 50% of the public offering price.

Competition and Rapid Technological Change

A new product or industry which is not yet dominated by a few large firms is subject to intense competition, both from startups and from major companies operating through subdivisions. The fact of competition and the risks of product obsolescence must be cited in the prospectus.

Dependence on Key Personnel

A new company usually hinges on the energy and brilliance of just a few individuals. This risk factor is the converse of the initiative that launched the company. The prospectus spells out the amount of key man insurance that has been taken out for officers who are central to the enterprise.

Control

After the offering, the founders and key executives will generally own the controlling shares in a corporation. The investor is made aware that a small group or one person may be able to elect the board of directors. By the same token, classes of stocks with multiple voting rights and owners of more than five percent of the shares are identified. All key players and their positions are revealed.

Lack of Patent Protection

This caveat is not listed solely for products vulnerable to imitation because they lack patent protection. The fact that a patent has been filed, or even awarded, does not exempt it from competition. The prospectus will spell out the fact that the patent can be challenged or superseded.

Need for Additional Financing

In spelling out the use of funds, the prospectus will also indicate how long they are intended to last and include the proviso that the firm may run out of funds or be unable to complete its project with only the funds generated by the offering.

Offering Price Arbitrarily Determined

The fact that the valuation of an IPO is a function of negotiations between the underwriter and the issuer must be specified because no public market has existed for the stock; hence the price has not been determined by demand and supply.

Shares Eligible for Future Sale

When a company goes public, the shares held by the founders, the principals of the company, the venture capitalists, and other insiders who have invested in the company will constitute restricted stock that cannot be sold, at the offering or at any other time, without being registered with the SEC. Moreover, the shares must be held for a minimum amount of time—two or three years, depending on the class of stock. There is also a limit to the amount of stock, relative to the total volume of trading, that may permissibly be sold within any particular three-month period (Rule 144).

Since insiders generally hold large blocks of stock, their sale can depress its price, despite all precautions, and investors are alerted to this possibility. In addition, underwriters will sometimes request that potential sellers hold on to their shares for some period after the offering (e.g., 13 months).

New Marketing Program (or Any Other Effort)

Although this sounds like a plus, if the issuer is inexperienced in the area, the prospectus will indicate the fact and the possibility that any given project may not work.

Outstanding Options and Underwriters' Warrants

The prospectus warns the investor about classes of securities that may *dilute* the shares—that is, increase the number of shares outstanding— and hence decrease per-share earnings.

Use of Proceeds

Every company going public must disclose the way it will use the funds that it raises. Home Shopping Network used the offering proceeds to purchase computer equipment, reduce its debt, acquire new offices, equipment, and inventory, and institute training and marketing programs. Management Technology used its funds to finance its marketing activities, establish sales offices, improve client services, and integrate its mainframe computer software system with the IBM Stratus system. Items to watch under *Use of Proceeds* are large amounts for working capital, overhead, and salary expenses. Generally, salaries over $50,000 and directors' fees are enumerated in the prospectus.

Dilution

As we have noted, when a company goes public, the insiders, having made a commitment far in advance of the public investors and at greater risk, expect to benefit from the offering through the appreciation of the share prices and from owning a large portion of the company. In addition, the public investors will likely be contributing much more than their proportionate share to the post-offering book value of the company. This dilution, or *water*, in the stock is specified not only in the list of risk factors but in a separate section of the prospectus.

Dilution is the difference between the purchase price of the shares and the net tangible book value per share after the offering. Table 14-2 shows the format for Management Technology. The company's per-share book value after the offering is obtained by adding up the former net worth of the company and the net proceeds of the offering and dividing the sum by the new number of shares outstanding. This is represented as the pro forma net tangible book value after the offering—in Management Technology's case $1.70. The insiders enjoyed an immediate increase of 67 cents in the value of their shares, while the outsiders, having paid $3 for shares that were worth $1.70 after the offering, experienced a book equity dilution of $1.30.

Dilution can also be expressed as a percentage. To derive it, divide the dollar figure for the dilution ($1.30) by the offering price ($3). In this case dilution was 43 percent. Even for early-stage companies, investment banks work for dilution of 50 percent or less, just as they work for public ownership of 50 percent or more of a company.

Some companies that went public with high dilution have done extremely well. When Apple Computer went public in December 1980, it already had an impressive earnings history. In the three years before the offering, earnings had jumped from 3 cents to 24 cents a share. Public investors paid a stiff premium for their shares. They spent $22 a share to buy stock whose book net worth after the offering was $1.95, for a dilution of $20.05 or 91 percent. They paid $101.2 million for seven and one-half percent of a company whose market value at the offering, $1.19 billion, was 100 times earnings of 22 cents a share (post-offering), and about 10 times annual sales of $117 million.

That was discounting the future, indeed. But by 1984, revenues were $1.5 billion, and earnings per share were 52 cents. In 1987, revenues were over $2.6 billion. Earnings per share for 1987, projected at $1.65, and book value per share was $6.63, on over 125 million shares out-

Table 14-2. Management Technology.

DILUTION

At January 31, 1987, the Common Stock had a net tangible book value per share of $1.03. "Net tangible book value per share" represents the amount of total tangible assets less total liabilities, divided by the number of shares of Common Stock outstanding. After giving effect to the sale hereunder of 1,400,000 Shares by the Company at the public offering price, (attributing no value to the warrants) the *pro forma* net tangible book value at January 31, 1987, would have been $1.70 per share, representing an immediate increase of $0.67 per share to existing shareholders and an immediate dilution (i.e., the difference between the purchase price of a share and the net tangible book value per share after the offering) of $1.30 per share to the persons purchasing such shares at the public offering price. The following table illustrates the per share dilution.

Public offering price per share		$3.00
Net tangible book value before offering	$1.03	
Increase attributable to investors	.67	
Pro forma net tangible book value after offering . .		1.70
Dilution to investors		$1.30

The following table sets forth the difference between the number of shares purchased from the Company, the total consideration paid and the average price per share paid by existing shareholders and that to be paid by investors:

	Shares Purchased		Total Consideration Paid		Average Price Per Share
	Number	Percentage	Amount	Percentage	
Existing shareholders	1,401,200	50.0%	$1,721,800	29.1%	$1.24
New investors	1,400,000	50.0	4,200,000	70.9	$3.00
Total	2,801,200	100.0%	$5,921,800	100.0%	

standing—roughly twice the number of shares that had been outstanding with the IPO. The price of the stock, in January 1988, was $38, after a year's high of $59.75. Adjusting for stock splits (to make a fair comparison to the IPO price of $22 per share), these share prices were $76 and $120, respectively.

In this case, the dilution and the multiple of earnings* anticipated subsequent performance. After seven years, the buyer at the IPO would have multiplied his investment almost 4 times. If he had sold at the 1987 high, he would have realized almost 6 times his original investment. Needless to say, the venture capitalists had far greater profits.

In Home Shopping Network, outsiders paid 99.8 percent of the proceeds for 16 percent of the company (including the overallotment). The company's net tangible book value before the offering was 46 cents a share. After the offering, the book value was $2.32, for a dilution of $15.68, or 87 percent, on the $18 shares. However, the earnings multiple* after dilution, based on the company's annualized earnings, was only about $18\frac{1}{2}$. In August 1986, the stock hit 133, and went to the equivalent of about 150. After several splits, there were about six times as many shares outstanding as there had been at the IPO, so that, even after a dramatic drop—due to a combination of market conditions, equipment problems, and fallen earnings, the shares in January 1988, at $4.25, were the equivalent of $25 at the IPO.

Not all companies are so well-known, the issues so hot, or the public premium as high as these were. Belvedere Corporation, underwritten in January 1987 by Donaldson, Lufkin & Jenrette and Merrill Lynch Capital Markets, raised $23.4 million for 2.6 million shares, giving it a $52 million market capitalization on a net worth of $39.8 million. Public investors paid 52 percent of the total consideration for 45 percent of the company. With shares priced at $9, dilution in book value was $2.15, and, as a percentage, 23.8 percent. (See Table 14-3.)

Planning the Process of Going Public

Once a company has decided to go public, the long and rigorous process of planning, preparing, and executing the IPO begins. The focus of the company's investment banker/lead manager—the terms are used

---

* The earnings multiple is the price of stock divided by the earnings per share. See Chapter 6.

Table 14-3. Belvedere Corporation.

DILUTION

	Price to the Public	Underwriting Discounts and Commissions	Proceeds to the Company
Per Share	$9.00	$.65	$8.35
Total(3)	$23,400,000	$1,690,000	$21,710,000

	Shares Purchased	Percent of Total Shares	Consideration Paid(1)	Percent of Total Consideration Paid(1)	Average Price Per Share
Existing stockholders	3,212,654	55%	$21,654,000	48%	$6.74
New Investors	2,600,000	45%	23,400,000	52%	$9.00
Total	5,812,654	100%	$45,054,000	100%	

Price to the public		$9.00
Pro forma net tangible book value per share before offering	$5.96	
Increase attributable to payments by new investors ...	.89	
Pro forma as adjusted net tangible book value per share after offering		$6.85
Dilution of book value per share of new investors		$2.15

CAPITALIZATION

The following table sets forth the consolidated capitalization of the Company at September 30, 1986 on an actual and pro forma basis, and as adjusted to give effect to the proposed issuance of the Common Stock offered hereby (assuming the Underwriters' over-allotment option is not exercised) and the application of the estimated net proceeds therefrom.

	Actual	Pro Forma (in thousands)	Pro Forma As Adjusted
Bank loans	$ 5,500	$15,000	$ 7,645
Stockholders' Equity:			
Preferred Stock, $.10 par value; 500,000 shares authorized; none issued	—	—	—
Common Stock, $.10 par value; 15,000,000 shares authorized; 2,064,005 shares outstanding, 3,212,654 shares issued pro forma and 5,812,654 shares issued pro forma as adjusted	206	321	581
Additional paid-in capital	4,095	12,480	32,899
Retained earnings	8,853	8,853	8,853
Total stockholders' equity	13,154	21,654	42,333
Total capitalization	$18,654	$36,654	$49,978

here interchangeably—who previously has been advising the company's owners on the pros and cons of going public, now shifts to taking the steps necessary to make the initial public offering a success.

After the decision is made to go public, the issuer and lead manager sometimes sign a letter of intent which spells out in detail the terms and conditions of the undertaking. Items covered often include, but are not limited to:

- offering size in shares
- filing price range
- maximum gross spread
- marketing plan
- out clause covering certain circumstances whereby the underwriter may not proceed with the offering

Firm Commitment Versus Best Efforts

Early in the IPO process, in so-called all hands meetings, the issuing company and its lead underwriter draft (but do not sign) one of two types of underwriting contracts. The first type is known as a *firm commitment* underwriting agreement, in which the underwriters agree to purchase the entire issue from the issuing company at a specified price for resale to the public. Here the underwriters take the full risk of sales and price.

The second type is called a *best efforts* underwriting agreement; here, the underwriter(s) only agree to act as the company's marketing agent. No undertaking to purchase the issue at a specified price is made; instead, shares are marketed at a fixed price for a specified period of time. The agreement usually stipulates that if a predetermined minimum number of shares are not sold by a specified end date, the offering will be cancelled.

Registration Statement

One of the principal tasks requiring immediate attention of all hands (including representatives of the lead manager and co-manager(s), underwriters' counsel, counsel and accountants for the issuer, and key company personnel) is the preparation and filing of the SEC registration statement.

Form S-1 or S-18

This document may be SEC Form S-1 or, for smaller businesses, SEC Form S-18; certain types of businesses may require other forms instead. Whichever form is used, the registration statement serves as both a legal document and the source of the preliminary prospectus (the so called *red herring*) for potential investors. It must therefore not only conform to the disclosure requirements of the SEC but also be clearly and convincingly written, presenting the company as an attractive investment opportunity.

Parts I and II

The registration statement consists of two parts. Usually only Part I is distributed to prospective investors. Part II, which contains a copy of the draft underwriting agreement and other legal documents, is made available for public inspection at SEC headquarters in Washington and, on microfiche, at other SEC regional branch office locations.

Disclosures

Disclosed in the registration statement are various kinds of information important for investors to consider in making their investment decisions. Such data include a summary of the offering, estimated share price when first issued (the filing range), estimated number of shares to be issued (the size), a company description, risk factors, intended use(s) to which IPO proceeds will be put, the company's current and pro forma capitalization, management information; financial data, names and ownership size of principal and selling shareholders (if any), lead underwriter and co-managers (if any), and certain legal opinions and accounting firm certifications concerning the company and the issue.

A key portion of Form S-1 is the management's discussion and analysis (MD&A) section, which examines the company's financial condition and the results of its operations and lays out in detail the company's business plan. (Form S-18 does not contain an MD&A section; smaller businesses are granted a year or more to file an MD&A equivalent.) The MD&A section typically attracts close scrutiny by prospective investors, as do any equity sales by insiders described in the prospectus under *Use of Proceeds* and *Principal and Selling Shareholders*, and, for obvious reasons, the data in *Pending Litigation*. A section usually entitled

Certain Transactions also gets close review as this portion covers many of the prior financial events of the company's history, including related party transactions, if any. (Related party transactions, such as the company leasing facilities from a founder or investor, can be revealing and should be scrutinized.)

SEC Review

Once the registration statement is filed, the SEC subjects it to an often lengthy review process, the purpose of which is to ensure that there are no material misstatements or omissions in the prospectus that might prevent an investor from making a fully informed investment decision. The issuer should understand, however, that the SEC review does not address the intrinsic worth of the company or the shares it plans to issue; that judgment is made by the marketplace.

Due Diligence

Among the many conferences that take place early in the IPO process is the first of what may ultimately be a number of due diligence meetings, in which the lead underwriter fulfills its legal responsibility to investigate issuer disclosures that are or properly should be made in the registration statement and prospectus. This process is accomplished, in part, by having underwriter's counsel question the issuer's managers and directors and investigate representations made in the statement as drafted. The due diligence process may also include exhaustive background checks of issuer management, meetings with customers, suppliers, and other business associates, and review of all the issuer's legal contracts.

Blue-Sky Laws

In addition to SEC regulations, many individual states have adopted so-called blue-sky laws to protect investors against securities fraud. These laws oblige companies to register their new stock offerings and provide prospective investors with all relevant financial and business data. Note that even after the SEC's Division of Corporation Finance has approved a registration statement, failure to satisfy a given state's blue-sky laws may block the initial issuance of stock in that state.

Liabilities and Defense

A prospectus is a liability document: What it says can hurt far more than it can help. As a rule, issuing companies generally and the board of directors and certain members of management specifically are legally responsible for all misstatements or material omissions in their registration statements, notwithstanding an error's origin, a lack of intent to deceive, or any due-diligence activities conducted by underwriters. Belief, however, is becoming an important defense. In litigation arising from investor assertion that a registration statement does not contain full disclosure and/or contains material misstatements and /or omissions, underwriters and other parties retained by the issuing company have in recent years mounted successful due-diligence defenses based on the fact that, after the underwriters had made an investigation, they had reason to believe and did believe that the information contained in the registration statement was indeed accurate.

The Marketing Effort

Once the registration statement has been prepared and filed, the marketing effort begins. This campaign, as much as anything that precedes or follows it, will determine the success or failure of the IPO. The key is to stimulate investor demand for the stock so that, as in basic economics, the demand will exceed the supply. Through the marketing effort, the underwriter (called the lead manager or lead underwriter when, as is usually the case, it forms an underwriting syndicate) attempts to create an imbalance in the supply/demand equation for the issue, so that there are more buyers than sellers when the stock is finally released for sale to the public. Key aspects of the marketing effort include creation of a marketing plan, distribution of the preliminary prospectus (commonly known as the red herring—so called because of the red-ink hedge clause that is printed on the left edge of the cover page), and the development of a roadshow.

From the preliminary prospectus, the issuer's senior management and the lead manager often develop a brief underwriter's memorandum or marketing memo for use by the sales force of the lead manager. This non-public document usually consists of a series of key sales points for use by brokers who will be soliciting indications of interest from prospective investors in the approaching IPO. Great care must be exercised both in the preparation of this memo, since it is not a formal part of the registration statement, and in its distribution—the memo is strictly for securities sales people and cannot be shown to the public in whole or in part.

Because of the importance of the marketing memo as a selling tool, public relations professionals are sometimes enlisted to sharpen its language and make it as effective as possible. Outside public relations counsel is also engaged by some issuers to advise and assist in many aspects of the IPO campaign, including drafting of press releases, press contacts, roadshows, and other public, professional, and media events. Moreover, because SEC rules and regulations limit corporate public relations during the time between the registration date and the effective date and the 25-day cooling-off period after the effective date (i.e., the time period during which no securities firms may publish research on the issuer), it is advisable for privately held companies to establish an active public relations program well in advance of going public. This action is often done with the help of a respected public relations firm, generally one specializing in financial matters.

The Roadshow

The roadshow (also known as the "dog-and-pony show") is the key marketing campaign event that precedes the IPO by several weeks and provides the issuer with the opportunity to present the company in person to prospective investors. As its name implies, the senior management of the issuer participating in the roadshow travel to major financial centers, giving investors a chance to size up issuer management, ask questions about the company, and, significantly, judge how warmly fellow investment professionals seem to regard the issue.

Increasingly, institutional and retail investors base their decision whether to purchase shares of an IPO on their opinion of management, an opinion often formed during a 25-minute roadshow presentation. Years of hard work and business progress can be undermined or even undone by an inept roadshow performance. The roadshow is thus a kind of trial for the issuer's business plan, where the verdict is rendered in the size of the investor's order and the maximum price at which the order will hold. No effort should be spared to ensure that the roadshow is a success.

By the end of the roadshow, the lead manager should have a good idea of the level of interest among investors in the company and the stock it plans to issue. Proper assessment of that level of interest will assist the managing underwriter in determining the final per-share price and ultimate size of the offering.

Allocation and Distribution Of Shares

The investor universe consists of three distinct groups: U.S. domestic institutions, U.S. domestic retail investors, and international investors (primarily institutional but increasing in breadth rapidly to encompass individuals as well). Issuers obviously prefer an investor base that will be loyal to the current management, and, believing retail investors to be more inclined to such loyalty, they often express a preference toward retail as opposed to institutional investor groups.

This perspective must be regarded as somewhat naive given the realities of today's equity markets. In the mid-1980s, institutions held more than 35 percent of all equities listed on the New York Stock Exchange (NYSE), which was double their share in 1960. By 1990, institutions are expected to hold 50 percent of all NYSE-listed equities. Institutions already hold between one-half and two-thirds of the stock of the nation's 200 largest corporations. In 1953, when institutions held 15 percent of listed stocks, their trades constituted about 25 percent of stock market transactions, in terms of both volume and value. Today that percentage approaches 90 percent.

For almost every offering in excess of $30 million, a separate international tranche whereby shares are marketed worldwide is now appropriate. Underwriters must also make known to issuers the existence of a whole coterie of buyers—so-called hedge funds, for example—who are professional players in the IPO market. These players do nothing but buy and sell shares of virtually every IPO, looking for the ones that appreciate quickly and return a fast profit. (A classic example of the quick-rising or so-called hot new issue was the initial public offering for Genentech, a south San Francisco biotechnology company which in 1980 was priced at $35 and skyrocketed to $88 in its first day of public trading.)

Although these IPO professional investors are not the elusive long-term investors issuers prefer, they are a reality with which underwriters must deal. The managing underwriter must also impress on the issuer that investor loyalty is contingent on how the company fares and is managed after as well as before the IPO.

Issuers often ask the lead manager what the ideal share distribution might be. In theory, the correct answer is: the distribution that will create the highest *sustainable* price that the market will bear on the issue date. However, the lead manager must not commit itself to a formulaic distribution at the outset. In the past several years, institutional investors have dominated the marketplace for IPOs—domestic institutions, primarily, but increasingly foreign institutions as well. However, there have also been periods when the individual investor was the only audience willing to listen and invest in IPOs. The lead manager who prejudges the allocation at the outset, before the marketing effort begins, makes a critical error.

Often, during a worldwide roadshow, the lead manager may get an indication that one of the three market segments may be willing to pay a higher price per share—an indication, for example, that European institutions may be willing to spend two dollars per share more than their Asian or American counterparts. If the lead manager can ensure that higher price in Europe and by means of an effective roadshow, still get a good domestic retail distribution, then, for example, American institutions might safely be excluded from the transaction. A useful principle for both issuer and lead manager is to be realistic about goals and, simultaneously, realistic about markets.

The Syndicate and Selling Group

The lead manager's own sales force (retail and institutional), secondary trading expertise, and aftermarket research coverage largely determine the success and aftermarket performance of an IPO. It is logical, therefore, for a lead manager to distribute a large portion of the offering through his own organization. However, the lead manager also has the responsibility to ensure some liquidity in the stock. If the lead manager distributes nearly all of the shares, locking out the rest of the street (i.e., Wall Street, the brokerage community) and providing little incentive for other firms to make a market in the stock (trade it in the secondary market) or follow it on a research basis, the stock probably has less of a chance to appreciate quickly and will have little liquidity in the immediate aftermarket.

It is thus customary for the principal underwriter to form a syndicate of underwriters, each of whom is committed to buying a portion of the IPO as specified in the registration statement. This underwriting syndicate is assembled during the time between the filing of the registration statement with the SEC and the effective date, when SEC approval is received and the offering may proceed.

The decision to distribute some shares outside its own organization requires courage on the lead manager's part. First of all, the firm has to make some economic concessions in sharing the underwriter's spread with its competitors. Secondly, today's fiercely competitive environment creates the risk that one of the syndicate members might outshine the lead manager on the distribution and thereby gain an edge in subsequent competition for any future offerings of the IPO company. (Note: Underwriting agreements or letters of intent, however, sometimes give the lead manager the right to handle any future equity offerings—the so-called right of first refusal.)

In general, the lead manager should try to find five or six other firms to participate in the distribution in a significant manner. It is up to the syndicate manager of the lead underwriter to select the appropriate firms. Its decision should be based on a solid distribution of the shares to strong investors, on ability of making a market in the stock, and on following it on a research basis.

The Final Stages

Some five to ten weeks after the S-1 registration statement is filed (usually somewhat less if an S-18 Form has been used), the IPO process enters its final stages. Since the initial filing, several things will have happened in addition to those already described. The SEC's Division of Corporation Finance will have reviewed the filing and sent a deficiency letter (also known as a letter of comment), indicating which sections of the preliminary prospectus require further revision or expansion. The issuer and underwriter and their professional associates will have acted to address the points raised in the deficiency letter, either by revising the registration statement or by clarifying for the SEC particular points raised in the deficiency letter.

The day before the effective date, which may average 30 to 45 days after the registration date, the final price of the stock is negotiated, and the underwriting agreement is signed the next morning. On the morning of the effective date, the independent auditor delivers to the issuer and the underwriter a comfort letter regarding the correctness of the accounting information in the registration statement and prospectus and certifying the absence of material changes made since it was prepared. Since the per-share fixed price is based on what the market will bear and other conditions at the time the pricing amendment is filed, underwriters in almost every case release the shares for sale to the public almost immediately after receiving word from the SEC that the registration statement has been declared effective.

Pricing

The last and most crucial step of the IPO transaction is the pricing of the issue. In a perfect world, the roadshow is finished, all indications of interest are in, and the allocation of the issue to investors is completed two or three days before the issuer gets the go-ahead from the SEC. The more likely scenario, however, is that the SEC grants approval before the issue is fully sold, or that the deal is fully sold but the SEC has not yet completed its review. Timing thus becomes critical.

Time of the Day

The actual price negotiation usually takes place in the afternoon, not necessarily before the market closes, and involves a meeting of the lead manager's syndicate manager and senior corporate finance representative and the issuer's senior officers. Together, this group determines the final offering price, the size (number of shares to be issued), and the underwriter's discount. These numbers get inserted into the registration statement, and the so-called pricing amendment to the registration statement gets printed that night.

The next morning, the issuer files the pricing amendment with the SEC, and the underwriter waits for the SEC to declare the amendment effective (this word is hopefully received before the opening of trading) and then releases the shares for sale to the public at the stated fixed price. All the underwriters and/or selling group members are bound by the so-called agreement among underwriters and/or the selected dealer agreement to sell the shares at that fixed price until the lead manager terminates price and trading restrictions, thereby allowing the stock to trade freely in the secondary market. Depending on market conditions and the policies of the lead manager, these restrictions might terminate immediately or one to several days after the issue is initially released (depending upon market receptivity to the issue and the progress of firm ticketing by retail brokers).

Factors to Consider

In pricing an IPO, the underwriter must consider a number of factors. One of the most important is the issuer's projected annual earnings per share, corrected to reflect the increased number of shares outstanding as a result of the IPO, and correlated with the price/earnings (P/E) ratio of comparable companies in similar industries.

In addition to the fundamental quality of the issuer's business and the caliber of its management team, important factors in final pricing include the general health of the issuer's industry, the performance of stocks of comparable companies already traded publicly and the status of the market as a whole. The response to the roadshow will figure in the decision.

Price Sensitivity of Prospective Investors

During the marketing period, issuer and managing underwriter alike must pay close attention to the price sensitivity of prospective investors. A given institutional investor, for example, may be prepared to purchase 80,000 shares priced at $10, but only 40,000 shares priced at $15. Certain retail investors may be willing to pay one price for a deal with a large institutional or international component but will pay a considerably lower price for a deal without broad institutional sponsorships. Other factors taken into account include the risk factors inherent in the issuer's business and the performance of issuer management during the roadshow.

Aftermarket Considerations

As we noted earlier, because a drop in a company's stock price immediately after the IPO can be an embarrassment (or worse) to both the issuer and the underwriters, and in order to provide potential investors with an added incentive to buy the stock, the final stock price of an IPO is usually set somewhat lower than the maximum price obtainable. Moreover, to make the IPO more attractive, the underwriter sometimes opts for a larger number of shares with a lower per-share price. Two million shares at $20 may generate no more capital than 4 million shares at $10, but the latter deal may seem a better buy, even to some sophisticated investors.

Finding the Market Window

The managing underwriter's aim is to time the IPO so that it occurs during an up market and positive industry cycle, to find the market window and launch the IPO before the window closes. (This task is anything but easy considering that the process of mounting an IPO ordinarily takes six to nine months from start to finish.) If the window should close before the IPO has taken place, the issuer and underwriter may quite properly decide to wait for a more propitious time to offer the stock, however painful this decision may be in the short run. Proceeding when the market does not want an issue is an open invitation to perhaps permanently damage the issuer's reputation in the market and thereby restrict or eliminate future financing alternatives.

Coordination and Timing

The lead manager, from experience and familiarity with SEC reviewers, must make a reasonable estimate of the length of the review process, which may range from four to six weeks. The time required generally depends on the SEC's backlog and the length and complexity of the registration statement. If the issuing company has no outstanding litigation, the *Certain Transactions* section is brief and straightforward, the financial statements are in order, and all outside directors are in place, then the review process should proceed smoothly.

The accuracy of the lead manager's estimate is critical. The stock cannot be priced and issued until SEC approval of the registration statement is in hand, but once approval has been granted, no time should be wasted in getting the shares into the market. Any time lag between SEC approval and stock issuance may expose the issue to changes in market conditions that might adversely affect the final size and price of the deal.

Ideally, the lead manager will be ready to price the issue the same day SEC approval is granted. Thus, estimating the length of the review period ultimately determines the agenda for the all-important marketing effort, timing, and scheduling of the roadshow.

The Green Shoe Option

After the issue has been released and is trading freely, the lead manager must consider whether demand for the stock is strong enough to call for exercising part or all of the overallotment (if granted); this is the so-called Green Shoe option. Now a fairly standard clause in registration statements for both IPOs and secondary offerings, the Green Shoe option permits underwriters to purchase additional shares up to a maximum of 15 percent of the original size of the deal at the same original fixed offering price less the full underwriter's spread. (The Green Shoe option takes its name from an early use of this type of option in an offering managed by PaineWebber in 1963 for the Green Shoe Company of Vermont.)

On a four million share offering, then, the maximum umber of additional shares available through a Green Shoe option would be 600,000. The actual size of this option, if granted, is firmly established in the registration statement and usually carries with it a maximum life of 30 days, although the life of the option can also vary and must itself be specified in the filing documents.

In the above example, the lead manager would probably allocate at least 4.6 million shares, thereby technically creating a short position of 600,000 shares. To cover this short, the lead manager can buy the shares from the issuer on the original price terms, using the Green Shoe option, or in the marketplace. This decision depends on market activity and the reception of the deal after the date of issue.

The short position effectively gives the lead manager a bid, known as a syndicate or stabilizing bid, to allow time for the market to adjust to the entry of the new issue and to facilitate the distribution of a fixed-price offering in a dynamic and increasingly volatile marketplace.

If the post-effective market is roaring and the IPO starts rising, the lead manager can use the Green Shoe option to cover the short at the fixed initial offering price, thereby avoiding the trading loss it would incur if it had to buy those shares in the market at higher levels.

Issuers should understand that the Green Shoe option is indeed an option, one granted *by* the company *to* the underwriters. Once granted, it becomes the sole province of the underwriters and cannot be revoked.

Perspective

In an IPO, it should be remembered, the lead manager must serve more than one master. In addition to the client issuer, who wishes to obtain the highest price for the equity being offered, the lead manger is also accountable to its own investor clients as well as the investor clients of the other members of the syndicate. Generally, the lead manager serves the best interests of all parties concerned by setting the goal of realizing the highest *sustainable* price on the date of issue.

To achieve this goal, both the issuer and the lead manager must invest a great deal of time and effort from the drafting of the registration statement to the final pricing meeting. From the issuer's perspective, the necessary decisions on an IPO must involve the chief executive officer. While decisions on a bond issue or a line of credit may be routinely made by a treasurer, an IPO requires the input of the company's senior management. As noted previously, this involvement often represents a significant hidden cost of the transaction.

An IPO is a management decision second in psychological impact only to a decision to sell the company. Most companies going public for the first time are run by founders or entrepreneurs who own large pieces of the enterprise. Often these individuals have spent most of their business lives in the enterprise and have developed powerful emotional ties to it. Now they are about to share part of their company with the public. Despite presumably sound business reasons and their own potential financial enrichment, they inevitably grapple with a reluctance to let go.

The lead manager must be cognizant that the principals' egos are on the line throughout the IPO process. These people are the ones who built the business and, in their own minds, the market reaction will be taken as a reflection of their own ability and worth, personal as well as financial.

There are instances in market cycles when a lead manager has the opportunity to deliver extraordinarily good news to the issuer (i.e., that the market will accommodate *more* shares at a *higher* price). In recent times, this phenomenon occurred most often during brief periods in early 1972, in late 1982 through early 1983, and in late 1986 through early 1987.

More often, however, the lead manager may find during the marketing effort that the contemplated price is too high or the contemplated size of the deal is too large. Delivering bad news is much more difficult, given the highly charged, emotional nature of the transaction.

The lead manager must also remember that it was probably chosen from a field of five or six investment banking competitors. News travels fast in the Wall Street community, so any rumors of problems with an IPO will reach those investment banks that didn't get the business. Those rival bankers, you can be sure, will not be afraid to call the company's CEO, offering help or criticism of the current state of affairs. Such conversations can undermine the CEO's confidence in the lead manager, and most certainly create another source of anxiety that may impede the orderly progress of the transaction.

The key to dealing with the anxieties that the IPO process generates is constant communication between the lead underwriter and the issuer.

If representatives of the managing underwriter spend time early in the process educating the issuer on the events that are to take place and then maintain an ongoing dialogue with the issuer throughout the process, the deal will proceed much more smoothly. This policy of *no surprises* works well. In the end, regardless of how many price/earnings (P/E) ratio comparisons are made, how many countless investors were visited worldwide, and how all participants perceive their own worth and value, *the market* prices all deals: The laws of supply and demand in the end will win out over all other factors.

While the risks inherent in any IPO are substantial, they are also manageable. A properly managed IPO will not only benefit the issuer and create immediate revenues for the underwriter, it will also establish a professional relationship between issuer and underwriter that can continue to deepen and develop over many years.

CHAPTER 15

Private Placements*

Companies of all sizes and credit qualities can access the private debt and equity markets to meet their capital needs. A private placement is the selling of equity or debt securities to institutional or individual investors without the rules, regulations, and requirements of a public offering. Typically, any security which can be issued in the public market can also be placed privately. In some instances, certain securities can only be sold in the private market due to the complexity of the situation, the nature of the issuer, or the size of the offering.

As recently as within the last decade, the private placement market has evolved from being the poor stepchild of financing vehicles to a sophisticated $124 billion capital market medium with over 2500 issues annually. This growth has been in large part the result of the increase in cash flow available at the major private placement lending institutions (i.e., insurance companies and pension funds). In an effort to satisfy these enormous cash flow needs, new product development has been directed as much to the private market as to the public market.

In keeping with the trend toward innovation already noted with regard to the public market, the traditional institutional marketplace and recent mezzanine financing funds have matured as they relate to analyzing and documenting new structures. The private placement departments at most of these institutions have filled their ranks with as many Ivy League MBAs as can be found on Wall Street.

---

*This chapter has been derived from "Private Placements" by Dorothy Dotson, Volume II (Capital Raising and Financial Structure), Dow Jones-Irwin's *The Library of Investment Banking* (1990), Robert Lawrence Kuhn, editor-in-chief.

In this chapter we summarize the standard operating procedures of a private placement, particularly the preparation of the private placement memorandum, the term sheet, and pertinent covenants.

Preparing Private Placement Memoranda

How do private placements avoid the registration requirements of the Securities and Exchange Commission (SEC)? Section 4(2) of the Securities Act of 1933 exempts from registration with the SEC "transactions by an issuer not involving any public offering," but does not provide definitive rules as to what constitutes a private placement. In early 1982, however, the SEC adopted Regulation D (Rules 501–506) which does provide specific guidelines. Rule 506 under Regulation D (Reg D) provides that offers and sales of securities by an issuer that satisfy all of the rule's conditions shall be deemed to be transactions not involving any public offering within the meaning of Section 4(2) of the Securities Act of 1933 and shall therefore be exempt from the registration requirements of that Act. There is no maximum dollar amount of securities which may be offered and sold under Rule 506, and as long as all purchasers are accredited investors, there is no limitation on the total number of purchasers nor any specific information which must be furnished to the purchasers.

Contents of the Memorandum

The private placement memorandum on a Regulation D offering can be compared with an initial registration statement filed for a public offering. The introduction to the memorandum typically consists of standard, boilerplate provisions describing the legal basis upon which the private placement is being offered and stating that the only representations to be relied upon are those which have been provided by the issuer and appear in the memorandum to follow. This language should be prepared by legal counsel and, once drafted, become standard for all private placement offering memoranda used by the firm.

The memorandum usually includes, but is not limited to, the following sections: summary of the offering, use of proceeds, summary financial statements and the management's discussion and analysis of the summary financial statements, pro forma capitalization, a full description of the business and industry, a description of management, and complete financial statements, including the most recently available audited statements and any available interim statements. If the issuer is a reporting company, all recent SEC filings should be appended to the memorandum.

The text of the memorandum is usually followed by a summary of proposed principal terms as well as exhibits which may include various projections (particularly for an equity or equity-related financing), public relations brochures further describing the issuing company's operations, and a subscription agreement, purchaser questionnaire, and purchaser representative questionnaire in the case of a private equity offering.

Critical Areas of Content

There are certain fundamental assumptions which, if taken into consideration in the preparation of the memorandum, should result in a better selling document. The first assumption which should be made is that the analysts at the lending institutions typically specialize in certain industries. Therefore, their knowledge of the issuer or its industry may go well beyond that of the private placement specialist marketing the issue. As a result, the body of the memorandum needs to be specific enough to satisfy this expertise and to provide the type and depth of data that the analysts will be looking for. Secondly, the private placement memorandum will in all likelihood become the basis for the analysts' internal committee memoranda (i.e., it will in essence become their selling document to the various internal portfolio managers). To the extent the memorandum can assist the analysts in this regard, the easier and quicker the commitment process.

In light of the foregoing, the body of the memorandum needs to provide enough detail to satisfy the institutional marketplace. Such information should include a description of the business, including sections focusing on each reportable industry segment; principal products and services rendered; principal markets and methods of distribution; sources and availability of raw materials; importance, duration, and effect of all patents, trademarks, licenses, franchises, and concessions held; seasonality or cyclicality factors; customers; backlog orders (compared with prior periods); a description of any material portion of the business that may be subject to renegotiation of profits or contract terminations; competitive conditions in the industry, including the number and identity of competitors, the issuer's competitive ranking, and the principal methods of competition (i.e., price, service, warranty, or quality); market share data; and research and development activities and compliance with federal, state, and local regulations.

A management section should briefly describe the board of directors and key senior personnel, including their backgrounds and qualifications, their remuneration for services rendered including incentives and stock options, any related party transactions, and management's ownership of the issuing company's equity securities. Finally, the body of the memorandum should include descriptions of the issuer's properties and any material legal proceedings.

Private Placement of Debt

The summary of proposed principal terms (the term sheet) accompanying the memorandum summarizes the offering by describing the nature of the securities being offered, the principal amount thereof, the maturity, the interest rate, any conversion features, the redemption or sinking fund schedule, and each affirmative and negative covenant.

Term Sheet

The term sheet begins by stating the issuer, the issue and amount, the maturity date, the price (typically par), the interest rate (typically payable semiannually), the takedown (i.e., when the company gets the funds), the use of proceeds, and the nature of the offering (i.e., a private placement without registration under the Securities Act of 1933).

The first key area addressed on the term sheet is the required or mandatory repayment of principal. Repayments typically take the form of either equal annual payments referred to as *sinking fund* payments (although payments are made directly to the lending institution rather than to a sinking fund) which begin after a certain number of years' grace period, or a single payment at final maturity (referred to as a *bullet maturity*). Because the proposed repayment schedule should be consistent with the issuer's projected cash flows, careful preparation and review of forecasts is mandatory.

Optional prepayments of principal at the issuer's option are also addressed, permitting a borrower to make an additional payment on each principal repayment date at par, up to a fixed amount but usually limited to an overall percentage (i.e., 25%–35%) of the total principal amount outstanding (in general, optional prepayments are allowed at an amount up to the required prepayment—hence known as a *double-up* provision). Optional prepayments are normally applied to the outstanding principal in the inverse order of maturity (i.e., early payments reduce the *last* payments due, not the first payments). During periods of high interest rates, lending institutions prefer to exclude or minimize this option in an effort to prevent reductions in the average lives of high-yielding loans and securities, while issuers prefer to have the option of reducing the average life of a high cost debt.

Call Protection

The term sheet will then summarize the call protection afforded to the purchaser. In return for investing and thereby foregoing the opportunity to make various alternative investments, the issuer is usually required to promise not to call the securities for redemption for a given period of time following issuance. Private placements are generally considered more risky than public offerings (due to the illiquidity) and hence demand a higher rate of interest. Since investors take their risk up front, it would be unfair if the company, when it has prospered and no longer needs the cash, could payoff the debt and thereby prevent the investors from realizing their expected return for the remainder of the instrument's life.

As a general rule, call protection is structured to match the average life that the securities are to be outstanding. Once callable, the debt may be redeemed at a premium equal to the interest rate declining ratably from the first year after issuance to par in the final year. An alternative to the standard call premium which allows for a shorter non-call period is what is known as a *make-whole* premium. This means that the company, in order to call the issue, must pay a compensating amount reflecting the present value of an interest-rate differential between the private placement instrument and some pre-set standard or formula.

Covenants Overview

Covenants have traditionally played a key role in private placement transactions, by providing institutional lenders with a means of monitoring their investments. The successful negotiation of covenants, however, can be a delicate balancing act. On the one hand, the purchaser's investment interests must be protected, particularly given the risks inherent in, for example, an unsecured, non-investment-grade private placement. On the other hand, it is not the intent of the purchaser to unduly restrict an issuer so that it cannot operate successfully or to structure covenants in such a fashion so that a minor misstep would trigger a loan default.

In formulating a term sheet and arriving at covenants, there are two key assumptions which must be made. Firstly, the nature of the issuer's business and its future strategy must be taken into account. For example, if the issuer is a company which grows via acquisition, the covenants (i.e., mergers and acquisitions or permitted investments) must address this inherent aspect of the issuer's ongoing operations. Secondly, the term sheet provides the basis from which the note agreement is drafted. The extent to which the covenants within the term sheet are specified and accurately defined will dictate the ease and clarity of documentation.

A term sheet will outline two principal types of covenants: affirmative covenants and negative covenants.

Affirmative Covenants

Affirmative covenants are fairly standard; they outline the general ground rules by which the parties agree to borrow and lend money, including but not limited to payment of principal and interest, maintenance of books and records, delivery of financial statements, and maintenance covenants (e.g., current ratio and net worth).

Negative Covenants

Negative covenants, on the other hand, are drafted specifically according to the issuer's financial status. The weaker the credit, the more stringent the covenants; the stronger the credit, the more closely the covenants match what are commonly referred to as public covenants which are similar to those of a general promissory note. Some of the major negative covenants are: permitted indebtedness, restricted payments, permitted liens, merger and consolidation, and sale of assets.

There are two principal types of debt covenants: (1) those restricting the incurrence of long-term debt (a leverage test limiting the borrower's total long-term debt to a percentage of total capitalization), and (2) those restricting the incurrence of short-term debt. To help reassure the lender that any short-term borrowing is not needed as a surreptitious substitute for long-term financing, a covenant may require the borrower to be free of bank debt for a stated period of time (e.g., 30 days) during any 12-month period—this is usually termed a *clean-up* provision.

Restricted Payments

Restricted payment covenants are generally intended to limit a borrower's ability to declare or pay any dividends on any shares of its capital stock, to purchase, retire, or redeem any shares of its capital stock, or to make any other payment or distribution with respect to its capital stock. The purpose of such covenants is to require the borrower to channel its earnings into its enterprise and to preserve and perhaps increase its net worth rather than allow the borrower to dissipate its earning power through dividend payouts.

An ancillary covenant covers restricted investments. Restrictions on investments are used to encourage borrowers to reinvest funds in their own business, to avoid dissipation of assets and earnings, and to ensure that the character of the enterprise does not change.

Permitted Liens

In cases where the lender is being asked to lend to the company on an unsecured basis, there is a restriction on the amount of borrowing which the company can incur on a secured basis. The pledging of receivables, inventory, or other current assets as security in exchange for credit accommodations is generally prohibitied. There is often a covenant to secure the note equally in cases where the company has no ability to secure other debt. (Usually there is a certain amount of permitted secured debt even after all specifics are outlined. This *basket* provision is typically stated as a dollar amount or a percentage of net tangible assets.)

Consolidation, Merger, or Disposition of Assets

The lender knows the character of the entity to which it is making the loan and wishes to reduce the likelihood of the company radically changing its complexion and financial characteristics, thereby increasing the risk of the loan. The lender often inserts a clause forbidding sale of a substantial portion of the company's assets outside of the ordinary course of business. In today's world of active merger and acquisition activity this covenant has taken on great importance. In some cases, it can be seen by the borrower as somewhat of a deterrence to corporate takeover.

Typically, merger or sale is permitted after a certain amount of reasonable discussion is held between borrower and lender. Usually if the two parties disagree the borrower can repay the lender at par and add a prepayment penalty amount (perhaps reduced).

Definition Section

The definition section defines all the significant terms used in the agreement such as *current assets*, *net tangible assets*, *funded debt*, *filed charges,* and *net income*. Most of these terms are used in establishing protective covenants and are according to generally accepted accounting principles (GAAP).

Private Placement of Equity

Given the amount of equity which is raised in the private market, it is good to be familiar with the document used in placing private equity, namely the Stock Purchase Agreement (which is most often arrived at by negotiation among the investment banker, the company, and the respective counsel of each). The purchase agreement is then offered to prospective purchasers of such privately placed common stock.

The introduction to the agreement should greet each investor and introduce the company which is issuing common stock. It should specifically name the amount of stock being offered, stating par value and the per share purchase price of the stock. Should there be any selling shareholders, the fact should be disclosed at this time (including the number of shares being sold). Typically the placement agent, if any, is disclosed up front.

Due Diligence Required before a Private Offering of Securities

As in any proposed offering of securities, the investment banker should exercise adequate due diligence on the proposed issuer of securities, its employees, and its financial statements. Once the investment bank has completed its due diligence and offered securities in a private placement, it is customary for proposed investors to complete their own due diligence before purchasing the securities being offered. In effect, the issuing company has had at least two thorough investigations into its business and financial affairs.

Timetable for a Private Placement

The time from the beginning to the end of a private placement—from the moment the investment banker receives a mandate to proceed until the payment of money by the investor for the securities purchased—varies with market conditions and familiarity of the issuing company with the private placement process. Elapsed time is estimated at 12–15 weeks. In summary, the private market is alive and well and flush with cash; it is *the* market upon which most institutions rely to meet their investment objectives consistently.

CHAPTER 16

Leveraged Buyouts*

How can you overpay and get rich? The answer is simple if you know what to buy and how to buy it, and when to sell and how to sell it. Mix financial leverage, managerial ownership, clever structure, and even more clever restructure. It's called a leveraged buyout (LBO), and what it does is cure the healthy.

Take a sound company strong with equity. Sell it. Make it sick, laden heavily with debt. Make it better by rebuilding equity—redeploy assets, cut overhead, pay back debt (not too much), and perhaps improve earnings. [1] Sell it again. Count your money.

How can ordinary mortals offer $25 billion for RJR Nabisco, the tobacco and food behemoth; $6.2 billion for Beatrice Companies, the food and consumer products giant; $1.6 billion for Metromedia, Inc. the broadcasting chain; or $648 million for Dr Pepper, the soft drink company—leverage to the teeth with mounds of debt—and hope to make a profit?

An LBO looks like it's done with mirrors. Remember one of the first barn burners? It was when William Simon (Westray) made a $50 + million bonanza in a period so short he might have been caught for ordinary income, not capital gains. Simon simply bought Gibson Greeting Cards

---

*This chapter has been derived from "Leveraged Buyouts I: Structure and Restructure" by Robert Lawrence Kuhn, Volume IV (Mergers, Acquisitions, and Leveraged Buyouts), Dow Jones-Irwin's *The Library of Investment Banking* (1990), Robert Lawrence Kuhn, editor-in-chief.

1. Note that improving earnings on profit and loss (P&L) statements are generally *not* critical for leveraged buyouts to succeed. Some LBOs have been known to lose money every year on the income statement until the time they were sold for an enormous profit. (Such P&L losses were due to huge depreciation and amortization as well as accrued interest on the highly leveraged balance sheet.) Cash flow, you can be sure, was quite positive.

from a tired RCA and then sold part of it back to a ravenous public at a much higher price/earnings multiple. Simon's timing was good, but his structure was better. What did the former Secretary of the Treasury put up? Only a few hundred thousand dollars, which, if you look closely, was hardly put up at all. (Would that he had performed such miracles with the national debt!)

Structure

How do LBOs work? To begin with, investors chip in preciously little cash—not much real money is ever put at risk. This equity (the cash contribution) is then leveraged 10, 20, or even 50 times with debt. Leverage, that's part of the secret. (Management, as we will see, is the other part.)

Where does all this debt come from, and how can conservative bankers take such risks? First of all, the debt is arrayed into multiple layers or strips, with higher levels in the capital structure (up toward senior debt) yielding lower risks and lower returns, and lower levels in the capital structure (down toward equity) yielding higher risks and higher returns.[2]

Senior debt is normally *secured* in LBOs. This means that the acquired firm's *own* assets are pledged to support the debt. Lending limits, for example, might be 80 percent of receivables, 50 percent of inventories, or 25 percent of plant and equipment. Mortgages of real estate and sale-leaseback of plant and equipment can raise additional cash. (Note that no matter how large the debt, the acquirers take no risks other than their initial, minimal equity investment.)

Often there need to be middle layers of subordinate debt to make the financing work. Such subordinate debt is called *mezzanine* money since it stands *between* the senior bank debt and the investor equity.

Who finances the subordinated debt? It can be taken back by the seller (common in LBOs of private companies—see Chapter 7), or it can be bought by third parties. Such third-party subordinated debt can be sold as private placements (e.g., to insurance companies—see Chapter 15) or as public offerings (i.e., high-yield debt—see Chapter 13). If bought by a third party, this mezzanine money demands a piece of the equity, called a *kicker*, in addition to a guaranteed rate of return higher than that of the senior debt (which is appropriate considering the higher risk). An example capital structure, showing sources and uses of cash in a stylized LBO, is shown in Table 16-1.

---

2. See Chapter 3 regarding the relationship between risk and return and its importance in analyzing the capital structure of enterprises.

Table 16–1. Example Capital Structure of a Leveraged Buyout.

Sources of Cash

Revolving line of credit	$ 200 million
Mortgage/sale-leaseback debt	100 million
Senior term loan[1]	600 million
Increasing rate notes[2]	250 million
Senior subordinated debt[3]	100 million
Junior subordinated debt[4]	75 million
Junior zero coupon notes[5]	50 million
Preferred stock (pay-in-kind)[6]	50 million
Preferred stock (convertible)[7]	50 million
Common equity	25 million
Total uses of cash	**$1,500 million**

Uses of Cash

Acquisition of common stock	$ 815 million
Acquisition of preferred stock	50 million
Refinancing of existing debt	460 million
Transactional fees and expenses	50 million
Working capital support	125 million
Total uses of cash	**$1,500 million**

[1]A senior term loan is usually structured for five to seven years, with a regular amortization schedule.

[2]Increasing rate notes are usually designed to be a bridging facility for asset disposition. The increasing rate, say 50 basis points per quarter, encourages speedy sale of the assets/divisions and rapid retirement of the notes. Delay in retiring these notes becomes very expensive very quickly.

[3]Senior subordinated debt may have a rate about 200 basis points over the senior term loan. It would pay interest currently but not require principal repayment for several years, say equal payments in six, seven, and eight (after the senior debt is completely repaid). The senior subordinated debt could only be called (i.e., paid off and retired) by the company by paying a premium (say 108 percent of par) to investors (this premium would decline in later years). After all, the investors took a significant risk in purchasing this piece of paper and should not be penalized for a successful company.

[4]Junior subordinated debt would have a rate slightly higher (say 50 basis points) than senior subordinated debt. It, too, would only pay interest currently and have an amortization schedule later than the senior subordinated debt, say equal payments in years seven, eight, and nine. Likewise, the junior subordinated debt could only be called (i.e., paid off and retired) by the company by paying a premium (say 108 percent of par) to investors (this premium would decline in later years). Again, the investors took a significant risk in purchasing this piece of paper and should not be penalized for a successful company.

[5]Zero coupon notes accrue interest over the life of the note, with all interest and principal paid at the end. Zero coupon notes are structured as deeply discounted original issues, with the implied interest rate being the accrual rate that brings the initial cash payment up to the face value at the maturity date. This maturity date might be just after the payment of all more senior indebtedness (including all current-pay subordinated debt), in this case say the tenth year. Naturally, the interest rate on zero coupons is higher (say 100 basis points) than the current-pay junior subordinated debt.

[6]Pay-in-kind preferred stock offers a high rate of dividends (15 to 20+ percent), with the understanding that for a period of years, the interest can be paid "in kind" (i.e., with additional pay-in-kind preferred stock). Redemption of this preferred stock would not be mandated for many years, probably not until after all more senior indebtedness, including the zero coupon bonds, are retired.

[7]Convertible preferred stock would pay a lower dividend rate than the pay-in-kind preferred stock but would expect an ultimately higher annual return (in the 25 to 40 percent range) as a result of its convertibility into a healthy amount of equity (say 15 to 30 percent of the company ownership).

Institutional Support

But who is supplying this hugh mountain of LBO debt? Equity players like talking about *OPM* (Other People's Money), but who are all these other people? Suckers they are not, of this you can be well assured.

In fact, many of the largest and most astute financial institutions in the country are the primary suppliers of LBO debt—and they get compensated very well, thank you, for taking these risks. [3] This is premium lending, with banking returns far outdistancing their typical commercial loans. By earning several hundred basis points (100 basis points equal one percent) over alternative investment opportunities for their assets,[4] LBO lenders give a tremendous boost to their own return on equity (since these financial institutions are themselves highly leveraged[5]).

Cash Flow

The touchstone of LBOs is cash flow. Almost nothing else matters. Profit and loss statements, surprisingly, are almost irrelevant. All that counts is whether, when, and with what safety you can meet interest coverage in the near term and can pay back principal in the long term. (Such payment schedules can be staged with endless variation to meet anticipated forecasts. The creative use of various layers and terms of debt, as discussed above and shown in Table 16-1, is essential for many deals to succeed.)

A nice feature in calculating cash flow is tax payments or, more accurately, the lack thereof. Paying an inflated price can thus present minimal problems. Interest is tax deductible, and if depreciation is high, that too becomes an effective tax shield. The acquirer could merely

---

3. For example, banks such as Citibank, Chemical Bank, Bankers Trust, Security Pacific, and Manufacturers Hanover, and insurance companies such as The Prudential, are large LBO lenders. (In the early days of LBOs, such lending was viewed as *fringe* lending—certainly not befitting the blue-chip institutions. The enormous returns eliminated such snobbery and today the blue-chippers are fierce competitors for the LBO business.)

4. Overall returns for the financial institutions include fees up front (perhaps 3% on the entire deal) plus participations in the equity layers in the form of being issued warrants to purchase common stock and/or making direct investments in the higher return instruments. Such structure generates a very healthy, blended rate of return for the LBO lenders.

5. For example, a bank that is leveraged 20 to 1 (assets to equity) would earn a 20 percent incremental return on equity (before direct expenses) for every one percent incremental return on assets.

write up company assets and generate higher write-offs for depreciation (far easier under the pre-1986 tax law)—in addition to already hefty deductions for interest.

Similarly, companies with net operating loss carryforwards (NOLs) have a competitive edge in LBO acquisitions. NOLs generate a powerful engine of payback power and dramatically shorten the time period of debt repayment (which both increases return and decreases risk).

Sensitivity

You only have to watch the windows. Downdrafts in this business cause quick pneumonia. Sensitivity analysis is critical. "What if" games are not games. LBO investors had better be awfully sure they can weather any storm. Default sits right overhead in those low-altitude rain clouds, especially during the first few years. If a slight change in market, pricing, margins, overheads, and especially interest rates occur, in blow the banks with their liens in one hand and auction blocks in the other. (Or do they? When you owe small money, you have a creditor; when you owe big money, you have a partner.)

Sensitivity analysis is required to assess and compare the alternative capital structures in order to determine which is most effective for financing the LBO. Which layers of debt (with what terms and conditions) have the greatest likelihood of initial appeal to investors and ultimate success for the issuer? The optimum captial structure improves robustness since the multiple layers of debt enhance flexibility.

Restructure

LBOs work, notwithstanding the extraordinary debt, because of the restructuring of the acquired company. Assets not being properly employed, such as current inventory, are shrunk down, thus making the operation more efficient. Conserving cash is the touchstone with which all business decisions are evaluated. Long-term thinking is a nice luxury; short-term cash management is an absolute necessity. Subsidiary businesses may be sold off for values far in excess of their cash-generating potential.

The key is to sell all assets, divisions, or subsidiaries whose price/earnings multiples (or, better yet, price/cash flow multiples) exceed the original multiples paid for the entire company. Those assets, divisions, or subsidiaries that generate a high degree of cash relative to the acquisition price (and possible sale price) should be kept. These *cash cows* will generate the dollars required to pay off the debt and build rapid shareholder value.

The restructuring process often reveals hidden assets in LBO acquisitions, such as real estate holdings (that have been long ago written off the books), lease values well in excess of lease costs, and smaller divisions that have significant potential. It is amazing how frequently these assets emerge, especially when mature public companies (e.g., conglomerates assembled years before) are taken private in management-led LBOs.

Cashing Out

LBO financiers always think about the exit before they walk through the entrance. "How do we get out? " is a question they must answer before investing their cash.

There are not many alternatives for cashing out; there are really only two. One is the public markets. It is the dream of every LBO investor to take the company public in a relatively short period of time (three years perhaps, but no later than five) and reap the enormous rewards of financial leverage. But the public markets are not always available: the market window may not be open and/or the company itself may not be ready.

The second option is a private sale to a new buyer. This new buyer may be another LBO investor group that seeks to purchase the entire company in a manner similar to how the original LBO group did it. The new buyer may be current management seeking to own all of their own company. Or the new buyer may be a corporate acquirer, seeking a market or operational fit with its overall strategy. From an American perspective, foreign corporations have been eager buyers of restructured LBOs (especially since the fall of the dollar).[6]

From the standpoint of the LBO financiers, corporate acquirers are often the most desirable (even if a public offering would appear to gen-

---

6. Foreign corporations are a natural buyer for many restructured LBOs. Cheap dollars are surely one reason, but there is also another. Many foreign corporations seek entry into the American market, often as a channel of distribution for their other products. They have long wanted to purchase various American public companies—*but*, by culture and custom, they would never have approached such a company when it had been traded on the stock market (prior to the LBO) and certainly would never have considered taking any hostile action. Here, then, may be the first opportunity for these foreign corporations to buy many long-sought companies. Foreign corporations will pay a healthy price to acquire access to the American market.

erate higher profits *on paper*).[7] Mergers with large coporations are most efficient; they are easier to structure and quicker to close. Consideration is normally all cash (or highly liquid securities) and generally the shareholders get it all at once. Furthermore, if a large corporation really wants the company it will not be afraid to pay top dollar.

Evaluating Returns On Equity (ROE)

Everyone speaks about returns on equity (ROE). It is LBO lingo personified. It is the Holy Grail of the LBO game. But there is more to ROE than is immediately obvious. Understanding the nature of returns on equity is fascinating: the leverage appears to create miracles.

Assume an LBO financing of $100 million, structured with $90 million in debt supported with $10 million (or 10 percent) in equity. Now assume the company is sold four years later for $130 million, after having paid back only $20 million of the debt. Doesn't it seem like a rather mediocre performance? Well, watch what happens.

The absolute, after-debt value of the deal is $60 million (the $130 million sale price minus the remaining debt of $70 million, which is the original $90 million in debt minus the $20 million paydown). But ROE, remember, is calculated on the original equity investment of $10 million. So the payback is 600 percent—figured as $60 million divided by $10 million (60/10), which equals a compound annual rate of return of about 56 percent (pre-tax) over the four years. (Not bad in any financial scheme.)

The evaluation of returns on equity is usually considered the key criterion in determining the viability and desirability of any LBO transaction. However, there is an inherent complexity, perhaps even a fallacy, that crops up in such analyses—the factor or time.

Almost always, the spreadsheet-calculated returns decrease as the time frame of evaluation increases. This means that the ROE might look best two years hence, and it declines progressively (and precipitously) as you look three, four, five, six, etc. years into the future.

Such a decline does *not* mean that the company is beoming less valuable. After all, the company is continuing to generate cash and pay off debt. The problem is that the rate of growth is far less than would be required to maintain the excessive returns. (The initial high returns are

---

7. From the standpoint of the operational managers of the LBO company, a corporate acquirer is often *not* the best alternative. Granted, the managers receive their profit—but now they are back working for others and suddenly the future becomes less certain and they become less committed.

the product of the leveraged structure.) So a declining ROE should be expected and should not discourage the potential acquirer. Nor should the decline suggest that the company be sold after two years to lock in those higher returns! Frankly, it is far better to earn a compounded ROE of 30 percent for ten years than a compounded ROE of 50 percent for two years.

Management

The key to successful LBOs is management. LBO financiers insist that operating executives take part in the action. The boys with the bucks require that management assume plenty of risk—making great gain on the upside and suffering painful loss on the downside. (Not known for their generosity, financiers seek only to solidify their own success.) Savvy investors hardly ever bankroll an LBO unless those who run target companies get a good hunk of the equity, generally 10 to 20 percent, and put up hard cash to buy it.

The critical transition, then, occurs inside the heads of these executives. Previously employees, they are suddenly owners. Professional managers with company-paid club memberships change mystically into personal entrepreneurs who scrutinize every expense. Participation and commitment become the essence of motivation. It is a transformation most remarkable.

To be general manager of a conglomerate division managing public money is one thing. To be president of an independent company building personal wealth is quite another. Take the decision-making process. Which will it be, a new corporate aircraft or an upgraded manufacturing facility? The decision is made in a microsecond. Care is exercised over every facet of the business. No cost savings are too minor. Dollar signs are seen everywhere. Lights are turned off and spirits are turned on. Think of the enhanced effort and reduced waste. When management is galvanized, the company is rejuvenated.

Public Policy

Debate about the socioeconomic value of leveraged buyouts continues to rage. LBOs have become a whipping boy of the mass media. It is easy to attack businesses where a few people make so much money so quickly—seemingly without doing, well, *anything*. Nothing new has been produced, it is argued, except untold stacks of paper have been shuffled and unseemly amounts of legal bills have been paid.

There is another side to the issue, and it focuses on the remarkable success rate of LBOs and the equally remarkable amount of money now committed to LBO funds. As of the middle of 1988, it was estimated that $25 billion had been invested in LBO funds ready for deals. At least six firms controlled more than $1 billion each, with several more approaching that figure.[8] The investors in these funds were some of the strongest and smartest institutions in the world. And considering a typical 10 to 1 leverage structure, this meant that $250 billion worth of deals could be completed. (Roughly $40 billion worth of LBOs were consummated in each of the years 1986 and 1987—Figure 16-1.)

The danger is competition. The intense rivalry on the buying side generates wild prices on the selling side. What will so many high-powered LBO funds do with so much cash? Their institutional investors do not want the money languishing in Treasury Bills—they expect a very healthy return on their investment. The result is predictable: with too much money chasing too few deals prices get bid up and the risk escalates geometrically.

LBO investors would like to pay between four to five times cash flow. Deals work quite well at those levels; debt service is comfortable and the financial structure is robust enough to withstand aberrations and shocks. But those days are gone, perhaps forever. It becomes hazardous, even perilous, to pay eight to twelve times cash flow (unless there is a clear opportunity to sell off available assets at even higher multiples). But such risk is precisely what current LBOs must absorb.

The first major LBO failure, the $1.5 billion collapse and Chapter 11 bankruptcy of Revco (the drug discount chain), exemplifies the problem. Even the initial, pre-deal (usually optimistic) projections showed that the company would have to sustain healthy, profitable growth in a highly competitive industry just to service its debt and pay its interest. Such growth seemed uncertain, even in the heady days prior to the transaction.[9]

---

8. Kohlberg Kravis Roberts (KKR), $5.6 billion; Forstmann Little, $2.7 billion; Morgan Stanley Group, $1.6 billion; Merrill Lynch Capital Appreciation Fund II, $1.5 billion; Shearson Lehman, $1.3–1.5 billion; Prudential-Bache, $800 million (capital) plus $500 million-$1.5 billion (fund); Wasserstein Perella, $750 million to $1 billion; Blackstone, $750 million; Gibbons Green van Amerongen, $600+ million.

9. As a matter of uncertain interest, the author, representing an institutional investor, rejected an opportunity to invest in Revco.

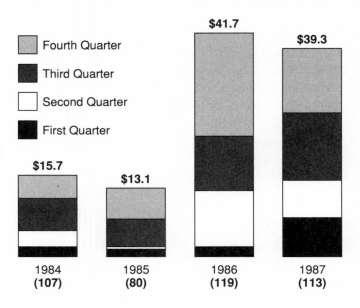

Figure 16-1. Value of Leveraged Buyouts.

Value of leveraged buyouts completed, in billions of dollars.
In parentheses are the number of deals completed each year.

Source: IDD Information Services

Yet so many of these highly leveraged companies survive and indeed prosper. They sparkle, operationally and financially. Why? How is it that, even with all that debt, many LBOs perform better as highly leveraged companies than they had ever performed as unleveraged companies?

The answer, as we have seen, is management—their spectacular change in attitude and increase in commitment. Businesses are not democratic organizations, and it is the top executives and managers that make them successful. This fact may not resonate with some folk's idealized sense of social structure, but it's the way the world really works.

One can argue that those equity-owning executives and managers should have been doing the same good things before the LBO as they are now doing after it. They should have done, sure. But they didn't do, sorry.

Managers and executives are people and not gods, and it is unreasonable to expect that they would act the same when they are owners with cash invested (after the LBO) as they did when they were just representing the stockholders' interests with no personal investment (before the LBO). People are people and no political philosophy will alter the powerful motivation of self-interest.

New Developments In LBOs

Stimulated by the enormous success of LBOs, creative investment bankers have sought to broaden the benefits of the same leveraging techniques. Could an LBO's financial returns be extended beyond the small group of top executives and canny investors? Two such developments have been receiving wide interest: *recapitalization of public companies* and *LBOs financed by Employee Stock Ownership Plans (ESOPs)*. Both are new and growing factors in the world of LBOs.

Recapitalizations of Public Companies

Recapitalizations of public companies (known as "recaps") can be envisioned, at least at first, as a company doing a leveraged buyout of itself. The public shareholders are given a large cash dividend, which is funded by the firms heavily encumbering itself with debt. Though its relative ownership percentage must drop (due to tax considerations), the public still retains a "stub" interest in the equity of the now highly leveraged company. Thus the public derives benefits on both sides of a leveraged recapitalization transaction: shareholders receive cash payments as if they were LBO sellers and enjoy ownership interests as if they were LBO buyers.

Management, for its part, must operate the business just as if it were a traditional LBO. All the same financial characteristics are required to do the deal (e.g., a consistent and predictable stream of earnings, good cash flows from operations, readily disposable assets or divisions), and all the same cash flow controls and cost containment concerns are required to make the deal work (e.g., working capital efficiencies, minimal capital expenditures, closing down unprofitable operations, downsizing businesses to meet market realities). Normally, management would have increased ownership (equity participation), and thus greater incentive to operate a lean, tight business—with the resulting financial benefits enriching the public as well as themselves.

Since its introduction by Metromedia in 1985, leveraged recapitalizations have been used as a defensive technique in the face of hostile takeover attempts. The dynamics here are clear. By replacing equity with debt, the company becomes much less desirable to the potential raider. Furthermore, since the proceeds of that debt have been already paid out to shareholders (and are gone forever), the raider has been cleverly cut off from the major source of his intended financing (i.e., the company's own borrowing capacity).

In general, the market performances of recapitalized public companies have been compelling. (See Tables 16–2 and 16–3.) The leveraged recap enables public shareholders to liquify a substantial part of their stock holdings ("cashing out"), while still retaining a significant part of the growth potential of equity ownership. (Under normal LBO conditions, shareholders must sell their shares to cash in their gains, thereby losing all future benefits of stock ownership.)

ESOP-Led LBOs

ESOPs maximize both the impact of active ownership and the sensitivities of public policy. ESOPs are complex structures in which *all* the employees of a company can participate in the new ownership. As such, these plans have been enjoying an increasing level of worker excitement, congressional support, and investment banking interest.

Considering their broad-based appeal, especially in the Congress, ESOPs now enjoy substantial and fascinating tax advantages. A powerful example is the significantly more lenient retention of carryforward tax

---

Table 16-2. Stub Performance of Leveraged Recapitalizations.

Company	Recap Date	Initial Price/Share	1 Year Post Recap Price/Share	% Change	DJIA % Change
Multimedia	Oct. 1985	19⅜	42	116.8%	36.6%
FMC Corp.	May 1986	19¼	36	87.0%	22.1%
Colt Industries	Oct. 1986	11⅝	42¾	26.9%	34.0%
Owens-Corning	Nov. 1986	12⅛	42½	16.0%	2.6%
Holiday Corp.	Feb. 1987	17⅛	42⅝*	67.2%	19.7%

*Six month post-recap data; *DJIA* = **Dow Jones Industrial Average**
Source: *Bank & Quotation Record*, *The Wall Street Journal*

Table 16-3. Impact of Leverage on Recapitalized Public Companies.

Company	Recap Date	Long-Term Debt ($Million)		Equity ($Million)		Interest Coverage		Current Ratio		Return on Investment (ROI)	
		Pre	Post	Pre	Post	Pre	Post	Pre	Post	Pre	Post
Multimedia	Oct. 1985	73.2	877.7	248.7	(576.4)	8.7x	2.3x	1.6x	1.3x	13.6%	17.0%
FMC Corp.	May 1986	303.2	1,783.3	2,806.7	(506.6)	7.7x	2.0x	1.1x	.97x	14.7	16.0
Colt Industries	Oct. 1986	342.4	1,643.1	414.3	(1,077.8)	16.3x	2.9x	2.4x	1.6x	17.9	22.0
Owens-Corning	Nov. 1986	543.0	1,645.2	944.7	(1,025.2)	5.9x	1.4x	1.9x	.95x	10.1	24.9
Holiday Corp.	Feb. 1987	992.5	2,542.5	1,024.5	638.7	3.7x	2.2x	.77x	.68x	8.8	10.2

benefits resulting from prior net operating losses of the company to be acquired—even after a total change in ownership of that company, which ordinarily would have eliminated these benefits completely. (NOL carryforward tax benefits are of enormous utility to LBOs, enabling the company to pay off its debt and accumulate cash much more rapidly.) ESOP-led LBOs are a wave of the future.[10]

Summary

From a public policy point of view, LBOs can be seen as the refresher of capitalism. They enhance efficiency, raise productivity, and reward creativity. One can make the case that the surge in LBOs is returning the economy to the early days of entrepreneurship and rugged individualism, when managers were owners and owners were managers—and when these corporate leaders worked best for themselves the system worked best for everyone.[11] Given the American way of thinking, the managerial ownership of enterprise is vital.[12]

---

10. As we go to press, Congress is considering restricting the tax benefits of ESOPs.

11. When we say that the system worked best for everyone, the reference is to relative economic growth and productivity compared to other nations, not necessarily to social fairness or political equality. We would be well-advised to allow the economy to function as efficiently as possible on its own terms (i.e., with management- and employee [ESOP]-led LBOs), and then cure social unfairness and political inequality through wealth reallocation policies (i.e., taxes) and entitlement programs.

12. There are obvious exceptions. For example, LBOs are much less appropriate in industries requiring substantial investment in research and development that will not generate commercial products for many years. Nonetheless, for these companies as for all companies, the principle of managerial ownership is indeed vital.

CHAPTER 17

Risk Arbitrage and the M&A Process*

Arbitrage means making money from price discrepancies. In its most general sense, arbitrage is the simultaneous buying and selling of the same or equivalent security, instrument, or commodity in order to profit from some price differential between or among them. As such, arbitrage profit relates to inherent price disparities (e.g., price differences between the same security in different markets or between similar securities in the same market) and does *not* relate to either speculation or market movements. Arbitrage by definition requires determination of a known or relatively known price for both the purchase and the sale before making either the purchase or the sale.

Arbitrage has become an important factor in the modern capital markets. In conventional form, it is a riskless transaction which acts to equate values in different markets. As sophisticated investors seek to benefit from the ever-present market disparities, their system of simultaneous buying and selling brings these markets closer to parity. It is a classic case of when the individual works strictly for himself, the process works well for everyone.

Arbitrage has also become a major force in determining the courses of companies in contemporary mergers and acquisitions (M&A). This is *risk* arbitrage, and it is the focus of this chapter. After discussing briefly

---

* This chapter has been derived from "Risk Arbitrage" by Robert Lawrence Kuhn and Emanuel Friedman, Volume I (Investing and Risk Management), Dow Jones-Irwin's *The Library of Investment Banking* (1990), Robert Lawrence Kuhn, editor-in-chief.

the two more traditional forms of arbitrage (riskless and perception), we present the various facets of risk arbitrage—explaining the analytical investment strategies and the intuitive market insights. The latter are the more intangible elements of risk arbitrage and involve an understanding of what makes mergers and acquisitions more or less likely to close. Since the consummation of an announced deal is the only way that risk arbitrage works, knowledge of what can go wrong is essential in assessing the risk of that deal not closing.

Three Kinds of Arbitrage

There are three kinds of arbitrage: (1) *Riskless* arbitrage, (2) *Perception* arbitrage, (3) *Risk* arbitrage. The key difference among them is *time*— the length of the period between the two ends of the transaction, between the time of the purchase and the time of the sale. Naturally, when time increases so do both cost and risk.

- *Riskless Arbitrage.* Riskless arbitrage involves the purchase and sale of diverse securities, instruments, and commodities and is a simultaneous transaction—the profit is certain and the risk is essentially zero.

- *Perception Arbitrage.* Perception arbitrage involves the purchase and sale of diverse securities, instruments, and commodities and is short term, perhaps a day—the risk is minimal but not zero.

- *Risk Arbitrage.* Risk arbitrage involves the purchase and sale of corporate securities of announced merger and acquisition companies and is long term—the transaction time between the purchase and the sale may involve several months.[1] (The reason risk arbitrage is still arbitrage and not simple investment is that the price in an announced merger or acquisition is predetermined: the purchase and sale prices are both known, even though the closing may be several months into the future and even uncertain.)

---

1. Several months is definitely long term in the world of arbitrage.

Riskless Arbitrage

Currency Arbitrage

The earliest emergence of arbitrage probably occurred in the currency market. For example, the French franc, selling in London against the British pound, might have had a slightly higher price in London that it did in Paris. To profit from this differential, an arbitrageur (arb) would buy francs in Paris and sell them in London at the same time. He would continue to do this until he had supplied London with enough francs to drive the price down to the same level as it was in Paris where he was pushing the price up by buying up the supply.

Due to a superior connumications system and the ability to trade in markets all over the world, the arb was able to make a profit without any significant risk. In addition, the arb was providing a benefit to the marketplace by helping to equalize the franc price in London and Paris.

Commodity Arbitrage

In the case of commodity arbitrage, the arbitrageur takes simultaneous and opposite positions in the futures and physical markets. If market conditions have established a differential between the current price for the physical product (i.e., spot price) and the current price for future deliveries of that product (i.e., future price), the arbitrageur will be able to lock in a certain profit, no matter how prices change. The arbitrageur will either (1) buy the physical commodity (go long) and sell the futures (go short) *or* (2) sell the physical commodity (go short) and buy the futures (go long).

For example, if the spot oil price this month is $15/barrel and the futures price for next month delivery is $15.25/barrel, the arbitrageur would buy (go long) the spot oil for $15 and sell (short) the futures contract for $15.25, locking in a profit of 0.25/barrel. (In this simplified example, transaction, storage, and interest costs are assumed to be negligible. In the real world, such costs are essential terms in what become complex equations.)

Stocks and Bonds

Riskless arbitrage is also possible with stocks and bonds. It was first implemented with stocks which traded in two different locations (i.e., two different stock exchanges) with small price differentials which occurred from time to time. For example, an arb would watch the prices of a stock trading on both the New York and Pacific Stocks Exchange. If Company A is selling at $10/share in New York and $10.25 on the Pacific exchange, the arb will simultaneously buy it on the New York and sell it on the Pacific. Despite the small spread (normally $\frac{1}{8}$ to $\frac{1}{4}$ points/share), the arb will make a substantial profit by dealing with large volumes. The arb will continue to trade until the spread has disappeared, pushing up the price in New York (by stock purchases) and driving the price down on the West Coast (by stock sales). Computers and instant telecommunications have largely eliminated such arbitrage.

The advent of increasing varieties of derivative securities and instruments—options, futures, and indices—offers additional opportunities for arbitrage. One can search out price discrepancies between baskets (combinations) of the primary securities and their multiple derivatives. For example, a discrepancy between a share of common stock and the price of its option can enable an arb to assure a profit by buying one and selling the other. Usually this profit is small and fleeting, but high volume can generate high annual rates of return on invested capital.

Another example involves the simultaneous buying and selling of stock indices and the basket of primary stocks which those indices reflect. Clearly, with the complex forms of derivative securities available today, arbitrage analysis has become exceedingly sophisticated, requiring computers and clever algorithms to manipulate the myriad variables.

Yet, riskless arbitrage has limited potential. The markets just do not allow riskless returns to be made continually above the established riskless rates (i.e., Treasuries). The profit potential of classic riskless arbitrage has been squeezed by several factors working together: the rise of instant worldwide communication, high-volume marketplaces in currencies and securities throughout the world, the common access to computers and those clever algorithms, and, energizing it all, the intense competition among investors and financial institutions.

Perception Arbitrage

The next step after riskless arbitrage is perception arbitrage, where the arb takes a small amount of risk by relying on his market sense. For example, he might sell (short) 10,000 shares of company A in New York on Monday. Since he does not have to deliver the shares until the next day, he waits until Tuesday morning and buys the shares in London, where he perceives the price would be lower. In this case, the arb feels the tendency of the market to move in one direction or another. (If it moves the wrong way, he will take a loss.)

Risk Arbitrage

Risk arbitrage has become a major force in the capital markets by concentrating on mergers and acquisitions. But the concept began differently.

Exchange Offers

During the depression, opportunities for arbitrage arose as bankrupt railroads and utilities reorganized, issuing new securities in exchange for old securities—but with a difference in value. After assessing the possible spreads between the old and the new security *which was still unissued*, the arb would buy the old security (if the price were low enough) and wait to exchange it for the new security when issued.

In this case there was a definite risk since the reorganizing company might take longer than anticipated to issue the new security. Since the arb usually operated with borrowed money, the longer the new issue took, the higher his costs were (i.e., the more interest he would pay). In addition, there was always a possibility that the reorganization would not go through at all. This was the critical change: The arb was now taking a position that assumed significant risk—he was engaged in risk arbitrage.

The arbitrage of the discounted securities of troubled companies continues today. There is a class of investors that specializes in buying up the securities of corporations in need of reorganization. The debt of such companies trades at a discount, often substantially below par. By purchasing this debt (which may be secured), the investors may take control of (or at least influence) the reorganization process. If the company engages in an exchange offer, giving one or more new securities in trade for the old, the investor profits since he bought the old securities at a low price.

Mergers and Acquisitions

The merger mania of the 1960s created new vistas for risk arbitrageurs. With most acquiring companies offering securities (not cash) for the target company, a spread would usually arise between the market price of the target's stock and the market price of the equivalent number of shares of the acquirer's stock that would be received as payment. This spread was derived from three factors: (1) the premium that the acquiring company would offer for the target company combined with the market delay in reflecting it, (2) the time delay between the announcement and the anticipated closing, and (3) the inherent uncertainty of the transaction.[2]

The arb would buy (go long) the securities of the target company, expecting them to rise in price and sell (short) the securities of the acquiring company, expecting them to decline in price. The two risks for the arbitrageur were (1) the possibility that the merger would not be consummated and (2) the length of time it would take. Following is an example of this kind of risk arbitrage.

A Merger and Acquistion Pricing Example

Assume Company X is trading at $100 per share and offers to exchange one share of its stock for two shares of Company Y, which is currently trading at $25 (i.e., $100 for $50—a 100% premium), with the merger to be consummated in 3 months. The arb, after researching the deal and determining that it will go through, offers the shareholder of Company Y $40 per share. Company Y's shareholders can immediately take a $15 per share profit from the proposed merger by selling to the arbitrageur. Or he can wait 3 months to receive one-half share of Company X stock currently valued at $50. The second choice yields an extra $10, but only if the deal goes through and only if Company X stock is still trading at $100.

Assume the Company Y stockholder decides to sell to the arbitrageur and take the immediate $15 per share profit. The arb who has bought the Company Y stock will sell short Company X stock at $100, thereby

---

2. There is another risk as well. It is possible that the structure of the deal will change so that the premerger market price would exceed the real value of the actual merger. This is often true with two-tier transactions.

locking in a profit of $20, assuming the deal is consummated 3 months later (i.e., $100 - [2 \times 40] = 20$). Two Company Y shares will be exchanged for one Company X share and used to cover the short sale. In this case, the arbitrageur's profit of $20 on a three month investment of $80 yields a gross annualized return of 100% (not considering interest payments for borrowed funds and transaction costs).[3]

The risks are clear. The primary risk is that the deal will not go through at all and the price of Company Y's shares will plunge back down to its original, pre-deal value of about $25 per share, pounding the arb with a huge loss ($15 per share deficit).

The secondary risk is the element of time: Perhaps the deal will go through but it will take nine months instead of three. Since the arb deals with borrowed money, the longer the deal takes to close, the greater the cost of capital (interest) and the lower the profit margin. In this case, the 100% annual return drops to 33.3%. (While a 30 + % return still looks great, arbs must factor into all their returns the probability that, on occasion, deals will fail completely. And it takes many 30 + % deals to make up for one huge loss.)

In this respect it is important for an arb to analyze *all* the factors in a transaction, including hidden obstacles such as antitrust violations and possible legal injunctions. In addition, an arb should assess the target company's *real* or *fundamental* value, independent of any M&A amplification. Such a detailed financial analysis (e.g., industrial, business, operational, managerial, financial, projections) provides a *floor* value should the transaction fall through.

Arbs like to determine a target company's break-up value—what it would be worth if all its divisions were sold individually and all assets and liabilities were tallied (see Chapter 6). A break-up value assessment will generally determine the likelihood of other bidders going after the company should the primary deal disappear. (There are tricks and traps here. For example, the value of off-balance-sheet assets [e.g., real estate] and liabilities [e.g., medical retiree expenses] must be considered.)

---

3. What would the annualized return be when interest charges and transactions costs are included? At 10 percent per year, interest on the $80 for three months is $2.00. Transaction costs should not exceed 10 cents per share for large traders. To be conservative, add in all logistics and expenses and assume $2.50. Thus the $20 profit per share becomes $17.50 and the annualized rate of return becomes 87.5 percent ($[17.5/80] \times 4 = .875$).

Levels of Complexity

Modern merger transactions can be frightfully complex, forcing the arbitrageur to make a number of calculations to determine the *workout value*. There are three general categories of M&A structures.

The first and most basic transaction is the exchange of stock for stock *or* cash for stock. Evaluating these mergers are straightforward.

The second and more complicated transaction is the two-tier offer. Cash is offered for an initial given percentage of stock to be tendered (e.g., 50%), while stock or new notes are exchanged for the remainder of the stock. In a two-tier offer, the value of the new notes must be assessed (they are almost always valued below par).

The third and still more complicated transaction offers cash *and* a combination of securities for stock (e.g., cash for 30% of the target company's outstanding stock plus a package of newly issued convertible preferred stock plus common stock of the acquiring company plus, perhaps, other exotic securities).

The Business of Risk Arbitrage

Mergers have always been part of corporate life in America. Up until the 1960s there were only a small group of people involved in risk arbitrage and the activity did not have a high profile, not even within the capital markets. However, in the late 1970s and through the 1980s (especially during the Reagan Administration), the whole game of arbitrage changed. With the relaxation in antitrust enforcement, the increase in deregulation, and the increase in the availability of high-yield financing, there has been a tremendous increase in buyouts, mergers, and acquisitions. Furthermore, takeovers grew more likely to be hostile in nature and higher in value.

In the 1970s, cash tender offers increased in popularity and it became nearly impossible to arbitrage away the risk of fluctuation in share price. No longer could securities of the acquiring company be sold short to lock in the spread. The risk arbitrageur had to buy stock in the target company and would make money only when—or, more importantly, *if*—the target company was taken over at a premium to market value. With little room left for classical arbitrage, detailed analysis was required by the arbitrageur before funds were committed to a target company.

Arbs have had tremendous influence on merger and acquisition activity. They have always been involved in tender offers and takeover situations. They have helped make the M&A market liquid and have given the investor a way to sell stock at a price *near* the tender price without waiting for the takeover to be consummated. As such, arbs transfer risk from the investor to themselves and consequently expect a commensurately high return.

Risk arbitrageurs had been doing very well indeed until the arrest of Ivan Boesky[4] for insider trading in late 1986 and the Black Monday stock market crash of October 19, 1987. As a result, particularly in October of 1987, many takeover stocks collapsed and arbitrageurs lost millions. The pool of money devoted to risk arbitrage fell from $15 billion in the summer of 1987 to $6 billion in the first quarter of 1988. Many of the arbitrageurs' losses were multiplied by their high leveraging. For example, Smith Barney Harris Upham & Co. left the arb business after losing $43 million.

But arbs claim to be contrarian—they like talking against the crowd (though they often march with the crowd). Since everybody took a beating in the crash and some arbs were driven out of the business, it was suggested that there would be more opportunities for those still in the business. Subsequent events confirmed the suggestion.

Following the October 1987 crash, there was a marked change in the entire takeover situation. In 1988, there were many well-financed takeover offers made by major corporations, but not as many bids from raiders backed by junk bonds. Arbs seemed to be pursuing the announced, solidly-financed transactions, and not the more risky, speculative, unannounced targets.

In addition, arbs adopted a more conservative posture, often changing their investment strategy in reaction to broader market news, input they had largely ignored in the past. Previously, arbs had assumed that the prices of stocks involved in takeovers and restructuring moved independently of market averages. Today, however, arbs are more likely to pay attention to the market and to become active traders getting in and out of general market positions as opposed to concentrating only on particular takeover stocks.

---

4. As an arb, Ivan Boesky reportedly made $50 million on the Texaco takeover of Getty, $65 million on the Chevron/Gulf deal, and perhaps as much as $150 million on Ted Turner's attempted takeover of CBS. On the other hand, he also lost $40–70 million when Phillips Petroleum bought off T. Boone Pickens.

Furthermore, arbs are now less highly leveraged. With the recent government crackdowns, arbs are tending to buy stock only after the deals have been announced. There is much less anticipation, much less seeking out of borderline insider information. But with the glut of more recent high-quality mergers, there has also been no shortage of action. The major worry is new legislation and possible changes in antitrust enforcement.

The business can be very profitable. For example, on January 4, 1988, Hoffman-LaRoche & Co. announced a $72 per share hostile takeover bid for Sterling Drug. The next day, Sterling's stock leaped $17\frac{1}{4}$ points to $74\frac{1}{8}$. On January 18, Sterling rejected the offer suggesting that it might seek a white knight.[5] With a bidding war in the offering, the market pumped the stock to $77\frac{3}{8}$. The following day, Hoffman-La Roche sweetened its offer to 76 and then raised it again to 81 just two days later. The war ended suddenly the next day when Sterling agreed to be bought by Eastman Kodak for $89.50 a share. The arbs had hit the jackpot.

Finally, arbs need mergers and acquisitions to do their work. As such they are like the armies of attorneys and investment bankers who do what they can to encourage such activity. It is not out of character for arbs to try to put companies *in play*. (A typical technique is to show that a company's break-up value is far greater than its market value [see Chapter 6]. Another ploy, immoral if not illegal, is just to start a rumor.)

The small group of approximately one dozen big-time arbs had grown by the mid 1980s to at least 50 major arbitrageurs with another 100 smaller operators. Ivan Boesky made risk arbitrage highly visible to the rest of the investment community, and unfortunately, would come to personify the field.

Arbitrageur Behavior

The Boesky scandal, however obscene, focuses attention on the fundamental issues of arbitrage—and they all circle around the concept of *information*. If cash is king for corporate raiding, information is king for risk arbitrage.

---

5. A white knight is a "friendly" company brought in to defeat a hostile takeover attempt by taking over the target company itself. Management hopes that since *they* brought in the white knight, the new owners will be more sensitive to the interests and concerns of prior management.

Information is the currency of arbitrage, and an arb's information network is his most vital business asset. Tens of millions of dollars are riding on the accuracy of what may, might, will, or will not happen. And with so many people being privy to so much inside information,[6] with the performance demand so high, and with competition so intense, some arbs went over the line to acquire that information.

It should be recognized that the arb is an investor with *no* interest in the corporation beyond a quick profit. Arbs invest in a particular transaction *not* in a particular company. They make their money from the deal's profits not from the firm's profits. The long term to an arb is measured in months if not weeks. Arbs generally leverage their capital by borrowing and need rapid turnaround due to compounding interest costs.

As such, the more stock that winds up in the hands of arbs after a hostile announcment is made, the more likely it is that the target company will be sold. Consequently, it is not uncommon—and it is not legal— for potential hostile acquirers to tip off the arbs in order to get as much stock as possible out of the control of longer-term shareholders and into the hands of the very short-term arbs. Arbs often hold the balance of power of contested battles and can determine the nature of the outcome. (It is not uncommone for arbs to hold 30 percent or more of a takeover target's shares.)

Arbs, for their part, try to get out ahead of the pack. It is no longer good enough to work with announced deals. Everyone can do that. A prime objective of risk arbitrage has been to take advantage of the big rise in price *before* the actual bid is made public (which is almost always the largest part of the price spurt). Thus, arbs routinely take positions in the stock of undervalued companies which they believe are ripe for takeover or the stock of companies in which a corporate raider is known to be quietly accumulating a position. (In fact, arbs are often suspected of spreading speculative stories in order to *tee up* a company.)

According to reports, there was no end to which arbs would go to ascertain the likelihood of a rumored M&A deal being announced and then closing successfully once it was announced. The insider trading scandals, with suitcases of cash changing hands in the back alleys of Wall Street, was the grossest testimony to greed and immorality. Yet

---

6. Dozens of people are aware of mergers before they are announced publicly. These include bankers assessing the proposed financing, several batteries of legal firms, and many support personnel inside the acquiring company.

there were other, more subtle forms of sleuthing. Some arbs, it is said, used to track the flight paths of corporate aircraft (to determine which companies were talking together) and monitor the night activity of certain law firms (whose clients might be preparing M&A acitivity, whether a takeover or a defense).

Megamergers

Many deals of the late 1970s and 1980s would never have been considered in the past. Billion-dollar takeover bidding contests have become common. In 1981, DuPont beat out Mobil and Seagram's for Conoco, paying $7.8 billion ($3 billion in cash and the rest in DuPont common stock). Since then large acquisitions have included: Chevron's purchase of Gulf Corp. ($13.3 billion), U.S. Steel grabbing Marathon Oil ($3.75 billion), Campeau's devouring Federated Stores ($6.6 billion), Texaco engulfing Getty ($10.1 billion), and Mobil swallowing Superior Oil ($5.7 billion). General Electric took over RCA for $6 billion, while Phillip Morris spent $5.7 billion for General Foods. In the largest M&A transaction in history, KKR, the most famous LBO investment firm, took RJR Nabisco private in a transaction valued at $25 billion.

With increased size and competitiveness in bidding, complex and creative bidding strategies have evolved. Risk arbitrageurs have become a critically important part of the process, in many cases controlling (and in most cases influencing) whether the deal is completed and at what price.

In the middle 1970s, hostile deals began to emerge with rival bidders raising the premium as if they were playing penny-ante poker. The hostile acquisition of Babcock and Wilcox occurred after a frenzied bidding war, with 11 separate bids by United Technologies and J. Ray McDermott (the white knight) before the latter won with a top offer of $750 million, 50 percent over the opening bid and almost twice the target price prior to the bidding war. This six-month battle generated the greatest amount of money arbs had ever made (at that time) and served to attract new arbs into the business.

Evaluating Mergers and Acquisitions

We now examine how the risk arbitrageur goes about his work. What exactly does an arb consider before deciding to get involved with a potential takeover situation? There are seven critical factors to evaluate in assessing the likelihood of success of any particular merger or acquisition:

1. Regulatory agencies and approvals.
2. Deal financing.
3. Attitude of management.
4. Tracking the particular industry.
5. Specifics of the acquiring and of the target company.
6. Timing of the M&A deal.
7. Potential deal deterrents.

Regulatory Agencies and Approvals

There are three general categories of laws which affect mergers and acquisitions:

1. The rules of the state in which the target company resides (which determine how corporate control may be transferred and exercised).
2. The rules of the federal government, particularly the securities laws (e.g., the Williams Act which establishes disclosure requirements and the minimum offering period before an acquisition can proceed).
3. The Hart-Scott-Rodino Antitrust Improvements Act of 1976 (Hart-Scott) which requires premerger waiting periods and notifications.

The two leading antitrust regulatory agencies are the Justice Department and the Federal Trade Commission (FTC). Under Hart-Scott, mergers must be submitted to the proper federal antitrust agency for review. What may or may not happen will affect the arb dramatically. Thus, for each merger, the arb will require the services of an expert lawyer or consultant to help evaluate the likely action of the given agency, the timing involved, the probable issues, the possible disputes, and the like.

Deal Financing

The cash tender is the most difficult offer for a target company to resist or defend. (Shareholders get premium values with no going-forward risks, and directors know that if they reject the offer the stock may well plunge in value and they can be sued.) The arbitrageur must evaluate the funding sources of the acquiring company (and the target company if necessary) for each particular deal. Is the buyer bona fide? Does the acquiring company have its own cash? Is the acquiror raising the funds by an equity offering? by junk bonds? Which investment banks are participating in the financing? which commercial banks? Has the buyer made deals with these investment or commercial banks before? Are bridge loans required? Are leveraged buyout pools involved? (For example, when Beazer PLC took over Koppers, the Beazer association with Shearson Lehman Hutton and NatWest Bank was an indication of the seriousness of the offer.[7])

Attitude of Management

The arb must evaluate the senior executives involved in potential mergers. (Note that this evaluation focuses strictly on how top management reacts in the pressured M&A environment, and does not relate at all to top management's ability to run the company.) Through library research and the opinion of analysts and other outside experts, the arb carefully checks out the past history and track record of each participant. Has a target's management been involved in previous hostile fights? Have they looked for a white knight or friendly buyer? Or did they recapitalize or restructure their firm? Did they try getting rid of raiders by paying greenmail, repurchasing a potential suitor's stock at a premium to market and thereby maintaining their own independence while allowing shareholders' stock to plummet in value?

The arb must determine the probability that each of the many options will occur. In friendly takeovers, it is important to know the plans of both acquiring and target managements. Who will control the negotiations? Do both sets of management have similar goals? Finally, how have the acquiring and target managements performed in previous deals, especially of the hostile kind?

Tracking the Particular Industry

Industry trends can have a significant effect on increasing or decreasing the value of a deal and on its probability of closing. A fundamental analysis of the industry (or industries) must be performed and forecasted

---

7. Shearson felt the sting when the city of Pittsburgh and the state of Pennsylvania, the home city and state of Koppers, attacked Shearson for its participation. See below.

over the lifetime of the deal (*lifetime* is defined as the length of time it takes for the arb to make his money—a time period usually measured in months).

There are industries where companies, which have not been profitable in the short run, have become exceptionally valuable based on anticipated jumps in revenues or margins. For example, changing commodity prices may dramatically affect the prices of companies dependent on those commodities; the enormous increase in metal prices in 1987 and 1988 increased the value of many primary producers.

As another example, outrageously high prices are being paid for cellular communications companies, which are being valued not by current earnings but rather by anticipated revenues (based on regional population and the absence of potential competition). Similarly, cable stocks are priced with respect to the number of subscribers, not the current profits. Deregulation has allowed increased subscriber rates, while lower interest rates have simplified acquisition financing. In these industries the awarding of new franchises can make a big difference in valuation (whether winning an unexpected territory or losing an expected one).

Specifics of the Acquiring and of the Target Company

In addition to the particular industry, both the acquiring company and the target company are analyzed in depth by the arb. He uses all available public reporting documents (e.g., 10K, 10Q) combined with the input of analysts and other outside experts until both businesses are well understood. The best arbs do not invest without maximum information.

Can the buyer afford the acquisition? Are funding sources lined up? Is due diligence an issue? Who are the accountants and lawyers for each company? Are there potential business problems on either side that might surface in the intervening period before closing? Does either company have any skeletons in the closet? The stock prices, the earnings forecasts, and the actual earnings during the course of the deal will be monitored by the arbitrageurs.

Timing of the M&A Deal

With arbs historically aiming at an annualized, all-in return of 25–30 percent per deal, the timing of the completion of the deal is crucial. The longer the deal takes to close (assuming no change in the final price), the lower the return. What is the sequence of events for M&A transactions?

Friendly Mergers.   A friendly merger begins with an announcement of a preliminary agreement in principle. Preliminary terms are set after extensive negotiations between the two companies. The merger proposal is then filed with the appropriate government agencies. SEC clearance is sought and approval generally takes four to six weeks.

After receipt of SEC clearance, a definitive agreement to merge is signed between the two companies. Proxy material will now be mailed to the shareholders of each company, setting a date for the shareholders' meeting. Generally one month is required before the vote. The ten-to fourteen-week period which has expired since the initial announcement does not take into account any of the delays that could be caused by regulatory review and legal problems.

Tender Offers.   Tender offers are governed by securities regulations and have specific timing requirements. A tender offer is a public solicitation by a potential acquiring company to stockholders of a target company in which cash and/or securities in the acquiring company are offered for the shares of the target company. A friendly tender averages 30 days, while a hostile bid will take 45-60 days. If the bid is changed, it must remain open for an additional 10 business or 30 calendar days.

According to the Hart-Scott-Rodino Act, after the filing of the takeover offer, the Justice Department and the FTC have 15 days to rule on whether or not the merger will be challenged. If the ruling agency asks for more information from the companies involved, up to 10 more days can pass before a decision is reached. If securities are offered instead of cash, the waiting period is 30 days (plus another 20 if more information is requested).

Hart-Scott was the key to Mobil's loss and Dupont's victory in the Conoco takeover in 1981. DuPont, which had offered securities plus cash, filed on July 8 and would become eligible on August 7. Mobil, with an all-cash offer, could have been approved by July 31, unless a request for more information delayed it until August 10. DuPont applied heavy political pressure and received its clearance on July 30. A few days later, a second information request would delay Mobil another 10 days. Despite Mobil increasing its bid twice to a final offer *above* Dupont's and going to court, Mobil lost—partly due to fear that the Justice Department would not allow the merger of the two oil giants. The highest bidder did not prevail.

While Mobil had made a higher bid with a cash offer, DuPont used a front-end-loaded, two-tier offer to pressure successfully the target shareholders of Conoco. The first step (tier one) was a cash tender offer, and the second step (tier two) was an offer to remaining shareholders of securities valued *below* the cash consideration offered in the first step. The front-end loading encouraged shareholders to tender quickly. (Despite the reduced value in the second tier, the two-tier merger is usually approved since the bidder company has usually acquired a controlling interest in the target company after the first tier and can force its way. Two-tier offers have been increasingly rejected by boards of directors and the courts.)

Other Regulatory Approvals. Other regulatory approvals may be required. For example, the takeover of a cable company with subscribers in 40 different municipalities could require 40 different approvals and delay deal closing for a whole year. Retail chains may require the consent of hundreds of leaseholding owners.

Potential Deal Deterrents

The proliferation of hostile bids for corporate control has resulted in the emergence of defensive and offensive maneuvers limited only by the ingenuity of both target and acquiring companies, their investment bankers and attorneys, and the ever-present arbitrageurs. The following are potential deal deterrents that must be monitored in every situation.

Legal Action.   In order to thwart unwanted suitors, target managements may seek access to the courts or the regulatory agencies. Oftentimes their motivation is not to defend shareholder interests, but rather to seek delay, thereby gathering the time needed to develop successful strategies for bolstering and perpetuating their own control.

When in a defensive posture, lawyers will try almost anything to slow the advance of an acquiring company and assist incumbent management to maintain independence. For example, target attorneys often try to convince the Justice Department or the Federal Trade Commission to invoke its antitrust authority to stop the transaction pending submission of additional premerger information. Or, they will sue the acquiring company and bring it into court under any and all pretexts, with the hearings, taking of evidence, judge's deliberation, and appeals process all taking up valuable time.

In one case (1981), Grumman successfully halted a merger with LTV by building up an antitrust case. In another case (1982), Carl

Icahn had started accumulating undervalued Marshall Field stock at $20. The target management responded with a lawsuit charging Icahn with being a racketeer because of securities violations under the Racketeer Influenced and Corrupt Organizations Act (RICO), since he had signed a consent decree for alleged violations after purchasing Hammerhill Paper Company shares. (Marshall Field was unsuccessful and forced to bring in a white knight.)

Poison Pill. A poison pill is a class of securities issued by the target company which is convertible into the common stock of the target or raider company at a rate highly deleterious to any hostile bidder. Convertibility may be triggered by consummation of any unfriendly merger (i.e., a merger not approved by the original board of directors) or any other specified, potentially unfriendly transaction (e.g., the accumulation of a specific percentage, say 20%, of the company's stock).

The convertibility factor is designed to be extremely favorable to current shareholders and makes the potential acquisition significantly more expensive to any possible buyer (e.g., the right for shareholders, other than the potential acquirer, to buy target company shares at half the market price). The idea is that the poison pill makes a hostile takeover so costly that few raiders would exhibit interest in swallowing the pill and mounting an unfriendly raid.

The pill may come in the form of a dividend of rights to buy the raider's stock at a bargain price. For example, Brown-Forman Distillers Corp. attempted to purchase Lenox, Inc. In self-defense, the latter issued preferred stock to all its stockholders, which, in the event of a takeover, could be converted into the stock of the newly merged company, thus ensuring that the Brown family would lose control of the company. It was only after Brown increased their bid and convinced Lenox that the offer was friendly, that Lenox removed the poison pill and allowed the merger to proceed.

Over 500 companies have poison pills. In a study by New York proxy solicitor Georgeson & Co., companies so protected received an increased purchase price when engaged in defending hostile takeovers.[8] Proponents

---

8. In the study, 27 companies with pills received final offers averaging 78.5 percent above where their stock had been trading six months before the takeover attempt started. The 21 companies without pills averaged a 56.7 percent gain.

of pills argue that they prevent takeover abuses, give bargaining power to management, and result in higher prices for shareholders. Critics contend that pills entrench current management, protect the sleepy status quo, and prevent shareholders from realizing their full value. Institutional investors in particular have been strong opponents of poison pills. (Many of the legislative initiatives to limit hostile takeovers also seek to curb the abuses of poison pills.)

Greenmail.   An unfriendly raider may purchase a substantial block of a target company's stock with the primary purpose of coercing the target into repurchasing the block at a premium over the amount paid. For example, Texaco repurchased $1.28 billion of its shares from the Bass brothers and Disney repurchased $325.3 million from Saul Steinberg's Reliance Holdings—both substantially over then current market prices. The T. Boone Pickens group made $800 million when Gulf was bought away from them by Socal in 1984.[9] On the other hand, many arbitrageurs lost a great deal of money when the Pickens group sold its stock back to Phillips, as the price of the stock dropped immediately thereafter.

Debt Schedules.   Now we discuss several different strategies for stopping a hostile takeover attempt. The first such defensive method is for a potential target to schedule all of its debts to come due immediately after takeover. This means that a company writes its debt covenants with its financial institutions so that a change of control results in a requirement to pay back all loans instantly.[10] (Raiders normally include the cost of refinancing all the debt along with the cost of acquiring all the equity as part of their takeover financing plan.)

Stock Buyback and Recapitalization.   Another method for resisting takeovers is for the target company to repurchase its own stock. This recapitalization technique accomplishes several things at the same time:

---

9. The raiders themselves never claim that their primary purpose is greenmail. In fact, many raiders have come out publicly against greenmail. The raiders' stated primary purpose is always to enhance the value of the target company, with full takeover the means to that end. Greenmail, they might admit privately, is a nice reward for second place.

10. The financial institutions themselves often require such covenants since they do not want to have their loans exposed to new managements whom they do not know.

By reducing the number of outstanding shares, it increases the earnings per share and as a result the market price; it removes a supply of shares from the grasp of any current or future raider; and it increases the percentage of the company that the insiders control. By using debt to buy in the equity, recapitalization also make the company both less desirable to raiders and harder for them to finance. (See Chapter 16.)

Leveraged Buyout.   The leveraged buyout (LBO) is a favorite corporate defense (see Chapter 16). Here management itself (often together with outside investors) purchases the company with borrowed funds, based on the company's cash flow and/or sale of assets. Dr Pepper performed a defensive LBO in 1984. In 1988, Macmillan management's initial response to a takeover bid from the Bass Group was a combination LBO and restructuring plan, proposing to split the company into two divisions.

LBOs put heavy burdens on companies. Southland, the convenience store chain which retired its stock at high prices (after overtures from the Belzbergs), when private in December 1987. It then had to service $5.5 billion of debt, cutting back spending and selling off assets in order to reduce this massive liability. (Before the LBO, Southland had had $2.2 billion of debt and $1.7 billion of equity.)

Antitrust.   An extreme mechanism for defending against a specific acquirer is for the target company to purchase another business similar to that of the bidding company, thereby creating an antitrust conflict for the potential acquirer.

Crown Jewel Option.   A *crown jewel* is the most prized asset of a corporation; it is often the critical element that makes the company an attractive takeover target. A defensive tactic against a hostile tender offer is to *sell* the crown jewel, thereby removing the key asset that the unfriendly bidder was hoping to acquire.

There is a problem here of possible director liability if a profitable division is sold suddenly below its fair market value. The issue, of course, is fair market value as compared to the selling price. If the sale is at or above fair market value, and especially if the price is at or above the capitalized value of the division's earnings (see Chapter 6), shareholder value should be enhanced and the transaction would be hard to criticize.

In 1984, Carter-Hawley Hale, the California department store chain, fended off The Limited, a fast-growing group of women's specialty stores, by resorting to the crown jewel strategy. They offered its crown jewel, the profitable Waldenbooks chain, to General Cinema.

Revlon lost its bid to avoid a takeover by Pantry Pride when the court limited its rights to lock up assets so as to favor one bidder over another. In another case, Marathon Oil gave U.S. Steel an option to purchase its Yates oil fields for $2.8 billion, if Mobil's tender offer succeeded (the option was upset by the Court).

Liquidation.   Perhaps the most violent way for discouraging raiders is to sell the entire business—closing plants, selling equipment, and writing down assets. For example, in 1980 UV Industries went into liquidation in reaction to a takeover attempt by Sharon Steel.

Pac-Man Defense.   In the Pac-Man Defense, the target firm makes a responding counter-offer to purchase the would-be acquiring company. (*Pac-Man* refers to the famous video game in which the object is to eat your adversaries before they eat you.) This maneuver was used by Martin-Marietta in its defense against Bendix. Heublein used a similar strategy to scare off General Cinema.

Staggered Board of Directors.   Target firms have changed corporate bylaws to stagger the terms of directors, thereby preventing the acquirer from acquiring full control of the target for years. (However, in an all-cash, high-premium offer, the acquiring company will generally win control due to potential director liability.)

Supermajority Vote.   Another defensive step is to require a supermajority vote of stockholders to approve a merger. For example, company bylaws may be amended to require 80 percent of the board of directors and shareholders to approve a change in control of the firm.

Different Classes of Common Stock.   Issuing different classes of common stock has become an increasingly popular technique for maintaining control.[11] Consider Resorts International, where 5.6 million shares

---

11. Whether companies with different classes of common stock can be listed on the major exchanges has been an issue.

of Class A stock have 90 percent of the equity but only 7 percent of the vote, while 800,000 shares of Class B stock have 10 percent of the equity but 93 percent of the votes.

New Legislation. With anti-takeover sentiment running high in the late 1980s, a large number of state and local laws were being passed. Furthermore, state and local governments became active in corporate defense (fearing the loss of jobs). For example, in the case of the Beazer PLC takeover of Koppers, there were such strong feelings in Pittsburgh and Pennsylvania that the State Treasurer cancelled over $7 billion of business normally handled by Shearson Lehman (Beazer's investment bankers). In Washington, some Pennsylvania legislators introduced measures trying to end Shearson's role in the bid.

Summary

Risk arbitrage is an invention of the capital markets. It is a derivative activity that mediates between long-term investors and acquiring companies, absorbing the risks of deals by giving current shareholders an early cash out and a guaranteed return. By providing this kind of increased liquidity for merger and acquisition transactions, arbs facilitate M&A activity and help enhance overall shareholder wealth.

Arbs take high risks and require high returns. Since information is central to success, there is a great tendency to maximize knowledge. Care must be taken to that such tendencies do not engender illegal behavior. Nonetheless, the fundamental value of risk arbitrage should be stressed: By making the merger and acquisition market more liquid, arbs enable long-term owners of corporations to make higher returns at lower levels of risk (see Chapter 3). Over time, this increase in wealth should facilitate capital formation and the building of economic enterprises.

CHAPTER 18

Futures and Options*

No financial phenomena have contributed more toward characterizing the 1980s than the unprecedented volatilities in short-term and long-term interest rates, equity prices, and currency exchange rates. The magnitude and duration of these volatilities have subjected every corporation to various degrees of financial risks which could severely impact a company's future competitive strength if left unmanaged.

Attempts at controlling such complex financial risks with conventional (pre-1980) techniques did not meet with much success. Traditional methods cannot provide the effectiveness and flexibility at reasonable costs that financial officers have been demanding. As a result, a variety of new markets and innovative techniques have emerged to satisfy and even exceed the most stringent corporate demands. Working together, investment bankers and finance managers can now achieve remarkable control over financial risks.

Conventional Techniques

Conventional alternatives for protecting an anticipated bond issue from interest rate volatility have frequently been ineffective and inflexible. In the past, a financial manager who was fearful that yields would be

---

*This chapter has been derived from "Financial Risk Management" by Oliver Abel IV, and "Risk Management with Futures and Options in Investment Banking" by Joanne Hill and Thomas Schneeweis, Volume I (Investing and Risk Management), Dow Jones-Irwin's *The Library of Investment Banking* (1990), Robert Lawrence Kuhn, editor-in-chief.

higher prior to the desired funding date had little alternative but to issue the bonds in advance of the original date—even though the funds may not have been deployed immediately, if at all. Of course, the financial manager with high coupon debt could eliminate those bonds via a tender offer, but historically that has been only partially effective and costly (a premium must be offered to attract the attention of the bondholders—rarely would all be attracted, and a commission must be paid to transact the bonds). In any event, an offering in advance of the date in which the funds are needed is permanent in spite of: (1) whether market fluctuations in the interim provide a more attractive yield, or (2) cause a different size or maturity bond issue to be preferred and, (3) whether the funds will be required at all, as originally assumed.

While an advanced funding is a common conventional technique, the most common alternative has been simply to wait, unprotected, until the first call date, at which time new bonds will be issued, or until the funds are required as for a corporate acquisition. While remaining unprotected has a significant amount of flexibility, it is completely ineffective in safeguarding current yields and any existing unrealized profits.

No matter which of the above techniques is selected, financial managers have been quick to note that the end result is frequently costly and ineffective, offering little flexibility to capitalize on market fluctuations or internal corporate needs.

Innovative Techniques

Financial futures contracts have been in existence since the middle 1970s, financial options since the early 1980s. Used together in a sophisticated program, they provide new avenues by which corporate financial officers can protect their anticipated debt offerings without limiting flexibility—and at times even enhancing it. The new avenues include *fixing, capping,* and *collaring* today's interest rates for a future financing.

Fixing Interest Rates

First, U.S. Treasury bond futures and Treasury note futures are utilized to *fix* today's interest rate on long-term debt and intermediate-term debt, respectively, without actually having to issue the bonds until a future date. If the financial manager is comfortable with current rates and is willing to forgo any further decline in rates, he can sell the appropriate number of futures contracts today and plan on purchasing them back on the anticipated financing date. Should interest rates rise (fall) then gains (losses) will be made in the futures markets to offset the higher (lower) interest expense for the life of the new bond issue.

Capping Interest Rates

Secondly, options on Treasury bond futures and options on Treasury note futures contracts are utilized not to fix today's rate but to *cap* it. If the financial manager is fearful that rates will rise but wishes to benefit should rates decline, then put options are purchased and held until the date the bonds are issued. Should interest rates rise while the options are held, then gains on the options contracts will be realized, offsetting the higher interest expense for the life of the bond issue. Should interest rates decline, the most that will be lost is the premium or up-front fee that was paid for the options, and more importantly, the lower bond yields existing in the markets are attained.

Collaring Interest Rates

Thirdly, options on Treasury bond and Treasury note futures contracts can also be utilized to *collar* today's interest rate rather than cap or fix it. If the financial manager is fearful that rates will rise and desires a ceiling and is willing to forgo any further decline in yields below a predetermined floor, then an equal number of put options are purchased and call options sold. Should interest rates rise above the ceiling, then gains will be realized on the put options, bringing the effective yield back to the ceiling level. Should interest rates decline below the floor, then losses will exist on the call options, bringing the effective yield back to the floor level. Should interest rates remain above the floor and below the ceiling, then both the put and the call options will exhibit little, if any, gain or loss. The most unique aspect of this type of protection is that there is little up-front fee, since the cost of purchasing the put options is approximately equal to the income received by selling the call options.

Costs

In utilizing futures contracts to fix today's rate for an upcoming bond issue, the overwhelming cost component is the negative cost of carry associated with a positively-sloped yield curve.[1] This cost-of-carry is nearly identical to the cost of hypothetically issuing the bonds today and investing the proceeds in lower-yielding, money market securities until the original date of funding. The negative spread resulting from paying high rates on the bonds and receiving lower interest income on the money market securities cannot be circumvented and is directly incorporated in the futures prices. In addition to this cost-of-carry component, there are also very modest commissions (which add less than two basis points to the final yield), a security deposit (which is returned when the protection is no longer needed), and a marked-to-market requirement which is nothing more than a cash realization of the changes in the future level of interest rates.

In utilizing options on futures contracts to cap today's rate for the upcoming bond issue, the major cost component is the premium paid to own the option. The size of this premium reflects:

1. how far above current rates the ceiling is established.

2. the maturity of the protection.

3. the volatility of interest rates.

Obviously, the lower the cap level is set, the higher the cost of the option; the longer the period of protection the higher the cost; and the greater the volatility the greater the cost. In addition to the premium, the only other cost incurred when using options is the commission expense, which, like futures, is quite modest, normally adding less than 2 basis points to the final yield.

In utilizing options on futures to collar today's rate for the upcoming bond issue, the largest cost component is based on the midpoint of the collar. This midpoint is the current futures rate (upon which the options are based) and not the current level of the coupon. Normally, the ceiling is the same distance away from the futures rate as the floor level. However, since the futures rate is higher than the current coupon in a positively-sloped yield curve environment, the ceiling will be further above the coupon rate than the floor is below it. As for any fee, the

---

1. The yield curve expresses the relationship between interest rates and maturity for bonds; a positively sloped yield curve means that as the maturity of bonds increase (say, from two years to ten years) the interest rates also increase (say, from 8.25% to 8.95%). A positively sloped yield curve is the normal expectation.

cost of the put option and the income received from the call option should combine to be equal or close to zero, assuming that the floor and ceiling are symmetrical. The only other costs are the commission expense, the security deposit, and the marked-to- market requirements for the call options sold.

Risks

Once the decision is made to protect the current interest rate level using either financial futures or options contracts, two major risks still exist.

Credit Risk

The first is credit risk which is caused by a weakening of the issuer's credit standing or a weakening of the issuer's overall industry. The spread over Treasury rates for a future issue cannot be hedged; only the Treasury component can be hedged. While credit risk is a major risk, it is one which the corporate officer realizes exists whether or not protection is established.

Yield Curve Risk

A second and smaller risk is a result of shifts in the slope of the yield curve. The Treasury note contract is based on a 10-year maturity Treasury rate and the Treasury bond contract is based on a 20–30 year maturity Treasury bond. The greater the maturity of the anticipated issue differs from that of the chosen futures or options contract, the greater the potential risk resulting from a change in the slope and not the level of the yield curve. As an example, a 3-year maturity issue may behave differently than a 10-year maturity. Should the yield curve flatten, then the final yield will be less effective. Should the yield curve steepen, then the final yield will be better than expected.

Of course, it should be noted that the risks due to credit and yield curve fluctuations could be dwarfed by the magnitude of the change in the Treasury yield component itself.

Flexibility

Financial futures and options contracts provide the corporate financial manager with flexibility for developing strategies other conventional markets cannot offer. For those corporations with high coupon debt, expenses need not be paid for a tender offer, assuming the first call date is within the time frame of the futures and options markets. In addition, the treasurer can wait until the first call date before selecting the maturity of the new issue. Should interest rates decline precipitously, a longer-term issue than originally contemplated may be offered; should rates rise significantly, a shorter-term issue than originally planned may be offered with excess gains arising from the futures or options markets. (Since the actual maturity of the bond issue is less than the originally anticipated maturity, only a partial amount of the gains from the futures or options contracts are utilized to offset the higher interest expense; the remaining gains are income for the corporation.) Of course, the options contracts provide additional flexibility not available in any other market—the ability to benefit from declines in the level of interest rates prior to the bond issue.

While these features are equally attractive to a corporate officer planning on issuing bonds to finance a proposed acquisition, the ability to lengthen, shorten, or even cancel the protection and alter the proposed bond issue (if one is still contemplated), are equally attractive. Financial managers are quick to realize that by employing futures or options contracts the protection can always be modified or cancelled altogether.

All of these features help to delay the necessary funding decisions until the final offering date is closer and the actual parameters are known with greater certainty. Why should a corporate financial officer who can protect against adverse changes in the future course of interest rates be forced to predict future funding needs with certainty? In today's financial world, such a prediction is no longer needed.

How Investment Banks Use Risk Management

The capital markets in the United States offer a means for lenders of capital to provide funds to corporations in exchange for financial assets offered by borrowers. In addition, investors can exchange financial assets as well as sell financial claims in order to meet current consumption needs. Investment bankers, security dealers, and security traders (e.g., market makers and block traders) are among the principal nonbank financial intermediaries in the capital markets—and they manage their financial risk with futures and options. In fact, investment bankers use risk management techniques for two purposes: to help their clients and to help themselves.

Investment banks help to provide financial capital to both private industry and federal, state, and local governments. In the primary market for new corporate and state and local issues, investment bankers often purchase (underwrite) the securities from a corporation or governmental unit and assume the risk of security placement.

Underwriting

As underwriters, investment bankers can use financial futures to hedge the risk of price changes on the value of these newly purchased issues. A classic demonstration of financial futures in hedging the risk of underwriting new security issues is Salomon Brothers' hedge of an IBM debt issue in 1979. After the Federal Reserve Board announced in October of 1979 that it was going to allow more freedom for the marketplace to establish interest rates, bond prices plunged. At the time, Salomon Brothers was acting as lead underwriter of a $1 billion IBM debt issue. They had sold interest rate futures short as a hedge against pure declines in fixed-income securities (which they had in inventory) and thus recovered in the futures markets a large part of the losses they realized in their temporary position in the IBM bond issue market.

Dealing and Trading

Most investment bankers also act as dealers in corporate, government, and municipal bonds and in equity issues. They offer and manage money market funds, mutual funds, and pension plans and also provide personal loans, insurance, and brokerage services. As such they maintain large inventories of financial products. The financial futures and options markets permit investment bankers to hedge the price risk of securities they wish to hold and to reduce the uncertainty associated with the cost of future securities they wish to purchase.

In their trading function, security dealers are also active in trading in futures and options for their own accounts, often in transactions aimed at capitalizing on price discrepancies across futures, options, and cash markets. Traders at investment banking firms become familiar with the intricacies of price interrelationships between futures, options, and cash instruments as they use these tools for inventory risk management. They are therefore well positioned to perceive and act on profitable trading opportunities across markets. These opportunities often occur when the release of some new information is reflected at different speeds in the various markets in which securities or derivative securities[2] with interest rate sensitivity are traded. By participating in arbitrage and other trading strategies that involve both derivative and cash markets, dealers and traders assist in keeping markets linked, reflecting relative values, and available for use by others for risk management activities.

As security dealers and security traders, investment bankers are highly exposed to unexpected changes in security prices. Financial futures not only help security dealers and traders to manage a security's price risk, but also provide a means to hedge quantity risk. Quantity risk refers to the risk that even very small changes in price may affect the aggregate value of an inventory position by a large dollar amount. This quantity risk may prevent security dealers and traders from taking large asset positions even in stable price environments. Financial futures enable security dealers and traders to hold large asset positions while greatly reducing the risk of losses in total inventory value from even small, unexpected price movements.

Costs and Risks

Given the degree of price and quantity risk in the capital market, it is not surprising that investment bankers, security traders, and security dealers are currently the largest users of financial futures. However, they do face potential costs in their use of financial futures and options as risk management tools.

First of all, a futures position designed to protect against unexpected and unfavorable interest rates or stock market moves also prevents gains on the cash position from unexpected yet favorable price changes. Hedging with options does allow for retention of a portion of the gains on the position being hedged, but it comes at a cost that is directly related to the price risk of the security position being hedged.

Second, due to basis risk, changes in futures or option prices may not correspond exactly with changes in the price of the security to be held or purchased.

Third, security dealers, security traders, and investment bankers provide a number of auxiliary services. They face the problem of deciding between the hedging of a net position across all their financial service

---

2. *Derivative securities* relate to other (primary) securities. For example, options are derivative securities to buy or sell common stock, which are primary securities. Derivative securities have no independent life of their own.

areas versus the hedging of individual asset positions. If the net exposure of the firm is not considered, a hedge may reduce the risk on an individual security position while increasing the total risk exposure of the investment banking firm.

In subsequent sections, we discuss the use of futures and options markets for security dealers and security traders as well as for investment bankers' underwriting activities.

How Corporations Use Risk Management

In contrast to financial institutions such as banks, brokerage firms, and investment management firms, most corporations are not primarily engaged in the business of managing or trading financial assets. Corporations are both suppliers and borrowers of financial capital. As borrowers they issue securities to obtain funds for investments in real assets. As suppliers of financial capital they lend acquired cash balances and in return obtain financial assets. These financial assets are held until they are used for inventory accumulation or capital projects.

Liability Management

The risk of financial liabilities such as short-term borrowings or debt is offset to some extent by financial assets held in the corporation. For example, long-term bonds held as pension assets can be considered to be a partial hedge against increases in pension liabilities associated with declines in interest rates. Therefore, the net interest rate or equity risk exposure of the balance sheet is the appropriate focus for risk assessment and management, and futures and options are one of many available tools to affect this exposure.

Hedging Purchases or Sales of Debt or Equity

The price uncertainty associated with anticipated purchases or sales of debt or equity assets can be partially eliminated by purchases and sales of financial futures contracts in related securities. A financial position that leaves a firm exposed to unexpected price declines in financial assets can be hedged with the sale of financial futures. The risk of unexpected increases in the value of financial liabilities can be hedged with the purchase of financial futures. Corporations involved in international business operations may also choose to use currency futures markets as an alternative to the forward market to hedge their currency exposure.

Financial Management

Financial management has generally separated capital decisions into two areas: (1) long-term financing and (2) working capital management. Long-term financing is principally concerned with obtaining funds to purchase long-term fixed assets. Working capital management deals primarily with cash, marketable securities, receivables, and inventories. Within these two areas of capital management, financial futures provide alternatives to other available methods of risk management.

Long-Term Financing   Most long-term debt is issued in large amounts with a fixed interest rate. Futures on intermediate and long-term Treasury securities can be sold to fix current yields up to two years forward. In addition, bond and note options can cap or collar current yields on securities. These anticipatory hedging techniques give corporate treasurers the flexibility to time the raising of capital independently from the application of that capital. For example, assume funds are needed for expansion one year from now but yields are currently at their cyclical lows. A corporate treasurer can either buy puts or sell futures on Treasury bonds in an amount based on the par value of the anticipated debt issue and the relative durations of the anticipated issue versus the future. This anticipatory strategy effectively locks in the portion of the cost of issuance that is related to Treasury yields. (No hedge is in place for the spread between the corporate yield and Treasury yield.)

Working Capital Management.   In working capital management, the gap between current assets and liabilities can be managed with the use of derivative securities. Eurodollar options can be employed to create a floor or collar around investment returns on net short-term asset positions. Eurodollar futures are useful in achieving a closer match between maturities or the timing of short-term outflows and inflows.

Foreign Exchange Exposure Management.

Foreign exchange exposure management is another area in which corporations have been active users of futures and options, as well as other over-the-counter risk management products such as forwards, swaps, cross rate options, collars, and the like. With the growth of foreign markets and production facilities and with the continued volatility of exchange rates, risk management in the currency area has become an essential component of the corporate treasurer's function. One of the great difficulties here is the measurement of the foreign exchange exposures a year of more in advance which must precede any carefully constructed hedging plan.

Pension Fund Management

In the area of pension fund management, futures and options have been used primarily for return enhancement in managing the risk of pension assets, in managing cash flow, and more recently in controlling the interest rate exposure of pension surplus. As investment managers, many pension funds have found stock index and Treasury bond futures valuable in cash management for the pension fund, getting inflows quickly invested in stocks and bond vehicles and protecting the value of anticipated withdrawals.

Short-Term Focus

The overriding feature of the use of financial futures in risk management is that these instruments tend to be most valuable when the risk control is needed for the short term (e.g., a year or less). Liquid futures and options contacts are typically limited to this time frame. Therefore, these vehicles tend to be the cheapest and most available for protecting against or benefiting from short-term changes in price or interest rate. Their low execution costs also make them suitable for frequent and short-term trading to more effectively and cheaply manage risk. Longer-term risk management problems, such as hedging a 5-year floating-rate debt commitment, are usually more easily hedged with an interest rate swap or collar agreement, which has the further advantage of off-balance-sheet treatment.

Dealing in Financial Futures and Options Markets

Futures and options on financial assets such as stocks, bonds, and currencies were introduced in the 1970s and 1980s and saw their most rapid growth in the last six years. Between 1983 and 1988, financial centers around the world such as Tokyo, London, Paris, Sydney, Hong Kong, Toronto, Stockholm, and Singapore have also opened futures and options exchanges. The most active financial futures are Treasury bond futures, Japanese Yen bond futures, Eurodollar futures, and futures on the Standard & Poor's 500 stock index. Options on the S&P 100 stock index, on Treasury bond and note futures, on currencies, and on individual stocks are also traded actively.

Initial Margin Deposits and Daily Coverage

Futures trading differs from trading in cash markets (stocks and bonds) because only a small deposit (called the *initial margin*) often representing under 10 percent of the value of a contract is required for opening a position. However, gains and losses in the value of the contract must be recognized and covered daily through a clearinghouse in which futures brokers participate. Through this arrangement of passing funds among position holders on a daily basis, the financial viability of the system is always intact and the credit exposure of a brokerage firm to a client or of a clearinghouse to a brokerage firm is limited to one day's potential price movement.

Trading Arena

The trading arena for futures and futures options is also different than that for stocks and bonds in U.S. markets. The open outcry system is used in which exchange members congregate in pits to compete for the right to participate in the order flow. In contrast to stock specialists, no one trader has a monopoly on trading activity; however, futures traders are also under no obligation to make orderly markets and can withdraw at any time.

Trading System and Regulation

To buy or to sell futures or options, a customer opens an account by a process similar to that involved in opening a stock or bond account. Brokerage firms are required to separate the funds associated with futures margins from those of the same or other customers in other trading activities. Also, the customers must acknowledge that the risk disclosure is understood, must make arrangements for handling cash flows in variation margin, and must identify themselves as hedgers or speculators. (Speculators face tighter position limits, more vigorous reporting requirements, and higher initial margins.) All futures trading and exchanges are regulated by the Commodity Futures Trading Commission which acts in a similar capacity as does the Securities and Exchange Commission for security transactions.

CHAPTER 19
Swaps*

At first blush swaps sound impossible. They seem to defy the laws of finance (if not nature) and just should not work. How can a financial transaction decrease risk and increase return at the same time to *all* parties? That's exactly what swaps do—with enough left over for an always-healthy investment banking fee.

Swap Definition

What are swaps? The general meaning of the word applies to the specific financial sense: Swaps are exchanges—exchanges of cash flow obligations among two or more parties. And due to inefficiencies in how financial markets evaluate different credits, there is opportunity to create what amounts to a virtual perpetual motion machine.

An interest rate swap is a contractual agreement between two (or more) parties to exchange differently structured interest rate obligations based on a notional principal amount. It is normally executed through a market-maker or broker—a large commercial or investment bank. The parties sign a legal contract which dictates the exchange of cash flows at a future date. Simply put, two parties exchange payment schedules in order to obtain one which better fits their particular cash flow requirements.

Originally developed to exploit the credit-spread differential that existed between fixed-rate and floating-rate funds, interest rate swaps

---

*This chapter has been derived from "Swaps I: Structures and Strategies" by Robert Lawrence Kuhn and Frank X. Stankard, Volume I (Investing and Risk Management), Dow Jones-Irwin's *The Library of Investment Banking* (1990), Robert Lawrence Kuhn, editor-in-chief.

have become indispensable tools for managing interest rate risk and asset/liability matching programs. Negotiated around the world and around the clock, these interest exchange agreements solve what had been a major problem—namely, staying locked into an interest rate that made sense last week, but not next month.

The Need and the Innovation

As financial markets became more volatile with respect to interest rates and currency exchange rates over the past two decades, investment bankers devised innovative financial instruments to reduce risk and enhance return. Swaps are one of the most powerful hedging methods. Their introduction has changed substantially and permanently the world of corporate and institutional finance.

Swaps are a truly remarkable innovation: the technology enables company chief executive officers, chief financial officers, and treasurers both to determine the level and character of assumed risk, and to establish new, more efficient frontiers of risk/return profile (i.e., reducing risk and enhancing return at the same time—that seemingly magical achievement). Swaps dramatically enhance the flexibility of choosing the most desirable financing environments and matching assets and liabilities with extreme precision.

The advance has not been made without a radical jump in financial complexity, both with respect to financial structure (i.e., the new instruments) and financial markets (i.e., globalization). Corporate financing decisions about how funds should be raised, matched, shifted, serviced, and paid back are now tied inextricably to these most sophisticated products. Although their continuing evolution and current implementation is not simple, the fundamental concept of swaps is not complicated.

How Swaps Work

The interest-rate swap works as follows: The party with access to, but with no demand for fixed-rate funds, raises them through a bond issuance; the party with demand for fixed-rate funds but access to only variable-rate funds, raises the variable-rate funds. Then, an interest rate contract is arranged between the two, whereby one party (the party wishing to borrow at a fixed rate) pays a fixed annuity in exchange for a variable-rate cash flow stream from the other party. The contract runs continuous with the underlying bond issue. The transaction is not a loan, but rather a mutual exchange of interest payments, one in which no principal is exchanged. The end result is floating-rate funding for the bond issuer on terms more attractive than otherwise available, and fixed-rate funding for the other party, again on better terms than the alternative, if indeed an alternative existed.

As stated by definition, an interest rate swap is an agreement to exchange on a periodic basis the differential between two interest rates; one of them fixed (the fixed rate) and one of them variable (the floating rate). The fixed rate is set on the commencement date and remains fixed for the entire term of the swap. The floating rate is attached to some floating index and it changes as other market interest rates change. A simplified schematic diagram of the most basic swap would appear as in Figure 19-1.

In this generic example, Company A has agreed to enter into an interest rate swap with Company B. A typical transaction of this sort would have Company A, the fixed rate payer, pay or receive the difference between some fixed interest rate (established at the time of the transaction) and a floating rate. In other words, if the fixed rate is below the floating rate, the fixed payer will receive the difference between these two rates; if the fixed rate should be above the floating rate, the fixed payer will pay the difference between these two rates.

To illustrate this classic interest-rate swap executed in the early years of the market assume the following: Company A, an AAA-rated U.S.

Figure 19–1. How Swaps Work (simplified).

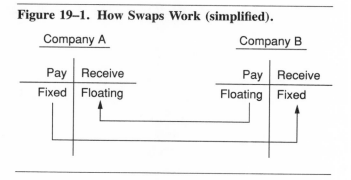

corporation, has access to seven-year, fixed-rate funds via the Eurobond market at a fixed rate of 14.6 percent, 0.1 percent above the U.S. Treasury yield. Company A has no appetite for funds at this rate, however. On the other hand, company A is currently funding in the commercial paper market at a cost equal to the 30-day commercial paper rate. Company B is an A-rated U.S. corporation desiring to raise fixed-rate funds. Company B does not have the credit strength demanded by Eurobond investors; hence a Eurobond issue is not an alternative. And a private placement or public note issue in the U.S. would provide funds at 15.75 percent, 1.25 percent above the seven-year Treasury yield. Alternatively, company B could raise funds in the commercial paper market at the benchmark, 30-day commercial paper rate (Federal Reserve Board composite rate for AA industrial issues) plus 0.25 percent.

Company A's comparative funding advantage is in the Eurobond market where its cost of funds is 1.15 percent lower than company B's. Company B's comparative advantage is in the commercial paper market where its cost is only 0.25 percent higher than company A's. The swap transaction permits each borrower to raise funds in the market where it enjoys the comparative advantage and use the swap agreement to transform the liability to the desired interest rate structure. The result is that each party saves .45 percent versus alternative funding costs. The case described is outlined in Figure 19-2.

ADVANTAGES OF SWAPS

Most interest rate and currency swaps are motivated by inefficiencies between markets. In the first case above, the differential on credit risk premiums charged to company B relative to those charged company A in the U.S. commercial paper market and the Eurobond market produced the arbitrage opportunity.

Another prominent advantage is the role swaps play in restructuring debt financing. A company that wishes to change its mixture of fixed- and floating-rate debt without refinancing its borrowings (e.g., through a noncallable fixed-rate note issue) can use an interest rate swap to convert the existing obligation from fixed to floating, or vice versa. A company may want to follow this type of interest exchange so as to reduce its interest rate sensitivity. Such reductions in sensitivity are especially important for leveraged buyouts where interest rate fluctuations could prove disastrous (see Chapter 16).

Figure 19–2. Mutual Benefits for Companies.

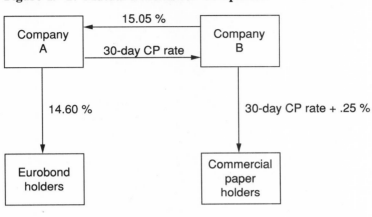

	Mutual Benefits for Companies	
	Company A	**Company B**
Inflow from swap:	15.05%	30-day Commercial Paper (CP) rate
Outflow under bond issue:	14.60%	—
Outflow to CP holders:	—	CP + .25%
Margin:	0.45%	−0.25%
Outflow under swap:	30-day CP rate	15.05%
Total cost:	CP rate − .45%	15.30%
Alternative Cost (without swap)	CP rate	15.75
Total Savings	.45%	45%

Results: Each party saves 0.45 percent versus alternative funding costs.

Limiting the impact of uncontrolled swings in interest rates is a major advantage. Corporations often arrange interest rate swaps to match debt costs against projected revenues. If a company has a fixed or predictable income stream but its costs of funds is based on a floating rate (such as commercial paper), the company may want to swap into a fixed-interest cost. Thus an interest rate swap permits a company to match interest costs with expected revenues.

The swap is not tied legally to the assets or liabilities of either firm, and normally no principal is exchanged. If one side defaults the other simply stops its own payment schedule. Unlike financial futures, little management is required for interest rate swaps. There are no worries over marking-to-market. In addition, swaps can often be conducted for longer periods than those available in the futures markets. Swaps and similar diversification strategies have the additional benefit of structurally changing the asset/liability structure of the firm.

Swaps, however, are not without their problems. No central marketplace exists for the trading of swap commitments. Equally as important is that no central clearinghouse exists to guarantee the payment of contracted debt.

CHAPTER 20

Asset Securitization*

Medieval alchemists sought to turn base metals into glistening gold. Modern alchemists—investment bankers—seek to turn illiquid assets that lie inertly on the balance sheet into liquid instruments that can be traded freely on the market. They began with the largest source of supply, the residential home mortgage debt, *rolling up* these small, consumer obligations into large, institutional securities. The story is a fascinating one. Color it gold.

Residential Mortgage Debt

The residential, mortgage-backed securities market has expanded many-fold over the past three decades. At $2.7 trillion in 1988, the amount of mortgage debt outstanding made it the largest domestic debt market as compared to Treasury debt at about $2.3 trillion and corporate debt at less than $1.5 trillion. Some $822 billion of the $2.7 trillion in mortgage debt has been securitized by the government or its agencies and instrumentalities (and that number increases if you add the various structured mortgage loans deals). The size of the mortgage market is a by-product of the creation of many innovative mortgage-related securities and the further proliferation of these and traditional mortgage securities in the

*This chapter has been derived from "Securitization Principles for Residential Real Estate" by Keith Maillard and Robert Lawrence Kuhn, Volume V (Mortgage and Asset Securitization), Dow Jones-Irwin's *The Library of Investment Banking* (1990), Robert Lawrence Kuhn, editor-in-chief.

marketplace. This growth was a direct result of several factors emerging in the primary mortgage (i.e., thrift and mortgage banking) industry.

The Thrift Industry

Initially, the mortgage business, as defined by the origination, purchase and sale of mortgage loans, was primarily the thrift industry.

Chartered Functions

Thrift institutions—the nation's savings and loan associations and savings banks—were chartered to provide two major functions: first of all, to accept and hold savings monies subject to federal government insurance; and secondly, to provide mortgage money for the purchasers of homes. The thrift industry was an integral part of the American dream, where owning a home was a principal axiom.

Initial Spread: Three Percent

When originally chartered, the thrift industry was mandated by law to maintain a spread of three percent (3%) between their cost of funds (primarily the amounts paid out on deposits) and the interest rates at which they lent mortgage money. In a relatively stable environment such as existed back then, where deposits and home ownership were not subject to constant turnover, the three hundred basis points was a comfortable margin within which the majority of the thrifts operated.

High Rates and Disintermediation

However, in the period commencing in the early 1960s, the world changed, and for the thrift industry, the change was dramatic. New regulations were promulgated for the commercial banks and for newly-created mutual funds that would signal the end to the thrift industry as it had been known. The most critical change was the enabling of commercial banks to offer the *money market accounts* and the establishment of mutual funds. This account, as well as the purchase of mutual fund shares, was the first to be introduced whereby an individual could participate in the changes in the overall interest rate changes in the capital markets. The longer-term savers who had traditionally maintained thrift accounts now saw the opportunity to improve the returns on their savings accounts. They began to remove their funds from the thrifts and place them with the higher-yielding accounts in the commercial banks and mutual funds. It was the time of double-digit inflation and very high interest rates—and everyone with money wanted to participate in the rise in rates.

The process was called *disintermediation* and it caused the 3 percent spread formerly earned by the thrifts to erode quickly. Bad then turned to worse: Thrift spreads became negative since they had to pay current high rates to attract short-term deposits and these rates (their costs) were *higher* than the rates they were earning on their previously made long-term loans (their revenues). (*Mismatched* assets and liabilities became a primary thrift problem, and matching them became a major investment banking opportunity.) Thrift capital stopped growing and in many cases started shrinking dramatically.

Reviving The Moribund Thrifts

It did not take long for the entire industry to become a severely weak-ened credit, especially as compared with the industrial and commercial banking sectors of the capital markets.

What was there to do? Over the past 20 years several new techniques have been introduced to help the thrift industry cope with the new finan-cial realities. Financial concepts such as conversions, subordinated debt, preferred stock, and the like were effective—but the largest impact came from mortgage-backed securities. In order to compete and remain viable, thrifts could only look to their *golden* assets—residential mortgages—to bolster their capital.

Homebuilding and Mortgage Banking
Look To Securitization

The changes in the regulatory environment to which the thrifts were subject were paralleled by changes in the general housing and capital markets. As the cycles of inflation waxed and waned, these two allied industries looked to securitization as a mechanism for bolstering their businesses. In order to combat the escalating interest rates and declining home prices, homebuilders began to provide their own mortgage monies. Because of the associated tax benefits for the homebuilders, the volume of securitized products rose. In addition, in order to offset the now higher funding costs that were ruining spreads (margins), the mortgage banking side of the business began using the pass-through market to provide liquidity.

Securitization

One of the underlying themes of the thrift industry is that the American family needs a home and will maintain that home over most any other possession. This deeply ingrained principle is one of the foundations that underlies the usability of mortgage loans to support investment-grade securities.

Aided by statistical research showing the predictable (and minimal) default rates on residential real estate, investment bankers saw a dramatic new way to generate liquidity. By *rolling up* hundreds of individual real estate mortgages into one large security, great confidence could be achieved in terms of the financial characteristics of the group. Whereas it would be virtually impossible (and certainly impractical) to guess the likely results for any individual mortgage (e.g., if and when it might default), one could quite reliably predict the average for the group based on historical studies of other similarly large pools of mortgage loans. This was the theory and practice engendering securitization.

Among other things, this chapter discusses the different paths the thrift industry (and later the mortgage industry) took to accomplish its capital and earnings improvement goals. We also discuss some of the nuances behind the structures of residential, mortgage-related products.

Mortgage Pass-Through Securities

Early efforts to utilize mortgage loans as a source of cash resulted in the purchase and sale of whole loan packages either with or without recourse for losses to the loan seller. The transaction is generally regarded as a sale for the seller unless the amount of recourse is material.

Whole Loans

The term *whole loan* describes a mortgage loan and all of the cash receipts associated with it (i.e., scheduled principal and interest payments, prepaid principal, insurance proceeds, and any proceeds received in a foreclosure and subsequent liquidation of the underlying property). The whole loan can represent an interest in several different classifications of residential real estate (i.e., owner occupied, nonowner occupied, multifamily, etc.).

In a whole loan sale, all rights and responsibilities connected with a mortgage loan are transferred to the purchaser. These rights include the collection of monthly principal and interest payments, the right to foreclose on the property if payments are not made on a timely basis on the underlying loan, and the capacity to amend the terms of the loan to correct a delinquent status.

Whole Loan Sales.   Whole loans can be sold whereby the seller retains the right to service the loans (collect the monthly principal and interest payments, garner a fee, and remit the remainder to the owner of the loans, as well as correct delinquent loan payment situations and administer foreclosure proceedings). Conversely, whole loans can be sold whereby the purchaser assumes the duties of servicing the loan.

Whole Loan Sales Structure.   The structure behind a whole loan sale is straightforward. The loan files are gathered for inspection by the purchaser, and the seller may make specific representations and warranties with respect to the loan such as the dollar size, coupon and maturity of each loan, the loan to value ratio, the breakdown of property types of each loan, the payment characteristics of each loan, and the status of ownership. Information regarding mortgage insurance (if any) and geographic location may be asked for as well. The notes and mortgage (or deeds of trust) are recorded in the name of the purchaser and legally assigned over to him. Subject to legal inspection and agreement on price, the loan files are then physically transferred to a location specified by the purchaser, and the sale is consummated.

Whole Loan Sales Participants.   The primary participants in whole loan sales were thrift institutions and mortgage bankers. These institutions were the most familiar with the underwriting and origination of a mortgage loan and therefore could best evaluate the quality of those functions as performed by others. Monies raised from these loan sales were used to fund further loan production and to prompt further sales.

Unfortunately, the initial buyers and sellers of the whole mortgage loans were members of the same community. As a result capital was shifted throughout the industry but new capital, the kind that would allow thrifts to really offset their problems, was not being introduced. The reason for this lack of more diversified investor interest was primarily a lack of understanding on the part of non–mortgage-related institutions regarding the mortgage market and the underlying mortgages themselves.

Mortgage Participation Certificate

The start of what was to become the securitized mortgage market was triggered by the introduction of the mortgage participation certificate.

Pools of Assets.   Mortgage participation certificates, the precursors to the pass-through certificates, were designed to reduce the amount of loan-by-loan review that needed to be performed by the purchaser of a *pool* of whole loans. Representations and warranties on a particular pool were made by the seller, who assumed the obligation to repurchase any loan that wound up in the pool that did not conform to these representatives and warranties.

Third-Party Involvement.   The loans were generally placed with custodians different from the seller and the loans were reviewed by that custodian as part of the transaction. The introduction of the third party review was one step in easing the entry of the mortgage security into the capital markets. Although the mortgage participation certificate addressed some of the concerns, the purchaser was still the full owner and therefore liable for all of the losses associated with the pool of loans.

Two Major Problems: Credit and Homogeneity.   Two major areas still presented themselves as resistance points for the capital market participant: the first was the question of the credit quality of the pool of individual loans and the second was the homogeneity (or consistency) of the product. Traditional, corporate, capital market purchasers were uncomfortable with the potential risks associated with ownership of mortgage loans as well as with the various and sundry quirks associated with mortgage loans—such as prepayment options, the monthly pay nature of the loans, and the poor level of financial strength in the thrift industry (especially in the cases of transactions with recourse).

Pass-Through Security Concept

To begin to assuage these concerns and encourage broad investor interest, the notion of the pass-through security was developed.

Initial Purposes.   The initial purposes behind the pass-through certificate were threefold: (1) to enhance the credit of the now somewhat familiar whole loan sale so as to better insulate the nontraditional mortgage purchaser from the possibility of loss, (2) to create a security that would be more freely tradeable and transferable, (3) to create a security that would not necessarily involve the labor-intensive process of loan file review associated with whole loan sales.

Trust Structure and Trustee Payments.   The pass-through certificates incorporated many of the concepts of the old equipment trust certificates. To create a pass-through, the loans, or pieces of *collateral*, are placed into a trust estate created and held by an independent trustee. The rights to any cash flows associated with the loans—principal and interest payments, insurance payments, insurance proceeds, prepaid principal— are assigned to the trustee for the benefit of the pass-through certificate holders.

Credit Ratings on the Securities

The other aspect that allowed for the introduction of the pass-through certificates into the corporate capital markets was the placement of a rating on these securities.

Criteria.   Each rating agency had constructed a series of criteria that must be adhered to in order to obtain its designated ratings. The nature of a rating in the secured transaction world is slightly different than that in the unsecured transactions world. With regard to secured financing, the tightness and security of cash flow from the mortgagors' hands to the hands of the ultimate pass-through certificate holder is of paramount importance as opposed to a judgment of expected earnings.

Reduced Exposure.   The credit rating given to a particular pass-through security is a reflection of the reduced credit exposure (loss of both principal and interest) to the pass-through certificate holder. Among other things, the rating agency will review the flow of payments as outlined in the pooling and servicing agreement, which is the operative document for a pass-through security. The agency's focus will be on the timely payment of principal and interest to the certificate holders and on the method established to cover any shortfalls that may arise due to deficiencies in the collateral. This coverage takes on two forms: (1) pool insurance and (2) a senior/subordinated structure.

Pool Insurance.   A pool insurance policy is an insurance policy that covers losses equal to a defined percentage of the pool.

Senior/Subordinated Structure.   The senior/subordinated structure (sometimes referred to as senior/junior) became the newest method of credit enhancement after the failure of several pass-through programs and mortgage issuers and the difficulty to obtain mortgage insurance after those lapses. The senior/junior structure, although a newly employed concept, is simply the use of overcollateralization to cover credit losses. The cash flows of a given class (the junior) are subordinated to those of another class (the senior) in order to provide the senior class with comparable protection as if there were a pool insurance policy.

Standardization

Although the private pass-through market has since flourished—as demonstrated by the $20 billion of securities outstanding in 1988—the private sector did not originally establish any standardization procedure nor did it create a large market-making entity.

Even into the 1970s, the private pass-through market was far from where it should have been. There needed to be some form of standardization in the mortgage market as well as a major clearinghouse for the purchase and sale of mortgage securities. In the late 1970s and early 1980s, three institutions were created to address this concern. Through the facilities of The Government National Mortgage Association (GNMA), Federal National Mortgage Association (FNMA), and Federal Home Loan Mortgage Corporation (FHLMC), the different characteristics of the loan that could be securitized were announced. Because of the large purchasing effort on the part of the agencies, these characteristics would become the standards of loan packages in the secondary market. GNMA, FHLMC, and FNMA would take mortgage loans and in turn create pass-through securities that could be sold in the secondary market. The influence of the rating agencies was helpful as well to extend these standards further in the marketplace.

Securitization Instruments

Although several steps beyond the pure whole loan security in terms of credit coverage, the mortgage pass-through securities had a structural weakness which was the same as that which existed in the underlying mortgage loan—their lack of call protection or poor predictability of cash flow—and that prevented acceptance by some capital market purchasers. Due to the ability of a home buyer to prepay his mortgage loan as a result of a change of job, refinancing, death, or purchase of a new home, the purchaser of a mortgage loan or pass-through security held an instrument that could have a maturity of 30 days instead of the expected 30 years.

Mortgage-Backed Bond

The mortgage-backed bond was one of the instruments created specifically to correct such cash flow unpredictability. A mortgage-backed bond is a collateralized term-debt offering. It is secured by collateral (usually mortgage related) that has a market value equal to 110–200 percent of the principal amount of the bond. Unlike the pass-through certificates, it is a financing (not a sale) of the collateral behind the bond (the issuer still owns the collateral). The terms of the debt are very much like other capital market debt securities—semiannual or quarterly payments of interest at floating or fixed rates and a final bullet payment of principal.

Thrift Issuers. Thrift institutions—or special-purpose, bankruptcy-proof subsidiaries established by them—have been the predominant issuers of mortgage-backed bonds. Although secured by collateral, the bonds are obligations of the issuer. As a result of this structure, the financial strength of the issuer or the parent of the issuer must be considered in determining the likelihood of an early termination of the bonds. The overcollateralization mechanism, however, will ensure that if such an early termination were to occur, then the full principal amount of the bonds and accrued interest would be payable.

Overcollateralization Initial Form.   Currently, two basic forms of mortgage-backed bonds exist in the marketplace. The older structure requires that the principal amount of the bonds plus accrued interest be overcollateralized on a market value basis. The amount of overcollateralization will vary as a result of the type of collateral chosen.

Overcollateralization Defeasance Form.   A new structure, which was first issued in 1987, is the defeasance mortgage-backed bonds. Here, instead of overcollateralizing the principal amount of the bonds, a pool of collateral is used that will, on a market value basis, pay for the purchase of a portfolio of Treasury securities that will, based upon their expected cash flow, pay the principal and interest on the mortgage-backed bonds.

Collateral Pledged.   Like other mortgage-backed financings, the collateral is pledged to an independent trustee. In most cases this ensures a relatively smooth liquidation of the collateral in the event of a default on the part of the issuer. This structure is utilized in the issuance of collateralized medium-term notes as well, which from a structural context resembles mortgage-backed bonds.

Inefficient Use of Collateral.   Although the mortgage-backed bond was a fine response to the capital market outcry, it was an extremely inefficient use of the collateral. The mortgage pass-through certificate had little if any overcollateralization as compared to the 110–200 percent for the mortgage-backed bond. The task then was clear: to design appealing instruments for the capital markets purchaser and to improve collateral efficiency for the issuer. The innovative solutions were the cash flow bonds and the collateralized mortgage obligation.

Cash Flow Bond

The first version of the cash flow bond looked very much like the conventional pass-through certificate. With the ability of some builders to recognize installment sales treatment of the loans that were financed through such a security and the ease of the pass-through mechanics, the cash flow bond was created. The installment sales treatment allowed the builders to recognize profits on the sale of homes as principal was paid on the homeowners' mortgage and not up front in the year of home sale, thus postponing the payment of taxes.

Collateral and Valuation.   The structure of the security was very similar to the mortgage-backed bond. The collateral was placed into the hands of a trustee, once again registered in the name of the trustee for the bondholders. The valuation methods for determining the amount of bonds issuable were referenced as coupon-to-coupon and the current method of bond value.[1]

Collateralized Mortgage Obligation (CMO)

The collateralized mortgage obligation (CMO) was created to address the call option of the mortgage loans. The CMO takes the same cash flows that the cash flow bond or conventional pass-through would generate and then carves them up into discrete maturities. The method of collateral valuation for the CMOs is similar to that of the cash flow bonds. The CMO, like the cash flow bond, allows for monthly, quarterly, and semiannual payments, making it look more like a corporate bond. However, while the CMO does not remove all of the uncertainty of the prepayment option, it does limit the amount of whipsawing a particular investor may get from that same group of collateral.

In general the CMO is structured with four classes, each of them appealing to a different buying public. The difference classes of the CMO have differing maturities and payment schedules. These differences are a result of the CMO structuring which is geared toward the average life and duration desires of the purchasers of the different classes.

One of the by-products of the CMO is the residual cash flow. These residual cash flows are a result of the disparity between the economic considerations received and the assumption used in structuring the CMO. The CMO, like other mortgage-backed securities, has gone through a considerable amount of change in response to market shifts. During the volatile periods in early 1986, floating-rate tranches along with tranches that had fairly determinable sinking fund schedules, were created.

---

1. The *coupon-to-coupon method* took the coupon on the collateral, divided it by the coupon on the bonds, and then used the number obtained and multiplied it by the principal balance to determine the number of bonds that could be issued. The *bond value method* provided additional bonds to be raised from a given group of collateral. The amount of the additional bonds was simply the present value (using the bond rate as a discount rate) of the expected receipts on the mortgage collateral. At the onset of the bonds issuance one could calculate a table to instruct the trustee how to pay the bondholders. This table was necessary since it was not a straight pass-through of the cash flow. Although this security was used primarily by the builder constituency, its initial appeal in the market place waned because it still reflected the call option of the mortgage loans.

Interest Only/Principal Only Securities

One of the most recent additions to the world of securitized, residential, mortgage loans is the STRIP (Separate Tranche Interest and Principal) security. We see in the creation of the STRIP a response to interest rate shifts. The first STRIP security was issued in 1986 and some $2 billion worth had been issued as of early 1988.

There is a clear relationship between the mortgage rate and the prepayment rate at different levels of market interest. Obviously, the higher-rate mortgages show the most rapid rise in prepayments as the interest rates fall. Homeowners, naturally, seek to refinance their current higher-rate mortgages with lower-rate money, thus boosting the prepayment percentage.

There is a lag period of time between changes in interest rates and the corresponding changes in prepayment rates. During this lag period a wide disparity with regard to prepayment rate can exist among purchasers of the mortgage-backed product. As a result of this disparity and with the introduction of the STRIP security, a security position can be taken in the market to best advance the buyer's theory on prepayments.

The STRIP security is created by taking the cash flows from the underlying collateral and splitting them into two or more classes that have the same maturity as the underlying collateral. Each of the newly created classes will be entitled to receive more or less principal or interest than the other classes. The resultant classes look like a discount (lower coupon) and a premium (higher coupon) security. Herein lies the attractiveness of the securities.

The purchaser of the interest only (I/O) portion of the STRIP security has bought the security that has the yield potential like that of a higher coupon piece of collateral. The hope of this investor is that interest rates continue to remain the same or rise. If rates remain the same or rise, prepayment rates should slow down while allowing the investor to receive his higher yield for a longer period of time. Likewise the purchaser of the discounted piece (the principal only, P/O) expects that interest rates will continue to fall and as a result prepayments will rise. As prepayments rise more of the investor's principal is returned to him faster than expected and his rate of return increases. Because the P/O is a security which is bought at a discount, this faster principal return results in a higher-than-expected yield due to the quicker discount amortization.

The performances of the two pieces of the STRIP security—P/O and I/O—change dramatically under varying interest rate environments.

These instruments are extremely volatile in response to small changes in interest rates and the resulting prepayment rates; there is a dramatic difference in investor yields—and they move in opposite directions for the P/O and I/O instruments (Figure 20-1).

For example, for one particular P/O instrument, a decrease of 100 basis points from the expected interest rate (base case) boosts the yield from 10.41 percent to 15.21 percent; with a decrease of 200 basis points the yield hits 25.35 percent, and when interest rates drop 300 basis points the yield reaches an astounding 42.22 percent. As stated, the driving factor is the projected prepayment rate, which is estimated to be almost three times faster than the base case when interest rates drop 300 basis points (roughly 24% of the mortgages are being prepaid per year in the low interest rate environment versus 9% in the base case environment). As the yields go up, however, the (weighted) average life

Figure 20–1. 9.5 Percent STRIP Yield Comparison (interest only vs. principal only).

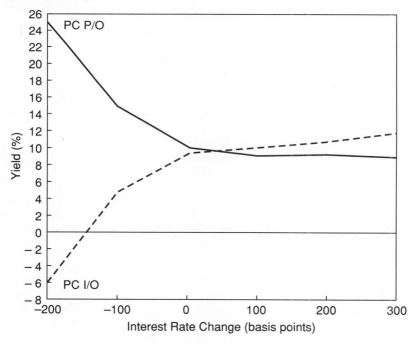

of the P/O instrument declines—this is logical since the prepayment rate is progressively higher. However, since the average life is smaller, this diminishes the luster of the very high yields, since they are earned only for a short time.

For one particular I/O instrument, a decrease of 100 basis points from the expected interest rate (base case) drops the yield from 9.75 percent to 4.39 percent; with a decrease of 200 basis points the yield becomes negative at −6.08 percent, and when interest rates drop 300 basis points the yield crashes to −22.26 percent. As above, the driving factor is the projected prepayment rate. When prepayments increase, this means that the amount of interest that you had expected to receive will not be forthcoming. When these future cash flows do not materialize the internal rate of return on your investment can become negative.[2] In essence, you have paid for streams of interest income that you had expected but will never receive.[3]

Thus, P/O and I/O instruments are both risky and fascinating. Considering the fact that sophisticated investors (including major financial institutions) have incurred substantial losses on I/O and P/O securities, proper use of these innovative synthetic instruments dictates careful hedging and not wild speculation.

---

2. A *negative* return on interest only instruments means that the internal rate of return on the investment is negative. In other words, the *net present value* of the investment is a negative—the discounted value of all future cash flows minus the initial investment is a negative number (i.e., the initial investment is *greater* than all discounted cash flows received in the future). This loss is generated by the fact that some of those interest cash flows do not materialize due to the higher prepayment rate. (Interestingly enough, it is generally not possible for the current structure of principal only instruments to become negative, since they are bought at a discount and are guaranteed by agency collateralization. For the returns on P/O instruments to become negative they would have to consist of whole loans which were not collateralized; these whole loans would have to default and the resulting foreclosures would have to sustain market value losses.)

3. It seems paradoxical for interest rate instruments to *lose* value if interest rates drop. Fixed-income securities, of course, *increase* in value when interest rates drop, since their now relatively higher coupon payment rates would make their principal worth more. The key difference with interest only instruments is the prepayment feature—so that a declining interest rate environment translates into the elimination of future cash payments.

Conclusion

The residential mortgage securitization market has undergone rapid evolution. Many of the innovations are a result of or a response to pressures from the capital markets, the rating agencies, and regulatory and accounting changes. The products that exist today will provide the foundations for further growth in the world of securitization. Newer products will be created to address further utilization of wasting assets on the balance sheets of not only the mortgage-related institutions but general corporate entities as well. This process will incorporate the popular forms of assets such as the adjustable rate loans, but will also involve the more esoteric classes.

The introduction of stricter capital requirements in the financial services industry will prompt many institutions to apply such securitization techniques to manage their businesses. Furthermore, many corporate entities (traditional and nontraditional) will utilize the same techniques for better balance sheet management. The securitization of other assets— such as automobile and credit card receivables from consumers as well as commercial real estate mortgages from companies—follows the basic tenets established in the residential mortgage world.

CHAPTER 21

Public Finance*

The economic system in the United States has two capital-raising processes. One raises funds for corporations in the equity and debt markets through the financial community headquartered on Wall Street. The other raises monies for state, local, and other governmental entities and is also developed and maintained by Wall Street financial institutions. Neither the corporate nor the public finance capital-raising method is more important than the other. Without a systematic way for profit-making corporations to secure funds to finance their businesses, the American economic system would be much different than it is now. Similar but usually unrecognized is the fact that without a systematic way for states, local governments, and public authorities to secure funds for a whole host of critically important public services, America as we know it today would simply cease to function.

For the last hundred and fifty years, state and local governments have financed long-term capital improvements by issuing municipal bonds. Approximately 37,000 different states, counties, school districts, towns, and other public issuing bodies have issued municipal bonds. By 1988 there were seven hundred billion dollars in municipal bonds outstanding. This is a huge market for investment bankers who represent issuers and investors alike.

---

*This chapter has been derived from "Public Finance as a Counterpart of Corporate Finance," by Stephen P. Rappaport, and "Municipal Securities I: Characteristics and Categories" by Sylvan G. Feldstein, Volume III (Corporate and Municipal Securities), Dow Jones-Irwin's *The Library of Investment Banking* (1990), Robert Kuhn, editor-in-chief.

It should therefore come as no surprise to those who work within corporate America and to citizens who receive government services of all types that the corporate and public finance infrastructure within the Wall Street community has become a vital part of the free world. Nowhere can this be seen more clearly than in the need of governments to raise funds and in the capacity of public finance departments to raise funds through the sale of municipal securities.

Motivations of Issuers and Investors

From the issuer's point of view, the virtue of financing long-term capital improvements such as schools and bridges with municipal bonds is that the burden of paying for the capital improvement in the community is spread-out over the useful life of that facility. Although some investors buy municipal bonds as a way of supporting public improvements such as schools, playgrounds, and parks, the vast majority of investors buy them because interest income from most bonds is exempt from federal income taxes. Consequently, municipal bonds are purchased by those who are in high marginal tax brackets, because on an after-tax basis they offer a yield that is greater than comparable bonds that are taxable. For example, if an investor is in the 28 percent tax bracket, a municipal bond selling at par to yield 7.2 percent is equivalent to a taxable bond's before-tax yield of ten percent. If otherwise comparable taxable bonds are offering a yield that is less than 10 percent, there is a yield advantage to purchasing municipal bonds; the higher the investor's tax bracket, the greater the advantage. This benefits issuers and taxpayers as well, for it lowers their cost of financing necessary capital improvements in their communities.

Public Finance and the Governmental Process

Just like corporations, state and local governments enter the securities markets principally through securities firms and other financial organizations. These kinds of financing opportunities have moved state and local governments beyond the simple pay-as-you-go system of by-gone years. In those times, governments throughout the country paid for the largest proportion of their services directly through tax-related revenues. As the population in the United States grew and as state and local revenue streams could no longer supply the funds needed to pay for basic services, state and local governments began to access the debt market through the orderly sale of securities in much the same way corporations had done.

Perhaps the most significant development, however, in this general transformation of funding governmental services came with the development of the public revenue authority. Through revenue authorities that issued bonds for services financed outside the normal governmental budgeting processes, there arose a quasi-corporate type of governmental entity that was not originally envisioned by the framers of the United States Constitution.

Today, revenue authorities issue securities to provide governmental services for a wide range of projects. These services are financed largely through some type of user-fee arrangement such as that employed by a revenue authority toll-road system. Many of these include such services as housing, transportation, water, wastewater, hospitals, public power, education, and resource recovery projects.

Such a user-fee repayment system is in sharp contrast to a governmental entity such as a state or local government of general jurisdiction pledging its general obligation and full faith and credit to the payment of debt service. This usually entails the local government's authority to levy ad valorem taxes within its defined geographic area. Access to the securities markets by state and local governments and the governmental creatures called public authorities has become woven deeply into the fabric of American society.

Why the World Would Stop

In recent years, the market for municipal securities has grown enormously, although in the late 1980s, the total annual new issue volume dropped to levels of earlier years (which most industry observers attribute to the Tax Reform Act of 1986). Yet the importance of the debt markets for state and local governments cannot be understated: Under the American economic system the ability of government to serve its citizens would simply be unavailable without the access to securities markets.

The market for state and local government securities is something of a bellwether of the national economy. The appetite for public services is a driving force in an ever-expanding state and local governmental financial system seeking to be self-sustaining. This is becoming even more pronounced due to the decrease in federal support for many state and local services that were previously financed in part by federal funds. The trend will also place an increasing strain on state and local financial systems at a time when elected and appointed officials have come to realize their basic infrastructure is in need of substantial repair and upgrading. As a result, not only will state and local governmental entities require a steady stream of funds, but many will undoubtedly seek to expand the use of the revenue authority. In all of this, securities firms and the entire industry stand at the threshold through which governments of all types access the capital markets.

When Governments Come to Wall Street

Wall Street performs a unique service for governments nationwide, although many would think that government and the securities industry are in fact worlds apart. Nothing could be further from the truth. The securities industry and the securities markets provide an orderly way to underwrite and sell the securities of state and local governments as well as those of public authorities to institutional and retail purchasers.

Investment Bankers Sell Securities

When governments come to Wall Street, they arrive via two principal financial routes for the sale of their securities. The first route is the securities sales process known as *competitive bidding;* this is the usual method for financing the general obligations of state and local governments where their full faith and credit is pledged. The second route is through the *negotiated sale* of municipal securities; this is the usual method for financing revenue bond issuers (and sometimes for general obligation bond issuers) in instances where the market is unfamiliar with the issue, the market is exceptionally volatile, the issue is of considerable size and complexity, or the issuer does not want to be tied to a specific time and date as would be the case in a competitive sale.

Investment Bankers Give Financial Advice

Another important reason why governments come to Wall Street is simply to receive financial advice. Securities firms provide state and local governments with financial advice on either an ad hoc basis or on one that is related to a specific sale of securities or a time frame during which the financial advice is provided. The normal financial advisory type of arrangement is between a government and a particular firm which provides specific securities-related advice that may include information related to structuring the deal, the credit implications of it, and the pricing of the deal.

The Process of Public Finance

More than anything else, public finance is a process. From the development of legislation that creates a governmental entity such as a transportation authority, to the selling of the securities to finance the project, and to the closing of the deal, public finance is a system of doing things. Public finance professionals, together with those in an investment bank's municipal bond departments which include the trading, underwriting, sales, and research areas are all involved at almost every stage of a government's financing program. The entire transaction is process-oriented: the estimates on expected interest rates upon which feasibility studies and debt service coverage ratios are calculated, the structure of the bond deal to achieve the highest credit rating possible and thus the lowest interest cost to the issuer, the research material that is prepared to educate investors about the issuer and its securities, the salespeople both institutional and retail who ultimately market the securities, and the risk taking by the underwriting departments of the securities firms involved in the deal. There are a number of basic stages in the general process of public finance.

Legislation

The first stage is the creation of enabling legislation that occurs in any given public finance deal when new projects and programs are being developed. Investment bankers, feasibility consultants, and attorneys work closely with state and local officials to develop legislation that will provide the skeletal framework upon which a particular project is developed and municipal securities are issued.

Request for Proposal

The next stage is called the request for proposal (RFP) process. In the RFP process, government officials send a questionnaire to prospective investment banking firms. In most cases, a small number of the firms are ultimately requested for an interview, and from these firms the investment bankers for the project are selected. This process often elicits creative financial suggestions as to how the project may be secured and the bonds or notes issued. It is as much an intellectual and discovery-like procedure as it is an effort on behalf of government officials to select the best securities firm and investment bankers.

Feasibility Study

Another part of the process is the development of a feasibility study; this is used for revenue bond or project-oriented types of municipal financings. (It is certainly critical for new public issuing agencies.) It is also important for those entities that are coming to market on a regular basis so that the feasibility of the project may be confirmed.

Structuring the Transaction: How the Issue is Secured

The next stage of the process is structuring the transaction, and this is a two-part job. The first part has to do with how the issue is to be secured and, for new projects, involves the creation of the appropriate indenture, covenants, and resolutions that are the documentary foundations of any bond issue.

Structuring the Transaction: How the Issue is Paid Back

The second part of the structuring process occurs at the time of the underwriting. This is when the pay-back schedule of the bond issue is set up, such as the number of maturities, the amount of the principal to be paid on each maturity date, and whether there will be any term bonds (or balloon payments) that come due during the later years. The issue is structured so as to gain the attention of investors and to achieve the lowest interest cost to the issuer while at the same time allowing the issuer to meet its bond covenants.

Underwriting and Sale

The last part of the public finance process involves the underwriting and the sale of the issue. This can take anywhere from a couple of hours to a couple of days. Sometimes the underwriting involves repricing a negotiated issue which means adjusting the maturities or interest rates so that the issue can be sold successfully.

Categories of Municipal Bonds

Municipal bonds come in a vast variety of types with different coupons and yields, maturities and amortization schedules, redemption features, security structures, and marketabilities. In short, there is a wide spectrum of risk/return profiles for municipal bonds, although not as wide as for corporate bonds.[*]

In terms of municipal bond security structures, there are basically two different types. The first type is the *general obligation bond*, and the second is the *revenue bond*.

General Obligation Bonds

General obligation bonds are debt instruments issued by states, counties, special districts, cities, towns, and school districts. They are secured by the issuer's general taxing powers. Usually, a general obligation bond is secured by the issuer's unlimited taxing power. For smaller governmental jurisdiction such as school districts and towns, the only available unlimited taxing power is on property. For larger general obligation bond issuers such as states and big cities, the tax revenues are more diverse and may include corporate and individual income taxes, sales taxes, and property taxes. The security pledges for these larger issuers such as states are sometimes referred to as being *full faith and credit obligations*.

Additionally, certain general obligation bonds are secured not only by the issuer's general taxing powers to create monies accumulated in the general fund but also from certain identified fees, grants, and special charges, which provide additional revenues from outside the general fund. Such bonds are known as being *double barreled* in security because of the dual nature of the revenue sources.

Also, not all general obligation bonds are secured by unlimited taxing powers. Some have pledged taxes that are limited as to revenue sources and maximum property tax millage amounts. Such bonds are known as *limited-tax general obligation bonds*.

Revenue Bonds

The second basic type of security structure is found in a revenue bond. Such bonds are issued for either project or enterprise financings in which

---

[*]For example, equity features such as convertibility are not meaningful for municipal bonds.

the bond issuers pledge to the bondholders the revenues generated by the operating projects so financed. (The *full faith and credit obligations* of the issuing municipally are *not* pledged for a revenue bond as they are for a general obligation bond.)

The following are some examples of the specific types of revenue bonds that have been issued over the years by creative investment bankers: airport, seaport, college and university, hospital, single-family mortgage, industrial development, pollution control, public power, resource recovery, sewer, sports complex, convention center, student loan, toll road, and water.

More unique security structures have features of both general obligation and revenue bonds. They include the following: federal savings and loan insurance corporation-backed bonds, lease-backed bonds, letter of credit-backed bonds, life care revenue bonds, new housing authority bonds, tax allocation bonds, and troubled city bailout bonds.

CHAPTER 22

International Finance*

International finance is a dynamic, growing, and relatively recent area of investment banking. It is a great cauldron in which financial creativity and competition boil hot. It is a vast arena where giant multinational financial institutions struggle and strive, wax and wane, and prosper and flourish.

This chapter is a brief introduction to major world financial markets, with particular emphasis on fixed-income securities. These markets have experienced rapid growth during the past two decades. At the same time they have also undergone significant structural changes in terms of competition and regulation, and they have experienced a high degree of integration of national markets, a phenomenon that has been labelled *globalization*. During this period, these markets have spawned a tremendous number of innovative instruments and techniques, creating new opportunities for issuers and investors.

Concepts and Terminology

We begin by trying to make sense of the sometimes confusing terminology surrounding global financial markets. The frequently used term *Eurocurrency market* illustrates the problem: while the term suggests a

---

*This chapter has been derived from "International Financial Markets" by Gunter Dufey and Taeyoung Chung, and "Eurocapital Markets" by Hung Q. Tran, Larry Andersen & Ernst-Ludwig Drayss, Volume VI (International Finance and Investing), Dow Jones-Irwin's *The Library of Investment Banking* (1990), Robert Lawrence Kuhn, editor in chief.

market for currencies in Europe, it actually refers to a market for bank deposits and loans in a variety of currencies that are mediated *outside* the country where the respective currency serves as a means of payment!

An overview of international financial markets must begin with the distinction between three markets according to the function they perform:

1. The market for international payments.
2. The market for international credit.
3. International markets for real assets.

Foreign Exchange Market

The *foreign exchange market* enables enterprises or individuals making transactions to make payments across borders efficiently. Technically speaking, this is done by exchanging the ownership of *demand deposits* in the respective national banking systems. Thus, a payment from the United States to Switzerland would involve the simultaneous debiting of the payer's demand deposit account in the United States and the crediting of the recipient's current account in a bank in Zurich.

As in every market, each transaction involves agreement on (1) the price, (i.e., the exchange rate) and (2) the delivery of the means of payments, (i.e., the *settlement* or value date). If settlement is on the second business day, it is usually referred to as a *spot* transaction and the exchange rate is then known as a *spot* rate. When settlement takes place on the third business day or further in the future (in major currencies that time of settlement may reach all the way out to ten years), the price is generally referred to as a *forward* rate.

Foreign Credit Markets

While the essence of the foreign exchange market is the movement of financial claims over *space, credit* transactions involve exchange of funds over *time*. Savers, whose income exceeds temporarily their use of funds, make the additional output that they have created available to borrowers, who have a shortage of funds because they commit resources to real assets (such as consumer durables, productive assets in the form of business investment, or government projects) in excess of their current income. Credit markets also aid in distributing risks among participants in this savings and investment process. By generating various types of financial claims, these markets permit savers and borrowers to fine-tune the combination of risks they are willing to bear.

Such transactions take on a variety of forms. To bring some semblance of order to chaos, it is useful to distinguish first between *fixed income securities* and *equity claims*. The essence of this distinction, of course, is that the former yield returns that are contractually fixed, while the latter provide returns that are dependent on the success of an enterprise. While this broad characterization is sufficient for most purposes, it is not as sharp as it appears because the markets have brought forth many hybrid securities that contain elements of both. Illustrative examples range from high-yield bonds (junk bonds) to convertible bonds, money market preferred bonds, and many others. (See Chapters 12 and 13.)

Foreign Real Assets Markets

Finally, there are international markets for claims on *real assets*. In this context, one usually refers to foreign direct investment (FDI), where the distinction between FDI and international portfolio investment through equities is not always apparent. Formally, a foreign subsidiary of a multinational enterprise is simply a company where the parent company holds a significant percentage of the equity claims in that firm. For an understanding of this type of investment, however, the pure risk and return concept is not sufficient; the essence lies in the exercise of managerial control over business assets abroad in order to exploit some technology or another enterprise-specific competitive advantage.

International Credit Markets

We begin with a simple conceptual scheme for classifying international credit markets. It is based on two dimensions: we ask *how* (i.e., through which financial channel) and *where* (i.e., in which governmental jurisdiction) funds are transferred from savers to borrowers.

Institutional Structure

The first dimension represents the channel (i.e., the institutional structure of market participants) through which funds are moved.

Resources can be transferred from savers to borrowers through two channels: (1) through *financial intermediaries* which attract funds from savers by issuing their own claims and in turn lend the funds to those who invest in real assets and (2) through organized *securities markets* in which savers and borrowers can link up directly (e.g., savers can purchase securities issued by ultimate borrowers). The organizational pattern of such markets is determined either by convention, the explicit agreement of the participating private entities, or by government regulation, or by both.

The proportions of funds that are channeled indirectly or directly through organized securities markets are important distinguishing characteristics of different credit markets. For one, the two channels for funds tend to react differently to external shocks. A capital market dominated by intermediaries is relatively better able to withstand external disturbances because financial intermediaries absorb some of the risk faced by both savers and ultimate investors. Therefore, different capital markets may react to the same shocks differently depending on whether the intermediated or the direct channel is more important. Furthermore, markets where intermediaries dominate are, for better or worse, much more susceptible to direct government guidance of credit flows.

National Jurisdictions

The other dimension of international credit markets concerns the *jurisdiction* where financial resources are transferred. Most credit transactions take place in domestic financial markets. However, many financial markets have extensive links abroad: Domestic investors purchase foreign securities and may invest funds in foreign financial institutions. Conversely, domestic banks may lend to foreign residents, and foreign residents may issue securities in the national market or deposit funds with resident financial intermediaries. These are the traditional foreign markets for international financial transactions.

The significant aspect of such traditional foreign lending and borrowing is that all transactions take place under the rules, customs, and institutional arrangements prevailing in the national market concerned. Most importantly, all these transactions are directly subject to public policy governing transactions with non-residents (foreign transactions) in a particular market. To illustrate, when savers purchase securities in a foreign market, they do so according to the rules, market practices, and regulatory precepts which govern such transactions in that particular market. The same applies to those who invest their funds with financial intermediaries abroad.

Likewise, borrowers from abroad who wish to issue securities in a national market must follow the rules and regulations of that market. Here we encounter an important phenomenon that is crucial to understanding international markets: the rules governing the access of foreign borrowers to national markets tend to be discriminatory and restrictive. The same is true with respect to financial intermediaries. The borrower who approaches a foreign financial institution for a loan obtains funds at rates and conditions imposed by the financial institutions of the foreign country, and he is directly affected by the authorities' policy on lending to foreign residents.

International Jurisdictions

During the 1960s, market methods were developed that removed international—and to a certain extent even national—borrowing and lending from the jurisdiction of national authorities. This was accomplished by locating the market for credit denominated in a particular currency *outside* the country where that currency is legal tender (i.e., into a jurisdiction that offers a more hospitable regulatory climate for such transactions). For example, markets for dollar-denominated loans, deposits, and securities in jurisdictions other than the United States—to a large extent—avoid U.S. banking and securities regulations.

We refer to these markets as Euromarkets—or more properly as *external* markets or *offshore* markets—in order to indicate that they are not part of the domestic (or national) financial system. Thus, the essence of this classification is the nature of regulation. Differences in interest rates, practices, and regulations that exist between domestic and external markets arise primarily from the extent to which regulatory constraints are different.

Structural Summary

Today, virtually all major capital markets, including those of the United States, exhibit a three-tiered structure:

1. **Domestic Market**. A domestic market which has special and unique procedures and institutions stemming from historical and regulatory determinants.

2. **Foreign Market**. A foreign market which is attached to the domestic market, where nonresidents participate as suppliers and takers of funds, but always under the specific conditions, rules, and regulations established for foreign participants in the national market.

3. **External or Offshore Market**. An external or offshore market which is located in a different political jurisdiction, with only the currency used to denominate the financial claims linking it to the national market.

The various external markets have more features in common with each other than with their respective national markets. Therefore, they are properly discussed as a common, integrated market where claims denominated in different currencies are exchanged and are therefore usually referred to as Euromarket(s).

National Credit Markets

The international role of a financial market and its prevailing regulatory climate are closely related. Appropriate regulation makes some markets more attractive than others (e.g., by minimizing the risk of loss through fraud, various conflict-of-interest situations, and lack of adequate disclosure). Unfortunately, the dividing line between regulatory measures that improve markets and those that have just the opposite effect is thin. Thus, when governments pursue ambitious social and political objectives by way of financial market policies (such as allocating credit according to political criteria) or when they discriminate against nonresident borrowers and issuers to a significant extent, markets become inefficient quickly. The result is that both foreign and domestic market participants escape by using markets in other jurisdictions (i.e., external markets).

Japan

The Japanese market, with a huge domestic segment, is second only to the U.S. market, reflecting the size of the Japanese economy (roughly one-half of that of the United States). Interestingly, the size of the total stock of Japanese government bonds (JGB) outstanding almost equals that of the market for U.S. Treasury bonds in absolute U.S. dollar terms.

Until the early 1980s, however, the external segment of the Japanese market was rather underdeveloped due to tight regulations, including extensive exchange and capital controls. Beginning slowly in the 1970s and greatly accelerating in the early 1980s, there has been considerable liberalization, especially with respect to discrimination against foreign borrowers and issuers as well as foreign financial institutions operating in the Tokyo market. By 1988, Tokyo had become the home of a modest offshore banking market for non-yen currencies, especially dollar deposits and interbank placements. Secondly, the so-called *Samurai* market, a market for foreign bond issues in Japan, had expanded considerably. Its growth would have been even greater had it not been for competition from the more efficient (i.e., less regulated) markets for Euroyen bonds.

Similar trends can be observed in the banking market.[1] While Japanese banks denominate most of their international business in dollars, they and their foreign competitors have begun to do a considerable volume in Euroyen deposits and loans. Indeed, this segment has been the fastest-growing of the Eurocurrency markets, albeit from a very low base.

The Teutonic Bloc: West Germany, Switzerland, and the Netherlands

Next to the U.S. dollar and the yen, the Deutschmark (DM) market ranks third in world importance. The international role of this currency is enhanced because the conservative, steady, monetary policy of the Bundesbank has effectively become the reference point for central bank policy of most other European countries which—with different degrees of success—align their monetary policies to that of the German central bank. Of course, this feature is reinforced by the fixed exchange rate targets with the European Monetary System, which the following countries comprise: Belgium, Denmark, France, West Germany, Ireland, Italy, Luxembourg, and the Netherlands.

In the international banking market, the Euro-DM market is, with considerable distance, second only to the United States. More significantly, markets for DM, Dutch Guilder, and Swissfranc bonds are sizable. However, the negative effect of market fragmentation on liquidity must also be noted. For international portfolio managers, only the market for German government securities (so-called *Bunds*) has the liquidity required to allow for continous 24-hour global trading.

---

1. Of the 20 largest banks in the world (in terms of assets), 13 are Japanese; of the top 10, 8 are Japanese; of the top 8, *all* are Japanese.

The financial markets in this bloc of countries are dominated by large financial intermediaries which engage in all aspects of banking (universal banks). Regulations are reasonably liberal by international standards, and the markets have a history of being reasonably open to foreign investors and borrowers.

The German bond market has some further interesting features. Most notable is the virtual absence of a domestic corporate bond market, as even German corporations find it less burdensome from a regulatory perspective—and cheaper due to the escape from withholding taxes—to use the facilities of the offshore market. Thus, there is no real distinction between the foreign market for DM bonds and the Euro-DM bond market. Other unique features are a relatively large market for the debentures of financial institutions (more than 50 percent of the total bond market) as well as a large market for *debt certificates* which have limited liquidity and are not securities in a legal sense.

The United Kingdom

The capital markets of the United Kingdom and France belong to the international middle weight class. The United Kingdom, particularly, has an active government market (the *gilt* market) but its international role is diminishing as the United Kingdom and—along with it—pound sterling have become a relatively minor part of the world economy.

In contrast, London has taken on a critical role as an international financial center as a home for the external markets denominated in other currencies. London is definitely the focus of the Eurocurrency market, particularly at the wholesale level. Interbank rates for various currencies (e.g., LIBOR— London Interbank Offered Rate) have become the pricing standards for bank funds worldwide, being frequently used even in domestic transactions. This is even more true for the bond markets, where London has managed to attract a large proportion of the international issuing business, as well as secondary market activity in fixed-income securities (Eurobonds and notes), major government securities markets, and even markets for equities of large companies from many countries. London has achieved this position largely due to the infrastructure already in existence, the conducive nature of the regulation, and the relatively free access to the market. Changes in the structure of the London market (Big Bang) during 1986 made the domestic market more efficient as measured by turnover and trading spreads, but the implementation of regulatory reforms called London's international dominance into question.

France

The French franc market is somewhat larger than the UK market. In addition, it comprises a sizeable corporate sector. However, the international role of the French market has been quite limited due to a long history of exchange and capital controls. The liberalization of both the external controls and the rules that govern internal markets has caused international investors and issuers to look at the French market more intensely. This potential has been enhanced with the growth of markets for derivative securities such as futures and options. If current liberalization and growth trends continue, the French market will turn into a significant regional market in Europe—not to speak of its potential as part of an integrated European market—provided the European Community will achieve monetary unification.

Financial Instruments in the Euromarkets

Following are several of the major categories of financial instruments available for issuers and investors in the Euromarkets.

Fixed-Income Instruments

Straight Bonds.   Traditionally, straight (or fixed-rate) bonds have been the mainstay of Eurocapital market financing. Straight bonds in the Euromarket are almost exclusively bearer instruments,[2] although some sovereign borrowers have floated large denomination registered bonds for tax reasons. Eurostraight bonds pay interest annually. (A significant volume of straight bonds have been issued with warrants attached which represent a securitized call, or in some instances, put options for currencies, commodities, debt, or equities.)

Debt Warrants.   Beginning in 1983, many issues of straight debt were floated with warrants attached allowing the holder to purchase further

---

2. Bearer bonds are not registered; ownership is determined strictly by possession.

debt of the borrower at a fixed price. These warrants were basically equivalent to long-term, interest rate call options. The high yields in the U.S. dollar sector made them attractive for investors since the perceived trend of interest rates was down and the call options offered a highly leveraged instrument which could produce spectacular returns.

Another motivation for investors to buy the warrants was a protection against a drop in the value of the U.S. dollar on the foreign exchange market, while at the same time they could participate in the rally on the U.S. dollar bond market. Through the warrant, a much larger bond position could be assumed and any gain would be made on the entire bond position, while any foreign exchange loss would be limited to the smaller amount paid for the warrant.

Currency Warrants.   The issuance of currency warrants in connection with the flotation of a Eurobond is usually an arbitrage operation. The borrower, and hence the writer of the currency option, is able to secure a higher premium on the options he is selling than the premium he has to pay for his hedge to cover his exposure.[3]

Commodity Warrants.   Gold and silver have been used as the basis for warrant issues in the Euromarket. Gold warrants attached to a fixed rate bond offer a particularly attractive package since the return on the package should be protected against inflation by the inclusion of the call options for gold.

Dual-Currency Bonds.   Dual-currency bonds pay interest in one currency while the bonds are redeemed in a different currency. They therefore resemble a portfolio of annuity and zero coupon bonds in two different currencies. Since it should be possible to replicate the cash flows in the different currencies, there are arbitrage possibilities which can

---

3. A net gain is only possible if there is some reason why investors cannot directly purchase the options used as the hedge. It may be that large denominations make the over-the-counter options unattractive for retail investors who may nevertheless be attracted to the warrants either as a hedge or as a leveraged investment instrument. Also, some institutional investors are prohibited by law or their own internal rules from purchasing securities which are not listed on an exchange. Listed warrants would consequently satisfy this requirement and the borrower can earn a profit by utilizing them.

be exploited. The most commonly used variety on the Euromarkets has been a bond which pays interest in yen and is redeemed in U.S. dollars.

Variable-Rate Debt Instruments in the Euromarkets

Variable-rate debt instruments in the Euromarket include capital market instruments (e.g., floating-rate notes) as well as money market instruments (e.g., Euronotes and Eurocommercial paper) with long facility lives.

Floating-Rate Notes

Floating-rate notes (FRNs) are typically long-term, variable-rate bonds linked to interest rates in the money markets and issued by banks, sovereign borrowers, U.S. savings and loan associations, and U.K. building societies. Normally, coupons on FRNs in the Euromarket are based upon one of the London interbank rates (LIBOR, LIMEAN, or LIBID), but other base rates have been used.

The following innovative structures have been used with EuroFRNS: mismatched, capped, and perpetual.

Mismatched FRNs.   Mismatched floaters (FRNs) exploit an investment technique that allows the issuer to achieve a reduction in the coupon paid. If the yield curve has a positive slope—its normal shape—financing an FRN with money shorter-dated than the coupon reset period will result in an increase in the return on the bond.[4]

Capped FRNs.   A capped FRN has a maximum coupon beyond which the adjustment to higher base rates no longer takes place. This is conceptually equal to a put option on the coupon at the capped rate. The

---

4. For example, if an FRN has a coupon of six-month LIBOR reset semi-annually, then financing the FRN position with three-month money will produce a pick-up in return (providing the yield curve remains positively sloped). Assume that at the coupon fixing, six-month LIBOR is eight percent, while three month LIBOR is seven and seven-eighths percent. The one-eighth percentage point differential between six-month and three-month money can be used to increase the return by financing at seven and seven-eights percent for three months and then rolling forward. The investor must accept that three-month LIBOR in three months may be above the eight percent coupon, thus reducing his return and perhaps producing a loss.

bond investor is the writer of the option and must be compensated for his risk by a higher return on this type of FRN compared with a conventional one. The issuer of the FRN can then either hold the option himself or sell it to a third party, thus reducing his total cost of financing. Numerous FRNs in the Euro-DM sector have been capped.

Perpetual FRNs.   Beginning in 1985 and continuing into 1986, a large volume of FRNs without a redemption date were launched by U.K., Canadian, and U.S. banks. These FRNs were structured in order to meet the guidelines of the respective central banks to be considered as part of the issuing banks' primary capital. In numerous cases the coupons were linked in some manner to the dividend on the bank's stock. In all cases, the FRNs were subordinated debt.[5]

Euronotes and Eurocommercial Paper

Note issuance facilities (NIFs) are credit facilities with long maturities (five to seven years usually) during which the borrower can obtain funds up to a maximum amount by issuing short-term money market paper over the life of the facility.

NIFs have been given a variety of other names to reflect small differences in their organization (e.g., revolving underwriting facilities [RUFs], transferable underwriting facilities [TRUFs],) but they all have the same basic structure: a banking consortium is required either to take up notes issued or to provide a credit to the borrower.[6]

Fixed Rate Bonds With Equity Warrants

Fixed rate bonds with equity warrants attached have been popular in the Euromarkets since the middle 1980s. The long period of rising

---

5. As of early 1988, prices in this sector of the FRN market experienced a major deterioration as investors became concerned about the liquidity of their assets and sold large quantities of bonds to the market makers. Prices declined to exceptionally large discounts and, even at these low prices, there was no significant investor interest. The primary market for perpetual FRNs had been effectively closed.

6. The fact that the standby credits involved in NIFs represent off-balance-sheet, contingent risks for banks caused regulatory authorities to begin requiring provisions be made for these risks by allocating a bank's primary capital to stand behind these contingent commitments, thus decreasing the attractiveness of this instrument for both the banks and the borrowers.

stock prices meant that investors preferred the leverage provided by the securitized call options to the downside protection offered by convertible bonds. Issuers found equity warrant issues attractive because of the low cost of debt—at times 500 to 600 basis points below capital market yields—and the advantageous swaps which these issues produced.[7]

Convertible Bonds

Convertible bonds have been used in the Euromarket almost from their inception, with U.S. corporations making extensive use of this instrument. Maturities on convertible bonds are usually longer than equity warrant issues, with 15 years being a common maturity. Convertible bonds are popular in the pound sterling sector, where equity warrant issues have been scarce.

---

7. For swap purposes, the equity warrant instrument is preferable to the convertible bond since the end maturity of the debt is known due to the fact that the warrants can be separated from the bond and traded— or exercised—separately.

APPENDIX

A Philosophy of
Investment Banking*

Investment banking is the business of money. Its primary purpose is to link users of capital with providers of capital, seeking optimum financial efficiency for both issuers and investors. It is the intermediary channel through which capital is distributed efficiently and exchanged effectively. As such, investment banking claims to be capitalism's critical mechanism for facilitating the resource allocation decisions that epitomize the free market system. To no small degree, investment bankers believe that they fuel the world economy.

But what actually *is* investment banking? It is transaction oriented, a service business. It manufacturers no goods and sells no merchandise — yet it influences virtually all enterprises that do just that. Its primary asset is financial intelligence and its primary product is financial advice and financial power.[1] Investment banks make things happen, energizing corporations to grow and expand and enrich their shareholders.

Some see investment banking as the indispensable hub of the wheel of commerce, the vital force of companies and industries, the market catalyst of economic productivity. Others consider investment banking —

---

* This Appendix has been derived from "A Philosophy of Investment Banking" by Robert Lawrence Kuhn, Volume I (Investing and Risk Management), Dow Jones-Irwin's *The Library of Investment Banking* (1990), Robert Lawrence Kuhn, editor-in-chief.

1. Power in physics is the ability to do physical work; power in investment banking is the ability to exert financial force. Virtually all aspects of investment banking manifest the importance of having financial power and exerting financial force. But such power and force are *not* simply a function of body and mass. They are more qualitative than quantitative, reflecting more insight and wisdom than size and strength.

why mince words—to be a parasitic profession, feeding off the productivity of its clients. Investment bankers, these critics complain, are
overcompensated and underproductive, a drag on the system. The results
are paradoxical: Investment banking is a powerful profession, and yet it
must continuously justify its own existence.

This appendix deals with that paradox. Our objective is to discern
the fundamental nature of investment banking, and thereby ascertain its
fundamental worth. We analyze not apologize, recognize not rationalize.
The search is for industry purpose, for intrinsic value and meaningful
contribution. We explore foundations, seeking the deep structure of
investment banking. The quest is for essence—a *philosophy*, if you
will—of investment banking.

What Is a Philosophy?

What is a philosophy of a profession, or more broadly, of any area of
human knowledge? First of all, let's start at a more basic level: What
is philosophy? In general, philosophy is the search for sense, meaning,
cause, and principle using modern methodologies of logical thinking
and rigorous thought. And when philosophy is applied to a specific area
of human knowledge, it is the search for sense, meaning, cause, and
principle in that specific area using those same modern methodologies.

Philosophy stresses being and mechanisms, or what things are and
how they work. It is an attempt to perceive what things *really* are, not
how they appear to be, and to discern how things *really* work, not how
they appear to work. Philosophy is the quest for ultimate, irreducible
truth.

A philosophy bores into the inner essence of an area and excavates the
foundation of the field. Elaborate philosophies have been constructed in
various fields including science, education, history, law, and religion. As
a backdrop for formulating a philosophy of investment banking, it is both
interesting and instructive to summarize a few of these other philosophies.
(See the Addendum: The Philosophies of Knowledge Areas.)

It is an awesome heritage, this philosophy stuff. Considering the context, one fears failure and hesitates. After all, a philosophy of investment
banking seems pretentious (or worse, silly) surrounded by such tower-
ing areas of human knowledge as the philosophies of science, education,
history, law, and religion. Yet we overcome the fear and continue the
venture—philosophy claims to be able to make sense out of any human

awareness or endeavor, however massive or minuscule,[2] and investment bankers are not known for their modesty, however appropriate or misplaced.

There are numerous pitfalls in attempting to devise a philosophy of investment banking—it is frighteningly easy to be overblown by ambition or deluded by complexity. Grandiosity is an enemy, intellectual obfuscation an error. Thus we promise no grand design or tightly reasoned system in our nascent philosophy. Our goal must remain limited. We will dig a little, explore the foundations of the field, and organize some aspects of the profession. Perhaps we will find a few interesting things about the nature of investment banking.

Appendix Organization

If we are to lay claim to constructing a philosophy of investment banking, we must begin by introducing some rigor into the process. Our construct is founded on five concepts.

1. *Definitions of Investment Banking.* A philosophy of a field must commence with clarity of language and precision of terms.

2. *Characteristics of a Profession.* Professions in the modern world have particular characteristics; does investment banking share these traits—and is it a profession?

3. *Field Paradigm of Investment Banking.* What good is investment banking; what does it do for the world? What is the industry's intrinsic worth and way of thinking?

4. *Professional Attributes of Investment Banking.* What are the special characteristics of investment banking as a profession and as an industry?

5. *Personal Attributes of Investment Banking.* What are the special characteristics of investment bankers as successful individuals?

---

2. I am ever enchanted by George Bernard Shaw's comparison of the scientist and the philosopher. The scientist is said to learn more and more about less and less, while the philosopher is said to learn less and less about more and more—so that in the end the scientist knows everything about nothing and the philosopher knows nothing about everything.

In this philosophy of investment banking we revisit and review many of the principle and techniques of investment banking presented earlier in the book, only we do it with the eye of the philosopher.

Definitions of Investment Banking

A philosophy flounders when language wobbles. Amorphous boundaries do not encourage clarity of thought. Progress is difficult without commonality of communication. So this is where we must begin: An incipient philosophy needs verbal precision.

Even within the finance community, the term *investment banking* is used rather loosely. Such uses range from those widely inclusive of virtually everything that large Wall Street firms do to those narrowly restrictive to only certain conventional investment banking functions, primarily underwriting. Part of the problem is the evolution of the field.

Traditional investment banking *was* the underwriting of basic common stock equity and investment-grade corporate bonds. But the financial world has changed dramatically and investment banking, the key catalyst of the metamorphosis, has widened its scope proportionately. This scope has become a very broad one, too broad in fact for our proposed philosophy to discern. Since loose uses of the term may generate different views of their profession, the target must be tightened.

We must know the dimensions of the area to be surveyed, the magnitude of the mass under the microscope. Consequently, we reiterate the four diverse definitions of investment banking made in Chapter 1 and articulate the differences among them. The order proceeds from the most broad to the most restrictive, from broadly inclusive of wide-ranging financial services to narrowly restrictive to traditional underwriting.

1) Investment Banking as Everything Major Firms Do

All Wall Street activities are encompassed here, including retail investments and personal financial products. Why should what are clearly consumer product functions be included within a definition of investment banking? The rather circular logic rotates as follows: Since Wall Street firms *are* investment banks (i.e., the a priori assumption), when these firms perform virtually *any* activity, then each of those activities must be ipso facto an integral part of investment banking.

As an example, let's consider one problematic facet of this broad definition: How can the management of the retail branch network be categorized as investment banking? The reasoning for inclusion is not illogical. Consider the process of selling primary-issue securities. Distribution is a critical function; indeed, it is often a comparative strength (or weakness) for competing underwriters. Investment banks that maintain a branch network of retail distribution can underwrite certain securities that other firms cannot—since there are many kinds of securities that can only be sold as retail products. The strategic benefit of a retail branch network is especially clear when an investment bank underwrites securities that are not attractive to institutional investors (such as high-risk, public venture capital.)

2) Investment Banking as All Capital Market Activities

Capital market activities include the wide range of capital raising and corporate finance functions (see Chapter 1). These activities would include functions such as mergers and acquisitions, merchant banking, fairness opinions, fund management, venture capital management, investment research, risk management, and the like—in addition to traditional underwriting of debt and equity securities. Activities would exclude other functions such as consumer markets, retail investments, branch management, and the like (but would include market making and institutional securities trading). (Note that this definition happily includes activities where investment bankers work for their own account—i.e., merchant banking.)

3) Investment Banking as Some Capital Market Activities

Some uses of *investment banking* restrict its connotation to only some capital market activities, stressing underwriting, mergers and acquisitions, fairness opinions, and the like. This definition does not consider certain capital market activities as true investment banking functions. Excluded, for example, might be those areas where investment bankers are working not just as third-party intermediaries but rather as money managers for clients or for their own accounts (e.g., institutional fund management, venture capital management, and merchant banking). Other areas that can be excluded in this third definition are research, commodities, and some elements of risk management (i.e., trading).

4) Investment Banking as Only Underwriting and Raising Capital

This is the most restrictive definition. It is also the traditional definition, the roots of the profession. Investment bankers raise capital for corporations in the public markets. They float securities in the primary market and trade securities in the secondary market. They set standards, conduct due diligence, and establish prices in the underwriting process (primary market), and they broker trades and make markets for the subsequent trading of those securities (secondary market).

Eliminated from this narrow definition are merchant banking, leveraged buyouts, fund management, venture capital management, and perhaps even merger and acquisitions. Interestingly enough, this classical definition would more likely admit securities trading and market making into the inner sanctum of core investment banking than it would mergers and acquisitions (although today it is hardly a defensible position not to include M&A as central to mainstream investment banking).

Restricting investment banking to underwriting is what some contemporary critics might recommend for the social redemption and restoration of the field. Others would contend that progress cannot be reversed, that what has changed cannot be changed back.

Personal Definition

Which definition do I favor? As noted in Chapter 1, considering the contemporary world of finance as it is, I prefer the second definition (i.e., investment banking as encompassing all capital market activities). I am not, however, constant in my convictions: sometimes I drift back into the purist (and elitist?) connotation of investment banking including only some capital market activities (third definition), while at other times I allow investment banking to expand upward to include all major firm functions (first definition). I am motivated to be more restrictive when I am overcome by antiseptic notions of economic efficiency. I am motivated to be more inclusive when I feel compelled to address diverse issues that impact investment banking in the real world.

Characteristics of a Profession

Contemporary professions are characterized by several primary attributes that provide cohesion and consistency:

Field Paradigm[3]

The field paradigm of a profession consists of its intrinsic worth, or the reason for its existence (i.e., raison d'etre), and its way of thinking, or the accepted system of reasoning and procedures that maintain the profession's consistency in producing quality output.

Professional Attributes

The professional attributes of a profession include the following elements: a body of knowledge, or a recognized amalgam of specialized information, education and certification, or the accepted procedures for learning and recognition; development and progress, or the need for continuous advance and adaptation; and client service and professional integrity, or an adherence to high standards of performance.

Personal Attributes

The personal attributes of a profession include the following elements: natural abilities and learned skills, or the individual traits that engender success; attributes and ethics, or how members of the profession should behave; and coping with professional tension, or handling the intrinsic conflicts that industry participants must face in the course of their duties.

To reflect on investment banking as a profession, we consider these three categories: field paradigm, professional attributes, and personal attributes.

Field Paradigm of Investment Banking

The field paradigm of investment banking consists of its *intrinsic worth* and its *way of thinking*. Clearly, these are the two most important justifications of the profession.

---

3. A paradigm is a particular pattern of thinking about a given area of human knowledge that is commonly accepted within a given social and temporal context. The term was popularized by Thomas S. Kuhn in his seminal book, *The Structure of Scientific Revolutions,* where he showed that the theories which are used to explain scientific facts are not absolute and immutable but are rather influenced by the conceptual environment of the then current system (i.e., the paradigm) and can change (i.e., paradigm shift) as that conceptual environment changes.

Intrinsic Worth

What is the fundamental basis for the investment banking profession? Why does a free market allow, indeed encourage, the existence of highly compensated financial intermediaries who make markets but not products? Following are several areas of high-value, added contribution that investment bankers provide for the financial markets.

Worth of Underwriting—The Primary Market.   If we focus on the traditional, restrictive sense (fourth definition), the answer emerges simply. As noted above, investment bankers link users of capital with providers of capital, seeking optimum financial efficiency for both issuers and investors. They raise money for client companies by providing the intermediary relationships. As such, investment bankers are the essential third-party—superbrokers—the independent interest that is necessary to establish the market between buyers and sellers.

As mentioned, there are two fundamental financing services that investment bankers provide in the process of raising capital in the financial markets. First of all, as underwriters, they float new issues; this is the primary market. Secondly, as dealers and brokers, they make a market in trading securities; this is the secondary market.

The primary market is the vehicle by which users of capital access the capital markets, and investment bankers assure the efficiency of this market by their issuer selection process, due diligence procedures, pricing mechanisms, distribution allocations, supply and demand equilibria, and the like. Thus, investment bankers provide significantly more than a simple brokerage function; they ensure confidence in the primary market for newly issued securities by putting their own reputation on the line in choosing the issuer, verifying the financial data and business claims, and making the mutually acceptable decisions regarding price.

Through the process of *syndication*, the risk of underwriting new securities is distributed among various firms; this process is a fundamental part of the primary markets. This participation process occurs when several (many) investment banking houses agree before the offering to purchase a pre-determined number of the securities at the offering. They would then resell these securities to their clients, making a spread between the gross price to the public and the net price to the issuer.

The syndication process is important in that it requires one investment bank to convince its peers of the efficacy of its proposed offering. A single investment banking firm rarely takes the entire burden and risk of selling an issue by itself—and almost never for large issues—and so if a syndicate cannot be put together the offering will not be made. As such, syndication builds checks and balances into the system for issuing primary securities.

Furthermore, by involving a number of firms in the primary market for issuing securities, greater interest and support is generated in the secondary market for trading securities. An investment bank is more likely to follow a stock or bond that it has underwritten and sold to clients.

Worth of Broker/Dealer Market Making—The Secondary Market. The secondary market provides liquidity for issued securities by enabling the continuous buying and selling of those securities to occur. Such liquidity is vital for giving investors confidence that their investment can be converted into cash easily and quickly. This investor confidence is essential in lowering the cost of capital for issuers of securities in the primary market as it lowers investor risk for every given level of required return (see Chapter 3).

Investment bankers ensure that a ready and efficient market exists for both buying and selling sides. They act as *brokers*, who are commissioned agents for buyers and sellers (brokers maintain no inventory and therefore assume no price risk); *dealers*, who set bid-and-ask prices for each security they offer for trade (dealers assume a price risk for all securities they maintain in inventory); and *market-makers*, who establish (and support) the entire market for a security, normally following its initial public offering.

Worth of Mergers and Acquisitions. If we focus on the contemporary, expanding sense of investment banking (third definition), we must broaden our justification of investment banking's intrinsic worth. For example, what is the fundamental value of facilitating mergers and acquisitions and arranging leveraged buyouts? Here the investment banker performs a service greatly desired by both buyers and sellers, helping each to achieve economic goals not attainable as efficiently through any other means. When corporate buyers and sellers have a ready, fluid (liquid) M&A market, there is greater incentive for entrepreneurs and investors to build companies (e.g., cashing out is easier and more lucrative) and greater opportunity for effective strategic planning (e.g., growth through acquisitions is more practical).

Worth of Merchant Banking. Finally, we consider merchant banking (second definition), where investment bankers work for their own account. Here the justification becomes more complex, since client and self-interest can conflict.[4] Nonetheless the rationale simply extends what we presented above for mergers and acquisitions. If one accepts that increasing M&A liquidity provides intrinsic worth to the economy, merchant banking adds still greater liquidity to the market. The investment bank risks its own capital to facilitate M&A, whether as short-term bridge financiers or as long-term equity players. The process enables more companies to be on the market and more deals to be completed, thus enlarging the M&A market and making it more liquid and more efficient.

Worth of a More Liquid M&A Market. But what is the real value of a more liquid M&A market to the entire economy? This is a value judgment, which is often based on political-economic ideology and one's personal position.[5] There is little doubt that when business executives worry more about buying and selling companies than about manufacturing and marketing products the result can be less productivity and more slack. This is especially true when current management considers itself under siege in a hostile takeovers.

The intrinsic worth of hostile takeovers (i.e., assessing and comparing the often competing interests of stockholders and management) is a complex issue. On the one hand, it is competitive suicide for executives to spend their time devising legal and financial pyrotechniques to defend their companies against unwanted suitors. On the other hand, an efficient market demands that underperforming corporate structures (e.g., many conglomerates) should be subject to restructure, and sleepy corporate managements (e.g., highly paid and perked executives who are long entrenched in their positions but own little stock in their companies) should be subject to change.

---

4. The accounting profession faces a somewhat similar conflict as it expands its consulting services. Consulting now accounts for a large and growing percentage of the major accounting firms' revenues relative to the traditional areas of audit and tax. Consulting for a company on the one hand and auditing it on the other is problematic — but it is being done as accounting firms become more aggressive in an increasingly competitive environment.

5. Personal opinion is often determined by personal position. Where someone stands on a particular issue is often determined by where he or she sits.

Worth of Fees and What They Mean. The enormous fees that investment bankers charge in mergers and acquisitions are often used to question M&A's value to the economy (e.g., critics contend that when investment bankers churn companies they increase personal fees and not industrial productivity). Yet, viewed from another perspective, these admittedly huge fees can demonstrate the desirability of the service. After all, chief executives are not easy marks; they are not in business to overpay; they are not suckers, nor are they easily bullied; and most of all they are used to getting what they want. If these seasoned corporate leaders are paying such spectacular sums and are paying it often, who's to say that they are not getting their money's worth?

Way of Thinking

All professions have a common way of thinking, an accepted system of reasoning and procedures that maintain the profession's consistency in generating quality output. The way of thinking in investment banking can be described by the following six categories: financial maximization, financial optimization and cost/benefit analysis, independent judgment and due diligence, financial innovation and new product development, capital availability and efficient utilization, and client service and development. The first two are client-centered, the third and fourth are market-centered, the fifth is both client- and self-centered, and the sixth is largely self-centered.

Financial Maximization. Financial maximization seeks to get the most while giving the least. In underwriting this means achieving the lowest cost of capital for issuers and the best risk/return ratio for investors. The lowest cost of capital for equity issuers results from the highest market capitalization;[6] the lowest cost of capital for debt issuers results from the lowest interest rate and most relaxed covenants. The best risk/return ratio for equity investors is achieved by the lowest market capitalization; the best risk/return ratio for debt investors is achieved by the highest interest rate and the strictest covenants. Investment bankers are usually on both sides of security transactions, and as such the market is cleared

---

6. The market capitalization is the current value of the entire company as determined by the public marketplace. It is computed by multiplying the total number of outstanding shares by the current price per share.

between issuers and investors at a rational intersection point between issuer cost of capital and investor risk/return (see Chapter 3).

The financial maximization process is exclusively quantitative, a numerical determination of how return can be maximized and cost minimized. This is basic business, the way of the economic world, and it expresses a healthy (and sometimes unhealthy) part of the investment banker's thinking when representing clients in financial transactions.

Obtaining the lowest cost of capital is the holy grail of investment banking. Raising the most net-net dollars for the least all-in costs is the key criterion and around this icon does the entire profession dance. The maximization method works by investment bankers choosing and/or designing highly specific financial instruments tailored to each highly specific financing situation.

The process of financial maximization is often analytical (e.g., the use of mathematical algorithms, computerized spreadsheets, and numerical simulations). It encourages the development of innovative approaches such as the expansion into new markets (e.g., international finance — see Chapter 22) and the use of sophisticated techniques (e.g., hedging and risk management — see Chapters 18 and 19).

Financial Optimization and Cost-Benefit Analysis.   For financial optimization to occur (given the specific given conditions), the ideal financial structure and financing methods are sought. Such thinking takes both a short-term and a long-term perspective, seeking to balance the sometimes conflicting pressures between the two poles. The process is partly qualitative, a nonnumerical determination of economic efficiency and best choices.

Investment bankers analyze all aspects of a client's company and formulate those financial strategies and implement those financial structures designed to produce the most effective overall outcome. Aspects that must be scrutinized include business as well as financial elements. Financing is one part of an enterprise's operations, and internal consistency among all parts is essential.

Note that optimization is not maximization in that what is best may not always be what is most. For example, if the least expensive financing requires a maturity or covenants not consistent with business requirements, then it is not optimal even though it is maximal. Another example is the setting of security prices in an initial public offering; if prices are too high and the aftermarket becomes weak, investors will sour on the company and sit out future financings, thus raising the long-term cost of capital.

Financial optimization can be considered a cost-benefit analysis. Cost-benefit analysis compares relative value between the pros and the cons of given alternatives in a given situation. Developed for situations where numerical analysis is not relevant (e.g., government agencies and eleemosynary organizations), cost-benefit analysis can be an effective technique for discerning optimization in situations where numerical analysis is relevant.

Independent Judgment and Due Diligence. Independent judgment establishes the credibility of investment bankers, and due diligence is the primary expression of this independence. Confidence is the primary building block of investment banking; without such trust on both sides of financings the profession cannot exist.

Investors realize that when investment bankers represent issuers they are committed to obtaining the best possible transaction for their clients (and it is common knowledge that best usually means most). But these investors must also be able to rely on the statements and presentations that the investment bankers make regarding the issuer. For the system to work, investors must believe that everything material the investment bankers state to be true is in fact true; investors must be able to trust the reasonable veracity of what investment bankers present. (In this context, investment bankers differ from attorneys in representing their clients.[7])

Due diligence is the process by which investment bankers validate the claims of their own clients. For example, in preparing an underwriting, investment bankers must make reasonable efforts in examining all material aspects of the client's company, however laborious or complex or expensive the process. Such detailed checking is required by law.

What would happen to an investment bank that gets a better deal for its issuer clients than the facts would justify? That investment bank would

---

7. It is interesting to compare the professional responsibilities of investment bankers and attorneys in representing the often conflicting interest of their clients and the outside world. Attorneys do not have any professional responsibility to make their clients tell the truth when it is not in their client's best interest to do so. In fact, if attorneys would coerce their clients to say something not in their own interests, even if those statements were wholly true, it could be cause for malpractice. Investment bankers, on the other hand, must make reasonably sure that everything that their clients state is in fact true. Investment bankers could be liable for any client misrepresentations.

sustain competitive *loss*, not achieve competitive gain. Not only would the investment bank suffer severely as an underwriter but it might also be exposed to legal liability.

A similar requirement for proper due diligence applies in mergers and acquisitions. If an investment bank makes exaggerated claims for its client seller, it risks ruining its credibility in future transactions and thereby losing its comparative strength in attracting new clients.

Financial Innovation and New Product Development.   Financial innovation is a relatively new component of the way of thinking in investment banking. In former decades, underwriting had little variety; stocks and bonds were plain vanilla, each having largely similar features. But the plethora of new financial instruments changed the old world forever. And, once started, such change cannot be contained.

Today, innovation is major competitive weapon of investment banks. Each tries to upstage the others in bringing to market more focused and more efficient instruments for its clients. Client service is certainly a motivation here, but the primary impetus is the investment bank's own reputation.

Capital Availability and Efficient Utilization.   The adequate availability and efficient use of capital is a recurring theme of modern finance, and investment bankers apply this fundamental principle both to client companies and to themselves. The availability of capital is critical for the successful implementation of all corporate strategies. Client companies need sufficient capital to finance their businesses, whether for fixed assets (e.g., plant and equipment), working capital (i.e., receivables and inventories), or building the company (e.g., marketing and advertising, research and development). Investment banks need sufficient capital to support their underwriting, securities dealing, and merchant banking functions.

The efficient use of capital is the central mediator of the financial markets. Capital is allocated to where it will produce the highest return for the lowest risk (i.e., the optimal risk/return relationship [see Chapter 3]). Regarding client companies, investment bankers always want to understand the use of proceeds (i.e., how will the monies that are generated from the underwriting be employed in the business). Issuers must be able to demonstrate that their use of proceeds will generate sufficiently high returns to justify the investment, and certainly the returns should be well in excess of the cost of that capital. (No investor wants to watch his or her invested money sitting idly in Treasury Bills — investors can earn Treasury returns themselves, with full control and no risk.)

Regarding the investment banks themselves, the same efficient use of capital is required. In recent years, investment banks have been scrambling to increase their capital bases in order to compete effectively, especially in firm commitment underwritings, the world securities markets, and merchant banking. Yet, returns on that capital must exceed significantly the cost of that capital. In bull markets for underwriting, trading, and merchant banking, the returns are appropriately high and heavy capital is essential. However, when these markets turn down, the returns decline rapidly since the capital base is so high. When returns on capital fall far enough to approach the costs of capital this can mean that there may be *too much* capital in the company. (The idea of having too much capital is not normally part of an investment bank's way of thinking regarding itself. Perhaps it should be.)

Client Service and Development. Investment banks are service organizations, and as such attending to clients is the highest ideal. In most investment banking transactions there are many organizations and individuals involved, but no matter the complexity, the best investment bankers never forget who are their clients and what are their needs.

Clients may be issuers or investors, depending on the power relationships in a given market. Clients are those with the independent power to generate opportunities for making money in a financing situation. Power is critical here because, given the specific condition, such power may reside with either the issuer or the investors.

Blue-chip, investment-grade companies or hot initial public offerings draw in their own investors and issues are sold (and oversold) rapidly; the clients here are the issuing companies, and investment banks compete to offer these issuers the best services. In the high-yield market, on the other hand, power resides with the investors, or those institutions that buy below-investment-grade paper. Generally, there is more investor demand in the investment-grade market and more issuer demand in the high-yield market.

Professional Attributes of Investment Banking

We suggest that there are four professional attributes of investment banking that are important in constructing our philosophy: body of professional knowledge, education and certification, development and progress, and client service and professional integrity.

Body of Professional Knowledge

Every profession has a standardized body of generally accepted knowledge that forms its foundation and unifies its members. Recognizing and appreciating this knowledge base in investment banking is essential in evaluating the nature of its characterization as a profession. (Note the two complementary orientations in the following description of the knowledge base. Some parts would apply to the collective profession of investment banking as a whole, while other parts would apply to an individual investment banker's personal knowledge base.)

Finance Theory. If finance is the intellectual foundation on which investment banking is built, then finance theory supplies the raw materials used in its construction. Knowing why a particular financing techniques works is often critical in knowing how to make it work better. Seeing deeply into the structure of financial instruments gives a definite competitive edge. But however necessary finance and finance theory are, they are not sufficient.

Financing Experience. Experience in financing is part of the knowledge base. The collective record of financial performance from thousands of financings is the firm platform on which to construct future financings. Similarly, a keen sense of the outcomes of innumerable mergers and acquisitions over the years provides insight into how to make current M&A clients more successful in the future. As another example, the cumulative experience of seeing how hundreds of fairness opinions appear in retrospect, with the perfect vision of hindsight, helps improve procedures for future opinions.

But wide experience in financial transactions, like technical competence (or even brilliance) in finance theory, is not enough. Together, they comprise only part of the complex body of knowledge that supports investment banking as a profession. To appreciate the full extent of the knowledge base that investment banking requires we must go further.

Business Savvy and Industry Expertise. The importance of business savvy and industry expertise must not be overlooked or underestimated. First-rate investment bankers understand general business principles and specific industry fundamentals. They are astute at analyzing companies — say, the changing competitive structure within given industries — and perceiving what it takes for enterprises of all kinds to be successful within their product/markets. They are expert at articulating a company's current business requirements with the technical features of various financial instruments in order to formulate and implement the optimum structure for the proposed financing. Likewise, the ability to evaluate management is vital. So much depends on the senior executives of issuer companies. Such insights are critical parts of an investment banker's professional knowledge base.

Market Savvy and Financing Insight. Investment banking is an art as well as a science, and perceptive insight is as important as technical analysis. The best investment bankers just seem to *know* when an underwriting makes sense, and at what time and price it makes sense. They can discern a hot property, the next big market winner. They also have a nose for the negative; they can sense a problem quickly, whether with the products, the markets, the systems, or the management.

Traders, dealers, and market makers have their own special sense of the world and the markets. They have instinctive feel when to get in and get out of securities and they trust their intuition as much as their analysis. This is especially true of arbitrageurs, who must make multimillion dollar decisions on rumors and rumors of rumors.

Interpersonal Skills. Furthermore, the importance of interpersonal skills — competence in working with people — also cannot be overstated. This too is part of the investment banking knowledge base. For example, really appreciating the subtleties of the deal-making process is often more valuable than really knowing the technical aspects of those deals (see Chapter 9). How to make things happen is a vital part of an investment banker's knowledge bank.

Education and Certification

Where do investment bankers come from? There are no graduate programs specifically dedicated to investment banking, and one is not required to major in finance or earn an MBA (although many do). While these courses of study may be the traditional entree to investment banking, they are neither necessary nor sufficient to achieve success in the industry. Investment bankers emerge from a multitude of academic backgrounds and professional experiences. (Indeed, I believe that the richness and creativity of the industry is derived, at least in part, from the diversity of backgrounds and academic orientations.)

There are no authoritative bodies in investment banking, no formal certification procedures that determine who is or who is not an investment banker; there are no accounting CPA examinations, no medical boards to pass, no legal bar associations to which one must be admitted. Granted, many large investment banks have training programs where new associates are rotated through the various departments, but such training is no guarantee of success nor is the lack of such training any real hindrance in career advancement.

Consequently, if one would define a *profession* strictly in terms of an official body to which one must be formally admitted for membership—an authoritative association that regulates the members of the profession by setting standards and maintaining rules—then investment banking would not qualify. In my opinion investment banking is a profession, but a different kind of profession—an *entrepreneurial* profession, one might call it, with all the dynamism and volatility that the term connotes.

Development and Progress

Development and progression are essential characteristics of modern professions. Excellence in client service cannot be sustained by stagnancy of skill or opaqueness of vision. A constant desire to do a better job must be mated with a continuous striving to develop better methods.

Investment bankers are ever vigilant regarding new products, processes, and client relationships. Their sensory receptors are attuned to competitors and their activities. What novel financial instruments are going effective? Which companies are changing investment bankers? What industries are getting hot?

Investment banks devote intense energy to monitoring other investment banks and are ever-ready to duplicate, replicate, or better what others are doing. Never satisfied with the status quo, the best banks are constantly searching for new ideas and methods and for improved versions of old ideas and methods. They never stop thinking and never stop improving.

Specialists. As the world of finance has grown ever more complex, investment banking has grown ever more specialized. As with other professions, state-of-the-art expertise can only be maintained by narrowing one's focus more tightly on the areas of one's interest; hence the current specialization of investment bankers in highly specific products (e.g., mortgage-backed securities), techniques (e.g., ESOP-financed LBOs), and industrial areas (e.g., savings and loan specialists).[8]

Generalists. Such intense specialization, however, has created the need for generalists, investment bankers who appreciate multiple areas and activities and can integrate them together into a coherent whole and who can build an effective organizational strategy in a dynamic, competitive environment. The best generalists understand the technical language, translating it among internal departments and external clients, and understand the technical people, getting diverse factions to communicate and cooperate together. It is vital that some must picture the forests before others can plant the trees.

Client Service and Professional Integrity

Client service is the essence of any profession. Primary regard for the client's interests and welfare is sacrosanct. But doing what is best for the client in the long run is not always what the client thinks is best right now.

Investment bankers are financial architects, engineers, and physicians. Like good architects they should work intimately with their clients, discerning what is needed even if it contradicts what is asked. Like good engineers, they should coordinate all aspects of the assignment, insisting on internal consistency among all functions and tasks. Like good physicians, they should always base their diagnosis strictly on the facts, never biasing their opinion because of client wishes.

Investment bankers design and plan financing mechanisms and then fashion and construct them. Formulating and implementing financial strategies and structures are what they do. Investment bankers should

---

8. Specialists rule the professions. The investment banker who specializes in ESOP-financed LBOs is similar to the medical doctor who specializes in neurochemical pathologies, the attorney who specializes in ERISA labor law, or the accountant who specializes in international tax treaties.

never be afraid to break beyond a specific assignment. What clients really require may differ from what they actually request.

The only thing more important than serving the client is upholding the profession. It is wrong to subvert professional standards, even for the cause of assisting a client. Such subversion undermines the profession and diminishes future service (see Chapter 10).

Personal Attributes of Investment Bankers

We suggest that there are three personal attributes of investment bankers that are important in constructing our philosophy: natural abilities and learned skills, attitudes and ethics, and coping with professional tension.

Natural Abilities and Learned Skills

It is an historical truism that those professions perched on the highest strata of society and/or enjoying the largest relative proportion of society's material benefits attract the best and brightest members of that society. In the past, such a profession might have been the priesthood, the military, or the foreign service. Today, investment banking makes a good claim for the honor. This is not intended as an absolute value judgment (i.e., we do not assert that investment banking *should* occupy the highest strata); the dubious question of intrinsic social superiority or relative moral position is not the issue. Where investment banking stands in our socio-economic system is a fact; this reality is the only point here.

By providing extraordinarily large compensation packages, investment banking is no exception to the historical rule of attraction many of the smartest and most ambitious young members of society—in this case, the graduates of America's leading business schools. Many critics lament the consequences of this magnetic draw, claiming that since investment banking promotes more paper shuffling than product productivity, the smarter the bankers the more shuffling will occur. The fact that investment banking has attracted the best and brightest has energized the field with high competitive energy and rapid dynamic change. The best and brightest are creative and innovative as well as dedicated and ambitious.

As discussed above, there is certainly a substantial body of knowledge that undergirds investment banking, but there are a myriad ways to achieve its mastery—and personality is often as important as intellect in the process. Having an intuitive sense for people and relationships is as important as having an inherent capacity for numbers and formulas. For example, those with the ability to bring in new clients (called *rainmakers*) are highly prized and rewarded in all professions. Knowing what to do is one thing; having the opportunity to do it is something else. You cannot show your stuff without getting the chance. Winning the assignment comes first: You must get the business before you can show your brilliance. So whereas technical competence may get the highest score, personal charisma gets you into the game.

There are different sets of skills that can lead to success in investment banking. The main categories are technical, insightful, personal, and managerial. These skills are neither complementary nor mutually exclusive. Though few are gifted in all four areas, many investment bankers show strengths in several.

Technical.   Technical types analyze financial situations and develop financial instruments. The paragons are the so-called rocket scientists, those mathematicians and scientists who have migrated to Wall Street (drawn by the tingle of tough competition and the heat of hot dollars). Computer technology has changed dramatically how Wall Street works, from market arbitrage to back-office administration. Quants, those who specialize in quantitative analysis, are the new gurus on the old Street.

Insightful.   Insightful types see behind numbers and beyond technical analysis. They are often creative in spirit and enjoy innovating new concepts and products. They devise fresh financial instruments, and they add novel bells and whistles to transform ordinary products into special instruments. They find unrecognized M&A candidates, and they devise fascinating ways to make impossible M&A deals possible. They are the ones with the sixth sense of market savvy, making the best trades with the right timing.

Admittedly, insightful investment bankers have a tendency to ignore facts; but this weakness is also their strength. Ideas fly with high frequency. But insight is optimized when analysis is not slighted. Do the analysis first, then have the confidence to leap beyond the logic.

Personal.   Personal types are the leaders of the investment banking world. They lead by making it rain, by developing client relationships and bringing in the business. They have a great deal of charisma; they attract people by their often magnetic personalities. They also lead by shaping the system, by influencing the personnel and events of the internal environment.

Managerial. Managerial types run the organizations. They maintain the delicate balance between the high-ego, individual investment bankers and the collective authority needed to ensure conformity with corporate objectives. Managing investment banks—and investment bankers—is more like running an opera company or academic department than a traditional manufacturing or service corporation. Not only do you have all the conventional business problems, you also have the added aspect of managing prima donnas. Managers of investment banks work to focus the independent dynamism of investment bankers toward achieving collective goals.

Attitudes and Ethics

Professions are characterized by specific standards of performance and codes of behavior to which their members must conform. Such standards and codes serve to unify diverse aspects of the field.

It is difficult to examine attitudes and ethics in investment banking except in the context of controversy. But the import of ethics must supersede its fractious recent history and intense media attention. Ethical standards are prime building blocks of investment banking. Ethical behavior generates confidence, and without the confidence of clients investment banking cannot exist.

The fact is that ethical issues in investment banking far transcend the garish gloss of insider trading. There are many moral question and few easy answers. Addressing ethics is an important facet of investment banking (see Chapter 10).

Coping with Professional Tension

Like law and medicine, investment banking is a profession where providing the best service to clients is the highest ideal. But investment banking is also a business, the business of finance, where money is not only used to keep score but it is also the product and service being sold. Furthermore, the money is massive, moving it around seems easy, the financial leverage is enticing—and investment bankers control the whole process. This atmosphere causes a certain tension to develop, a tension perhaps unique to investment banking.

Client service and private benefit can conflict. Although present in all professions, such strain can become exceedingly intense in investment banking. Why is there a greater problem here? The prime reasons are the huge stakes and the competitive environment. The pie is so spectacularly large that even a vanishingly small piece translates into grand personal compensation. And in the world of investment bankers, perhaps more than in any other profession, public status and personal success is judged in terms of compensation comparisons with peers. Such a numerical assessment of human worth may seem silly, immature or immoral—but we kid ourselves if we pretend that it is not so.

Furthermore, many investment bankers would envision themselves as entrepreneurs, where personal productivity and creativity should lead to professional advancement and personal wealth. This desire, like most human emotions, has both an upside and a downside. The upside is enhanced individual effort; the downside is increased conflict of interest. Coping with such professional tension—resolving the conflicts that will certainly appear—is vital.

Addendum: The Philosophies of Knowledge Areas

A philosophy of an area seeks deeper understanding of that area by combining clarity of content with rigor of process. A philosophy disaggregates the area into several primary components or problems which are then subjected to a reasoning methodology that must be logical, analytical, rational, and reputable. The objective is to discern the fundamental essence or nature of the area. The search is for being and mechanisms, what the area really is and how it really works. A word of caution must be added: Progress may be obscured by what may seem to be excessive complexity. Often, however, such complexity is the manifestation of real progress.

In light of our fledgling first efforts to construct a philosophy of investment banking, it is instructive to summarize the more traditional philosophies of several areas: science, education, history, law, and religion. (For further information on each philosophy, see *The Encyclopedia of Philosophy*, Volume 5, Macmillan Publishing Company, Inc. and The Free Press, New York, 1967, from which much of the following was derived.)

Philosophy of Science

The philosophy of science covers a broad range of subjects from specific scientific solutions within one branch of science taken in isolation to general philosophical implications encompassing all branches of science taken as a class. The unifying factor is the methodology—a profound concern for fundamental essence, empirical data gathering, experimental testing and verification, rigor of analysis, and depth of explanation.

Issues explored within the philosophy of science include: language and terms (e.g., problems of precision in definitions and descriptions, and the limitations of language); the nature of laws (e.g., problems of absolute truth and formal logic); theory and hypothesis (e.g., problems of evidence and experimentation); the nature of proof (e.g., problems of reasoning, logic, and analysis).

Philosophy of Education

A philosophy of education means any body of cohesive thought that includes a theory of education, an ethic that justifies the goals that the theory adopts, a metaphysics that explains the psychological and sociological parts of the theory of education, and an epistemology that explains why certain methods and learning are effective and demonstrates our ability to know the truth of any thought whatsoever.

Using Plato's philosophy of education for illustration, we note that he sets forth an education theory—a foundational set of facts and world views about human nature and society on which he constructs his approved curriculum, methods, and administration of education—which collectively he regards as the means to the ultimate goal of just and good citizens living in a just and good society. Plato's ethical theory justifies this goal; his metaphysical theory sustains the recommendations supporting the goal; and his epistemology explains the effectiveness of some of the teaching methods he advocates as well as the human capacity to perceive truth in general.

Philosophy of History

The philosophy of history is composed of two different but related branches of philosophical inquiry: (1) a study of what historians actually do—the logical, conceptual, and epistemological characterization of the process of historical investigation—and (2) an attempt to discern the deeper meaning of history, either in the overall course of human events or in the general nature of the historical process, some meaning or significance of which transcends the intelligibility achieved by ordinary historical work.

Philosophy of Law

The philosophy of law deals with the problems of authority, law and order, duties and obligations, self-interest, individual versus collective rights, adjudication and enforcement, and recognition and change. Conceptualizing the essence or nature of law and legal system involves a host of questions regarding definition and role, such as how rules are formulated or how evidence is evaluated. Noncentral areas such as international law and primitive law are also included.

A philosophy of law articulates an understanding of the sources of law: (1) the general rules made by an authoritative or ruling body (e.g., legislature) and (2) particular precedents or past decisions of empowered entities (e.g., courts). The two types of legal reasoning methodologies — deductive and inductive — are also studied.

Philosophy of Religion

The emergence of doubts concerning society's religious tradition, beliefs and conceptions — questions that have always stimulated philosophical reflections — engendered the philosophy of religion as a distinct branch of philosophy. In general, the philosophy of religion is concerned with the consideration of reasons for and against various fundamental religious beliefs, a prime example being arguments defending or denying the existence of God. Other topics include: the essence and motivation of religion, the nature of religious faith as a mode of belief and/or awareness, the nature and significance of religious experience, the relationship between religion and science, the nature of revelation and its relation to human experience and reflection, the place of religion in human culture as a whole, the logical analysis of religious language, the nature and significance of religious symbolism, and possibilities for reconstructing religion along nontraditional lines.

The reason why all these diverse topics can be grouped together under the philosophy of religion rubric relates to the common methodology employed in their analysis. This methodology — logical, analytical, rational, and repeatable — scrutinizes the claims of religion in general (or one religion in particular) and critically examines these claims in the light of whatever considerations are relevant.

Index

Abraham, 174
Acquisition timing (M&A), 117
Acquisition valuation formula, 121–122
Adam and Eve, 174
Adler, Fred, 250
Affirmative covenants, 286
Aftermarket, 255–256, 275
Agent or principal, 55
Alchemy, 345
Alternatives and solution sets, 170, 172–173
Antitrust defense, 324
Appearance is reality, 197
Apple Computer, 249, 262
Arbitrage, 42, 305–326
Arbitrage, commodity, 307
Arbitrage, currency, 307
Arbitrage, stocks and bonds, 307–308
Arley Merchandise Corporation, 240
Asset-based finance, 42
Asset management, 42
Asset monetarization, 14
Assets, old-time, 86
Attitudes and ethics, 404
Auction-rate preferred stock, 8, 216, 217

Babcock and Wilcox, 316
Banks and leveraged buyouts, 294
Bass brothers, 323, 324
Beatrice Companies, 291
Beazer PLC, 318, 326
Belvedere Corporation, 264–265
Belzbergs, 324
Bendix, 325
Best efforts, 7, 266
Bible, deal making in, 174–175
Bid-and-ask, 10
Big Bang (London deregulation), 38, 376
Black-Scholes option valuation formula, 219
Blackstone, 21
Blue Sky laws, 247, 268
Boesky, Ivan, 313, 314
Bonds with warrants, 214, 220
Book value (M&A)(accounting), 104, 234
Boycotts and social conscience, 191–192

Breakup value (M&A), 105
British pound, 376
Brokers (stock), 10, 293
Brown-Forman Distillers, 322
Bulge-bracket firms, 20
Bullet maturity, 284
Bunds, 375
Bunny bonds, 220
Business timing (M&A), 116
Business savvy and industry expertise, 399
Busted deal fee, 149

Call protection, 285
Campeau, 316
Capital, 207
    availability and efficiency, 396–397
Capital (investment banking), 56
    firms by rank, 21–25
Capital markets, 38–44, 387–397
Capped floating-rate notes, 379–380
Capping interest rates, 329
Carter-Hawley Hale, 325
Cash flow, 63–64, 79–81, 234, 294
Cash flow bond, 354–355
Cash flow statements, 80–81
Chevron, 316
Churning mergers and acquisitions, 187
Churning securities, 187
Classification of financial instruments
    payment pattern, 216–218
    primary characteristics, 213–216
    security hierarchy, 209–210
Client relationships, 185, 401–402
Client service and development, 397
Codes and traditions, 181
Collaring interest rates, 329
Collateralized mortgage obligation (CMO), 354–355
Commissions, fees, and spreads, 145–153, 393
Commitment, 90
Commodity arbitrage, 307
Commodity Futures Trading Commission, 338

409

About the Author

Dr. Robert Lawrence Kuhn is an investment banker and corporate strategist specializing in mergers and acquisitions, financial strategy and structure, and new business formation. He is also a university professor and public speaker, scientist and scholar, and author and editor at home in the complementary worlds of finance, business academia, government, and media. He is editor in chief of Dow Jones-Irwin's seven-volume *The Library of Investment Banking* (1990), and McGraw-Hill's *Handbook for Creative and Innovative Managers* (1988). Trained in brain research, he speaks and lectures frequently and is quoted and published widely.

Investment Banking: As an independent investment banker, Dr. Kuhn arranges mergers and acquisitions, international ventures and investments, leveraged buyouts, and venture capital. He represents public and private companies, investment groups, and works with various investment banks. He has consummated deals in diverse industries, from high technology to basic manufacturing, natural resources to computer software, and retail to publishing. He worked with Charles Hurwitz in the acquisition of Kaiser tech (Kaiser Aluminum). He is active in Japan, where he is working with major financial institutions on cross-border mergers and acquisitions. He enjoys structuring innovative financial transactions.

Public/Policy Speaker: Dr. Kuhn has advised several governments on financing and commercializing technology. He chaired a symposium bringing together presidents and directors of leading research centers, advanced study institutes, and universities exploring the nature of creativity and innovation. He is a featured speaker for numerous corporate and public groups (e.g., IBM, U.S. Air Force, Japanese Institutions). He is planning several television series on international business and creative business. His public speaking and media interviews in Japan focus on business and financial strategies, stressing alliances between American and Japanese companies.

Academic Positions: Senior Research Fellow in Creative and Innovative Management, IC^2 Institute, University of Texas at Austin. Adjunct Professor (corporate strategy and policy), Department of Management and Organizational Behavior, Stern School of Business, New York University.

Education: B.A., Human Biology, The Johns Hopkins University (Phi Beta Kappa); Ph.D., Neurophysiology, Department of Anatomy and Brain Research Institute, UCLA; M.S. (Sloan Fellow), Management, Sloan School of Management, MIT; Research Affiliate, Psychology Department, MIT.

Editor in Chief: The Library of Investment Banking (Volumes I — VII: the leading reference work on investment banking, contributions from senior Wall Street bankers and financiers, Dow Jones-Irwin, 1990); *Handbook for Creative and Innovative Managers* (contributions from CEOs and well-known thinkers, McGraw-Hill, 1988).

Author: Investment Banking in the United States (Nikkei Business Publications [Japanese], 1990); *DealMaker: All the Negotiating Skills and Secrets You Need* (John Wiley, 1988); *The Creativity Infusion* (Ballinger/Harper & Row, 1990); *To Flourish Among Giants: Creative Management for Mid-Sized Firms* (John Wiley, 1985; Macmillan Book Club; Japanese edition, TBS-Britannica); *Creativity and Strategy in Mid-Sized Firms* (Prentice-Hall business school textbook, 1989); *Micromanaging: Transforming Business Leaders with Personal Computers* (Prentice-Hall books/disk, 1987); *The Firm Bond: Linking Meaning and Mission in Business and Religion* (Praeger, 1984); *Mid-Sized Firms: Success Strategies and Methodology* (Praeger, 1982).

Editor: Frontiers   in   Creative   and   Innovative   Management (Ballinger/Harper & Row, 1985); *New Directions in Creative and Innovative Management: Theory and Practice* (Ballinger/Harper & Row, 1988); *Commercializing Defense-Related Technology* (Praeger, 1984); *Commercializing SDI [Star Wars] Technologies* (Praeger, 1987); *Medical Information Sciences* (Praeger, 1987); *Corporate Creativity: Robust Companies and Entrepreneurial Spirit* (Praeger, 1985); *Managing Take-Off in Fast-Growth Companies* (Praeger, 1985); *Technology Venturing: American Innovation and Risk Taking* (Praeger, 1985); *Regulatory Reform* (Praeger, 1984). Columnist and Contributing Editor, *Journal of Business Strategy.*

Personal: Dr. Kuhn lives in New York City and Pasadena, California. His wife, Dora is a concert pianist. They have three children: Aaron, Adam, and Daniella.